HUMAN RIGHTS IN THE 'WAR ON TERROR'

Since the 9/11 attacks and the 'war on terror', have human rights become a luxury that we can no longer afford, or must rights always remain a fundamental part of democratic politics since they define the boundary between individual freedom and government tyranny? This volume brings together leading international lawyers, policy-makers, activists and scholars in the field of human rights to evaluate the impact on human rights of the 'war on terror', as well as to develop a counter-terror strategy which takes human rights seriously. While some contributors argue that war is necessary in defence of liberal democracy, others assert that it is time to move away from the war model towards a new paradigm based upon respect for human rights, an internationally coordinated anti-terror justice strategy and a long-term political vision that can reduce the global tensions that generate a political constituency for terrorists.

Richard Ashby Wilson is the Gladstein Distinguished Chair of Human Rights and Director of the Human Rights Institute at the University of Connecticut. He has a PhD from the London School of Economics and Political Science and is the author of numerous publications on how successor regimes and courts and truth commissions deal with past human rights violations, and on questions of human rights, culture and globalization. His most recent books are *The Politics of Truth and Reconciliation in South Africa* (2001, Cambridge University Press) and *Human Rights in Global Perspective* (co-edited, 2003, Routledge).

Human Rights in the 'War on Terror'

Edited by

RICHARD ASHBY WILSON

University of Connecticut

CAMBRIDGE UNIVERSITY PRESS
Cambridge, New York, Melbourne, Madrid, Cape Town, Singapore, São Paulo

Cambridge University Press
40 West 20th Street, New York, NY 10011–4211, USA
www.cambridge.org
Information on this title: www.cambridge.org/9780521853194

© Cambridge University Press 2005

First published 2005
Reprinted 2006

Printed in the United States of America

A catalogue record for this book is available from the British Library.

Library of Congress Cataloging-in-Publication Data

Human rights in the War on Terror / edited by Richard Ashby Wilson.
p. cm.
Includes bibliographical references and index.
ISBN 0-521-85319-2 (hardcover) – ISBN 0-521-61833-9 (pbk.)
1. Human rights. 2. Civil rights. 3. War on Terrorism, 2001 – 4. Terrorism – Prevention.
5. Iraq War, 2003. 6. International law. I. Wilson, Richard, 1964 – II. Title
JC 585.H865   2005
323'.09'0511 – dc22   2005013325

ISBN-13 978-0-521-85319-4 hardback
ISBN-10 0-521-85319-2 hardback

ISBN-13 978-0-521-61833-5 paperback
ISBN-10 0-521-61833-9 paperback

For Margaret Wilkinson Wilson

Contents

Contributors

Thomas Cushman is Professor of Sociology at Wellesley College. He is the author of numerous books and articles on topics ranging from cultural dissidence in Russia to the war in Bosnia and Hercegovina. He is the founding editor of *Human Rights Review*, and the founding editor and current editor-in-chief of *The Journal of Human Rights*. Prof. Cushman was Mellon Foundation New Directions Fellow in 2002, and is a Faculty Associate at the Center for Cultural Sociology at Yale University. His most current work is an edited volume entitled *A Matter of Principle: Humanitarian Arguments for the War in Iraq*, University of California Press, 2005.

Richard Falk is the Albert G. Milbank Professor of International Law and Practice at Princeton University. His most recent books are *The Great Terror War* (2003), *Religion and Humane Global Governance* (2002) and *Human Rights Horizons* (2001). He served as Chairman of the Consultative Council, Lawyers' Committee on American Policy Toward Vietnam (1967–75) and he has been a member of international panels of jurors addressing 'Marcos' Policies in the Philippines', 'The Armenian Genocide', 'Reagan's War Against Nicaragua', 'Nuclear Warfare', 'Puerto Rico: A History of Repression and Struggle', and 'Amazonia: Development and Human Rights'.

Michael Freeman is a Research Professor in the Department of Government at the University of Essex. He was the Deputy Director of the Human Rights Centre from 1989 to 1999 and the Director of the MA in the Theory and Practice of Human Rights from 1991 to 2002. In addition, he served as the Vice President of the Association of Genocide Studies and Chair of the Human Rights Research Committee of the International Political Science Association (1997–2000). He is the author of *Human Rights: An Interdisciplinary Approach*

(2002); *Edmund Burke and the Critique of Political Radicalism* (1980); *Frontiers of Political Theory* (co-Ed.) (1980); and *Nationalism and Minorities* (1995).

Peter Galison is the Mallinckrodt Professor of the History of Science and of Physics at Harvard University. In 1997, he was named a John D. and Catherine T. MacArthur Foundation Fellow; in 1999, he was a winner of the Max Planck Prize given by the Max Planck Gesellschaft and Humboldt Stiftung. His books include *How Experiments End* (1987), *Image and Logic* (1997) and *Einstein's Clocks, Poincare's Maps* (2003). In addition, he has instigated several projects examining the cross-currents between physics and other fields which include a series of co-edited volumes on the relations between science, art and architecture.

Richard Goldstone was appointed Justice of the Constitutional Court of South Africa in 1994 after the first multiracial elections. From August 1994 to September 1996 he served as the Chief Prosecutor of the United Nations International Criminal Tribunals for the former Yugoslavia and Rwanda. During 1998, he was the chairperson of a group of international experts who drafted a Declaration of Human Duties and Responsibilities for the Director General of UNESCO (the Valencia Declaration). From 1999 to 2001 he was the chairperson of the International Independent Inquiry on Kosovo. In 2001, he was appointed as the chairperson of the International Task Force on Terrorism established by the International Bar Association. He has been appointed by the Secretary-General of the United Nations to a three-person Committee of Inquiry into the Iraq Oil for Food Program headed by Paul Volcker.

Carol J. Greenhouse is a Professor of Anthropology at Princeton University. A cultural anthropologist, she has served as president of both the Law and Society Association and the Association for Political and Legal Anthropology, and has served as editor of *American Ethnologist*. Her major publications include *Praying for Justice: Faith, Hope and Order in an American Town* (1986), *Law and Community in Three American Towns* (1994, with David Engel and Barbara Yngvesson), *A Moment's Notice: Time Politics Across Cultures* (1996) and edited volumes *Democracy and Ethnography* (1998) and *Ethnography in Unstable Places* (2002, with Elizabeth Mertz and Kay Warren).

Neil Hicks is the Director of Human Rights First's International Programs and Human Rights Defenders Program. He also created and runs the Human Rights First Middle East Initiative, a project to assist local human rights defenders in the closed societies of the region. In 2000 and 2001, Mr. Hicks was a Senior Fellow in the Jennings Randolph Fellowship Program of the United States Institute of Peace in Washington, D.C. His forthcoming book is *The Crisis of Human Rights Implementation in the Middle East*, and he is the author of many reports and scholarly articles, including 'Human Rights in Turkey, Some Legal Aspects' in *Human Rights Review* (January 2002) and 'Does Islamic Human Rights Activism Provide a Remedy to the Crisis of Human Rights Implementation in the Middle East?' in *Human Rights Quarterly* (May 2002).

David Luban is the Frederick J. Haas Professor of Law and Philosophy at Georgetown University's Law Center and Department of Philosophy. He received his B.A. from University of Chicago, and his M.A., M.Phil. and Ph.D. from Yale. His recent publications include *The Ethics of Lawyers* (Ed.), *Legal Modernism* and *Legal Ethics* (co-authored). Dr. Luban has been a Woodrow Wilson Graduate Fellow, a Guggenheim Fellow, a Danforth Fellow, a Keck Foundation Distinguished Senior Fellow in Legal Ethics and Professional Culture at Yale Law School and a Fellow of the Woodrow Wilson International Center for Scholars.

Julie A. Mertus is an Associate Professor of International Relations at American University, where she is also Co-Director of the Ethics, Peace and Global Affairs Program. Her books include *Bait and Switch: Human Rights and U.S. Foreign Policy* (2004); *Kosovo: How Myths and Truths Started a War* (1999); *War's Offensive Against Women: The Humanitarian Challenge in Bosnia, Kosovo, and Afghanistan* (2000); *The Suitcase: Refugees' Voices from Bosnia and Croatia* (1999); and *Local Action/Global Change* (1999, with Mallika Dutt and Nancy Flowers). She is presently completing a new text on U.N. Human Rights Mechanisms (2005), a revised English version of *Local Action/Global Change*, and a co-edited volume, *Human Rights and Conflict* (2005, with Jeffrey Helsing).

Martha Minow is the William Henry Bloomberg Professor of Law at Harvard University, where she has taught since 1981. Her books include *Breaking the Cycles of Hatred* (2003); *Partners, Not Rivals: Privatization and the Public Good* (2003); *Between Vengeance and Forgiveness: Facing History After Genocide and Mass Violence* (1998); *Not Only for Myself: Identity Politics and Law* (1997); and *Making All the Difference: Inclusion, Exclusion, and American Law* (1990). She served on the Independent International Commission on Kosovo and worked as an advisor to the U.N. High Commissioner for Refugees. She is a member of the Harvard University Press Board, the Harvard Society of Fellows and the American Academy of Arts and Sciences.

Aryeh Neier spent twelve years as Executive Director of Human Rights Watch, of which he was a founder, before joining the Open Society Institute (OSI) and the Soros Foundations Network as president in September 1993. Prior to that, he worked for the American Civil Liberties Union for fifteen years, including eight as National Director. Neier is the author of six books: *Dossier: The Secret Files They Keep on You* (1975); *Crime and Punishment: A Radical Solution* (1976); *Defending My Enemy: American Nazis in Skokie, Illinois, and the Risks of Freedom* (1979); *Only Judgment: The Limits of Litigation in Social Change* (1982); *War Crimes: Brutality, Genocide, Terror, and the Struggle for Justice* (1998); and *Taking Liberties: Four Decades in the Struggle for Rights* (2003). He played a leading role in the establishment of the international tribunal to prosecute those responsible for war crimes and crimes against humanity in the former Yugoslavia.

Wiktor Osiatynski is a Professor at the Central European University, and also serves as counsel to the Open Society Foundation. Between 1991 and 1997, Osiatynski was a co-director of the Center for the Study of Constitutionalism in Eastern Europe at the Chicago Law School. Since 2001, he has been a member of Academic Council of the Riga School of Law. Dr. Osiatynski is also a Board member of the Open Society Institute, as well as of the Law and Human Rights and Public Health sub-Boards of the OSI Foundation network. He has written seventeen books, the majority of which address the comparative history of social and political thought. From 1990 to 1997, Dr. Osiatynski served as an advisor to a number of Constitutional Committees of Poland's Parliament, and he has been a co-editor of the *East European Constitutional Review*.

Geoffrey Robertson, QC, has appeared as counsel in many landmark trials and human rights appeals in Britain, Europe and the British Commonwealth. He has served for the past decade as a Recorder (part-time Judge) in London, and he is currently an Appeal Judge for the U.N. War Crimes Court in Sierra Leone, as well as a visiting Professor in Human Rights Law at the University of London. His books include *Crimes Against Humanity: The Struggle for Global Justice* (2002); *Media Law* (2002); *Freedom, the Individual and the Law* (1994, 7th ed.); and *The Justice Game* (1999). His book, *The Tyrranicide Brief* (Knopf 2005), is a study of how Cromwell's lawyers prepared the first war crimes trial of a head of state. Hon. Robertson is a Master of the Middle Temple, has led a number of missions for Amnesty International and has received awards for his writing and broadcasting on human rights issues.

Mary Robinson was U.N. High Commissioner for Human Rights between 1997 and 2002. Mrs. Robinson came to the United Nations after a distinguished seven-year tenure as President of Ireland. She was the first Head of State to visit Rwanda in the aftermath of the 1994 genocide. She was also the first Head of State to visit Somalia following the crisis there in 1992, receiving the CARE Humanitarian Award in recognition of her efforts for that country. Before her election as President in 1990, Mrs. Robinson served as Senator, holding that office for twenty years. In 1969, she became the youngest Reid Professor of Constitutional Law at Trinity College, Dublin. She was called to the bar in 1967, becoming a Senior Counsel in 1980, and a member of the English Bar (Middle Temple) in 1973. She also served as a member of the International Commission of Jurists (1987–90) and the Advisory Commission of Inter-Rights (1984–90).

Kenneth Roth is the executive director of Human Rights Watch, a post he has held since 1993. The largest U.S.-based international human rights organization, Human Rights Watch investigates, reports on and seeks to curb human rights abuses in some seventy countries. Previously, Mr. Roth was a federal prosecutor for the U.S. Attorney's Office for the Southern District of New York and the Iran-Contra investigation in Washington. He has written over seventy articles and chapters on a range of human rights topics in such publications as the *New York Times*, the *Washington Post, Foreign Affairs*, the *International Herald Tribune* and the *New York Review of Books*.

Fernando R. Tesón is the Tobias Simon Eminent Scholar at the Florida State University College of Law. In addition, he serves as a permanent Visiting Professor, Universidad Torcuato Di Tella, Buenos Aires, Argentina. He is author of *A Philosophy of International Law* (1998) and *Humanitarian Intervention: An Inquiry into Law and Morality* (1997). Before entering academia, Professor Tesón was a career diplomat for the Argentina Foreign Ministry in Buenos Aires for four years, and Second Secretary, Argentina Embassy in Brussels for two years. He resigned from the Argentine foreign service in 1981 to protest against the human rights abuses of the Argentine government.

John R. Wallach is Associate Professor of Political Science and Acting Director of the Human Rights Program at Hunter College, CUNY. His areas of study include the history of political thought, democratic theory, human rights and the philosophy of the social sciences. Prof. Wallach is the author of *The Platonic Political Art: A Study of Critical Reason and Democracy* (2001), and co-editor of *Athenian Political Thought and the Reconstruction of American Democracy* (1994). His most recent work is a book entitled *Perspectives on Democratic Virtue: Toward a Critical Ethics of Equality and Power*, forthcoming.

Richard Ashby Wilson is the Gladstein Chair of Human Rights, Professor of Anthropology and Director of the Human Rights Institute at the University of Connecticut. He is the author of *Maya Resurgence in Guatemala* (1995) and *The Politics of Truth and Reconciliation in South Africa: Legitimizing the Post-Apartheid State* (2001) and he has edited or co-edited four books: *Low Intensity Democracy* (1993); *Human Rights, Culture and Context* (1997); *Culture and Rights* (2001); and *Human Rights in Global Perspective* (2003). He was editor of the journal *Anthropological Theory* between 2001 and 2004 and presently serves on the editorial boards of *Journal of Human Rights, Social Justice* and the *Journal of the Royal Anthropological Institute*.

Acknowledgements

This edited volume arises out of the Inaugural Conference of the Human Rights Institute of the University of Connecticut, held on September 9–11, 2004. The effort to establish a human rights program that aspires to international excellence has received a remarkable level of support and encouragement from alumnus Gary Gladstein and his wife Judi. We are also grateful for the generous support for this conference provided by the Raymond and Beverley Sackler Foundation. The human rights program at the University of Connecticut could not have thrived without the involvement of the senior administration, and in particular President Philip Austin, Provost John Petersen, Interim Provost Fred Maryanski, Dean Ross Mackinnon and Tom Wilsted, Director of the Thomas J. Dodd Research Center, as well as a number of faculty in the College of Liberal Arts and Sciences, notably the Chairs of the Gladstein Committee Altina Waller and Diana Meyers, and Mark Janis at the Law School. I thank Fine Arts Dean David Wood and Drama Head Gary English for allowing us to use the Nafe Katter Theater as the ideal venue for the conference. In thinking through the issues contained in this volume, I benefited enormously from discussions with Saul Dubow and Wiktor Osiatynski. Tom Cushman provided generous counsel and lively debate throughout this project and thereby placed his distinctive stamp upon the proceedings. The Human Rights Institute Administrator Rachel Jackson did a superb job in the actual organization of the conference, and Joshua Jackson proved to be a meticulous copy editor of the manuscript. University of Connecticut students Matt Dickhoff, Megan McDonald and David Pildis were diligent and conscientious research assistants. Finally, thanks are due to Cambridge University Press Editor John Berger for his encouragement and guidance.

HUMAN RIGHTS IN THE 'WAR ON TERROR'

Human Rights in the 'War on Terror'

RICHARD ASHBY WILSON

Introduction

Since the end of the cold war, human rights has become the dominant vocabulary in foreign affairs. The question after September 11 is whether the era of human rights has come and gone.

Michael Ignatieff, *New York Times*, 5 February 2002

The idea of rights is nothing but the concept of virtue applied to the world of politics. By means of the idea of rights men have defined the nature of license and of tyranny . . . no man can be great without virtue, nor any nation great without respect for rights.

Alexis de Tocqueville, *Democracy in America*, [1835]1991: 219

After the 9/11 attacks and the subsequent 'war on terror'[1], have human rights irretrievably lost their status in international affairs and national policy-making? Or, as de Tocqueville declares, must rights always remain a fundamental part of democratic politics since they define the boundary between individual license and government tyranny? There now exists a plethora of books on international affairs after 9/11, too many to cite here, which examine the political fallout of the attacks on the United States and the subsequent U.S. response. Many are concerned with judging the proportionality of the U.S.

---

[1] Although no less normative than other ideas such as security or human rights, the 'war on terror' is rather more identified with the specific counter-terror policies of successive Bush Administrations since 9/11, and therefore I keep it in quotation marks throughout.

Thanks are due to Thomas Cushman, Saul Dubow, Michael Freeman and John Wallach for their comments on an early version of this chapter. Paul Bloomfield provided useful advice on utilitarianism and ethics. All errors of fact or interpretation are my own.

1

response to Islamist terrorism[2], and in particular determining the justness or otherwise of U.S. military interventions in Afghanistan and Iraq.

In this literature, human rights issues such as the treatment of terror suspects may appear in passing, but usually to the extent that they impinge on other, wider political aims, such as holding credible elections in Iraq. Human rights and questions of national and global security have become disconnected in these discussions, as if they were independent of one another. This volume builds upon a body of literature that evaluates the implications for human rights of the military actions and anti-terror legislation that constitute the 'war on terror', in the United States as well as globally[3]. What have been the repercussions of the 'war on terror' for the individual human rights of Afghanis, Iraqis, Britons, Americans, Spaniards and others? In what specific ways have their rights been violated or protected by counter-terror measures?

In addition to determining the impact of the new counter-terror context on human rights, there is a further need to identify the ways in which human rights and security concerns can be reconciled in the future. This is more than just a question of expediency, as when anti-terror experts conduct a pragmatist calculus to determine which government policies are most efficient in combating terrorism[4]. While knowing which measures are effective is valuable and necessary, I am referring to a rather different kind of project, one which takes seriously the security threat of Islamist terrorism whilst advancing the normative case for respecting human rights in the international order.

This volume brings together leading international lawyers, policy-makers, activists and scholars in the field of human rights to evaluate counter-terrorist policies since 9/11, as well as to develop a counter-terror strategy which takes human rights seriously. We should note that human rights scholars, lawyers and advocates, whilst sharing a primary commitment to individual rights and liberties, have adopted different stances on the 'war on terror', and not all of them are fully compatible. Our first observation, therefore, is that just valuing human rights does not answer the question of how best to respond to terrorism. Despite their differences over major issues such as the war in Iraq, all the contributors agree that governments need to uphold human rights

---

[2] By 'terrorism' I mean deliberate and systematic attacks by state or non-state actors upon civilian non-combatants with the intent to create a generalized state of terror in order to further an ideological cause. See Freeman in this volume for a discussion of definitions of terrorism.

[3] Including Cole 2003; Dworkin 2003; Leone & Anrig 2003; Neier 2002; and Schulz 2002, 2003.

[4] See Freeman 2003.

from the outset, and integrate human rights into the core of government anti-terror policies.

The contributors do not advance the case for human rights by mounting an absolutist defence; for instance, by asserting that human rights are 'trumps' or transcendental claims or privileges that can never be questioned[5]. Instead, human rights matter because they are an indispensable component of the liberal democratic politics required in emergency situations, a politics which insists upon the importance of individual rights, the separation of powers and a systematic review of executive power by the judicial and legislative branches. Borrowing from de Tocqueville, rights allow us to define and regulate the nature of both licence and tyranny. For democracies to counteract terrorists without losing their democratic souls, they have to continually review the threshold between unfettered individual licence on the one hand, and unnecessary governmental coercion on the other. At a time of seemingly perpetual 'war', a politics of human rights promotes the establishing of reasonable review procedures and constraints upon the conduct of the executive branch and its military command structure. This approach resonates with the majority position adopted by the U.S. Supreme Court, as articulated by Judge Sandra Day O'Connor. In the 2004 *Hamdi* decision, Judge O'Connor wrote that the executive's detention of terror suspects without trial during wartime 'serves only to *condense* power in a single branch of government. We have long since made clear that a state of war is not a blank check for the President' (124 S. Ct. 2633, 2650 (2004) (emphasis in original)).

Global Security Through Human Rights: The 1990s in Retrospect

The present disjuncture between rights and security in public and political discourse is all the more remarkable given that it comes after a decade in which human rights occupied a more prominent position in international affairs than at any other point in history. Whereas during the Cold War, human rights were often idealistic aspirations obstructed by a deadlocked U.N. Security Council, in the post-Cold War 1990s, human rights values and institutions played a greater role in establishing stability in the global order and ensuring more democratic forms of political and economic participation at the local level. During this time, significant advances were made in establishing international legal institutions which could actually pursue accountability,

---

[5] See Dworkin 1977 on rights as trumps. The classic view of universal constitutional right within a vision of cosmopolitanism comes from Immanuel Kant (1983) in his 'Perpetual Peace' essay, written in 1784.

albeit after most of the mass human rights violations had been committed. After 9/11, the emergent project of international legal justice is in danger of being derailed entirely.

In the 1990s, two significant factors propelled human rights to a more prominent role in the conceptualization and realization of collective security concerns. Firstly, in the context of rapid economic and political globalization, a greater premium was placed on global solutions to international security, and a contingent consensus emerged that human rights could play a greater role in promoting stability[6]. The United Nations and government overseas aid agencies came to insist upon basic human rights, the rule of law and accountability as a central part of their reconstruction strategy in post-conflict zones.

Secondly, with the ending of the Cold War, there was more scope for international responses to prevent further mass human rights abuses. In some instances such as Sierra Leone and East Timor, the United Nations successfully intervened militarily to prevent further violence against civilian populations[7], and embarked upon a relatively comprehensive reconstruction of those countries. In other cases such as Kosovo in 1999, there was no consensus at the level of the U.N. Security Council and NATO carried out a bombing campaign against Serb forces which contravened international law, but according to Samantha Power likely saved hundreds of thousands of lives (2002: 472).

The human rights agenda went beyond questions of geopolitical stability and shaped debates in other areas such as development, the environment and participation in political processes. For governments as well as social movements, human rights came to justify a range of activities in diverse fields such as economic development, reconstruction and political reform. Intergovernmental agencies such as the World Bank and International Monetary Fund, along with an array of non-governmental organisations advocated a rights-based approach to economic and social development, to replace top-down models of modernization. The brilliance of Nobel Prize winner Amartya Sen's (1999) thesis lay in the connections it drew between economic development and human rights, and in Sen's demonstration of how human rights were not just desirable political freedoms, but necessary preconditions for social justice and material development in impoverished countries.

Finally, and most importantly for this volume, the foundations were laid in the 1990s for a global system of legal justice. In contrast to the 'paper tiger' conventions on human rights during the Cold War, there were significant

---

[6] Brysk 2002; Falk 2003; Soros 2002.   [7] See Robertson 2001.

advances in the implementation of human rights. Governments, with policy guidance from human rights organizations, began constructing intergovernmental instruments of accountability for mass atrocities such as tribunals and truth commissions. The International Criminal Tribunals for the Former Yugoslavia and Rwanda advanced international criminal law to another level, and they secured the first international convictions for crimes against humanity since the Nuremberg and Tokyo trials, including the first conviction of a head of state (Jean Kambanda of Rwanda) for genocide. The 1998 Rome Statute, ratified by 120 countries but opposed by the United States, Israel and China, created the mandate for an International Criminal Court (ICC) that would have jurisdiction over four categories of crimes: war crimes, crimes against humanity, genocide and aggression[8].

These worldwide developments were underlined by decisions of national courts, which asserted 'universal jurisdiction' to try crimes against humanity. In the Pinochet extradition proceedings of 1998, Spanish and British courts ruled that Pinochet could be tried for offences such as torture, even though they were committed elsewhere and against non-nationals. The British House of Lords waived the centuries-old concept of 'sovereign immunity' to define the legitimate exercise of power of a head of state and concluded that torture did not fall within the official duties of a head of state[9]. In this era, individual human rights edged slightly closer to Immanuel Kant's late eighteenth-century vision of cosmopolitan justice which could, in certain cases of genocide and torture, override the traditional boundaries of national sovereignty.

Yet this would be a Whig history of human rights in the 1990s unless tempered by a recognition of the profound failures of the emergent human rights system, the most notable being the inability to prevent two (repeatedly predicted) genocides in the former Yugoslavia and in Rwanda. There still exists no permanent international mechanism to enforce the prevention requirements of the 1948 Convention on the Prevention and Punishment of the Crime of Genocide, a fact that is painfully evident as a genocide unfolded in 2004 in Darfur, Sudan. Politicians such as U.S. Secretary of State Colin Powell recognized in September 2004 that the slaughter was indeed 'genocide' but failed to take the necessary steps to put a stop to it (Kessler & Lynch 2004). Worse still, during 2004 politicians from the African Union and Arab League and China denied that genocide was occurring and the European Union sat on the fence, saying it did not have enough information.

---

[8]　See Schabas 2001.
[9]　On the Pinochet case, see Richard J. Wilson 1999 and Woodhouse 2000.

In trying to fathom the complexities of the 1990s, John Wallach makes the case in this volume that human rights talk rose to such prominence because their ideological fluidity and ambiguity allowed them to become a 'tool of the powerful.' On the one hand, they represent stasis, constraining political actors and institutions within a universal and international code, and on the other hand they represent a powerful moral charter to pursue social change. In the 1990s, the definition of rights shifted from the former to the latter, thus furnishing states with an 'ethics of power' that permitted them to reshape domestic policies, as well as to refashion foreign policy and intervene militarily in regions of political instability. While it is true that human rights came to coincide with the national self-interest of powerful states, in so doing, national self-interest was itself transformed. This was especially the case in a Europe pursuing greater economic and political integration, where seeking intergovernmental solutions to political conflicts became an ingrained way of conducting international affairs.

Unprecedented Challenges to Rights and Security?

After 2001, the Bush Administration advanced a formulation of international security that detached rights from security concerns. The gulf between human rights and international security manifested itself in a number of different ways, including the U.S. government's hostility to the International Criminal Court (ICC) and its attempts to undermine the ICC through bilateral agreements which grant a special exemption from prosecution for U.S. soldiers[10]. The reorientation of U.S. foreign policy away from multilateral institutions had already begun in early 2001 but gathered pace after 9/11. Secondly, in contrast to the humanitarian interventions of the 1990s, post-war reconstruction efforts in war-torn countries like Afghanistan and Iraq placed much less emphasis on re-establishing basic rights, the rule of law and accountability. Making the world safe from terrorism quickly became seen as antithetical to strong international human rights institutions.

Although it is tempting to explain the diminished role of human rights by reference to the neo-conservative nature of the Bush Administration, the reasons go deeper than the political complexion of one particular administration and result at least in part from the changing nature of the security threats since 2001. The new anti-terror doctrine responds to real security threats which existing international institutions were not originally designed to deal with. United Nations agencies are intended to prevent mass human rights

[10] This opposition to key tenets of the ICC existed during the Clinton Administration also.

violations and/or an unfolding genocide in an internal conflict, where a temporary U.N. peacekeeping force might help preserve a negotiated peace and prevent further atrocities against civilians after hostilities have ended.

The 1990s system of international criminal justice was not constructed with international terrorism in mind. The 1998 Rome Statute of the ICC does not mention global terrorism as a category of crimes it has jurisdiction over. Since the court's inception in July 2002, the prosecutor Luis Moreno Ocampo has carried out his investigations primarily in weak states such as the Central African Republic, the Democratic Republic of the Congo and Colombia. It could be argued that the 9/11 attacks might be dealt with under the rubric of 'crimes against humanity' but the ICC can only deal with crimes committed after 2002. Global anti-terror policing would therefore require a profound overhaul of the ICC mandate and operating structures. Further, the ICC relies (e.g., for powers of search, seizure and arrest) on a state sovereignty model that seems outmoded when faced with global Islamist terrorist networks. Many observers note that what makes al Qaeda unique is that it is a deterritorialized terrorist network spread across dozens of countries in different regions of the world, and instead of being highly centralized (e.g., the Shining Path in Peru), it is based upon a loose cell structure. It has a global reach and has demonstrated its capacity to strike at the heart of U.S. government and financial institutions.

Not only is the structure of 9/11 terrorist groups unique, but so is the particular strain of radical Islam motivating them. The religious fanaticism of Islamic Jihad or Jamal Islamiya or al Qaeda engenders unquestionable ideological unanimity and dedication among its followers, and engenders an apocalyptic vision that is singularly unyielding. The core aims of Islamist terrorists are quite unlike the secular political objectives of most nationalist groups which have used terrorist methods. The political platforms of Irish or Basque nationalists at least allowed the possibility of pragmatic concessions and power-sharing agreements.

In contrast, Osama bin Laden's 1998 declaration of war against the United States called on all Muslims to go forth, sword in hand, to kill all infidels in a 'Jihad Against Jews and Crusaders' and thereby to restore the Seventh-Century Islamic Caliphate. Regarding the extremist ideology of al Qaeda, the 9/11 Commission concluded: 'It is not a position with which Americans can bargain or negotiate. With it there is no common ground – not even respect for life – on which to begin a dialogue. It can only be destroyed or utterly isolated' (2004: 362). And yet, other core Islamist terrorist aims potentially do have political solutions and are quietly being resolved, such as the withdrawal of U.S. troops from Saudi Arabia. The official position of Tony Blair and the

British government has been that a peaceful and negotiated settlement to the Israeli-Palestinian conflict is a crucial part of the 'war on terror' insofar as it would undermine sympathy for Islamist terror networks (Freedland 2002).

The methods of Islamist terrorists also indicate how religious zealotry differs from broadly secular nationalist political violence. While the Irish Republican Army (IRA) targeted civilian non-combatants, the IRA never deployed any suicide bombers in a thirty-year terrorist bombing campaign, although IRA prisoners such as Bobby Sands did undertake 'suicide fasting'. Irish nationalists planting bombs in London railway stations or crowded shopping districts in Belfast always sought to evade capture and to avoid death. Operatives of al Qaeda or Jordanian Abu Musab al-Zarqawi's group are enmeshed in a cult of death that leaves them unbound by such restraints, and this makes their attacks potentially more devastating.

In a number of ways, then, the U.N. and other intergovernmental agencies, based upon a state sovereignty model, oriented to internal civil wars in developing countries and driven by a *post facto* law enforcement model, are not fully adequate for the new security challenges raised by global Islamist terrorism. Despite the emergent consensus and multilateralism of the 1990s, we cannot simply hark back to the institutions of that era and expect them to function adequately for present needs, without a comprehensive re-orientation and reconceptualization. It should be possible to recognize this without sanctioning the Bush Administration's antipathy to multilateral solutions to international terrorism.

While we are in some respects in a new era with new challenges, it is also important to recognize the historical precedents to our present deliberations on rights, the rule of law, war and security. We only have to consider the two-thousand-year-old Roman maxim *Inter arma silent leges* ('In times of war, the laws are silent') to know that these issues are not being faced for the first time[11]. One could even go further back to the origins of Western democracy and the Peloponnesian war between democratic Athens and oligarchic Sparta and chart the struggle between Athenian oligarchs such as Critias and democrats such as Pericles who held fast to democratic and humanitarian principles, as they were then conceived[12].

America's relatively short history also provides instances of emergency wartime powers which curtailed basic legal rights. Supreme Court Justice

---

[11] See Walzer 2004: ix for a discussion of this proposition.

[12] See, for instance, Pericles' Funeral Oration. One has to recognize, of course, that the Athenian conception of democracy did not extend to women and slaves. For a philosophical deliberation on the political debates in Athens during and after the two wars with Sparta, written at a time of war with totalitarian Germany, see Popper [1945] 1962: chapter 10.

William Rehnquist's (1998) book *All the Laws But One: Civil Liberties in Wartime* scrutinizes the early phase of the U.S. Civil War, when Abraham Lincoln sought to suspend the writ of habeas corpus in the U.S. Constitution to allow the military to detain individuals accused of sabotaging the war effort. This attempt was temporarily thwarted by the Supreme Court, but eventually certain civil liberties were curtailed for the duration of the Civil War, as they were again in World Wars I and II. Few now question the restrictions on press freedoms during those wars. Other executive decisions are now utterly discredited and have become a source of national embarrassment, such as the internment of Japanese Americans during World War II, upheld in 1944 by the U.S. Supreme Court in the *Korematsu* decision. Yet Rehnquist's conclusions are important, since he commends the historic trend in the United States against the 'least justified' curtailment of civil liberties in wartime: 'The laws will thus not be silent in time of war, but they will speak with a somewhat different voice' (1998: 224–5).

The debate about law and rights during wartime, then, is very, very old and we can learn something from its historical twists and turns. Michael Freeman's chapter in this volume takes us back to the classic distinction scholars have drawn between the writings of Thomas Hobbes and John Locke. Both wrote their treatises during the political and social ferment of seventeenth-century England, a century distinguished both by civil war and violent upheaval (including the beheading of Charles I in 1649 and ferocious clashes between religious fanatics), as well as by the consolidation of parliamentary authority and individual rights (e.g., the Habeas Corpus Act of 1679).

Thomas Hobbes famously believed the state of nature to be 'nasty, brutish and short' and characterized by the war of all against all, thus requiring a strong central sovereign authority (preferably a monarchy) to provide the order and security. For Hobbes, then, order is the fundamental prerequisite for all social institutions and civil society, requiring individuals to surrender their natural rights in exchange for security. John Locke appreciated the significance of a strong government in providing order, but he was more attentive to the penchant of governments to abuse their authority. Governments must therefore be accountable to their citizens, and among their primary responsibilities are the establishment of legislative power and the rule of law, the legitimacy of which derives from the consent of society. Freeman evaluates Locke's prescient theory of emergency powers, or 'executive prerogative' which grants the executive the power to suspend the rule of law in order to defend the public good from unforeseen threats. While Locke was fully aware that executive prerogative can be dangerous in the hands of unscrupulous rulers, he never proposed a system of checks and balances upon emergency powers. In balancing security and human rights in the present context, Freeman seeks to amend that oversight and he recommends a Lockean view of prerogative power, reinforced with robust protections for basic human rights.

Thus, we are confronted with questions which have been encountered before in the English Civil War, by the United States during the Civil War and two World Wars, and by many other democratic countries facing terror threats in the twentieth century, the most basic of which is, how do we safeguard security whilst preserving the human rights that are essential to democratic government? If in war some rights are suspended, which rights may be legitimately suspended in the 'war on terror', which most would accept is not like other more conventional wars? What fundamental principles of reasoning guide our decisions on which rights may be suspended and which rights are, to use the legal parlance, non-derogable in the context of democratic rule?

The Lockean executive prerogative question asks: If we grant governments the authority to temporarily curtail certain liberties in emergency situations, how can we positively ensure (rather than blindly trust) that governments will not overstep the boundaries? Regarding the conduct of war, how are foreign prisoners of war and our own citizens to be treated? Do individuals in either or both groups hold any rights to due process within the domestic legal system? Is ordinary law robust enough to judge their guilt or innocence? If not, then what special review procedures are to be introduced, and for what duration? Should terror suspects have access to the evidence against them, to a lawyer, to a trial and if so, then to the right to cross-examine witnesses? Despite the incessant references to the uniqueness of the post 9/11 context, the hoary questions of habeas corpus and the legal rights of detainees – questions which fueled political upheaval in seventeenth-century England – are the ones that have generated incendiary disagreements in twenty-first-century human rights debates.

Human Rights Arguments for War

> Prepare you, generals.
> The enemy comes on in gallant show.
> Their bloody sign of battle is hung out,
> And something to be done immediately.
>
> *Julius Caesar*, Act 5, Scene 1

Whereas human rights overtly inspired the humanitarian interventions of the 1990s, the two governments most dedicated to the 'war on terror' – America and Britain – have by and large deployed human rights as a subsidiary and *ex post facto* rationalization for military intervention in the post 9/11 era. Where human rights have featured, it is because they have been incorporated into just war theory, or at least one aspect of it, that being *jus ad bellum* (whether the decision to go to war is warranted in the original instance) rather than *jus in bello* (whether a war is fought using just means)[13].

Rather than being portrayed as a humanitarian intervention, the war in Afghanistan in late 2001 was a war of self-defence, undertaken, justifiably in the view of many, on the grounds that the Taliban regime had harbored, aided and abetted a terrorist grouping that had declared war upon and physically attacked the United States. Human rights were limited to a secondary, some would say propagandistic, supporting function as political leaders (and their wives, Cherie Blair and Laura Bush) pointed to the potentially beneficial effects of removing the Taliban for Afghani women's right to education and the right to religious freedom (Ward 2001). To be sure, these are important rights, but they are not ones that would satisfy many people's criteria of *casus belli*.

The war in Iraq was somewhat different, being less a war of self-defence than a preemptive war based upon a perception of Saddam Hussein's possession of, and intent to possess, weapons of mass destruction (WMD), and his regime's putative support for terrorist groups such as al Qaeda and his documented support for the families of Palestinian suicide bombers. Leaving aside the question of whether the evidence for WMD or an al Qaeda link appeared credible at the time, both grounds for war turned out to be based on flawed intelligence[14]. Saddam Hussein's appalling human rights record was used as a rationalization for war in the early part of 2003, but this was secondary. In March 2003, great emphasis was placed by both U.K. Prime Minister Tony Blair and President George W. Bush on Saddam Hussein's treatment of dissidents and his genocidal attacks on Kurds in 1988 and Marsh Arabs in the aftermath of the 1991 Gulf War[15]. However, human rights became a much more significant line of justification after the invasion, when the other cases for war had crumbled.

While one might expect that international policies based upon a security doctrine and backed by unilateral military invasions would appeal primarily to those of a conservative disposition, intriguingly, a number of liberal

---

[13] On just war theory and the 'war on terror', see Elshtain 2003 and Walzer 2004.

[14] Al-Zarqawi's public declaration of affiliation to al Qaeda in December 2004 was an unintended result of the U.S. military intervention and therefore cannot be used as plausible grounds for the original decision to go to war. Before the U.S. presence in Iraq, Abu Musab al-Zarqawi and Osama bin Laden were publicly sworn adversaries.

[15] See, for instance, President George W. Bush's radio address of March 15, 2003; Bumiller 2003, March 16.

commentators such as Paul Berman (2003), Thomas Friedman (2003) and Michael Ignatieff (2004) have supported the Bush Administration's 'war on terror'. These so-called 'Liberal Hawks' have endorsed American and British anti-terror wars on the grounds that open societies are faced with a threat from religious fundamentalists commensurate with the struggle against fascism in the mid-twentieth century. In the present global context, holding fast to liberal and democratic principles means seeing Muslim totalitarianism for what it is, and using all the available means to defeat it. These writers all agree on one point; that given the lassitude and ineffectiveness of the U.N. Security Council, the United States and United Kingdom are compelled to defend global security militarily and unilaterally, if necessary.

After the U.S. invasion of Iraq, commentators such as Michael Ignatieff argued that regardless of U.S. motives, which are not always pure, Iraqis are less likely to be tortured and gassed with Saddam gone (2003). Human rights advocates, having urged governments to act against repressive dictators for decades, should accept the result as a positive step for the freedom of Iraqis. Ignatieff asserted that those who opposed the Iraq war because U.S. foreign policy only belatedly came to focus upon the human rights record of Saddam's regime have adopted a self-defeating position which 'values good intentions more than good consequences'. Consequentialist reasoning, rather than a concern for intentions or motivations, is central to the arguments in Ignatieff's influential book *The Lesser Evil: Political Ethics in an Age of Terrorism* (2004).

While he protests the confused and inconsistent nature of U.S. foreign policy, Ignatieff nonetheless supports the global exercise of U.S. military power to defend liberal democracy. The 'war on terror' requires a new 'ethics of emergency' that may require the suspension of many cherished human rights except the prohibition on torture[16]. Ignatieff appreciates that this is not an ideal state of affairs, but emergency powers and radical counter-terror measures are lesser evils 'forced on unwilling liberal democracies by the exigencies of their own survival' (2004: 137).

In their embrace of just war theory, many liberal writers have edged away from their earlier reliance on rights-based arguments, in exchange for a political ethics suitable to an 'age of terror'. Human rights are certainly much less central to Michael Ignatieff's political vision after 9/11 than in the 1990s 'era of human rights'. John Wallach remarks upon this transformation away from a rights-based political framework for international affairs and he notes that

---

[16] And even here, Ignatieff allows the possibility that democratic survival may require liberal governments to revise their conception of what constitutes torture (2004: 136–43).

in Ignatieff's ethics of 'the lesser evil', human rights are unable to provide a clear political compass. Therefore human rights must give way to other, higher public goods, such as security and the survival of the liberal democratic political system.

What remains undeveloped in the writings of liberal 'war on terror' proponents is a fully fledged human rights validation of counter-terror measures. What would an argument which endorses counter-terror measures on human rights grounds look like? Can there be a humanitarian justification of the Iraq war and if so, what philosophical and political principles would it be based upon? In this volume, Fernando Tesón breaks new conceptual ground by contending that human rights and security are not as antithetical as either neo-conservatives or their detractors would propose. Both conspire to frame the debate in terms of the Hobbesian Dilemma – how do we defend liberty from imminent threats without compromising our hard-won freedoms?

As an alternative, Tesón thinks it eminently possible to integrate a human rights perspective into Hobbesian thinking about order, and thereby to make rights and security complementary. He maintains that restrictions on freedoms are warranted, but *only* if they are dedicated towards preserving freedom itself, and not as a means to attain other values such as security. Unlike in the classic conservative view, order is not an intrinsic value in Tesón's framework. Only the higher moral values of freedom, dignity and rights can underpin the legitimacy of the state and as a result, the state is compelled to protect and uphold the liberal constitution and the vision of liberty and human rights it contains. According to Tesón, liberal security measures are only justified by security threats perpetrated by 'principled evildoers' such as those Islamist terrorists who seek to destroy liberal-democratic society and its institutions in their entirety. The majority of other kinds of security threats usually do not meet this threshold, and Tesón is clear to distinguish his approach from the national security doctrine of repressive authoritarian regimes.

Thomas Cushman complements Tesón's philosophical thesis with a sociological analysis of public opinion polls in Iraq after the U.S. invasion. The extensive empirical evidence leads him to the view that the war in Iraq was seen by many Iraqis, at least early on, as a humanitarian war. Cushman presents a liberal critique of both the Bush Administration and the left opposition to the war. Since the Bush Administration was primarily motivated by realist security considerations, it only invoked the rights of Iraqis as a minor justification within a wider preventative war. The war's left critics, on the other hand, did not give sufficient consideration to the human rights arguments for the war and were too rigid in their devotion to international statutory law and ineffectual multilateral institutions. Had they been motivated more by the ethical imperative to defend human rights, they would have supported the war as an opportunity to advance the human rights of the Iraqi people by liberating them from the tyrannical regime of Saddam Hussein. Cushman grounds his humanitarian thesis in neo-Kantian theories of international relations and he concludes that while American unilateralism is not the ideal way to promote human rights, it is preferable to a passive multilateralism which settles for an unjust peace and the appeasement of dictators.

Human Rights Critiques of the 'War on Terror'

'Here is a mourning Rome, a dangerous Rome.'
Antony, *Julius Caesar*, Act 3, Scene 1

It must be conceded at the outset that the temptations to ignore international human rights norms when dealing with political violence will be strong. Nevertheless, two reasons may be provided for compliance. First, the apparent conflict between security and rights may not be real. Next, the consequences of failure to observe rights may be counter-productive in security terms in that there may be damage to the reputation of the state and an increase in support for its opponents.

G. Hogan and C. Walker, *Political Violence and the Law in Ireland* (1989: 36)

While we have seen that it is possible to build a comprehensive human rights case for many of the global counter-terror measures conducted since 9/11, by and large the majority of scholars, activists and lawyers in the human rights field have been critical of the 'war on terror', and perceive it to be damaging the cause of human rights, both abroad and at home. The various dimensions of the human rights case against the Bush Administration's anti-terror policies are laid out in Aryeh Neier's chapter in this volume. For Neier, the 'war on terror' is not the way to build democracy and promote human rights globally. The invasion and counter-insurgency war in Iraq have resulted in unprecedented levels of anti-Americanism, to the point where even liberalizing reformists and democrats in the Arab and Muslim world have to distance themselves from U.S. policy in order to survive[17]. Secondly, the United States itself has violated human rights in the treatment of terror suspects at Guantanamo

---

[17] A *Financial Times* [London] editorial, 'They do not hate us for our freedoms', refers to a U.S. Defence Science Board report which included public opinion polls in America's main Arab allies, Egypt and Saudi Arabia, giving America a 98% and 94% unfavorable rating, respectively. Defence Secretary Donald Rumsfeld has stated that we 'lack metrics' to measure success or failure in the war on terror (*Observer* 8 August 2004), but the precipitous decline in support for U.S. policies on the Arab street is one metric in the 'war on terror' which we might pay more attention to.

Naval Base and Abu Ghraib prison, and now faces charges of hypocrisy if it seeks to take up questions of human rights and democratic freedoms with foreign governments. Aryeh Neier does not question the official commitment of the Bush Administration to human rights, and he judges that on balance, America has been a force for democratization in the world since World War II, but he concludes that the Bush Administration's policies have been counter-productive and have done a profound disservice to the cause of international human rights.

While there was only relatively muted opposition to a war in Afghanistan that was largely seen as inevitable, and by some liberals such as Richard Falk (2003: xxii) as justified, there has been much greater antipathy from human rights organizations to the U.S. invasion of Iraq. In Kenneth Roth's statement of official Human Rights Watch policy, military intervention in Iraq did not meet the criteria of a 'humanitarian' intervention on par with the military interventions in places such as East Timor or, more recently, the Democratic Republic of the Congo. According to Roth, the U.S. invasion was not driven primarily by humanitarian concerns, which were minor compared with other motivations. There was no compelling and credible evidence that Saddam Hussein had weapons of mass destruction and was planning to supply them to international terrorists. The invasion was not approved by the U.N. Security Council, and while such approval is not essential in all cases, the Bush government did not exhaust all the alternatives, and it therefore weakened the international legal order that human rights rely upon. The war was not conducted in a manner that was compliant with international humanitarian law, particularly in the bombing of civilian centers and the use of cluster bombs. Most importantly of all, while Roth recognizes the ruthlessness and brutality of Saddam Hussein's regime, there was not an ongoing genocide or program of mass slaughter of a magnitude that could justify the death and disorder unleashed by a military intervention. Such a case could have been made during the 1988 *Anfal* genocide, when 100,000 Kurds were systematically murdered, but no such slaughter was taking place or imminent in 2003.

While *jus ad bellum* questions have divided human rights scholars, lawyers and activists, there has been a great deal more unanimity on matters relating to the actual conduct of war, and this is where the human rights critiques have been most incisive and foresighted. While consequentialist arguments have enjoyed a higher profile when considering the rationale for war, they carry much less weight in deliberations on the legal rights of terror suspects. Here, especially among international jurists such as Richard Goldstone and Geoffrey Robertson, the consequences of particular counter-terror policies are less compelling than maintaining the integrity of the rule of law.

Richard Goldstone begins his chapter by charting the American contribution since World War II to the building of a global justice system. From Nuremberg to the Geneva Conventions of 1949 to the International Criminal Tribunals for the former Yugoslavia and Rwanda, the United States supported measures designed to extend the principle of universal criminal jurisdiction for crimes against humanity. Thus Goldstone expresses consternation that the United States has contravened a number of principles of the rule of law (the presumption of innocence, the right to a trial before a competent court) by keeping detainees at Guantanamo Bay and holding hearings before special 'military commissions', detaining illegal immigrants and conducting secret deportation hearings, denying legal representation to two U.S. citizens, and maintaining prisons in Afghanistan and Iraq where prisoners were routinely abused. Rather than appealing to international customary law, Goldstone points to the richness of the American constitutional tradition of the rule of law, and urges the United States to return to its historic commitment to constitutional rights.

Geoffrey Robertson also begins his chapter with an historical perspective on legal trials of terrorists, beginning with the grotesque tortures and executions of the Star Chamber in seventeenth-century England. In rejecting such unchecked cruelty, the essential, non-derogable rights of the Anglo-American legal tradition were established; the right to know the charges being brought, the right to a public hearing, the right to be heard by judges who are independent of the executive branch, the right to silence and so on. The justice mechanisms put in place by the United States for trying terror suspects fall far below the accepted standards of both Anglo-American law and international criminal law. For example, the 'special military commissions' in Guantanamo Bay, while open, and to an extent adversarial, were heard by military officers who were not legally qualified[18] and whose authority was an extension of the executive power of a president who preemptively denounced them publicly as 'bad men'. Robertson observes with alarm Vice President Cheney's utterance in November 2001 that terror suspects, if convicted, 'deserve to be executed in relatively rapid order...by a special military commission'. Since terrorism succeeds when it persuades us to abandon the legal preconditions to democracy, we must look for models of justice resilient enough to weather the storm[19]. Robertson offers as an alternative the multilateral war

---

[18] With the possible exception of Col. Brownback, but even he let his legal license lapse and admitted that he would need to go to night school before practicing law again.

[19] Even accepting that this might deviate temporarily from standard practice, for example, by not providing trial by jury.

crimes tribunals established in the 1990s which developed a set of durable procedures (e.g., to protect intelligence sources) and legal norms created by international, and independent, judges.

At this point, we might profitably examine the philosophical principles at stake in the suspension of the legal rights of terror suspects. How do we decide when 'the public good' can be allowed to supercede the rights of individuals to a fair trial? In examining the philosophical foundations for the 'war on terror', one is struck by the resurgence of utilitarianism as a framework to make arguments about the common good that emphasize collective security and dismiss rights as a luxury we can no longer endure. Since 9/11 we have been inundated with utilitarian justifications for departing from the accepted military standards for conducting warfare that have been in place since World War II.

One example illustrates this clearly: the August 1, 2002 Memorandum on 'Standards of Conduct for Interrogation [under 18 U.S.C. §§ 2340–2340A]' from the Justice Department's Office of Legal Counsel for Alberto R. Gonzalez, legal counsel to President George W. Bush[20]. The memo was written at the request of the Central Intelligence Agency, whose operatives were using more aggressive interrogation methods on alleged al Qaeda members. Concerned that they might be prosecuted later, they asked for legal authority from the White House. The Department of Justice (DOJ) memo infamously claimed that any attempt by Congress to regulate the interrogation of combatants or any attempt to prosecute U.S. officials for torturing combatants 'would represent an unconstitutional infringement of the President's authority to conduct war' (2002: 2, 39). In addition, the memo redefines torture to refer only to that physical pain which is equivalent to the pain 'accompanying serious physical injury, such as organ failure, impairment of bodily function, or even death'. This may have been read by official U.S. interrogators as allowing interrogation practices such as mock executions or acts of sexual humiliation.

The author of the August 1 memo, U.S. Assistant Attorney General Jay Bybee, rationalizes the unparalleled suspension of suspects' rights in the new 'war on terror' by reference to a legal textbook, *Substantive Criminal Law*, by W. LaFave and A. Scott, citing a passage which reads, 'the law ought to promote the achievement of higher values at the expense of lesser values, and sometimes the greater good for society will be accomplished by violating the literal language of the criminal law' (1986: 629). The textbook invokes a classic

---

[20] Alberto Gonzalez was also legal counsel to George W. Bush when he was governor of Texas. For an account of Gonzalez's record as legal adviser to Bush in death penalty cases, see Prejean 2005.

test case of utilitarian thinking on law and morals – the 'necessity defence'. In this case, a person is justified in intentionally killing one person to save two others, on the calculus that; 'it is better that two lives be saved and one lost than two be lost and one saved' (Ibid. at 10). The memo explicitly presents the choice using the language of the lesser of two evils: 'the evil involved in violating the terms of the criminal law [. . . even taking another's life] may be less than that which would result from literal compliance with the law [. . . two lives lost]' (Ibid.).

Complicated moral choices in dealing with detainees are really not so complicated if one applies the simple logic of two are better than one. Yet moral clarity is not the primary aim of the necessity defence – that would be avoiding prosecution for torture. The memo declares that 'even if an interrogation method might violate Section 2340A (i.e., the section incorporating the Convention Against Torture into U.S. law), necessity or self-defense could provide justifications that would eliminate any criminal liability' (Ibid. at 46). Thus, the DOJ memo reads, in the words of Anthony Lewis (2004: 4), 'like the advice of a mob lawyer to a mafia don on how to skirt the law and stay out of prison'.

Some observers such as Human Rights Watch (2004), Mark Danner (2004) and the *New Yorker* journalist Seymour Hersh (2004) have drawn a connection between the DOJ memo, the legal reasoning of which was later integrated into the March 6, 2003, Defense Department memo on interrogation guidelines for Guantanamo Bay, and the systematic torture documented at U.S.-controlled facilities at Abu Ghraib and Guantanamo Bay. While Bush Administration officials have sought to distance themselves from the two memos and argue that they were never implemented, U.S. court orders forced a steady trickle of internal administration documents published in *The Torture Papers* (Greenberg & Dratel 2005), which illustrate a conscious lifting of standard legal constraints on interrogation in U.S. military prisons.

In the second Bush Administration, and despite further evidence of torture at Guantanamo Naval Base in late 2004, Alberto Gonzalez succeeded John Ashcroft as Attorney General, the senior law enforcement officer in the land. It was not only dyed-in-the-wool human rights activists who expressed concern. General James Cullen, along with twelve former U.S. military generals, opposed Gonzalez's nomination to Attorney General, stating that such a pattern of torture in U.S. military prisons would not have occurred without explicit authorization by civilian politicians (*Financial Times* 6 January 2005). During his questioning by the Senate Judicial Committee in early 2005, Gonzalez was unrepentant and stated that granting prisoner of war status to terror suspects would 'honor and reward bad conduct' and 'limit our ability to solicit information from detainees' (*Financial Times* 7 January 2005).

There is a notable correlation between the reasoning of some intellectuals who have supported the 'war on terror' and the legal thinking contained in the August 1 DOJ memo. Choosing the 'lesser evil' through a moral calculus is a hallmark of utilitarian moral reasoning as expounded by its central figure, the nineteenth-century English philosopher Jeremy Bentham. Jeremy Bentham, as the reader is no doubt aware, famously derided of the idea of human rights as natural rights, calling them 'nonsense upon stilts'. Indeed, it is worth noting that Bentham produced his 'principle of utility' as a direct challenge to the Declaration of the Rights of Man of the French Revolution[21].

Michael Ignatieff's 'lesser evil' ethics and overreliance on a consequentialist ethics place him much closer to the anti-rights philosophical tradition of utilitarianism than the liberal tradition of human rights. Philosophically and politically, utilitarian consequentialism is about as far from an ethics of human rights as one can travel, and this is borne out in the DOJ memo's dramatic bolstering of executive power and the sweeping away of the rights of prisoners of war. Jonathan Raban might have a point in suggesting that Ignatieff has become the 'in-house philosopher' of the 'terror warriors' (2005: 22). Lesser evil reasoning makes a virtue out of lowering accepted standards and surrendering safeguards on individual liberties. In the hands of government officials, it enables unrestrained presidential authority and a disregard for long-standing restraints on the conduct of war. Anyone remotely familiar with the history of twentieth-century Latin America will also be accustomed to 'lesser evil' excuses for human rights abuses, given their pervasiveness in the National Security Doctrine of numerous military dictatorships[22].

Ignatieff is aware that a lesser evil ethics can take us down a slippery slope: 'If a war on terror may require lesser evils, what will keep them from slowly becoming the greater evil? The only answer is democracy itself . . . The system of checks and balances and the division of powers assume the possibility of venality or incapacity in one institution or the other' (2004: 10–11). This argument now seems rather credulous. Evidence gathered from Abu Ghraib, Guantanamo Bay and U.S. prisons in Afghanistan suggests that torture, the keeping of 'ghost detainees' and other violations of the Geneva Conventions were endemic within the system of military custody. By the time government

---

[21] A point noted by Gledhill 1997: 83.
[22] Perhaps the most famous incidence of this was when Jorge Luis Borges referred to the murderous Argentine military junta as a 'necessary evil', a position he later distanced himself from (Williamson 2004).

officials weakly diverted blame by denouncing a few low-ranking 'bad apples' in the 372nd Military Police Company[23], the damage had already been done, to the prisoners and to America's standing in Iraq and the world. Even if the connection between a lesser evil ethics and a disregard for prisoners' human rights is coincidental rather than intrinsic, lesser evil advocates have been wildly overconfident about the probity of government and the ability of democratic institutions to monitor closely the boundary between coercion and torture. The evidence points to the contrary view; that the executive branch, at the very least, fostered a legal setting in which prisoner abuse could flourish and excluded any congressional oversight. The monitoring procedures that were in place did not prevent such abuse from becoming widespread and systematic[24].

The 'lesser evil' moral calculus that simplifies difficult decision making in an 'age of terrorism' is a little more complicated for others, and the DOJ memo should have at least demonstrated an awareness that the standard necessity defence case has been challenged comprehensively in jurisprudence and moral philosophy. In the 1970s, the late philosopher Bernard Williams carried out a critique of utilitarianism's philosophy of the law so devastating that he concluded 'the simple-mindedness of utilitarianism disqualifies it totally...the day cannot be far off in which we hear no more of it' (1973: 150)[25]. Alas, this was the only part of Williams' critique that was wide of the mark, since utilitarianism will probably always appeal to those longing for greater executive power.

Williams examines a scenario analogous to the necessity defence cases found in the DOJ memo. He considers the case of a man, Jim, who is dropped into a South American village where he is the guest of honor. There, a soldier, Pedro, presents him with the dilemma of intentionally killing one man and saving another nineteen souls, whom Pedro was about to execute. Williams finds the utilitarian answer, that obviously Jim should kill one man to save nineteen, inadequate on a number of grounds. Generally stated, Williams' position is that utilitarianism ignores individual integrity in its quest for the general good and it neglects the point that each of us are morally responsible for what we do, not what others do. Jim is responsible for his own actions

---

[23] All the signs are that the prosecutions will stop with junior Army reservists such as Spc. Jeremy Sivits and Spc. Charles Graner, with no indictments further up the chain of command. See the *Economist*, 22 January 2005, pp. 29–30.

[24] See especially Danner 2004; Greenberg & Dratel 2005.

[25] See Stocker 1976 for a view that also critiques utilitarian ethics as dehumanizing and which values intentions and motivations in ethical reasoning. See Railton 1984 for a critical response to Williams.

and his not killing one man is not causal to Pedro's subsequent killing of twenty.

To advise Jim to torture or kill the one to save the many is to treat Jim as an impersonal and empty channel for effects in the world, or in Williams' words, as a janitor of a system of values whose role is not to think or feel, but just to mop up the moral mess. The utilitarian perspective portrays any anxiety about the long-term psychological effects on the agent, say, a person's feelings of remorse for an act of murder, as self-indulgent. It ignores the life projects to which Jim is committed, and his obligations to friends and family to act in a certain way. It treats these commitments as irrational and of no consequence in its moral calculus of the greater good. In this critique, utilitarianism, of the kind that has characterized the legal counsel to President George Bush in the 'war on terror', ignores individual moral agency and strips human life of what makes it worthwhile.

Seeing persons as ends in themselves and not as means to other ends corresponds with a Kantian defence of human rights and liberal democracy more generally[26]. In the struggle against Islamist terrorists, we are well advised to temper our desire for good consequences (which can seldom be predicted in advance) with an equal concern with intentions and integrity of motives. Consequences matter and integrity and good intentions are not in themselves sufficient. Yet developing an approach that is not overreliant on consequentialism and which foregrounds human agency, motivations and intentions could provide enduring grounds for defending human rights in the present climate. It could better equip us with the fundamental ethical principles to go about recombining human rights and security, and work through more carefully which suspensions of ordinary domestic laws and international rule of law are defensible, and which are not.

One principle that guides human rights thinking holds that the rule of law matters, not only because of its implications for a democratic political system, but also because individual human agency and the constitutional rights that allow expression of an irreducible individual agency matter. Space does not allow me here to work through all the implications of this philosophical position for international affairs, and others can do it better[27]. Since the end of the Cold War, parallels have been drawn between America and the Roman Empire – that they are two unchallengeable empires wielding

---

[26] For a classic Kantian defence of human rights, see Gewirth 1978.
[27] David Held is one of the leading exponents of a neo-Kantian, liberal internationalism and Held persuasively advocates a new global covenant which would 'be the basis of a rule-based and justice oriented, democratic multilateral order' (2004: xv).

unprecedented power. Thinking about Shakespeare's portrayal of imperial Rome in *Julius Caesar* allows us to reflect on what distinguishes modern America from ancient Rome. For a start, the United States possesses a constitutional framework of individual rights, and an independent judiciary that can constrain the power of the sovereign.

We have seen the beginning of the reassertion of the rule of law and constitutional accountability in the June 2004 Supreme Court decisions in the *Padilla* and *Hamdi* cases, which grant the right to judicial review for all U.S. and non-U.S. citizens held by the U.S. military[28]. As Justice Stevens writes in *Padilla*,

> At stake in this case is nothing less than the essence of a free society... Unconstrained Executive detention for the purpose of investigating and preventing subversive activities is the hallmark of the Star Chamber. Access to counsel for the purpose of protecting the citizen from official mistakes and mistreatment is the hallmark of due process... For if a Nation is to remain true to the ideals symbolized by its flag, it must not wield the tools of tyranny even to resist an assault by the forces of tyranny (124 S. Ct. 2711, 2735 (2004)).

The majority argument found in the two U.S. Supreme Court decisions then inspired the December 2004 British House of Lords ruling that the British government had violated the European Convention on Human Rights by detaining seventeen foreigners suspected of terror offences under the Anti-Terrorism, Crime and Security Act without charging or trying them (*New York Times* 17 December 2004)[29]. It is down this path – of respect for basic legal norms that prevents governments from creating black holes of authoritarian legality – that we shall see a proper integration of human rights into a defensible security framework.

The conditions at prisons holding terror detainees and political prisoners, from Robben Island in South Africa to the Maze prison in Northern Ireland to Camp Delta in Guantanamo Naval Base, serve as a litmus test for a democratic political system. By this test, the United States has faltered badly. The abuse of prisoners at Guantanamo Naval Base and Abu Ghraib was not random or accidental insofar as the evidence directs responsibility towards the internal policy formulations of two key U.S. government departments. The abuse of prisoners has cast a pall of illegitimacy over American justice that will take decades to repair, and this ultimately undermines Americans'

---

[28] *Hamdi v. Rumsfeld*, 124 S. Ct. 2633, 159 L. Ed. 2d 578 (2004); *Rumsfeld v. Padilla*, 124 S. Ct. 2711, 159 L. Ed. 2d 513 (2004).

[29] See the full judgement at *A (FC) and others (FC) (Appellants) v. Secretary of State for the Home Department, UKHL 56 (2004).*

security by undermining legitimacy and cooperation abroad. By respecting the human rights of detainees and prisoners of war, not to mention wider civilian populations in zones of conflict, the United States can demonstrate that it is genuinely committed to the ideals of liberty and democracy that it officially espouses. Recognizing terror suspects as prisoners of war and acceding to their right under the Geneva Conventions to a genuinely independent and fair judicial review would undercut arguments that human rights are simply a smokescreen for American imperial or geo-strategic designs.

In the absence of respect for the basic legal rights of terror suspects, it is too easy to construe politicians' declarations on human rights as the mendacity of Shakespeare's Brutus. *Julius Caesar* is an object lesson on the dissembling potential of political oratory, and politicians' fondness for deceptive euphemisms, or what is now commonly called 'spin'. In *Caesar*, the conspiratorial senators invoke the sanctity of the law to oppose Caesar's rise and cloak their subterfuge in the language of virtue and the public good. As Brutus and Cassius plot Caesar's assassination in Act 2, Scene 1, Brutus grasps for the right-sounding expressions which will convincingly obscure from the Roman plebeians his true will to power, 'This shall make our purpose necessary and not envious, which so appearing to the common eyes we shall be called purgers, not murderers'.

The 'War on Terror', Globalization and Global Governance

Sovereignty can no longer be understood in terms of the categories of untrammeled effective power. Rather a legitimate state must increasingly be understood through the language of democracy and human rights. Legitimate authority has become linked, in moral and legal terms, with the maintenance of human rights values and democratic standards. The latter set a limit on the range of acceptable diversity among the political constitutions of states.

David Held, *Global Covenant* (2004: 137)

A number of contributors to this volume address the global impact of the 'war on terror' on questions of national and transnational governance. They conclude that the new counter-terror strategy has had deleterious consequences, reinforcing anti-democratic political trends and making the work of human rights activists that much harder. Examining the newfound alliances between the United States and countries such as Pakistan, one can draw clear parallels with the Cold War, when geopolitical advantage would regularly outweigh ethical concerns about human rights, as it did with a rogues gallery of Latin American military dictators such as Nicaragua's Samoza, Argentina's Galtieri, Chile's Pinochet and Guatemala's Rios Montt.

Carol Greenhouse points out that while the 'war on terror' has been described primarily as an international alliance, it also involves an important vertical dimension within the participating countries. She examines the effects of the 'war on terror' on domestic politics in Spain, Italy and the United States, and focuses on how the war has led to a restructuring of the relationship between national and local political parties. The 'war on terror' has been used to justify the consolidation of executive power and national party control at the expense of opposition and grassroots parties, thus widening the 'democracy deficit'. Executives have also seized the opportunity to accelerate a neo-liberal economic and political agenda, as well as to eliminate, or weaken, local resistance to emergency counter-terror legal measures. In this way, the opposition between security and rights is less a clash of incompatible concepts than it is an expression of heightened political contestation since 9/11 between executive power ('security') and grassroots opposition (denoted by 'rights' and 'civil liberties').

In his wide-ranging survey, Neil Hicks confirms Carol Greenhouse's findings by noting that new national security laws have increased executive power and paved the way for governments (e.g., in Russia, the Philippines) to redefine long-standing separatist or nationalist conflicts as part of the global 'war on terror'. Considering the examples of Indonesia and Malaysia, Hicks reflects on how some governments have even stopped pretending to adhere to international human rights standards, and peer governments are even less likely to raise objections to authoritarian measures against opposition groups. Human rights defenders now find themselves in a deteriorating situation in countries such as Thailand and Colombia, where they are equated with terrorists, censored or silenced, and on occasion targeted for repression. Hicks asserts that it need not be so, and he recognizes certain positive developments that integrate human rights into a new security strategy, such as the Indian government's repeal of the poorly conceived Prevention of Terrorism Act.

In his assessment of global responses to 9/11, Richard Falk comments on the United States' return to a foreign policy markedly similar to the Cold War, but he also identifies more constructive counter-terror policies in Turkey and Spain. In Turkey, the desire to join the European Union has led the government to improve its human rights record, including dropping the death penalty and improving prison conditions, as well as developing better relations with the Kurdish minority by granting certain linguistic and cultural rights. Despite its membership in NATO, the Turkish government bowed to popular opinion and parliamentary sovereignty and rejected U.S. requests to launch an invasion of Iraq from its territory. Turkey has preferred to adopt a law enforcement model in its struggle against Islamist terrorism, an approach that also characterized Spanish politics after the elections which removed the Aznar government. For Falk, these countries demonstrate that it is possible to be both anti-terrorist and opposed to the 'war on terror', whilst at the same time improving a domestic human rights record.

One of the main drawbacks of the 'war on terror' is that it has diverted attention away from long-standing global problems and two chapters in the volume seek to redress this imbalance by focusing on questions that dominated human rights discussions in the 1990s, namely whether human rights are universal and how the human rights paradigm might be employed to reduce poverty and economic exclusion. These issues have not gone away, and while order and security have seemingly trumped all other concerns, economic indicators, health conditions and democratic empowerment continue to deteriorate in many countries.

Wiktor Osiatynski analyzes the traditional arguments for and against the universality of human rights and identifies new threats to human rights in the context of Islamist terrorism. He seeks to understand the growing North-South divide over human rights by juxtaposing two diverging perspectives: the political agendas of states and the focus of human rights organizations. Osiatynski argues that the debate about the universality of human rights reflects how societies respond differently to the pressures of globalization and seek to pursue alternative paths to modernity. It may well be impossible to reach a cross-cultural consensus on the universality of the philosophical foundations for human rights. This does not preclude, however, the possibility of universal agreement on the rules that would protect basic rights. Osiatynski notes that present human rights conventions are obfuscating insofar as they conflate philosophical principles and legal rules, and he suggests creating two new covenants or codes which follow Isaiah Berlin's famous essay on two concepts of liberty. One negative rights code would list prohibited behaviors – what states cannot do to their citizens. The other, positive rights code, would list what governments are obliged to do for their citizens.

Mary Robinson does not accept that the era of human rights has come and gone, and she endorses the International Commission of Jurists' Berlin Declaration that calls on governments to rigorously uphold international human rights standards in their struggle against terrorism. Yet the international community must go beyond simply observing the rule of law and tackle the conditions of deprivation that create a constituency for terrorists. Robinson recognizes the threat of Islamist terrorism but acknowledges that this is not the main security threat faced by the majority of the world's population who experience 'the comprehensive insecurity of the powerless' resulting from poverty, disease and violence. Building a truly secure world will require, as Amartya Sen and Sadako Ogata have argued in *Human Security Now* (2003), broadening the concept of security beyond the state security paradigm to take into account the security of individuals and communities. Human security combines economic empowerment and adherence to democratic freedoms and legal standards, including non-derogable rights in times of crisis. This relatively new concept gives greater impetus to internationally agreed objectives found in human development targets.

Civil Liberties in the United States

The focus of the discussion so far has been on the place of human rights in foreign policy, and the treatment of (mostly) foreign terror suspects in U.S. custody, but three chapters remind us of the damaging implications of counter-terror measures on the rights of American citizens. There is now an established literature on the flaws and limitations of the USA PATRIOT Act of 2001 which grants unprecedented powers for homeland security agencies to invade the privacy of individual citizens on the slimmest of circumstantial evidence, and with few mechanisms of accountability[30]. This volume includes two essays of a more conceptual nature which scrutinize the core assumptions underlying the new security measures, with David Luban taking issue with whole language of trade-offs between human rights and security, and Peter Galison and Martha Minow evaluating the state of 'privacy' since 9/11. Julie Mertus concentrates on more practical and policy-oriented matters, asking why Americans are so badly informed about human rights and how this might change.

David Luban notes that discussions of human rights and security since 9/11 have been framed in terms of the question 'How much liberty should be sacrificed for security?' This question rests on a number of fallacies, including, *inter alia*, the mistaken assumption that other people's rights (e.g., foreign terror suspects) are being sacrificed for 'our' security; that being tough-minded means being pro-security; that questions of guilt and innocence are best decided by the president and that emergency counter-terror measures are demanded by military exigency and are only short-term. Luban disputes each of these premises, asserting that Americans are giving up their own protections from government error and abuse, that being skeptical of government is hardly idealistic, that it is almost impossible to calculate the degree to which the loss of liberties actually makes us any safer, and that the judicial

---

[30] For starters, see ACLU 2003; Brown 2003; Hentoff 2003; and LCHR 2003.

branch should not defer to the executive on the classification of legal facts. He concludes by reframing the question: How many of your own personal protections against government errors or malice are you willing to sacrifice for what are likely to be minute increments in security?

Galison and Minow demonstrate a similar concern for individual civil liberties and focus upon government responses to terrorism which intrude on privacy in unprecedented ways. They examine a Department of Defense project called the Terrorist Information Awareness System, designed to search databases of personal records even in the absence of specific suspicions. Galison and Minow draw out the wider implications for privacy as a legal right, and even more basically as a concept. As a right, the privacy of one's person, home and genetic information deserves robust protections from governmental intrusions, even in a context of heightened security concerns. Such protections might include technical limitations on the collection of financial, DNA, travel or communication data, as well as more careful safeguards requiring that data remain in anonymized forms, with audit trails tracking its use. Galison and Minow hold that consequentialist concerns about inefficiency cannot fully capture how 'privacy' has come to be a value in human lives. Privacy embraces a diverse array of aspirations, including political independence, individual dignity and a sense of a personal freedom. Given privacy's conceptual complexity and the rapidity of technological innovation, the authors argue for a plural and flexible strategy that can safeguard the aspirations contained in this concept.

Julie Mertus furnishes valuable insights into why Americans have not reacted more vigorously to defend their basic civil liberties since 9/11. During the 1990s, human rights NGOs (non-governmental organizations) entered the corridors of power in Washington and American foreign policy became increasingly characterized by human rights talk. Meanwhile, Americans' knowledge of their own human rights has remained very thin on the ground and one survey demonstrated that only 6 per cent of American adults are even aware of the Universal Declaration of Human Rights. Mertus explains this divergence by looking at how the long-standing doctrine of U.S. exceptionalism ('human rights are for others') has facilitated the suppression of a human rights culture at home. She contests the accepted view in human rights circles advocated by Risse and Sikkink, that the answer is more effective socialization and persuasion of official policy-makers. While persuasive lobbying is vital, it must be complemented by greater public education in the United States so that Americans compel their political leaders to make rights-based policy choices. As a number of U.S.-based organizations such as the Ford Foundation and Global Justice recognize, there is no substitute for a vibrant civil society and an informed electorate that insists upon the integration of international human rights norms into domestic laws.

Conclusions

We must find ways of reconciling security with liberty, since the success of one helps the other. The choice between security and liberty is a false choice . . . Our history has shown us that insecurity threatens liberty. Yet if our liberties are curtailed, we lose the values that we are struggling to defend.

The 9/11 Commission Report (2004: 395)

From this volume there emerges the clear outline of a counter-terror strategy based upon the view that human rights matter not because they are absolute, but because they represent the kind of democratic political values most needed at a time of war. If pursued, a human rights agenda would lead to a significant departure from the dominant 'war on terror' model, as presently conceived. Necessary conditions would be placed on (*jus ad bellum*) decisions to go to war. While not all wars are humanitarian wars (e.g., Afghanistan)[31], if politicians invoke humanitarian concerns in justifying a war, then certain criteria must be met: There must be verifiable evidence of an unfolding humanitarian catastrophe of impending genocide or mass slaughter, humanitarian considerations must be primary though not necessarily paramount, and security cannot be an end in itself, but only a means to protect basic constitutional freedoms and liberties. The decision to go to war must be a last resort and undertaken only after all means have failed.

Genuine and sustained efforts should be made to operate within the framework of international law. Countries retain the right to unilateral self-defence, but the main thrust of policy over the long term will have to be based upon international consensus. That means making more of a diplomatic effort at the United Nations, recognizing that it is in need of radical overhaul, particularly with regard to the membership and voting system of the Security Council. To paraphrase U.S. Defense Secretary Donald Rumsfeld, you don't build an international consensus on terrorism with the international institution you want, but with the one you've got. These conditions accompany all the usual pragmatic conditions that must also be met, including a realistic assessment of victory, a comprehensive plan for reconstruction, a feasible prospect of building democratic institutions (including the judiciary and rule of law) and a clear exit strategy within a defined time period.

---

[31] This war was fought on the grounds of retribution against the Taliban regime for harboring, aiding and abetting al Qaeda, planned and launched attacks on the United States from its own soil, and to prevent future attacks. It therefore had no specifically human rights *jus ad bellum* considerations, although of course *jus in bello* considerations did apply.

The *jus in bello* principles contained within human rights conventions are of a more unconditional nature, and they require that wars be fought justly. The intention to conduct a war with maximum effort to avoid civil casualties is easier to uphold if the conduct of troops is reviewable by complementary international justice institutions. Next, prisoners of war must be accorded their rights under the Geneva Conventions, including their legal rights to a fair and independent judicial review within a reasonable time frame. Commentators with political positions as divergent as Clinton State Department official Harold Koh and Homeland Security Secretary Michael Chertoff have maintained that civilian courts in liberal democracies are robust and flexible enough to withstand the special pressures of terror trials and fair enough to ensure the legitimacy of convictions and acquittals[32].

Instead of half-baked commissions cooked up by the executive branch, we are better served by independent civilian courts relying on well-tested and time-honored jurisprudential principles and established legal procedures. Where there are departures from ordinary law, for instance regarding the treatment of intelligence witnesses, a greater burden of proof must fall on governments to justify measures, and to explain how each measure actually enhances security. Legal modifications are to be kept to a minimum and should last the shortest possible duration. Alterations to laws and procedures are to be reviewable by the judiciary and legislative branch.

One of the most crucial recommendations of the 9/11 Commission is that there must be more monitoring and review of governmental counter-terror measures and it recommends creating a system to review the exercise of executive prerogative and, if necessary, raise questions regarding any unjustified encroachments on civil liberties and human rights. Richard Goldstone rightly proposes setting up a non-partisan Congressional oversight committee mandated to review the U.S. government's violation of constitutional guarantees and its compliance with international human rights conventions to which the United States is a party. The committee would set a limiting principle on the derogation of regular laws and regularly scrutinize the derogations in existence. More specifically, a congressional oversight committee, based upon Section 8 powers granted to Congress by the U.S. Constitution, would oversee the conditions of detention and treatment of all terror suspects in U.S. custody[33]. Other countries could design the appropriate institutional framework for their political system to carry out similar functions. The parallel structure in the United Kingdom would probably be an independent

---

[32] Koh 2001, November 23. On Chertoff's views, see *New York Times* 29 January 2005.
[33] U.S. Constitution, Section 8, 'Congress shall have the power to declare war, grant letters of Marque and reprisal, and make rules concerning Captures on Land and Water'.

parliamentary standing committee to investigate and report upon all aspects of laws against terrorism and the condition of detainees in U.K. police and military custody.

These conditions seek to highlight the human rights constraints on the 'war on terror', but as the 9/11 Commission recognizes, there needs to be more joined up thinking about how to go beyond the war model. In the view of many contributors to this volume, we need to replace the war model over the long term with an enhanced law enforcement strategy[34]. War must remain an option of last resort, but a state of permanent war without end is not a strategy any country can sustain, or afford. At the national level, enhancing law enforcement means working within constitutional parameters and integrating law enforcement and intelligence agencies – a process already underway in the United States. At the international level it means greater cooperation and coordination between the intelligence and policing services of various countries and the coordination of the various efforts into a single coherent strategy.

A justice model would also mean categorizing terrorist crimes less as acts of war and more as crimes against humanity and seeking, where possible, to deal with them using both national and international institutions of justice. National jurisdictions could be valuably complemented by intergovernmental justice institutions which have demonstrated their ability to prosecute successfully individuals that have committed mass atrocities. New international legal institutions might be needed to address the terror threat and Laura Dickinson (2002) has worked through the implications of three alternative models of international justice. These include establishing a new fully fledged international terrorism tribunal, a multilateral military commission (established along the lines of the International Military Tribunal at Nuremberg) and finally a hybrid domestic/international court based in Afghanistan or Iraq[35]. These institutions would not replace national courts or law enforcement agencies, and indeed both would rely upon them for their powers of search, seizure, subpoena and arrest, and strengthen them by building cooperation between national intelligence agencies and in the case of the hybrid court, rebuilding the infrastructure of a functional criminal justice system.

---

[34] Luban delineates the war model vs. the justice model, and goes on to argue that the Bush Administration has pursued a hybrid law/justice model that violates the integrity of both paradigms (2003).

[35] Based upon the model used by the United Nations in Kosovo and East Timor. Since Dickinson was writing before the Iraq war, she considers the model for Afghanistan, but in my view it is also applicable to the Iraq case.

Since law enforcement agencies are properly trained in respecting suspects' rights, an overhauled international law enforcement system is less likely to abuse detainees' human rights. This would go some way towards building support for resistance to terrorist methods among a moderate Muslim public, a constituency whose support is vital. Replacing the 'war' model with an international justice model involves designing the architecture for global governance that can deal with a number of issues that transcend individual nation-states, such as international crime, terrorism, migration, the environment and natural disasters. If reinforced and reoriented, the system of multilateral justice could allow democratic countries to project ideals of liberal democracy through more defensible and, in the end, more effective methods than letting slip the dogs of war and wreaking havoc.

Pro-Iraq war advocates tend to dismiss arguments for less war and more legality as political naiveté. Jean Bethke Elshtain (2003) opens her book with a section titled 'Politics Is Not the Nursery' where she excoriates liberal American opponents of the 'war on terror' as weak-willed and idealistic 'humanists' who ignore the gathering storm. What Elshtain's approach neglects is the number of observers making human rights arguments, including about half of the contributors to this volume, who have lived most of their lives in societies wracked by terrorism, and who have a firsthand understanding of which kinds of government responses are effective and which are counterproductive. To take forward the lessons from previous historical experiences of terrorism is neither naïve nor idealistic as Elshtain contends. Rather, it is pragmatic and commonsensical and most likely to produce a strategy that will succeed.

What is remarkable about the state of the debate on terrorism in the United States is how the doctrine of U.S. exceptionalism has prevented policy-makers and intellectuals from learning from the historical experiences of other countries that have faced terrorism and political violence for decades or even centuries[36]. It has been argued that al Qaeda represents something wholly new, but this argument is overstated, since many aspects of its ideology, methods and organisation have been seen before. Northern Ireland also had its share of 'no-surrender' psychopaths, some motivated by religious fervor, and Italy and Germany were plagued by apocalyptic Marxist terrorist groups in the 1970s. In the case of the IRA, several hundred terrorists were organised after 1978 into secret cells that could strike at the heart of British political and economic institutions pretty much indefinitely. The IRA was embedded within

---

[36] See Paul Wilkinson 2000 for a discussion of terrorism and liberalism.

a deterritorialized and global terror network that included Marxist guerrillas in South America, ETA in Spain and foreign governments such as Libya.

Even a passing familiarity with the history of Northern Ireland would provide unambiguous lessons on how not to deal with Islamist terrorists[37]. First, when anti-terror legislation was introduced as a reaction to a single violent event, it was more often than not a symbolic concession to public outrage rather than a careful and measured response to a long-term problem. In Northern Ireland, heavy-handed laws that were meant to be temporary soon became permanent and these were notoriously ineffective and often damaging[38]. Between 1761 and 1972, the British government passed twenty-six legislative acts containing features designed to combat Irish nationalists, including the setting up of special courts to hear terrorist suspects, as well as measures seen in the USA PATRIOT Act such as detention without trial and the suspension of *habeas corpus*. These coercive measures were counterproductive, created new sources of grievance and failed to prevent the recurrence of terrorist atrocities. They created enclaves of authoritarian legality which had adverse effects upon the wider, democratic legal system[39].

Further, in the 1970s the British security services came to use excessively harsh interrogation methods such as hooding, subjecting suspects to loud noise, sleep deprivation, prolonged standing in 'stress positions', slaps to the face and deprivation of food and water. According to the 1978 ruling of the European Court of Human Rights, such practices amounted to 'inhuman and degrading treatment'[40] and even though the British government moved to end abuse, by then the humiliation of terror suspects had delegitimated counter-terror policies, and created new constituencies of sympathizers. Repressive British government policies and actions in the 1970s, from the massacre on 'Bloody Sunday' to the internment of terror suspects without trial, and an alleged 'shoot-to-kill' policy in the 1980s, opened up a wellspring of support for violent terror groups such as the IRA and INLA that may not have existed otherwise. Here, then, is a clear illustration of how legal coercion and police and military repression pushed moderates into the camp of the extremists.

While Britain suspended basic legal rights of terror suspects such as *habeas corpus* and interned terror suspects without trial, these measures were abandoned when it became apparent that many innocents had been detained. A measure of review was then introduced, but special ad hoc courts and military

---

[37] As contained in *Political Violence and the Law in Ireland* by Hogan and Walker (1989), which provides much of the basis for the discussion that follows.
[38] See terror expert M. Freeman 2003.   [39] Thornton 1989.
[40] *Ireland v. The United Kingdom* (1978).

tribunals also ran into problems of due process and a lack of neutrality. Special tribunals such as the Diplock courts convicted numerous suspects, but a large percentage were eventually released since procedural irregularities (including confessions produced under duress) meant that convictions could not be sustained. In the end, it was only when the British government began to address the sources of political grievances, and to move from a military intervention to a law enforcement model that it began to win the struggle against Irish nationalist terror groups.

In adopting the model of the 'war on terror', suspending basic legal rights and ushering in unnecessary emergency powers, the U.S. government has managed to make nearly all of the unforced errors that governments commonly make when they respond to a terror threat. What is perhaps most surprising is that the U.K. government, with lengthy experience of containing a terrorist threat, also adopted the war model and has ended up investigating nearly two dozen of its own soldiers for alleged acts of abuse and torture of Iraqi detainees[41].

After the Iraq war, there exists an opportunity to correct major strategic errors and to develop a framework that combines security and rights in a more justifiable and effective way. It is time to move away from the 'war on terror', the flaws in which have become apparent to all, towards a new paradigm based upon respect for human rights, an internationally coordinated anti-terror justice strategy, and a long-term political vision that can reduce the global tensions that generate a political constituency for terrorists.

REFERENCES

The 9/11 Commission Report: Final Report of the National Commission on Terrorist Attacks Upon the United States. (2004). New York: W. W. Norton and Co.

American Civil Liberties Union. (2003, July). *Unpatriotic Acts: The FBI's Power to Rifle Through your Records and Personal Belongings Without Telling You.* New York: ACLU. Available at: www.aclu.org/.

Berman, P. (2003). *Terror and Liberalism.* New York: W. W. Norton and Co.

Brown, C. (Ed.). (2003). *Lost Liberties: Ashcroft and the Assault on Personal Freedom.* New York: New Press.

Brysk, A. (2002). *Human Rights and Globalization.* Berkeley: University of California Press.

Bumiller, E. (2003, March 16). 'US Names Iraqis Who Would Face War Crimes Tribunal'. *New York Times.* Late Edition, Final, Section 1, Col. 6, Foreign Desk, p. 1.

Cole, D. (2003). *Enemy Aliens: Double Standards and Constitutional Freedoms in the War on Terrorism.* New York: New Press.

---

[41] Williamson & Eaglesham 2005, January 20; *Financial Times* 20 January 2005.

Commission on Human Security (CHS). (2003). *Human Security Now.* New York. Available at: http://www.humansecurity-chs.org/finalreport/index.html.

Danner, M. (2004). *Torture and Truth: America, Abu Ghraib, and the War on Terror.* New York: New York Review of Books.

Department of Justice (DOJ), Office of Legal Counsel. (2002, August 1). 'Memorandum for Albert Gonzalez, Counsel to the President'. Available at http://www.washingtonpost.com/wp-srv/nation/documents/dojinterrogation-memo20020801.pdf.

Dickinson, L. A. (2002, September). 'Using Legal Process to Fight Terrorism: Detentions, Military Commissions, International Tribunals and the Rule of Law'. *Southern California Law Review.* vol. 75, no. 6, pp. 1407–92.

Dworkin, R. (1977). *Taking Rights Seriously.* London: Duckworth.

———. (2003, November 6). 'Terror and the Attack on Civil Liberties'. *New York Review of Books.*

Economist. 'Just a Few Bad Apples?' 22 January 2005, pp. 29–30.

Elshtain, J. B. (2003). *Just War Against Terror: The Burden of American Power in a Violent World.* New York: Basic Books.

Falk, R. (2003). *The Great Terror War.* New York: Olive Branch Press.

Financial Times. 'Gonzalez Faces Sharp Senate Scrutiny on "Torture" Memos'. 6 January 2005.

———. 'Gonzalez Defends Policy on Detainees'. 7 January 2005.

———. 'Britain's Shame'. 20 January 2005.

Freedland, J. (2002, September 26). 'The Man for the Job'. *The Guardian* [UK].

Freeman, M. (2003). *Freedom or Security: The Consequences for Democracies Using Emergency Powers to Fight Terror.* Westport, CT: Praeger Publishers.

Friedman, T. (2003). *Longitudes and Attitudes: Exploring the World after September 11.* New York: Farrar, Straus and Giroux.

Gewirth, A. (1978). *Reason and Morality.* Chicago: University of Chicago Press.

Gledhill, J. (1997). 'Liberalism, Socio-Economic Rights and the Politics of Identity'. In R. A. Wilson (Ed.), *Human Rights Culture and Context.* London: Pluto Press.

Greenberg, K. J. & Dratel, J. L. (Eds.). (2005). *The Torture Papers: The Road to Abu Ghraib.* Cambridge: Cambridge University Press.

Hamdi v. Rumsfeld, 124 S. Ct. 2633, 159 L. Ed. 2d 578 (2004).

Held, D. (2004). *Global Covenant: The Social Democratic Alternative to the Washington Consensus.* Cambridge: Polity Press.

Hentoff, N. (2003). *The War on the Bill of Rights and the Gathering Resistance.* New York: Seven Stories Press.

Hersh, S. (2004). *Chain of Command: The Road from 9/11 to Abu Ghraib.* New York: Harper Collins.

Hogan, G. & Walker, C. (1989). *Political Violence and the Law in Ireland.* New York, Manchester: Manchester University Press.

Human Rights Watch. (2004, June). *The Road to Abu Ghraib.* New York: Human Rights Watch. Available at: http://www.hrw.org/reports/2004/usa0604/usa0604.pdf.

Ignatieff, M. (2002, February 5). 'Is the Human Rights Era Ending?' *New York Times.*

———. (2003, September 7). 'Why Are We In Iraq?' *New York Times Magazine,* pp. 38–85.

———. (2004). *The Lesser Evil: Political Ethics in an Age of Terror.* Princeton: Princeton University Press.

Ireland v. The United Kingdom (5310/71) [1978] ECHRI (18 January 1978).

Kant, I. (1983). *Perpetual Peace and Other Essays on Politics, History and Morals.* (T. Humphrey, Trans.). Indianapolis, IN: Hackett.

Kessler, G. & Lynch, C. (2004, September 10). 'U.S. Calls Killings in Sudan Genocide'. *Washington Post*, p. A01.

Koh, H. (2001, November 23). 'We Have the Right Courts for Bin Laden'. *New York Times*. Late Edition, Final, Section A, Col. 1, p. 39.

LaFave, W. & Scott, A. (1986). *Substantive Criminal Law.* Eagan, MN: Thomson West Group.

Lawyers Committee for Human Rights (LCHR). (2003). *Assessing the New Normal: Liberty and Security for the Post-September 11 United States.* New York: Lawyers Committee for Human Rights.

Leone, R. C. & Anrig, G., Jr. (Eds.). (2003). *The War on Our Freedoms: Civil Liberties in an Age of Terrorism.* New York: BBS Public Affairs.

Lewis, A. (2004, July 15). 'Making Torture Legal'. *New York Review of Books*, pp. 4–8.

Luban, D. (2003). 'The War on Terrorism and the End of Human Rights'. In V. V. Gehring (Ed.), *War After September 11.* New York: Rowman and Littlefield.

Neier, A. (2002, February 14). 'The Military Tribunals on Trial'. *New York Review of Books*, p. 11(5).

New York Times. 'British Court Says Detentions Violate Rights'. 17 December 2004.

———. 'Nominee Gave Advice to CIA on Torture Law.' 29 January 2005.

Observer [London]. 'Editorial: Tough choices in the war on terror'. 8 August 2004.

Popper, K. ([1945] 1962). *The Open Society and Its Enemies. Vol. 1, Plato.* London: Routledge.

Power, S. (2002). *A Problem from Hell: America and the Age of Genocide.* New York: Basic Books.

Prejean, H. (2005, January 13). 'Death in Texas'. *New York Review of Books*, vol. LII, no. 1, pp. 4–6.

President George W. Bush. Radio Address, March 15, 2003. Available at http://www.whitehouse.gov/news/releases/2003/03/20030315.html.

Raban, J. (2005, January 13). 'The Truth About Terrorism.' *New York Review of Books*, vol. LII, no. 1, pp. 22–6.

Railton, P. (1984, Spring). 'Alienation, Consequentialism, and the Demands of Morality'. *Philosophy and Public Affairs*, vol. 13, no. 2, pp. 134–71.

Rehnquist, W. H. (1998). *All the Laws But One: Civil Liberties in Wartime.* New York: Alfred A. Knopf.

Robertson, G. (2001). *Crimes Against Humanity.* London: Penguin.

Rumsfeld v. Padilla, 124 S. Ct. 2711, 159 L. Ed. 2d 513 (2004).

Schabas, W. (2001). *An Introduction to the International Criminal Court.* Cambridge: Cambridge University Press.

Schulz, W. F. (2002). *In Our Own Best Interest: How Defending Human Rights Benefits Us All.* Boston: Beacon Press.

———. (2003). *Tainted Legacy: 9/11 and the Ruin of Human Rights.* New York: Nation Books.

Sen, A. (1999). *Development as Freedom.* New York: Alfred A. Knopf.

Soros, G. (2002). *On Globalization.* New York: Public Affairs.

Stocker, M. (1976). 'The Schizophrenia of Modern Ethical Theories'. *Journal of Philosophy*, vol. 73, pp. 453–66.

Thornton, P. (1989). *Decade of Decline: Civil Liberties in the Thatcher Years.* London: National Council for Civil Liberties.

Tocqueville, A. de. ([1835] 1991). *Democracy in America*, Vol. 1, (J. P. Mayer & M. Lerner, Eds.; G. Lawrence, Trans.). Norwalk, CT: Easton Press.

Walzer, M. (2004). *Arguing About War.* New Haven: Yale University Press.

Ward, L. (2001, November 17). 'Leaders' wives join propaganda war'. *The Guardian* [UK].

Wilkinson, P. (2000). *Terrorism versus Democracy: The Liberal State Response.* London: Frank Cass.

Williams, B. (1973). 'A Critique of Utilitarianism.' In J. J. C. Smart & B. Williams (Eds.), *Utilitarianism: For and Against.* Cambridge: Cambridge University Press.

Williamson, E. (2004). *Borges: A Life.* New York: Viking.

Williamson, H. & Eaglesham, J. (2005, January 20). 'UK Soldiers in Dock for "Following Order" in Iraq'. *Financial Times.*

Wilson, R. J. (1999). 'Prosecuting Pinochet: International Crimes in Spanish Domestic Law'. *Human Rights Quarterly*, vol. 21(4), pp. 927–79.

Woodhouse, D. (Ed.). (2000). *The Pinochet Case: A Legal and Constitutional Analysis.* Portland, OR: Hart Publishing.

1. Order, Rights and Threats: Terrorism and Global Justice

MICHAEL FREEMAN

1. The Challenge of Terrorism

In 2002, the International Council on Human Rights Policy published a report entitled *Human Rights After September 11*, based on an international seminar of distinguished human-rights scholars and practitioners (International Council on Human Rights Policy, hereafter ICHRP, 2002). The title implied that human rights after 9/11 were different from human rights before 9/11. How could that be?

Human rights are commonly thought to be 'timeless', because they are grounded in 'the dignity and worth of the human person'. However, they have a history. After the adoption of the Universal Declaration of Human Rights in 1948, the struggle for human rights took place in a world dominated by the Cold War and the consequences of decolonization. The period from the mid-1980s to 2001 witnessed a surge of human-rights optimism, as many countries made the transition from authoritarianism to democracy. There were human-rights disasters in this period, such as the Rwandan genocide and the conflicts in the former Yugoslavia, but, overall, the idea of human rights moved from the margins to the centre of international politics. The events of 9/11 seemed to bring an abrupt change. The dominant terms of political discourse became 'terrorism', 'security' and 'war'. It is true that 'terrorism' was represented as a threat to Western values, including human rights, and the wars in Afghanistan and Iraq toppled two regimes that had been massive human-rights violators. Nevertheless, human-rights activists have generally believed that the 'war on terrorism' has created new challenges for their cause.

Terrorism is, however, not new. Several democracies have had to deal with terrorism in recent decades. Sometimes they have introduced special legislation, and sometimes this has been controversial. No one thought, however, that this changed the global context for human rights. The need to fight 'terrorism' has also been a familiar defence of repressive governments accused of human-rights violations. Now, the Western democracies are using a similar justification for human-rights restrictions. Perhaps nothing has changed except that the societies ostensibly committed to human rights feel less secure than they did previously.

A common view is that 9/11 changed the world because we are now faced with the threat of what some scholars have called 'superterrorism'. This is said to differ from 'traditional' terrorism in that its ideology is 'apocalyptic', its aims global, and its means war-like. Consequently, political negotiation with superterrorists is said to be impossible. The novelty and magnitude of this threat, several commentators have suggested, may require us to revise our conception of human rights.

Some scholars are sceptical about the idea of the 'new terrorism'. Freedman has reminded us that the leftist terrorism of the 1970s was global and 'apocalyptic' (Freedman 2002b: 42). 9/11 appears to have had several traditional terrorist aims: punishing the 'enemy', terrorising its population, inspiring sympathisers, exposing the enemy's vulnerability and provoking an aggressive response. Gearson admits that the scale of the 9/11 attack was unprecedented, but argues that excessive emphasis on its novelty led to a confused policy response. The problem of 'terrorism' was conflated with that of 'rogue states' and weapons of mass destruction (Gearson 2002: 12, 20–3).

However much novelty we attribute to contemporary terrorist challenge, I shall argue that the challenge, and the counter-terrorist response to it, require a two-dimensional analysis. The first dimension is provided by the classical political theory of human rights, that seeks to find a just balance between order, rights and threats. The second dimension is provided by a conception of global justice. This second dimension is required, both because the concept of human rights claims a global reach, and because the dialectic of terrorism and counter-terrorism has a global impact. This is recognized in principle, to some extent, by Western policy-makers, but so far it has hardly influenced their practice. Locating the problem of terrorism in the context of global justice may seem uncontroversial, but, in doing so, I shall have to show that some strong objections to this approach are mistaken.

2. The Virtues of Society

'Justice', John Rawls famously wrote, 'is the first virtue of social institutions' (Rawls 1972: 3). There is a tradition, however, that holds *order* to be first virtue of social institutions. Hobbes assumed that security was a universal and fundamental value. He argued that, without a 'common power', the 'natural condition of mankind' would be a war of all against all. He thought that, in this condition, each would be such a great threat to every other person that we ought to give as much power to government as it needed to maintain order. On this view, we must give up all our 'natural' rights in order to be safe (Hobbes [1651] 1996).

Locke argued, by contrast, that if each of us were so dangerous to others, we would not be safe from the threat of oppression by an all-powerful government. He held that we had 'natural rights' to life, liberty and property in the 'state of nature'. Hobbes had been correct to believe that natural rights were not safe in the absence of a 'common power'. They would remain unsafe, however, Locke thought, unless government was accountable to the people and subject to the rule of law. Locke anticipated thereby the framework for the modern conception of human rights, including the idea that government was both necessary for, and a danger to, the protection of these rights (Locke [1689] 1970).

The threat to human security derived, for Hobbes, from the unregulated desires of others, but especially dangerous, it is interesting for us now to note, were religious fanatics. Locke thought that danger arose from those who were 'no strict observers of equity and justice', but also from governments that breached the trust placed in them. Locke also believed religious extremists to be a threat to order and to the people's rights (Marshall 1994). The solution to the problem of threats to human security, for Hobbes, was strong government. The solution for Locke was the rule of law, and, if this was not observed, the right of resistance to tyranny. Terrorists could be located in Hobbesian theory as threats to order, for whom the government should provide appropriate punishments, but Lockean theory provides a basis for distinguishing between 'terrorists' and 'freedom fighters': the latter resist tyranny by force when resort to law is impossible, whereas the former resort to force when legal remedies are available.

Locke affirmed that the 'first and fundamental natural law' was the preservation of society, and, as far as was consistent with the public good, of every person in it. The first and fundamental *positive* law of all commonwealths was the establishment of the legislative power. This legislative was the supreme power of the commonwealth, and no edict of anyone else could have the force of law, if it lacked the sanction of the legislative that the public had chosen. Otherwise, the law could not have that which was necessary to its being law, that is, the consent of society. The people could not violate the natural rights of anyone, and therefore could not give the legislative the power to violate the natural rights of anyone. The legislative could not assume to itself the power to rule by extemporary arbitrary decrees, but was bound to dispense justice by 'promulgated standing laws' (Locke [1689] 1970: §§134–8, 142).

Hobbes's sovereign was simply 'tasked' to defend the safety of the people both from internal and external threats. Locke's theory of foreign policy was more complex. He thought that political society would need a 'federative' power to manage all transactions with persons and communities outside the commonwealth. This federative power was much more difficult than the legislative to exercise by antecedent, standing, positive laws, and so must be left to the prudence of the executive. Foreigners, Locke implied, were more unpredictable than citizens, and therefore the executive had to be allowed discretion if foreigners posed a threat to the public good. A modern Lockean would allow the executive considerable discretion in responding to the threat of international terrorism.

It was, however, not only foreign affairs that Locke thought should be left to executive discretion. *Prerogative* was the power of the executive to provide for the public good in unforeseen and uncertain circumstances, in which certain and unalterable laws could not safely direct what should be done for the good of the people. It was indeed right that the laws themselves should, in some cases, give way to the executive power, if this were necessary to preserve society. The prerogative power was the power to act, according to discretion, for the public good, without the prescription of law, and sometimes even against it. The prerogative power might be necessary for good rulers, but it was dangerous in the hands of bad rulers. If a ruler exercised the prerogative to harm the people, such a ruler would have acted wrongfully. How, then, was the distinction between the rightful and wrongful use of the prerogative to be made? If the question were to arise, Locke said, the people could only 'appeal to heaven' (Locke [1689] 1970: §§146–7, 158–60, 166, 168).

This may be interpreted as transferring the issue from philosophy to politics and/or relying on the 'judgement of history'[1], but this leaves us with the dilemma of either protecting human rights regardless of the consequences or restricting human rights for the sake of fighting terrorism. Kofi Annan has insisted that no trade-off can be made between effective action against terrorism and the protection of human rights (ICHRP 2002: 19). Locke's executive prerogative, which, on his own account, is insufficiently checked, and Annan's no trade-off principle, which begs the question as to whether

---

[1] I am indebted to a participant in the conference on 'The United States and Global Human Rights', held at the Rothermere American Institute, University of Oxford, on 13 November 2004, for suggesting this interpretation.

we can counter terrorism effectively with no cost to human rights, define the boundaries within which the reconciliation between the defence of human rights and rational responses to terrorism must be found.

3. Global Justice

Executive prerogative, in Locke's theory, defends the public good, including the rights of the people, so far as possible. Human rights, however, are *universal*, and this raises the question of societies' obligations to outsiders. The Universal Declaration says that the recognition of human rights is the foundation of justice *in the world*. What implications, if any, does this have for the policies of governments faced with the threat of superterrorism?

Some believe that 9/11 was a protest against global injustice, even if the means chosen were horribly wrong (ICHRP 2002: 44). Others have strongly disputed this view on the ground that representing terrorists as agents of justice excuses their crimes and blames their victims. The thesis that poverty and oppression are causes of terrorism has been met with the further objection that the 9/11 terrorists, like many terrorists, were not poor, not oppressed, and not champions of justice. Fukuyama has found the root causes of Islamic extremism in the poverty and authoritarian politics of the Muslim Middle East, but argued that the West was not to blame for this, because it had provided a considerable amount of aid to the region. The fault, he maintained, was internal to the region, because it had failed to develop as a number of Asian and Latin American countries had done (Fukuyama 2002: 33–4). This argument applies to the Muslim Middle East – Rawls's general thesis that the causes of the wealth of a people lie in their own character, culture and institutions (Rawls 1999: 108).

Dershowitz has argued that the principal cause of terrorism is its success in convincing many that those who use extreme methods must have just grievances. He concedes that we ought to remedy injustice, but not in response to, and/or as a reward for terrorism (Dershowitz 2002: 24–8). Elshtain criticises those who interpret 9/11 as 'blowback' – that is, as a response to injustice – not only because this blames the victims for the crimes perpetrated against them, but also because it overlooks the fact that the attack was motivated by religious fanaticism. She concedes, however, that the United States has a responsibility to 'respond to the cries of the aggrieved', and that changes in U.S. foreign policy might reduce the attraction of radical Islamism, although it would not disarm it completely (Elshtain 2003).

These arguments confuse explanation and justification. Whether or not U.S. foreign policy is a *cause* of terrorism is an empirical question. Whatever the answer, it neither blames nor excuses anyone. If, however, we wish to combat terrorism effectively, we should investigate its causes (Andrews 2003). Although 'justice' is a normative concept, there may be a causal relation between a social condition that is reasonably deemed to be unjust – for example, one in which there are massive violations of human rights – and terrorism. There are two mutually independent reasons, therefore, for considering the relations between global injustice and terrorism. The first is that we have a moral obligation to rectify injustice when we can at a reasonable cost. The second is that injustice may be causally related to terrorism. It may be, for example, that Western policy towards the Muslim Middle East has been, *pace* Fukuyama, unjust, and that it has also contributed to the causation of terrorism. If we concluded this, we would be committed neither to excusing terrorism nor to blaming its victims. To identify a policy or state of affairs as unjust does not entail support for a rectification of the injustice through terrorism. To criticise Western foreign policy as (sometimes) unjust does not entail blaming the immediate victims of terrorism for that policy, still less concluding that they 'deserve' the terrible fate that the terrorists have chosen to inflict upon them.

There is no consensus on what the obligations of global justice are, but the following is an attempt to provide a relatively uncontroversial, working outline. We share a common humanity, and we have collectively created a global social structure of complex interdependence. The rich and the powerful benefit from this structure more than the poor and the weak, and the former have a considerable ability to determine the fate of the latter. Everyone has a basic negative moral duty not to harm others (in the absence of a special justification), and complex interdependence generates positive duties for all to support just institutions. These obligations are endorsed by the principles of the United Nations, including those of international human-rights law (Buchanan 2004: 85, 95; Pogge 2001: 14, 22; Wenar 2001: 87–8).

If we fail to meet our obligations of global justice, we have some moral responsibility for the unjust consequences. Western imperialism has been unjust and causally responsible for some of the unjust inequalities that still exist in the world. Contemporary Western governments support unjust governments around the world, economically, politically and militarily. The West has, therefore, not only been an accomplice in the exploitation of the global poor, but also helped to finance tyrannical government. Poor countries are sometimes deemed to be responsible for their poverty, because they have corrupt governments. Rich countries have, however, played a part in corrupting the governments of poor countries by condoning bribery. The rich are also causally connected to the poor through international institutions. In the World Trade Organization, for example, power is very unequally distributed, with the result that WTO agreements are unduly favourable to the rich and powerful nations (Wenar 2001; Pogge 2001). Elshtain's view that 9/11 was not 'blowback', because it was motivated by religious fanaticism, ignores the possibility that Western policies have been among the causes of religious fanaticism. The view that Western policy towards the Muslim Middle East has been unjust and has played a causal role in the emergence of terrorism is very plausible, but neither excuses the terrorists nor blames their victims.

The causal connection between global injustice and terrorism is not direct because many responses to injustice are possible other than terrorism, and terrorists may have motives other than the rectification of injustice. Since terrorists subscribe to ideologies that differ from the principles of human rights, the rectification of what they consider to be injustice would not necessarily be favourable to the advancement of human rights. They may favour, for example, discrimination against women and those who do not share their religious views; their conceptions of criminal procedure and humane punishment may not conform with international human-rights standards; and they may not be democrats. Promoting human rights more urgently might, therefore, remove some of the support for terrorism, but it might leave ideological cleavages that were expressed sometimes through terrorist acts (Falk 2003: xxiii). Promoting human rights is, however, good for its own sake, not only as a means to fight terrorism, and respect for human rights worldwide should lessen the appeal of terrorism.

The causes of terrorism are, therefore, complex, and the causes of particular terrorist actions, such as that of 9/11, are likely to involve unique, individual and contingent factors. There is nevertheless a plausible general causal link between Western foreign policy and Islamic terrorism. Over the last few centuries, the West has become politically, economically and culturally dominant. The experience of domination is generally humiliating, and undermines self-respect (Beitz 2001: 115). There is consequently a dialectic of domination and resentment. Islam is a powerful source of self-respect for Muslims. Relations between the West and Islam have left many Muslims with a sense of injustice. The struggle against the Soviet Union in Afghanistan gave some Muslims a sense of empowerment. Humiliation empowered may seek revenge. This is an explanation-sketch of 9/11. It points us in the direction of the sources of superterrorism, and of possible solutions to the problems that it poses for us.

4. 'Terrorism'

President Bush, in his address to the U.N. General Assembly on November 10, 2001, said: 'We unite in opposing all terrorists' (Falk 2003: 120). There is, however, no agreed definition of 'terrorist'. Even the U.S. government uses different definitions (Kapitan 2003: 48). There is no correct definition, and different definitions have different ethical and political implications. The best we can do is to stay as close to common understandings of the concept as possible without reproducing common confusions; identify the main problems in defining 'terrorism'; and settle as little as possible by definition, rather than by argument and evidence.

The most contentious definitional issue is probably whether 'terrorists' are necessarily non-state actors, or whether states can be 'terrorists'. Governments, unsurprisingly, usually define 'terrorists' as those who use violence against the state, directly or indirectly. Several writers maintain that the concept of 'state terrorism' makes perfectly good sense (Gearson 2002: 9; Waldron 2004: 18–19). Falk has argued that the U.S. Administration, by defining 'terrorism' as anti-state terrorism, and representing the 'war on terrorism' as a struggle of good against evil, has undermined the struggle against state terrorism, and thereby the struggle for human rights (Falk 2003: 143).

It seems obvious that 'terrorists' seek to cause terror, and this is commonly included in definitions of 'terrorism'. The essence of terrorism, according to Gearson, is 'the breaking of the enemy's will through the exploitation of fear'. This means that states responding to terrorism can increase the fear intended by the terrorists (Gearson 2002: 8). Freedman points out, however, that, whatever the intentions of the terrorists, terrorism does not always *in fact* cause terror: IRA attacks on economic targets in 'mainland' Britain caused little terror (Freedman 2002b: 47). Waldron suggests that a terrorist act may be an act of war and no more terror-inducing than, say, firing a mortar in battle (Waldron 2004: 8–9, 25).

Terrorists may have various aims. They may seek to punish their enemies, publicise their cause, inflict economic damage, assert their dignity (as they see it), mobilize their supporters, undermine the state's credibility, and/or shake (what they perceive to be) the moral complacency of a population thought to be unjustly privileged (Valls 2000: 67; Waldron 2004: 26–32; Elshtain 2003: 22; Gearson 2002: 11–12). None of these involves the creation of terror, except incidentally.

The wrongness of terrorism is often thought to consist in the fact that terrorists harm persons whom they have no right to harm, who are in this sense 'innocent' (Boyle 2003: 156; Freedman 2002b: 48; Elshtain 2003:

18–19; Ignatieff 2004: 94–5, 110–11). This makes 'terrorism' wrong *by definition*, not by argument. To avoid this problem, 'terrorism' is sometimes defined as indiscriminate or intended to kill civilians. Such definitions do not wholly conform to common usage, however. They would mean that the 9/11 attack on the World Trade Centre was 'terrorism', but that on the Pentagon was not. Also, some terrorists discriminate between 'legitimate' and 'illegitimate' targets. This confusion between definition and ethical judgement may reflect confusion in our ethical judgements. Modern warfare involves both killers and supporters, and the supporters may or may not be soldiers. The line that divides 'combatants' from 'civilians' has become blurred. There is a danger that 'terrorism' is so defined that 'we' are never terrorists, and only our enemies can be terrorists. We should not confuse definitions with ethical judgements, and we should make neither in a self-serving way. The contemporary discourse of 'terrorism' fails to meet these requirements.

The definition of 'terrorism' is often political, that is, an exercise of power. The Nazis called the French Resistance in the Second World War 'terrorists'. The apartheid regime in South Africa called the African National Congress 'terrorists'. Freedman points out that even 'terrorists' call their opponents 'terrorists' (2002b: 46). So, when President Bush called on the United Nations to unite against 'all' terrorists, his call was less than clear. Terrorists are neither the same as, nor necessarily different from, freedom fighters. Terrorists use 'terror' (whatever that is), while freedom fighters fight for freedom (whatever that is). Freedom fighters may be terrorists (use terror in the cause of freedom), an obvious truth that is often overlooked (Gearson 2002: 10–11). Terrorists use political violence, but not all those who use political violence are 'terrorists'. To distinguish between the two we need a theory of justified political violence. We are not likely to agree completely on such a theory, and this is at least one of the reasons why the definition of 'terrorism' will remain unclear.

5. Having Rights and Being Safe

Mainstream human-rights opinion holds that a 'fair balance' should be struck between national security and human rights (ICHRP 2002: 19). The International Covenant on Civil and Political Rights strikes this balance by allowing states, in time of public emergency 'which threatens the life of the nation', to derogate from their obligations under the Covenant 'to the extent strictly required by the exigencies of the situation'. Certain human rights are protected from derogation. They include, principally, the rights to life, to be free from torture, cruel, inhuman or degrading punishment, slavery and retroactive criminal laws, to freedom of thought, conscience and religion, and not to be subject to discrimination solely on the ground of race, colour, sex, language, religion or social origin.

The general idea of 'fair balance' as defensible is we recognize that the protection of some human rights can endanger other human rights or values other than human rights. Nickel has proposed three tests for evaluating the restriction of rights:

1) *The consistency test* specifies that, if a right (R1) is necessary to another right (R2), it is inconsistent to restrict R1 but not R2.
2) *The importance test* says that the weight of the values that *justify* a right provide guidance as to the conditions under which it might be restricted. The importance of particular rights is always subject to controversy.
3) *The cost-efficiency test* takes into account the cost of implementing a right. If a proposed restriction meets the consistency test, and we have to choose between restricting two equally important rights, we should protect the right with the lower costs, that is, the one whose implementation does less damage to legitimate values.

Nickel concludes that these tests generally support the derogation provisions of international law. The right not to be murdered, for example, meets the consistency test, because those who live in fear of their lives are disempowered from protecting their other human rights. It is also clear that the non-derogable rights are extremely important. It may be that banning extrajudicial killing and torture has costs in the fight against terrorism, but Nickel believes that these costs ought to be borne, because the cost of allowing such derogations would be extremely high. Convincing those who believe that targeted assassinations or torture can be justified in the post-9/11 world would require arguments showing that the costs of these policies would be excessive, or the cost test would have to be abandoned.

Nickel suggests that, if the right against retroactive criminal laws is non-derogable, other due-process rights, such as those to a fair trial, should also be non-derogable. However, in times of emergency, governments may reasonably believe that they ought to detain persons who are believed to be dangerous without trial where fair trials are impractical. This suggests that due-process rights might justifiably be limited during emergencies. Due-process rights might have great weight on grounds of consistency and importance, but might have high costs during emergencies, and therefore might be derogable. The rights to freedom of speech and assembly might be derogable for similar reasons. Since such restrictions of rights are subject to abuse and error, the right to petition ought to be non-derogable (Nickel 1987: 133–46). Ignatieff argues, in contrast, that derogable and non-derogable rights are indivisible in the sense that exercising derogable rights may be necessary to protect the non-derogable rights. The rights to freedom of expression, association and assembly may, for example, be necessary to prevent the use of torture (Ignatieff 2004: 47). In Nickel's terms, Ignatieff argues that consistency requires a larger set of non-derogable rights than international law recognises. Nickel draws our attention, not only to consistency, but also to *costs*, but costs are difficult to estimate. The consistency test itself does not settle disagreements. If there were no freedom of speech, it would indeed be difficult to defend the right against torture, but not *all* limitations of free speech would have this effect. Nickel's criteria may be appropriate, but they are indeterminate.

Ignatieff proposes several principles to help us choose 'the lesser evil' in time of emergency: 1) we should protect human dignity, which means, for example, that we should not countenance torture; 2) we should protect due process, make detention subject to judicial review and ensure that those detained have access to lawyers; 3) we should insist that exceptional measures will make the people more secure; 4) exceptional measures should be a last resort; 5) exceptional measures should be subject to open adversarial review by legislative and judicial bodies; 6) the state should respect its international obligations; and 7) exceptional measures should have 'sunset clauses' that subject them to time limits (2004: 18, 23–4, 39). These principles would provide relatively strong protection for human rights in times of terrorist threat, but it is hard to know whether the principles would be mutually compatible in practice, and whether their cost in vulnerability to the threat of 'superterrorism' would be tolerable.

Scanlon agrees with Nickel that the *justification* for a particular right helps to clarify what is at stake when we balance a right with its costs. In defending the claim that a certain right ought to be protected, we have to compare the expected advantages of protecting the right with the expected advantages of restricting it. We respect human rights because we believe that the benefits of protecting them are high, and that the costs of violating them are generally high. We become uncertain to the extent that we come to believe that the cost of protecting some rights might also be high. The threat of 'superterrorism' raises this possibility (Scanlon 2003: 35–9). Waldron points out that free societies always strike a balance between liberty and security: the right to a fair trial has the cost that a dangerous criminal may be freed. When people say that 9/11 requires 'striking a new balance between liberty and security', they mean that they now think that the cost of liberty that they enjoyed on 9/10 was *too high*. Two responses are possible: 1) we can reduce our liberty to achieve the amount of security we (mistakenly) thought we had on 9/10, or 2) we can accept less security, but also accept less liberty so that the security costs should not be unbearably high. This should not be seen as striking a balance between security and human rights, because there is a human right to security (Waldron 2003). This approach is consequentialist, because it takes seriously the moral consequences of protecting and limiting rights. It contrasts with Kofi Annan's view that the fight against terrorism should not involve trading rights.

Talk of 'balancing' two goods, such as liberty and security, ignores the question of how these goods should be *justly distributed* (Waldron 2003). Ignatieff points out that the threat of terrorism may lead to a defence of the security of some by sacrificing the liberty of others. The security of the majority in the United States and the United Kingdom after 9/11 has been balanced, not so much with *their* liberty, which has been reduced only marginally, but with that of adult Muslim males, especially those subject to immigration control. Human rights are the rights of everyone, but an important part of their justification is to protect unpopular minorities from unjust treatment. The unequal distribution of liberty and security that has been justified by the supposed need to 'balance' these two values may have aggravated ethnic prejudice, and may even prove to be counter-productive in the 'war on terrorism' as it alienates Muslim citizens from the rest of society, and increases sympathy for terrorists, if only among a small minority (Ignatieff 2004: 32, 44; Waldron 2003: 200–4).

Where liberty is reduced, the state's power is increased. This increased power can be used to fight terrorism, but Waldron points out that this is not the only thing that it can be used for. An increase in the threat from terrorists does not reduce the threat of state oppression. The fear that 9/11 has evoked may make us forget the dangers of state power. We should agree to reductions in our liberty, and increases in state power, only if these changes really are likely to increase our security, and the trade-off required is morally reasonable (Waldron 2003).

Human-rights supporters are sometimes accused of ignoring the consequences of protecting human rights, but consequentialist arguments do not necessarily favour those who wish to restrict human rights. Waldron points out that increasing the power of the state to combat terrorism is not the same as an actual decrease in the terrorist threat. A decrease in liberty can be justified by an increase in security only if security is actually increased. It may be that the increase in security is *uncertain*, but this means that the value of decreasing liberty is uncertain. Violating rights, especially of unpopular groups, may make people feel safer without actually making them safer. Making prejudiced people feel good does not justify violating human rights. Respect for human rights is an integral part of a 'good society', and any proposed trade-off must be evaluated for its effect on the overall quality of society (Waldron 2003: 208–10; Ignatieff 2004: 49, 54).

In evaluating restrictions of human rights for the sake of security, we must evaluate the threat from which we are said to need protection. This raises several difficulties. The threat may be uncertain; public information about it may be unreliable; important information may be secret. Ignatieff argues that, although secrecy is unavoidable, it should be accountable to legislative and judicial oversight (2004: 2–4, 11, 51). Such oversight is better than no oversight, but we should be aware of its limitations. Judges commonly defer to governments on matters of national security, although they do not always do so, and governments can manipulate legislatures by their control of information. A robust free press is necessary to hold these state institutions to account. Human-rights non-governmental organizations (NGOs) have an important role to play in minimizing the chances that governments will restrict human rights without good cause.

6. The War on Terrorism

The 'war on terrorism' is sometimes described as a struggle between liberal democracy and its uncompromising enemies (Ignatieff 2004: 125–6, 131; Berman 2003: 182–3). The ideology of Al Qaeda may indeed be 'apocalyptic', and this must be taken seriously. Yet many of its supporters may be motivated by political concerns that can be addressed by mundane, enlightened policies (Ignatieff 2004: 132). The response to 9/11 has been, as Gearson argued, to 'statify' the terrorist threat, and to translate it into the familiar discourse of 'war' by conflating the problems of terrorism, 'rogue states' and weapons of mass destruction. This has led to a controversial war against Iraq, and the detention of prisoners at Guantánamo Bay, who are neither prisoners of war nor suspected criminals with rights of due process. The threat of terrorism has been confused with various problems of inter-state relations, thereby vitiating policy responses to both. The unexpected persistence of instability in Iraq is only the most obvious manifestation of these policy errors.

The U.S. response to 9/11 has been criticised for being 'unilateralist', but it has, in fact, wavered between unilateralism and multilateralism. The United States has wanted to control the war on terrorism, but has needed the legitimacy provided by multilateralism, whether this comes from the United Nations or elsewhere. The attack on Al Qaeda and the overthrow of the Taliban regime in Afghanistan have been justified as legitimate measures of self-defence (Elshtain 2003). Although the sight of the world's most powerful state bombing one of the world's poorest countries was unattractive to some (including many Muslims), the argument that the United States should have confined itself to police measures and to working through the United Nations lacked conviction (Falk 2003). Nevertheless, the United States and its allies might be criticised for not taking their human-rights obligations towards the people of Afghanistan seriously. The war on Al Qaeda and the Taliban implied, misleadingly, that the West's allies in Afghanistan were champions of human rights. Concern for the rights of Afghan women was somewhat tentative. Arguments for self-defence were mixed with arguments for regime change. Ethical and legal arguments for 'humanitarian interventions' to change regimes that are gross violators of human rights have been in a state of uncertainty since the Kosovo war of 1999. The war on Iraq has proved especially controversial because, although it removed a brutal dictator, it was justified principally by his alleged possession of weapons of mass destruction. This justification was undermined because its factual assumptions were false. The outcome of this war remains uncertain, and its connection with the war on terrorism tenuous.

It may be that events since 9/11 have intensified, rather than changed, the principal dynamics of global politics since the end of the Cold War. The U.S. doctrine of preventive self-defence, the willingness to resort to war, the reluctance to submit to international regulation, even on human rights and arms control, the substitution of the 'coalition of the willing' for multilateral action and the disregard for inconvenient international laws have given the United States a dominant posture that predictably causes resentment. The United States has by no means withdrawn from the international system and its rule of law, but its commitment to them is selective. Realists will say that hegemonic powers always behave like this. This may be true, but such behaviour also always generates resistance. This resistance may occasionally take the form of terrorism, but, perhaps more often, the coalition of the willing will become the coalition of the reluctant. Excessive assertion of U.S. power may undermine the war on terrorism, and, possibly, co-operation on human-rights issues. The U.S. hegemonic project assumes trust in unaccountable power that contradicts the assumptions of the Western, liberal-democratic tradition. Power tends to rationalise self-interest as moral superiority. The 'war on terrorism' affirms both U.S. superiority and the global common good. Its tensions derive from doubts as to whether these are perfectly compatible (ICHRP 2002: 3, 33, 35; Freedman 2002a: 5; Wallace 2002: 117–18; Falk 2003: 32).

Some commentators fear that U.S. foreign policy since 9/11 will have harmful consequences for human rights. The United States is providing military support for local anti-terrorist campaigns in various countries, some of which are serious human-rights violators. Ironically, the United States is now backing authoritarian post-Communist regimes against putative Islamic terrorists, having, not so long ago, backed Islamic fighters against Communist regimes[2]. The fact that the United States, as well as other Western states, previously supported the regime of Saddam Hussein in Iraq, and the Islamic resistance in Afghanistan, of which Al Qaeda formed a part, makes it vulnerable to the charge of inconsistency. Even its policy on weapons of mass destruction (WMD) does not appear coherent, since the most likely source for terrorist groups to obtain WMD is not Iraq, but the former USSR, and perhaps Pakistan, but only limited resources have been devoted to preventing this (Dombey 2004). If Iraq had possessed WMD materials, the war in Iraq might have increased, rather than decreased, their distribution to terrorists. Guantánamo Bay and Abu Ghraib call into question the claim that the war on terrorism is a war for human rights. The former also calls into question the claim that official policy was not somehow responsible for the latter (ICHRP 2002: 2, 36–7; Reitan 2003: 52–4; Falk 2003: 147–8; Forsythe 2004).

There are several reasons why foreign policies may be inconsistent: interests are diverse and not always compatible; principles are diverse and not always compatible; democratic governments must heed public opinion that may be inconsistent; democracies change governments and so may change policies; even the richest government has insufficient resources to devote to all issues of justice and human rights simultaneously, and so must be selective; the external environments of governments change in complex and unpredictable ways; foreign-policy decisions require the exercise of judgement, and judgement is not subject to determinate rules (Brown 2003). Consistency is not always as good as is commonly thought: it is not a good reason not to do the right thing now, for example, that you did the wrong thing in the past (Halliday 1996: 83). However, inconsistency in foreign policy may be perceived as hypocrisy, and this may undermine the legitimacy of the war on terrorism, as well as the struggle for human rights (Falk 2003: 96–7; ICHRP 2002: 4, 60; Halliday 1996: 145–6).

9/11 evoked a rare moment of consensus on universal, humane values, comparable to the spirit that launched the Universal Declaration of Human Rights. Post-9/11 U.S. foreign policy has fractured this consensus (Halliday 2002: 239). Hegemons are always likely to be unpopular, and, because they are also likely to be self-righteous, will be puzzled by their unpopularity. There

---

[2] Some have argued that the human-rights foreign policy of the Bush Administration of 2000–4 has been underestimated, and that pressure has been put on such human-rights violating regimes as those of Uzbekistan and Egypt. The evaluation of this claim would require detailed analysis, but there is a general structural similarity between 'the war on terrorism' and the Cold War on Communism that should cause concern for human-rights supporters.

is a long history of Western intrusion into the Islamic world that has always been self-righteous and always provoked resistance. The post-9/11 Western intrusion into Muslim countries is not likely to be different. The United States claim that it has the right to preventive self-defence could not be recognized as a universal right, for, if it were, Iran and North Korea would have the right to attack the United States! Insofar as the United States is claiming rights that it could not allow to others, its foreign policy is unjust. Those who say that the United States, as the only superpower, must impose order on the world, like a Hobbesian sovereign, forget that the authority of the Hobbesian sovereign was based on consent, as well as the Lockean objection that Hobbesian sovereigns cannot be trusted not to promote their own interests at the expense of the rights of the people (Held 2004: 2, 146–7, 151; Buchanan 2004: 452, 466).

Since 'terrorism' is 'evil', or a violation of human rights, a war on 'terrorism' seems justified, and even obligatory (Elshtain 2003; Berman 2003). But the *idea* of a 'war on terrorism' is morally dangerous. It demonises the opponent. Some may respond that, if the opponent is Al Qaeda, this may be no bad thing. But the 'war on terrorism' is a war on all 'terrorists', and consequently an indefinite number of groups is thereby demonised. Demonisation is a barrier to understanding, and understanding is necessary to just and effective solutions to political problems. As it demonises the enemy, so it sanctifies the warrior. As in the war against Communism, U.S. foreign policy appears like a Western *jihad* (An-Na'im 2002; Klusmeyer & Suhrke 2002). This is undermined by the previous willingness of the United States to support Islamic extremism and other forms of terrorism, such as that of the Contras in Nicaragua, as well as by the contempt shown for human rights in the war on terrorism (Kassam 2003: 118; Kapitan 2003: 50; Forsythe 2004). The problem of defining 'terrorism', which may appear to be a technical, academic question, becomes a serious question of global justice, when enormous human and material resources are devoted to a global 'war on terrorism' with at least some harmful consequences for the rule of international law and human rights.

7. Conclusions

It is difficult to 'strike a balance' between human rights and security in 'an age of terrorism', because it requires complex and uncertain judgements, and information that is hard to obtain. Nevertheless, we can be more rather than less rational in our choice of policies if we keep certain points clear.

There is a human right to security, and therefore what we have to 'balance' are, in part, different sets of human rights that are not completely compatible.

The universal right to certain freedoms and protections puts us, or others, at risk, and this risk may threaten human rights. We need to analyse clearly which human rights are at stake under the threat of terrorism, and which risks we ought to take. This requires us to know the risk of the threat of terrorism, and this makes us vulnerable to manipulation by governments that control this information. It is generally accepted that, even in democracies, governments may keep some information secret, because such secrecy is necessary to protect the rights of the people. Locke's classic theory of rights protection would certainly allow the government considerable discretion in this matter. The recent handling of intelligence about Iraq's supposed weapons of mass destruction is a reminder that democratic politicians should not be trusted too much. Ignatieff emphasises the importance of legislative and judicial oversight. This is not wrong, but it may be insufficient. A robust civil society is necessary to challenge all the institutions of the state, even if civil society itself may err. The International Council on Human Rights Policy sees a special role for professional human-rights organizations, which have justifiably acquired a reputation for combining humane objectives with careful and responsible analysis. 'Superterrorism' is scary, and we are not irrational to be afraid. Against terrorism, and against the fear that it generates, our best defence is a judicious distrust of government and a commitment to the reasoned, analytical defence of human rights.

The problem of 'blaming the victim' is especially challenging. We must affirm that, from the perspective of a commitment to human rights, the attack on the United States on September 11, 2001, was an atrocity. We should go further, and maintain that the extremist Islamic ideology of Al Qaeda is a grave threat to human rights. There is, nevertheless, room for a complex debate about the origins of this crisis, and the best way to deal with it. Western powers are not very good at 'aftermaths'. They have a history of imperial intrusions into other parts of the world, and have been reluctant to acknowledge their responsibility for the consequences. In particular, the West fought the Cold War, with a mixture of just and unjust measures, but has been reluctant to attend to its aftermath. This seems to link the former Yugoslavia and Afghanistan. The West was involved in both to defend its interests in the Cold War. Having achieved its objectives, it was careless regarding the aftermaths. NATO bombed Yugoslavia to save Kosovo, but NATO political leaders are reticent about the aftermath. The United States backed the Islamist resistance to the USSR in Afghanistan, but became careless about its aftermath. It bombed Afghanistan to defeat Al Qaeda and topple the Taliban, but risks inattention to the aftermath. The war against Saddam Hussein was won, but its aftermath is uncertain.

The United Nations has a global vision, which risks fatal weakness because of excessive idealism. Yet a narrow, and pragmatic, emphasis on 'the terrorist threat', and the human rights of particular populations, may ignore wider issues of justice, that demand our attention for their own sake, and because they may be causally linked to terrorism. At the heart of these difficulties is the commitment to universal human rights and the difficulty of implementing that commitment peacefully (Freeman 2004). The current situation in Sudan exemplifies these dilemmas. We have the right to expect our governments to protect us from terrorists. We have the obligation to ensure, so far as possible, that they do so with due respect to our human rights, but also with due respect to the claims of global justice. This obligation cannot be fulfilled cheaply. If democratic governments are unwilling to pay the price, the fault is partly ours.

The challenge of terrorism to human rights requires a response that is two-dimensional. On the first dimension, we have to balance order and rights in the face of threats. We cannot specify, theoretically, precisely how this ought to be done, because threats are particular (as well as uncertain), and thus require judgements, on which reasonable persons may differ. The best response, however, lies somewhere between the Lockean prerogative power and the refusal to reconsider human rights in the face of threats to the right of security. Allowing discretion to government must be balanced with a rational distrust of government. The second dimension is that of global justice. Large claims have been made for the war on terrorism as a fight for global justice. It may, however, be criticised on this dimension for its disregard of human rights. 'Superterrorism' has changed the environment of the struggle for human rights. It has not changed the validity of that struggle. The idea of human rights defends the critical spirit. That critical spirit should be reflexive. The values of human rights are extremely robust. 9/11 and the war on terrorism call on us to rethink the strategies for human rights in this new world disorder in which we unexpectedly find ourselves.

REFERENCES

Andrews, K. (2003). 'Why Bush Should Explain 11 September'. In P. Hayden, T. Lansford and R. P. Watson (Eds.), *America's War on Terror*, pp. 29–40. Aldershot: Ashgate.

An-Na'im, A. A. (2002). 'Upholding International Legality Against Islamic and American *Jihad*'. In K. Booth and T. Dunne (Eds.), *Worlds in Collision: Terror and the Future of Global Order*, pp. 162–71. Basingstoke: Palgrave Macmillan.

Beitz, C. R. (2001). 'Does Global Inequality Matter?' In T. W. Pogge (Ed.), *Global Justice*, pp. 106–22. Oxford: Blackwell.

Berman, P. (2003). *Terror and Liberalism*. New York: Norton.

Boyle, J. (2003). 'Just War Doctrine and the Military Response to Terrorism'. *The Journal of Political Philosophy*, 11 (2), pp. 153–70.

Brown, C. (2003). 'Selective Humanitarianism: In Defence of Inconsistency'. In D. K. Chatterjee and D. E. Scheid (Eds.), *Ethics and Foreign Intervention*, pp. 31–50. Cambridge: Cambridge University Press.

Buchanan, A. (2004). *Justice, Legitimacy, and Self-Determination: Moral Foundations for International Law*. Oxford: Oxford University Press.

Dershowitz, A. M. (2002). *Why Terrorism Works: Understanding the Threat, Responding to the Challenge*. New Haven, CT: Yale University Press.

Dombey, N. (2004, September 2). 'Not Iran, Not North Korea, Not Libya, but Pakistan'. *London Review of Books*, 26 (17).

Elshtain, J. B. (2003). *Just War Against Terror: The Burden of American Power in a Violent World*. New York: Basic Books.

Falk, R. (2003). *The Great Terror War*. Moreton-in-the-Marsh: Arris Books.

Forsythe, D. P. (2004, August 26). 'The U.S. and Treatment of Prisoners: Only Part of the Story'. *Lincoln Journal Star*.

Freedman, L. (2002a). 'Introduction'. In L. Freedman (Ed.), *Superterrorism: Policy Responses*, pp. 1–6. Oxford: Blackwell.

Freedman, L. (2002b). 'The Coming War on Terrorism'. In L. Freedman (Ed.), *Superterrorism: Policy Responses*, pp. 40–56. Oxford: Blackwell.

Freeman, M. A. (2004). 'Human Rights and Force: Revisiting the Question of Intervention'. Paper presented to the Annual Convention of the International Studies Association, Montréal, Québec, Canada, 17–20 March.

Fukuyama, F. (2002). 'History and September 11'. In K. Booth and T. Dunne (Eds.), *Worlds in Collision: Terror and the Future of Global Order*, pp. 27–36. Basingstoke: Palgrave Macmillan.

Gearson, J. (2002). 'The Nature of Modern Terrorism'. In L. Freedman (Ed.), *Superterrorism: Policy Responses*, pp. 7–24. Oxford: Blackwell.

Halliday, F. (1996). *Islam and the Myth of Confrontation: Religion and Politics in the Middle East*. London: I. B. Tauris.

Halliday, F. (2002). 'A New Global Configuration'. In K. Booth and T. Dunne (Eds.), *Worlds in Collision: Terror and the Future of Global Order*, pp. 235–41. Basingstoke: Palgrave Macmillan.

Held, D. (2004). *Global Covenant: The Social Democratic Alternative to the Washington Consensus*. Cambridge: Polity.

Hobbes, T. ([1651]1996). *Leviathan*. Cambridge: Cambridge University Press, revised student edition, edited by R. Tuck.

Ignatieff, M. (2004). *The Lesser Evil: Political Ethics in an Age of Terror*. Princeton: Princeton University Press.

International Council on Human Rights Policy. (2002). *Human Rights After September 11*. Versoix, Switzerland: International Council on Human Rights Policy.

Kapitan, T. (2003). 'The Terrorism of "Terrorism"'. In J. P. Sterba (Ed.), *Terrorism and International Justice*, pp. 47–66. Oxford: Oxford University Press.

Kassam, Z. (2003). 'Can a Muslim Be a Terrorist?' In J. P. Sterba (Ed.), *Terrorism and International Justice*, p. 114–31. New York: Oxford University Press.

Klusmeyer, D. & Suhrke, A. (2002). 'Comprehending "Evil": Challenges for Law and Policy'. *Ethics and International Affairs*, 16 (1), pp. 27–42.

Locke, J. ([1689]1970). *Two Treatises of Government.* Cambridge: Cambridge University Press.

Marshall, J. (1994). *John Locke: Resistance, Religion and Responsibility.* Cambridge: Cambridge University Press.

Nickel, J. W. (1987). *Making Sense of Human Rights: Philosophical Reflections on the Universal Declaration of Human Rights.* Berkeley, CA: University of California Press.

Pogge, T. W. (2001). 'Priorities of Global Justice'. In T. W. Pogge (Ed.), *Global Justice*, pp. 6–23. Oxford: Blackwell.

Rawls, J. (1972). *A Theory of Justice.* Oxford: Oxford University Press.

Rawls, J. (1999). *The Law of Peoples.* Cambridge, MA: Harvard University Press.

Reitan, R. (2003). 'Human Rights in U.S. Policy: A Casualty of the "War on Terrorism"?' *The International Journal of Human Rights*, 7 (4), pp. 51–62.

Scanlon, T. M. (2003). *The Difficulty of Tolerance.* Cambridge: Cambridge University Press.

Valls, A. (2000). 'Can Terrorism Be Justified?' In A. Valls (Ed.), *Ethics in International Affairs: Theories and Cases*, pp. 65–79. Lanham, MD: Rowman & Littlefield.

Waldron, J. (2003). 'Security and Liberty: The Image of Balance'. *The Journal of Political Philosophy*, 11 (2), pp. 191–210.

Waldron, J. (2004). 'Terrorism and the Uses of Terror'. *The Journal of Ethics*, 8 (1), pp. 5–35.

Wallace, W. (2002). 'American Hegemony: European Dilemmas'. In L. Freedman (Ed.), *Superterrorism: Policy Responses*, pp. 105–18. Oxford: Blackwell.

Wenar, L. (2001). 'Contractualism and Global Economic Justice'. In T. W. Pogge (Ed.), *Global Justice*, pp. 76–90. Oxford: Blackwell.

2. Liberal Security

FERNANDO R. TESÓN

How should democracies[1] respond to security threats?[2] How can governments respond to heightened forms of violence, such as terrorism,[3] internal uprising, or external aggression, while remaining true to the rule of law, human rights, and democratic values? Commentators and courts in democratic countries, while divided on important issues, seem reluctantly to converge on the view that *some* adjustment on our individual freedoms is justified to face these threats.[4] But when, if ever, is such a curtailment defensible? And isn't curtailment of human rights self-defeating – as the cliché goes, aren't governments who curtail freedom destroying democracy under the guise of defending it?

---

[1] By democracies I mean societies committed to individual freedom (human rights, civil rights) and to democratic and periodic election of their government.

[2] I define "security threat" below. My definition is in line with standard treatment. Article 15 of the European Convention of Human Rights defines "emergency" as "war or other public emergency threatening the life of the nation," a concept that has been refined by the case-law of the European Court of Human Rights. See especially the cases *Lawless v. Ireland* (1961) and *Ireland v. The United Kingdom* (1978). The attacks of September 11, 2001, are, of course, at the heart of my concern in this chapter.

[3] The word "terrorist" is of course problematic, not the least because it is not merely descriptive but normative. See the discussions in Fullkwinder 2001: 9; Kapitan 2003: 47; and Coady 2002. While the choice of words is important, in this chapter I define "terrorism" *ostensively*: it is the kind of unconventional attack carried out by the September 11 attackers. That someone is a terrorist implies, in this chapter, at least two things: that he does not have a just cause for his attack, and that he targets innocents in violation of basic rules of morality, international conventions, and the doctrine of double effect.

[4] Compare Ackerman 2004 with Cole 2004. While some vigorously deny that altering constitutional rights is required to face the new threat, see, for example, Bovard 2003, passim., there seems to be a consensus that after the attacks of September 11, 2001, "some adjustment in our scheme of civil liberties is inevitable" (Waldron 2003: 191). See also Ackerman 2004. On the other hand, commentators disagree vigorously about where that balance should be drawn, as the Ackerman-Cole debate in the *Yale Law Journal* demonstrates. For the decisions of the United States Supreme Court and the British House of Lords, see note 13.

I tackle this subject with great trepidation. I am Argentine, and lived through the horrors of the military régime that ruled Argentina between 1976 and 1984. The government then argued that unless civil liberties were restricted, Argentine society would succumb to the terrorist threat (posed then by violent radical left-wing groups). The result is well known: the government unleashed abominable forms of state terror, torturing and murdering between 10,000 and 30,000 persons (see *Nunca Más* 1984).[5] What is worse, the government, vile as it was, could not be accused of manufacturing the terrorist threat: there *was* one. When the smoke cleared, I joined most Argentines of my generation in the view that human rights should *never* be violated, regardless of the magnitude of the threat. Lifting restraints on state action is the surest way to tyranny, and governments should never be allowed to invoke threats as a justification for trampling on human rights. But is this position reasonable? The lessons from history should certainly make us constantly vigilant, and we should be slow to renounce in any significant measure the great achievements of the Enlightenment, human rights, and democracy. Yet perhaps one should not generalize from the grotesque Argentine experience. Europe, for example, has a better record than Latin America: governments in general did a good job of defeating terrorist organizations during the 1970s and 1980s within the rule of law, although the threats were less substantial (Alexander & Myers 1982). And, on this side of the Atlantic, one should hope that American institutions are strong enough to countenance the readjustment that might be necessary (if it is) to face the terrorist onslaught while preserving freedom.

In this chapter I do not examine what specific restrictions to freedom, if any, can be justified by security threats. Rather, my purpose is mainly conceptual. I argue, first, that restrictions on liberty are justified, if they are, *only* by the need to preserve liberty itself, and not by other values such as order or security. I argue, secondly, that the terrorist attacks of September 11 pose the kind of threat that, subject to the usual requirements of necessity and proportionality, might justify some temporary restrictions to our freedoms. One important corollary is that a properly tailored fight against terror is a fight *for* human rights, not antithetical to them.

Conventional thinking poses the problem as a dilemma: democratic governments have to choose between two competing values, freedom and order.[6] The more freedom civil society enjoys, the closer it is to anarchy, as it allows

---

[5] There is an English translation: *Nunca más (Never Again): A Report by Argentina's National Commission on Disappeared People.* (1986). London : Faber and Faber.

[6] See, in addition to works cited in note 4, the thoughtful analysis by Heymann 2003: 87–113.

room for predators to victimize others. Conversely, if civil society wishes to curb predatory behavior, it runs the risk of sacrificing the very freedoms that justify its existence in the first place. Let us call this the Hobbesian Dilemma. I argue that the starkness of the dilemma is overstated by all sides in the current debate about liberal security. Human rights and security are *not* antithetical values. Contrary to appearances, security measures are *not* justified by values *other* than freedom, such as order or stability. Security measures can only be justified by the very moral principles that legitimize the state in the first place: the imperative to preserve and protect the liberal constitution – whether this idea derives from human dignity, human rights, natural rights, or any such liberal principles of justice. I suggest that *whatever that balance may be*, it should be justified, if it is, by an appeal to freedom itself, not to order. Liberal security is the flip side of freedom.

In this chapter I define "security threats" as *actual or foreseeable acts of massive violence against the lives or liberties of citizens of a democratic state.* Thus, the state has to face a genuine threat against the lives or liberties of its citizens, threats that, because of their large scale (such as a war) or the danger of repetition (such as terrorist attacks of the kind suffered by the United States in 2001), affect the democratic society as a whole and, quite often, democratic institutions themselves. *A contrario sensu,* a democratic state must tolerate anti-democratic behavior (such as speech) that falls short of a threat. This is one of the reasons why the infamous "national security doctrine," espoused by the Latin American dictatorships of the 1970s, falls outside the acceptable realm of liberal security. Liberal security measures are, then, those that would be justified to counter genuine security threats.

Must all security threats be political in nature, in the sense that the perpetrators must seek the destruction of liberal-democratic values in the name of an illiberal undemocratic ideology? I don't believe so. Democratic societies can be besieged as much by fundamentalist Islamic terrorists as by, say, the Mafia or drug lords (think about Colombia). However, the illiberal intent of the attackers may aggravate the threat in the sense that it may make it transparently directed, not only against life, limb, or property, but against liberal-democratic institutions themselves. We can therefore distinguish between *physical threats* and *moral threats.* Any threat that is eligible for security measures must be *massive* in terms of the harm threatened. This is a physical threat. If the threat is not massive, the liberal state can use the normal mechanisms of criminal justice. But some of those physical threats are, in addition, intended by the perpetrators against the liberal institutions themselves. I define as *moral threats* those threats that pose danger to the lives and property of citizens in a democracy and, furthermore, are carried out in the name of illiberal principles or values. (I elaborate on this concept later in this chapter.)

As is well known, Thomas Hobbes thought that stabilizing civil society, itself a precondition for mutually beneficial social cooperation, required the establishment of absolute government (1651: chapter 17). To him, people cannot cooperate spontaneously, because the temptation to prey on others is too great. The state of nature is, for Hobbes, a gigantic Prisoner's Dilemma: in the absence of strong governmental coercion people enjoy excessive freedom, and their selfish instincts cancel whatever cooperative impulses they may have (Kavka 1986). Chaos emerges. Hobbes's influence endures in the popular view that order and freedom are in unavoidable tension: what we gain by strengthening one we lose by weakening the other. On one reading, Hobbes was too obsessed with social compliance and stability; that is why he thought that the imposition of order was the paramount task of the state. (Alternatively, of course, one can read his project simply as an account of the inherent obstacles to social cooperation.) In the Hobbesian vision, we must secure social cooperation with whatever force is necessary because the alternative is chaos and, ultimately, mutual destruction. Therefore, we sacrifice freedom if we must, because liberty can easily turn into license to prey on others. A milder way of putting this is to say that institutions should be designed, first and foremost, to secure order. For purposes of this chapter, I call this the conservative conception of society. To be sure, conservatism in this sense can be quite complex and sophisticated, and modern versions of it would give an important place to civil liberties. But the Hobbesian insight remains: the supreme value of society is order. Only after securing a modicum of order can we, cautiously and incrementally, allow individual freedom as a sort of by-product, or luxury, of an orderly society.[7]

I would like to identify here two liberal positions antagonistic to the conservative view. The first one, endorsed by Locke, Kant, and their followers, places liberty as the ultimate justification of government, and especially as the ultimate justification for any form of coercion over our fellow citizens. These authors reject Hobbes's solution to the dilemma. For them, Hobbes misconceives the question of justification. Order is not, and cannot be, an intrinsic value. We need order, that is, we need to control interpersonal violence, *for* some other purpose, perhaps to enable us to pursuit autonomous life plans (as the Kantian tradition suggests), perhaps to secure natural rights (as the Lockean tradition prefers). Therefore, the state, its constitution, and its

---

[7] For a survey of conservative views and replies after 9/11, see Baker 2003.

political practices can only be justified by reference to those higher moral values (liberty, dignity, natural rights). Let us call this position then Liberalism$_1$.

The second position accepts Liberalism$_1$ but goes further: it defines human rights in a particularly strong deontological way. On this view, human rights are so important that they may never yield to values such as order or security. Supporters of this view may believe that a life with diminished rights is not worth living. Succumbing to the threat is preferable than degrading freedom in any substantial way. Let us call this position Liberalism$_2$. It is illustrated by the reaction (mine included) to the Argentine tragedy, mentioned above. Sometimes liberals$_2$ are identified as "human rights absolutists," a title that most of them carry with pride. Both liberal positions are critical of conservatism because fairly strong conservative view of society (in the sense here defined, that places social order above liberty) will tend to undermine human rights, and thus run counter to the very principle that justifies the state in the first place. By allowing just that amount of freedom that is compatible with the maintenance of order, the conservative view undermines the moral foundations of democracy. In this light, then, it does seem that conservatives on one hand, and liberals$_1$ and liberals$_2$ on the other, have a genuine moral disagreement: when facing a security threat, conservatives choose the suppression of the threat over the preservation of freedoms; whereas both liberal views are skeptical about restrictions of human rights, either because human rights form the basis of a justified society (Liberalism$_1$ and Liberalism$_2$), or, further, because human rights should be (almost) absolute (Liberalism$_2$). In the current political scene the debate seems often posed in that way. Conservatives and liberals$_2$ try to force the public into accepting one horn of the dilemma and rejecting the other. Conservatives thus often brand the specter of the terrorist threat and urge Americans to be brave and give up some of their freedom as the only way to be safe. Liberals$_2$, on the other hand, insist that our freedoms define us as a nation, and that a life without them is not worth living, even if it is safe.

I want to argue for Liberalism$_1$ and against both conservatism and Liberalism$_2$, and suggest some conclusions for thinking about the problem of security. Conservatives overestimate the dangers of noncompliance, underestimate the dangers of authoritarian rule, and misapprehend the moral foundations of civil society. The conservative view misses crucial features of the justification of the liberal order and, by extension, the justification of violence and coercion. Hobbes overlooked (or purposefully avoided) the question of the moral justification of the state. Like Hobbes, conservatives are all too ready to regard security as an intrinsic goal, and human rights as luxuries or by-products that should be set aside when our security is threatened. In doing so, they underestimate the devastating effect of authoritarianism and the importance that human rights have as the centerpiece of our democracy. Importantly, conservatives overlook the fact that a free society *must* pay a safety price in order to have freedom. The Soviet Union and Nazi Germany were safer, I suppose, than present-day Russia and Germany. Crime control is an important goal of a free society, but it is not its paramount goal. Absolute safety can only be achieved in a police state. Perhaps Hobbesian conservatism is at its best in cases of *total* collapse of the social order, of anarchy, where liberty arguably should take a second seat to survival. Even then I have my doubts, but at any rate this is obviously not the case in modern-day democratic societies. As I suggest below, the security threats are genuine and must be countered, but they do not threaten *collapse* of the social order itself.

But liberals$_2$ are also mistaken. While they are right to criticize conservatives for their insistence on order and security above all, they overlook the fact that certain threats (such as current forms of terrorism) *are directed against the very freedoms they want to preserve.* Liberals$_2$ often argue as if the terrorist threats were irrelevant to the preservation of our freedoms, as if security and freedom were two separate domains where, again, an increase in one means a decrease in the other.[8] Like conservatives, liberals$_2$ buy into the Hobbesian dilemma, except that they, unlike conservatives, choose the liberty horn of it. They treat almost any attempt to strengthen national security as an infringement on our freedoms and oppose it for that reason. The assumption seems to be that a life with reduced liberty is not worth living, threat or no threat. My objection to liberals$_2$, I want to make clear, is not that they are wrong in criticizing *actual* security measures in the United States and elsewhere. Rather, I question the view that appeal to liberal values can *never* justify temporary restrictions to the current level of enjoyment of freedoms.

What both sides miss is the simple point that *security measures, whatever they are, have to be justified by reference to one purpose, and one purpose only: the need to preserve our freedoms.* Liberals$_1$ are thus correct: all laws have to be justified by reference to the need to protect liberty. But the corollary is that sometimes restrictions on freedom are justified, namely when they are the only means to protect the liberal constitution, that is, freedom itself. To be sure, such restrictions are to be interpreted in the strictest way, and subject

---

[8] Bruce Ackerman describes this position (without endorsement) thus: "No matter how large the event, no matter how great the ensuing panic, we must insist on the strict protection of all rights all of the time" (2004: 1030). In addition to James Bovard (2003) and David Cole (2004) the ACLU may be included in this camp. The various ACLU reports on this matter are available at www.aclu.org.

to the usual stringent requirements of necessity and proportionality.[9] Thus, conservatives are wrong to assume that there is a value, such as order or safety or security, that is *independent* of the concern for freedom; and liberals$_2$ are wrong to assume that the only possible argument for restricting freedom is the conservative emphasis on order. In a democracy, *security and freedom are not antithetical but complementary*. The purpose of any measures adopted in times of war or other emergency is the preservation of the freedoms that define the democratic way of life. When, in a democracy, citizens endure rationing or curfews in times of war, they understand that the fighting that justifies those constraints has itself to be justified. And thus the cliché is exactly right: pursuing security is simply taking the necessary steps to protect democracy and human rights from enemies who threaten them.

If this point seems too obvious to be belabored, consider a common way in which conservatives sometimes justify security measures. They are necessary, they claim, to protect the nation; they are required by patriotism. They then sometimes accuse liberals (of all sorts) of lack of patriotism. They point out that the liberals' neglect of national security means that liberals are somehow disloyal, that everyone has a duty is to defend *the nation* against the terrorist threat. But this accusation cannot withstand scrutiny, and not just because it is unfair to liberals (in the sense that liberals might also be patriotic). The accusation is unwarranted because *patriotism itself is morally suspect*. Security measures cannot be morally justified simply by appeal to patriotism *tout court*. They should be justified by appealing to the principles that alone can justify defending the nation. The principle of patriotism fails in a number of ways. First, some nations and régimes are not worth defending. It is significant that dictators often appeal to patriotism to stir the public against outside pressures for political reform.[10] The message in this is obvious: "whatever you think about me, the government, and my lack of legitimacy, surely we have to unite against this threat to our nation." The patriotic argument here dilutes the question of moral justification of the régime itself. Second, legitimate states and governments sometimes do immoral things (think about the Iraqi prisoners' abuse scandal). Here again, a moral citizen should not endorse such acts in the name of patriotism. A citizen who, on reflection, believes that a war waged by its otherwise legitimate government is unjust should oppose the war

---

[9] In the European Convention of Human Rights, the requirement for suspension of liberties in times of emergency is heightened: governments can do it only "to the extent strictly required by the exigencies of the situation" (Article 15).

[10] The cases of the Argentine generals in the 1970s (besieged by the Carter Administration's pressures), and of Cuba and China today are good examples of this technique.

on moral grounds. Appeal to patriotism is out of place, because to the extent that patriotism is a value, it is subordinated to liberal principles of justice, which alone can infuse life into the concept of nation. That is why, in the debate in the United States about the war in Iraq, the view that the war is unjust but that U.S. troops should nonetheless stay for patriotic reasons rings hollow. If one thinks the war is unjust, or otherwise not justified as part of the war against terrorism, then one should advocate withdrawal of the troops.[11] In short, security measures are morally justified if, and only if, the principles in the name of which they are undertaken are themselves justified. The conservative view that patriotism, without more, requires support for security measures thus fails. Love of liberty, not love of country, should motivate moral citizens to support appropriate security measures.

Conversely, liberals$_2$ do not always take the flip side of this argument. They do not always argue with their opponents, as they should, that this or that security proposal (say, the USA PATRIOT Act), as an empirical matter, simply does not help us protect our freedoms. Rather, they often point out that the proposal impinges on our freedoms, which of course any security measure will do. The crucial issue is whether or not that particular measure requires temporary restraint on our freedoms in order to save those same freedoms from the attack by those determined to destroy them. The test, in its abstract form, is this: *A security measure is justified if, and only if, the amount of freedom it restricts is necessary to preserve the total system of freedom threatened by internal or external enemies.* I would like to defend this test against possible objections, in particular the objection that it ignores the special moral weight of human rights.

Human Rights and Deontological Ethics

One argument that liberals$_2$ might offer in support of the claim that security threats virtually never justify curtailment of civil liberties is this: Human rights are deontological concepts. We conceive them, not as shortcuts for maximizing utility or the general welfare, but on the contrary as trumping the pursuit of utility or the general welfare. As Jeremy Waldron put it, "rights are often resolutely anti-consequentialist" (2003: 194). Yet (the objection

---

[11] This chapter is not about the war in Iraq, but I should point out here another anomaly in the debate on that subject. Someone who believes that the U.S.-U.K. invasion of Iraq is illegitimate is committed to praising the Iraqi resistance as legitimate defensive action. Yet critics of the war have lacked the courage to say this. Thomas Franck (2003) and Mary Ellen O'Connell (2002), for example, firmly condemn the war but keep silent on the disturbing inference: the legitimacy of the Iraqi insurgency.

goes) talk about balancing substitutes calculation of costs and benefits for deontological ethics. The point about having rights is precisely to preclude those calculations. To say that someone has a right is to say that his interest cannot be overridden by societal benefits. The argument that we need to improve security is an appeal to the general welfare, and as such it cannot succeed against the imperative to respect rights. This well-known insight can be formulated in a number of ways: we may not sacrifice persons for the general good; the pursuit of aggregate goals must respect moral side constraints, and so forth. The test above (so the objection goes) violates this essential feature of rights, because it recommends violating the rights of some in order to maximize the total system of liberties. The point of having a bill of rights is precisely to forbid the government from making these types of calculations.

The contrast between consequentialist and non-consequentialist ethics has been the subject of a voluminous literature, and I cannot revisit it here in all its complexity (classic treatments include Williams 1973: 94–5; Nozick 1974: 30–3; and Scheffler 1994). However, in order to assess the strength of the deontological objection to my test, I need to clarify the different meanings that philosophers have given to the proposition that "rights trump utility."

1) **Strong Deontologism.** There are a number of contexts where many would agree that moral principles, and rights in particular, trump almost all other considerations. Consider the famous example of a villain who asks me to shoot an innocent person, and if I refuse, he will shoot two innocent persons. Suppose I refuse. I can justify my refusal to kill (with the certain consequence of the death of the two others) in two ways. I may say that the right to life (held by innocent persons, etc.) is absolute and therefore I may not violate it even if bad consequences occur. My duty not to kill an innocent person is so strong that it is not overridden by the bad consequences of complying with the duty – not even if those consequences are the murder (by others) of more innocent persons.

A second (and I believe, more accurate) justification is to say that *I* am prohibited from violating the right to life of this innocent person, regardless of what *others* do. Philosophers sometimes say that when rights are seen in this way, the duties they impose are *agent-relative* (see Kamm 1996: 207–353; Nagel 1986: ch. 9; Nozick 1974; Scheffler 1994; Spector 1992: ch. 5; Williams 1973). Liberals$_2$ may seize on this idea and suggest that this is exactly what happens in the debate over security measures. The government's violating individual rights is much more serious than the government's allowing, through inaction, deaths caused by terrorist attacks. We cannot simply count the number of victims, because the moral nature of *committing* a violation, on one hand,

and the moral nature of *omitting things to prevent violations by others*, on the other hand, are different. A democratic government has an agent-relative duty to respect individual rights, even if doing so allows others to violate more rights.

But is it sensible for supporters of this strong deontological approach to be insensitive to consequences in this way? I believe there is no general answer to this question. Whether or not we may legitimately insist that government respect a right knowing that its doing so will unleash bad consequences depends on the nature of the interest protected by the right, the seriousness of the bad consequences, and, perhaps, the kind of intent or purpose evinced by governmental behavior.[12] There is an important class of cases where this strong deontological approach to human rights works well. These cases centrally animate the argument mounted by liberals$_2$ against governmental attempts to restrict freedom in times of emergency. Think about the rights of the criminal defendant. Suppose the government proposes to relax the rules about police interrogation. Suppose further that the government responds to criticism by civil rights advocates by pointing out that keeping current stringent protections for suspects of crime demonstrably increases crime through underdeterrence. Civil rights advocates, correctly in my view, are entitled to disregard, at least to some extent, these bad consequences of stringent protections. They are willing to live with an increased crime rate for the sake of freedom. This is so, in part because crime control is not the paramount goal of the liberal state; in part because the kind of invasion of human dignity entailed by more severe forms of interrogation should be subject to the highest level of prohibition that a legal system affords. But the opposition to relaxation of criminal procedural rights is also grounded on the moral distinction between action and omission just described. *I* cannot allow my government, which represents *me*, to violate rights, even if others, who do not represent me, will predictably violate rights. Crucially, by observing stringent rights of defendants, the state is not *causing* the increase in crime; rather, the criminals' (freely chosen) behavior does. The distinction between action and omission grounds a moral difference, on this view, between rights violations by the government and rights violations by private persons. This is a case (and there are surely others) where the right in question successfully withstands competition against unpalatable consequences. We may not torture people, even if our not doing so creates incentives for criminals (through underdeterrence) in turn to torture and kill their victims.

[12] Elsewhere Guido Pincione and I claim that, in politics, citizens often inappropriately disregard consequences when making moral judgments (2005: ch. 6).

One example of a persuasive strong deontological approach is the recent decision of the House of Lords invalidating British legislation that allowed indefinite detention as part of the war against terrorism. While acknowledging the need to accept some restrictions to individual liberties in the wake of the terrorist attacks in the United States, the Law Lords found unacceptable the practice of detaining suspects indefinitely. Lord Nichols of Birkenhead wrote: "Indefinite imprisonment without charge or trial is anathema in any country which observes the rule of law."[13] The word "anathema" captures the idea of a right so strong that it cannot be outweighed by the urgency to protect citizens from terrorist attacks. The importance of the House of Lords opinion is its insight that there are certain things governments cannot do even in times of urgency because doing it would betray their very democratic nature. The curtailment of individual liberties, in these cases, is self-defeating.

2) Weak Deontologism. But the list of quasi-absolute rights is relatively short. Many rights, important as they are, are not as strong as, say, the freedom against torture or against indefinite detention, and thus it is less clear that they should always remain untouched by the need to protect total liberty. Politics is concerned with the design and the practice of political institutions meant for large numbers of people, and the kind of moral dilemmas illustrated in the previous section are not representative of many situations where democratic governments must make choices between competing social goals.

What is, then, the role of the principle "rights trump utility" in a democracy? Simply this: *political justice* demands that basic rights and interests of individuals not be sacrificed to the general welfare. This view is defended, in different ways, by two leading political philosophers, John Rawls and Ronald Dworkin. In *A Theory of Justice*, Rawls proposes his two principles of justice in lexical ordering: equal liberty and the difference principle, with priority to equal liberty. Central to this assumption is the insight that society is not like an individual in the sense that the gains of some can be weighed against the loss of others. Such an undifferentiated calculation ignores the "separateness of persons." This view, however, is deontological only in a weaker sense. It implies that we may not sacrifice freedom for economic gains and that we may not design institutions so that some, even many, prosper without regard to distributional effects, such as the impact of those institutions on the poor. But it does *not* imply that freedom may not be restrained *for the sake of freedom*

---

[13] A and others v Secretary of State for the Home Department; X and another v Secretary of State for the Home Department, House of Lords [2004] UKHL 56, [2004] All ER (D) 271 (Dec), para. 74.

itself. In fact, Rawls expressly writes that freedom may be restricted for the sake of freedom, so that what matters for justice (and for institutional design) is to maximize the *total* system of freedoms enjoyed by citizens (1971: 203–4). If this is correct, the deontological objection can block some, but not all, restrictions to freedom. A democratic society may restrict freedom to the extent required by the preservation of the total system of liberty. If this is correct, in Rawls the primacy of rights is closer to a "utilitarianism of rights" than to a strong deontological view of rights where they prevail regardless of consequences. Rawls' point is simply that principles of justice and institutional design should be sensitive to distributional concerns. Justice requires that government and citizens be attentive to the way burdens and benefits in society are distributed. Political institutions should be designed to maximize the total enjoyment of political freedoms. It is still not utilitarianism *tout court*, as it is not aimed at maximized general welfare or utility. The good to be maximized is a normatively qualified good: individual freedom, or autonomy, not just any undifferentiated cluster of preferences. And even the label "utilitarianism of rights" is misleading, because it is certainly false that we can do just *anything* to maximize rights enjoyment. As we saw, it is morally prohibited to torture people even if that would enhance the enjoyment of human rights of everyone else. So this weaker deontological approach is still subject to principles of necessity, proportionality, and the *differential deontological weight of various rights.*

Ronald Dworkin's early work on rights is particularly helpful here. As he argued a long time ago, a right is best defined as an interest that cannot be outweighed by just *any* appeal to the general welfare (Dworkin 1978: 92). Conceptually, a right cannot be defined as such if it can be set aside by any policy consideration. Rights must have a *threshold* below which calculations of costs and benefits or appeals to general welfare are not allowed. This is, in Dworkin's terms, the right's weight; I prefer to call it the right's *deontological bite*. It is the right's ability to trump the pursuit of social goals, to block trade-offs. If this analysis is sound, it follows that the fact that someone's interest is protected by a right does not mean that the interest can *never* be overridden by an appeal to the general welfare, or to the rights of others, or to the need to maximize rights-enjoyment in society.[14] Thus, Dworkin's analysis of rights converges on this point with Rawls' views on the priority of

---

[14] As Dworkin writes, "[r]ights may . . . be less than absolute; one principle may have to yield to another, or even to an urgent policy with which it competes on particular facts" (1978: 92). It is a mere verbal question whether we call the need to enhance the total system of liberties ("utilitarianism of rights") a policy or a principle in Dworkin's sense.

liberty. That someone has a right means that he has a special kind of interest, one entitled to special deference and not simply automatically subject to cost-benefit analysis. Whether and when the right can be set aside will depend on its deontological bite. Simply put: some rights are stronger than others; some are absolute, others quasi-absolute, yet others are weaker. The right not to be tortured is most likely absolute; the right to life is very strong but perhaps not absolute; the right to speak freely is quite strong; whereas, say, the right of a journalist to shield her confidential sources of information is arguably weaker and may perhaps be overridden by requirements of fair trial; and so forth.

The upshot is that the statement "rights trump utility" does not literally mean what it says, if by "utility" we understand a sufficiently rich notion of normatively upgraded social goals, and not just the general welfare. Whatever we can say about run-of-the-mill, socially desirable goals such as economic prosperity, or better transportation, or improving the quality of air and water, certainly preserving the total system of liberties in a democracy is as lofty, or urgent, as any social goal can be. It seems plausible, therefore, to suggest, at least initially, that some rights will sometimes have to yield to achieve that goal. Only absolute rights will operate in the strongest deontological sense that they may never be set aside, for any reason. Rights with lower thresholds may sometimes be legitimately set aside for morally sufficient reasons, such as enhancing the total system of liberties.

In summary: there are a number of ways in which respecting rights may lead to conflict with other values (I confine myself to governmental behavior):

a) The government's respecting my (or everyone's) right to X may reduce general welfare or some such aggregative policy – rights v. policy.

b) The government's observance of my right to X may conflict with your right to Y. This is the classical conflict of rights – individual right v. individual right.

c) The government's respecting everyone's right to X may reduce the *total* system of liberties in society – right v. total rights enjoyment ("utilitarianism of right").

Generally speaking, the solution of the conflict in a) should tend to favor the individual right, for the reasons given by Rawls and Dworkin: the primacy of liberty. The conflict in b) can only be solved by the kind of delicate balancing of reasons that courts in democratic countries invoke in deciding cases of conflicts of individual rights. The conflict in c) is the one that is central to the inquiry here. There is no automatic solution, but I suggest that only the most stringent rights should be immune to competition against the need to preserve the total system of liberties in a democratic society. One thing is certain: the fact that rights have deontological bite makes institutional design in situations like post-9/11 complex and non-automatic. Indeed, "adjustments in rights require structured arguments for their justification – arguments that pay attention to their special character" (Waldron 2003: 200). It is not *mere* balancing between undifferentiated social goals. Thus, the United States Supreme Court got it exactly right when it wrote on this very issue:

> Striking the proper constitutional balance here is of great importance to the Nation during this period of ongoing combat. But it is equally vital that our calculus not give short shrift to the values that this country holds dear or to the privilege that is American citizenship. It is during our most challenging and uncertain moments that our Nation's commitment to due process is most severely tested; and it is in those times that *we must preserve our commitment at home to the principles for which we fight abroad* (*Hamdi*, 124 S. Ct. at 2648) (emphasis added).

Moral Threat and Evil

The differential deontological bite of rights may be seen at work, as I said, in times of genuine security threats, such as internal uprising, war, and the presence of terrorist threats. The conduct of war, for example, requires some sacrifice by the public, including, but not limited to, a temporary limitation of their freedoms.[15] Now it is plain that such limitation can only be justified if the war itself is a just war. A war in turn is just if it is waged for the right reasons and complies with the well-known requirements of proportionality and with additional moral requirements, such as the strictures of the doctrine of double effect (see Walzer 2001; for a more critical view see Holmes 1989: 183–213). One of such right reasons is national self-defense. But defense against what? Against those who threaten our lives, our property, and our free institutions. So a war in self-defense is as much a direct defense of persons as a defense of democratic institutions.[16] If we assume that those who attacked the United States on September 11, 2001, intended to harm the United States and the values it stands for – notably freedom and democracy – a number of things follow. For one thing, the enemy (radical Islam) can only be defeated by the sword. There is no peaceful way out of the war against terrorism, given the determination and ferocity of the enemy. We are perhaps less determined

[15] *Hamdi* 2004; For the similar approach of the House of Lords see note 13.
[16] See Tesón 2004 (responding to Rodin 2003). Rodin's rejoinder is on the same issue (2003: 93).

and certainly less ferocious, but luckily we are still more powerful. There are factual differences between this war and World War II, but there are, in my view, few *moral* differences. In that instance, the morally right thing to do was to fight and defeat tyranny (as Winston Churchill clearly saw). Similarly today, the morally right thing to do is to defeat the enemies. Not murder or slaughter them: defeat them. There is no compromise, because that requires a conceivable basis for a peaceful modus vivendi, and there is none here.

Understanding the nature of the threat sheds light on the problem of the curtailment of liberties. As we saw, some threats are not just physical threats, but moral threats as well. A moral threat occurs when, in addition to the massive nature of the (actual or threatened) attacks, and the consequent dangers to the lives of the citizens of the democratic state (a physical threat), the perpetrators act *in the name of illiberal principles or values.* The attacks of September 11, 2001, were more than acts of murder. They were attacks against our most fundamental values, our commitment to human dignity, freedom, and human rights, because they were perpetrated in the name of principles that expressly negate those fundamental values.

But if this is so, it seems that the *intent* of the attackers – in this case, the intent to destroy or undermine liberal values – has a role in the analysis of the problem that occupies us. An intent to destroy liberal values is an *evil* intent. One reason why the human rights community rightly insists that tyrants such as Pinochet, Milosevic, and Saddam Hussein be held accountable is that their deeds were informed by evil intent. They evinced a particular kind of perversity.[17] I want to distinguish between two kinds of evil: *opportunistic* evil and *principled* evil. Opportunistic evildoers seek some advantage with their actions. They harm others to gain something. An opportunistic evildoer (say, a bank robber) confronted with the immorality of his behavior has no inclination to justify it, except by pointing out to his ill-gotten gains. Thus, Saddam Hussein or Stalin were arguably opportunistic evildoers. These agents weigh costs and benefits of their behavior. They are typically not willing to die or sacrifice themselves for a cause, because they seek to advance their self-interest. By the same token, they can be bribed (although if they are very powerful, bribing them may be hard, as no bribe will compensate them for, say, the loss of political power). They are sensitive to cost, and so to strategic considerations. They may be deterred. That is precisely one of the points of the criminal justice system: to put a price tag on crime in order to deter would-be opportunistic evildoers. The criminal law presupposes opportunistic evildoers.

---

[17] For an account of evil with special application to tyranny, see Nino 1996. On evil generally, see the collection of essays in Lara 2001.

These persons understand the maxim of right behavior, but choose to disregard it when, rightly or wrongly, they estimate that the benefit of the crime is well worth the risk of being caught.

Principled evildoers are very different. They act out of a maxim, a principle, albeit an evil one.[18] They want to realize a universal value, a value other than self-interest, a cause larger than themselves. They do not generally calculate costs and benefits, except in the narrower sense that costly behavior (for example, resulting in their death) might prevent them from advancing the cause in the future. But they typically persist in their crusade at a high personal cost. Suicide attacks are of this sort. The attacker immolates himself for the cause, gives up his life for his ideals. Principled evildoers cannot be bribed; if they are bribed, they cease to be principled. They can rarely be convinced or dissuaded. This aspect is more interesting: at first blush, we think that principled people are sensitive to rational argument, but this is not generally the case. Most principled evildoers are fanatics. A fanatic can be defined as someone who believes in something and (1) will not accept argument or evidence to the contrary, and (2) is willing to incur great cost in the pursuit of his belief. So, while the opportunistic evildoer understands the maxim of right behavior but chooses to ignore it out of self-interest, the principled evildoer acts out of a mistaken maxim. Hitler and Pol Pot were arguably principled evildoers.

Who is worse? There are arguments on both sides. Someone might say that principled evildoers, while mistaken, at least evince commitment and courage, the willingness to die for what they believe. On this view, principled evildoers, while they can cause horrendous harm to persons, show a better character. They are just wrong about the cause they pursue, but at least they try to be moral. The popularity of Che Guevara in some circles is an instance of this attitude. Someone who admires Che Guevara might say that she thinks Guevara (1) stood for the right principle (say, justice for the poor in Latin America), and (2) was willing to fight for that cause, disdaining personal gain and at great risk for his life. But most sensible people do not think Guevara endorsed a right cause. That is, most people do not think that imposing a communist dictatorship in Latin America (which is what Guevara fought for) was such a great idea. Still, these people admire him "for the strength of his convictions."

---

[18] Immanuel Kant's notion of radical evil does not capture this idea, because Kant thought that evil maxims were simply subjective maxims of the will and could not aspire to generality (because they would violate the categorical imperative). Kant's belief that human beings have a natural propensity to evil means simply that they are too ready to abandon the moral law for opportunistic reasons – whether or not embodied in "subjective maxims of the will" (1960: 27–8).

I think this is gravely mistaken, a sign of Kantianism gone awry (see Berman 2004). Commitment and courage are not primary but *secondary* virtues. We admire the courage of a soldier if he is fighting for a just cause. If he is *not* fighting for a just cause, we certainly prefer him to be a coward. The same is true about people who have strong convictions. We do not admire the racist who engages in civil disobedience and is willing to go to jail while he demonstrates against integrated schools. The value of principled behavior is *entirely parasitic* on the substantive moral validity of the principle. The racist's integrity, understood as commitment to principle, is entirely worthless, because the principle (racism) is entirely worthless. Also, at least the opportunistic evildoer can sometimes be prevented from hurting others, if given the right incentives. The fanatic, however, is impervious to incentives. Finally, I disagree with those who have an exaggerated admiration for principled people. It certainly depends on the case. Someone who sticks to a good principle while remaining open to argument is, of course, praiseworthy. But someone whose convictions are *too* strong does not evince a particularly attractive character. He comes close to fanaticism, because the stronger his convictions are the less amenable he will be to persuasion. There is a point where strength of conviction in a cause becomes irrational attachment to that cause.

The September 11 attackers are principled evildoers. They act out of an evil maxim, one that mandates the destruction of the West, or the infidel, or Great Satan, or "permissive" democracy, or some such thing, and are willing to incur great personal cost, including death. There are, of course, a number of interpretations about the nature of the conflict between the West and radical Islam,[19] but one thing is clear: the September 11 attackers were targeting democratic values, presumably because they see those values as a threat to the pre-modern beliefs and political institutions that radical Islam holds central. It is not a passing strategic threat, or a difference of a geopolitical kind that would allow for compromise, negotiation, and peaceful resolution. Nor is it an opportunistic threat, say, from a tyrant wishing to gain some advantage or other. It is, in a sense, a principled threat in the sense I described, a threat posed by persons who act on evil principles. And, for the reasons I gave in the previous paragraph, their extreme integrity and courage (showed by their willingness to die in the attack) deserve abhorrence, not admiration.

---

[19] Whether the current war against terrorism is part of a "clash of civilizations" in Samuel Huntington's sense is a matter that exceeds the scope of this chapter. While reaffirming the need to defeat the enemy, I tend to distrust broad generalizations about cultures or religions in favor of a universalist conception of human nature (Tesón 1998; see generally Huntington 1996). For differing views on this issue, compare Cohen 2003 with Jervis 2002.

What is the import of this discussion of evil to the question asked in this chapter? Has the fact that a democratic society is threatened by evil enemies any bearing on whether or not it is permissible to curtail some freedoms in order to face the threat? We may distinguish here two approaches. The first one is to say that whatever governments may permissibly do to face emergencies, it is unrelated to the intent, or lack thereof, of whoever poses the threat. Indeed, the legitimacy of governmental behavior is measured purely in terms of the principles of necessity and proportionality. Whether the threat is purely physical (like the recent tsunamis in Southeast Asia) or moral (like terrorist threats) is irrelevant to the question of the acceptable reductions of liberties. On this view, it is not the business of the government to evaluate intentions. Its job is simply to help people overcome the threat, regardless of whether it is posed by Al-Qaeda or by an earthquake. (There is a certain tension between this view and the view that gives pride of place to human rights, because the latter requires taking fairly strong positions about intentional structure of behavior, but perhaps this tension is not fatal.)

However, I think this view overlooks the moral urgency of fighting evil. Other things being equal, and subject to a number of constraints, the fact that someone's behavior is evil is an added reason for us to counter that behavior. I hasten to say that the fact that someone's behavior is evil is neither a necessary nor a sufficient reason to react to it. It is not a necessary condition because we may react to dangerous but innocent threatening behavior (someone who threatens us when sleepwalking, for example). And it is not a sufficient condition because we should not react violently against behavior that, while arguably evil, does not harm anyone. To fix ideas, take two situations. In the first, a number of people are threatened by an earthquake. Let us assume that we have an obligation to help them. The predicament of the victims in the face of that natural threat grounds that obligation. In the second, the same people are threatened with extermination by an evil tyrant. I suggest that our obligation to help is *heightened* in this second case. It is not merely the predicament of the victims that we take into consideration when deciding to act, but the need to prevent or undo a *moral wrong*. I consider only situations that meet the following two conditions: (1) there is a genuine security threat; (2) posed by principled evildoers. Take World War II. The greatness of the Allied victory was not simply marked by the defeat of the strategic threat posed by Germany, Italy, and Japan, ominous as it was. The Allied victory was a victory of good against evil, unfashionable as it may be to talk in these terms these days. Similarly, the fight against those who directed the September 11 attacks is a fight of good against evil. That is why it must be won.

It follows that the case for defending the total system of liberties – the case contemplated by Rawls as the only one that justifies a temporary curtailment of liberty to the extent strictly required by the threat – is strengthened by our need to fight and defeat evil. Thus, much as I sympathize with the humanitarianism that (as usual) animates it, I disagree with David Luban's view in this volume that the only relevant issue here is the degree of risk that each of us have of becoming the victims of a future attacks. In addition, a democratic society must defend the attacks against its values and institutions perpetrated by persons who in the name of evil principles, morally analogous to those espoused by our enemies in World War II.

Summary and Concluding Thoughts

I have argued for the following propositions:

(1) The imperative to protect the total systems of freedoms in a democratic society is *the only* justification for security measures that restrict liberty. Order and security are thus not independent values: they are parasitic on our commitment to liberty.

(2) Security measures are constrained by the principles of necessity and proportionality, so any proposal in that direction is vulnerable to the objection that, as a factual matter, it will not enhance the total system of freedoms.

(3) A genuine threat may be purely physical, or it may be, in addition, a moral threat. A moral threat is defined as one that is directed against liberal values.

(4) The evil intent of the attackers strengthens the urgency to respond to the attack. Evil intent may be opportunistic or principled.

(5) The attacks of September 11, 2001, against the United States posed a genuine physical and moral threat. They were attacks conducted by principled evildoers against the people and the institutions of our democracy.

(6) None of the above demonstrates the appropriateness of any *specific* degree of curtailment of liberty.

(7) The argument here is of course conditional: *if* point (5) is correct, then some restrictions to liberty *may* be justified. If it is not, then the standard tools of the criminal law should suffice, and there is no need to limit freedom in any way.

Much has been said about the proper way to respond to terrorism, and unfortunately the debate was polluted, in the United States, by politics during an electoral year, and many others have added to the confusion by mingling this issue with the debate over the legitimacy or wisdom of the Iraq war. But I have no doubt in my mind that this is a fight of good versus evil; that the threat does not merely pose physical risks to our citizenry but, crucially, that it is a profound attack against the values that, despite our differences, we hold dear; and that the democratic community, led by the United States, has the right and the obligation to defeat the enemy. The struggle against terrorism is not one that is in tension with human rights. It is a struggle, perhaps the most important one of our time, *for* human rights.

REFERENCES

Ackerman, B. (2004). 'The Emergency Constitution'. *Yale Law Journal*, vol. 113, p. 1029.

Alexander, Y. & Myers, K. A. (Eds.). (1982). *Terrorism in Europe*. London: Center for Strategic and International Studies.

Baker, N. V. (2003). 'National Security versus Civil Liberties'. *Presidential Studies Quarterly*, vol. 33, no. 3, p. 547–67.

Berman, P. (2004, September 24). 'The Cult of Che: Don't Applaud The Motorcycle Diaries'. Available at: http://slate.msn.com/id/2107100.

Bovard, J. (2003). *Terrorism and Tyranny*. New York: Palgrave.

Coady, C. A. J. (2002). 'Terrorism, Just War, and Supreme Emergency'. In C. A. J. Coady and Michael P. O'Keefe (Eds.), *Terrorism and Justice*. Melbourne: Melbourne University Press.

Cohen, A. (2003). 'Promoting Freedom and Democracy: Fighting the War of Ideas Against Islamic Terrorism'. *Comparative Strategy*, vol. 22, no. 3, p. 207.

Cole, D. (2004). 'The Priority of Morality: The Emergency Constitution's Blind Spot'. *Yale Law Journal*, vol. 113, p. 1753.

Dworkin, R. (1978). *Taking Rights Seriously*. Cambridge, MA: Harvard University Press.

European Convention of Human Rights. Available at: http://www.hrcr.org/docs/Eur_Convention/euroconv.html.

Franck, T. M. (2003). 'What Happens Now? The United Nations after Iraq'. *American Journal of International Law*, vol. 97, p. 607.

Fullkwinder, R. K. (2001, Fall). 'Terrorism, Innocence, and War'. *Philosophy and Public Policy Quarterly*, vol. 21, p. 9.

Hamdi v. Rumsfeld, 124 S. Ct. 2633, 2648, 159 L. Ed. 2d 578, 601, 2004 U.S. LEXIS 4761 (2004).

Heymann, P. B. (2003). *Terrorism, Freedom and Security: Winning Without War*. Cambridge, MA: MIT Press, pp. 87–113.

Hobbes, T. ([1651] 1998). *Leviathan*. J. C. Gaskin (Ed.). Oxford: Oxford University Press.

Holmes, R. (1989). *On War and Morality*. Princeton: Princeton Universty Press.

Huntington, S. P. (1996). *The Clash of Civilizations and the Remaking of World Order*. New York: Simon & Schuster.

Ireland v. The United Kingdom (5310/71) [1978] ECHRI (18 January 1978).

Jervis, R. (2002). 'An Interim Assessment of September 11: What Has Changed and What Has Not'. *Political Science Quarterly*, vol. 117, no. 1.

Kamm, F. M. (1996). *Morality, Mortality*. Vol. II. New York: Oxford University Press.

Kant, I. (1960). *Religion Within the Limits of Reason Alone*. New York: Harper.

Kapitan, T. (2003). 'The Terrorism in "Terrorism"'. In J. S. Sterba (Ed.), *Terrorism and International Justice*, vol. 21, p. 47. Oxford: Oxford University Press.

Kavka, G. (1986). *Hobbesian Moral and Political Theory*. Princeton: Princeton University Press.

Lara, M. P. (2001). *Rethinking Evil: Contemporary Perspectives*. Berkeley: University of California Press.

Lawless v. Ireland (No. 2)(332/57) [1961] ECHRI (7 April 1961).

Nagel, T. (1986). *The View from Nowhere*. Oxford: Oxford University Press.

Nino, C. S. (1996). *Radical Evil on Trial*. New Haven: Yale University Press.

Nozick, R. (1974). *Anarchy, State, and Utopia*. New York: Basic Books.

Nunca Más: Informe de la Comisión Nacional sobre la desaparición de personas, 3rd ed. (1984). Buenos Aires, Argentina: EUDEBA.

O'Connell, M. E. (2002, August 6). 'The Myth of Preemptive Self-Defense'. Available at: http://www.asil.org/taskforce/oconnell.pdf.

Pincione, G. & Tesón, F. R. (2005). *Discourse Failure: A Philosophical Essay on Deliberation, Democracy, and Consent*, ch. 6. Unpublished.

Rawls, J. (1971). *A Theory of Justice*. Cambridge, MA: Harvard University Press.

Rodin, D. (2003). *War and Self-Defense*. Oxford: Oxford University Press.

Scheffler, S. (1994). *The Rejection of Consequentialism*, rev. ed. Oxford: Clarendon Press.

Spector, H. (1992). *Autonomy and Rights*. Oxford: Oxford University Press.

Tesón, F. R. (2004). 'Self-Defense in International Law and Rights of Persons'. *Ethics and International Affairs*, vol. 18, no. 1, p. 87.

_____. (1998). *A Philosophy of International Law*. Boulder, CO: Westview Press.

Waldron, J. (2003). 'Security and Liberty: The Image of Balance'. *The Journal of Political Philosophy*, vol. 11, no. 2, p. 191.

Walzer, M. (2001). 'Double Effect'. In P. A. Woodward (Ed.), *The Doctrine of Double Effect*, p. 261. Notre Dame, IN: University of Notre Dame Press.

Williams, B. (1973). 'A Critique of Utilitarianism'. In J. J. C. Smart and B. Williams (Eds.), *Utilitarianism: For & Against*. Cambridge: Cambridge University Press.

3. The Human Rights Case for the War in Iraq: A Consequentialist View

THOMAS CUSHMAN

"It may well be that under international law, a regime can systematically brutalize and oppress its people and there is nothing anyone can do, when dialogue, diplomacy and even sanctions fail."

Tony Blair[1]

The purpose of this chapter is to provide a moral and ethical defense of the war in Iraq. The principal argument of this defense is that the war – while probably illegal from the point of view of most bodies of statutory international law – was morally defensible in its overall consequence: it has objectively liberated a people from an oppressive, long-standing tyranny; destroyed an outlaw state that was a threat to the peace and security of the Middle East and the larger global arena in which terrorists operated, sponsored materially and ideologically by Iraq; brought the dictator Saddam Hussein to justice for his genocides and crimes against humanity; prevented the possibility of another genocide by a leader who has already committed this crime against his own subjects; restored sovereignty to the Iraqi people; laid the foundation for the possibility of Iraq becoming a liberal republic; created the conditions for the entrance of this republic as a *bona fide* member into what John Rawls termed the "Society of Peoples"; and opened up the possibility for the citizens of Iraq to claim, as autonomous agents, those human rights guaranteed to them by the United Nations Declaration of Human Rights, but denied to them by the very mechanisms of international law that are supposed to be the formal guarantors of such rights. Overall, this chapter presents what I call the "human rights case" for the war. I think it is necessary to make such a case in this particular volume, because most of the chapters herein provide critical

---

[1] From a speech given by Prime Minister Tony Blair. Full text can be found at: http://www.pm. gov.uk/output/Page5461.asp.

reflections on human rights issues in the United States, or alleged abuses that have occurred in the prosecution of the war on terror and the war in Iraq. Such critiques are important and necessary, but serve to obscure violations of human rights in Iraq under Saddam Hussein's regime and forestall discussion of the possibility that the war has had positive moral consequences.

I would like to begin by stressing that the human rights case for the war has been difficult to make. The principal reason for this is that the Bush Administration failed to strongly present its own rationale for the war, especially in the months leading up to the war. As the primary mechanism of global governance, international law rendered the Bush Administration's first attempts to justify the war primarily legal in nature. The legal case was twofold. First, the United States argued that Iraq was in breach of sixteen separate U.N. Security Council resolutions, and that, according to international law, the Security Council was obligated to enforce its own resolutions. This was a fairly straightforward argument, which – to Saddam Hussein's advantage – was more or less ignored by the Security Council. The second argument was based on considerations of national interest: this was a war of anticipatory self-defense, or what has, in this case, been called "preemptive war." Based on intelligence reports that documented Saddam's efforts to acquire weapons of mass destruction (WMD), as well as evidence about Saddam Hussein's support of international terrorism, the Bush Administration argued that the Iraqi ruler was an imminent threat to the national security of the United States and a more general threat to world peace and security. This second argument has been very difficult to sustain in light of the failure to find appreciable quantities of weapons of mass destruction and the somewhat indeterminate evidence of Iraqi connections with al-Qaeda, the presumptive enemy of the United States in the war on terror.

For the most part, critics of the war have focused almost exclusively on the shaky case for preemptive war, while at the same time ignoring the failure of the United Nations to uphold its own resolutions or the principles of the United Nations Declaration of Human Rights. Absent from the debate on the war is a serious discussion of the moral legitimacy of the war in terms of human rights. I would like to argue that the war can be seen in positive terms, as an advance for human rights, both for the Iraqi people themselves and for the overall program of human rights more globally. Given the vitriolic opposition to the war and the fact that most major human rights lawyers, scholars, and activists were against it, this is a rather contentious argument. It is, however, one that must be made, because a stance of opposition to the war cannot in any sense be seen as an advance for human rights either. To have been opposed to this war – or to war in general – on the principle that the rule of law and peace is the most desirable state of affairs in the international community is a principled stance, which carries much weight. It is, however, a stance that has moral and ethical consequences, which extend beyond the virtue of pacifism or the issue of the rightness of obeying international law. The choice to adhere to international laws – even if such laws are unjust – and to prefer peace absolutely, forces the question of justice and human rights for the Iraqi people to take second place. Such an emphasis also begs the question of the relationship between violence and human rights, and when the use of the former is appropriate for achieving the latter. While this is a subject for another paper, it is important to consider that human rights have often been achieved through the use of violence against oppressive social systems and practices, some obvious examples being the French Revolution, the American Revolution, the struggle against apartheid in South Africa, and the prevention of genocide in Kosovo (all which took place in opposition to unjust laws).

There are those who would argue that a commitment to justice and human rights is the first and most fundamental ethical principle, to which laws and other ideological positions must be held accountable. To have stood against the war – even on the most virtuous of legalistic or pacifistic grounds – was, at the most basic ontological level, to have tolerated Saddam Hussein's violation of international law and human rights; his manipulation of legal procedures for his own advantage; and his ongoing threat to peace and security. This is an unpleasant fact for those who were against the war, but it is a fact that I insist on as a crucial starting point for my argument. That the war was badly legitimated and badly managed – so that it resulted in the loss of civilian life and the alienation of certain (but certainly not all, as some would have us believe) states in the world – does not diminish the fact that opposing the war also represented a moral choice. It represented a moral choice that involved the sublimation of human rights and justice for those who suffer to other concerns: concern about American imperial ambitions, the hatred of George W. Bush and anti-Americanism on the part of the global left; concern about the sanctity rule of law; concern about innocent victims; concern for peace (or the absence of war); and concern about the possibility of jeopardizing "authentic" humanitarian interventions in the future.

The basic argument of this chapter is that there are substantive moral and ethical imperatives that, at times, supersede the strict requirement of obeying formal bodies of law – especially those laws that are not made with the consent of those who are subject to them. The logic of this position should not be foreign to those liberals who, for instance, participated in the Civil Rights Movement and sought to overturn perfectly legal, but also perfectly unjust laws, which denied African Americans fundamental human rights. More generally, though, the central argument here is similar to that which many people made about the humanitarian intervention in Kosovo: that, strictly speaking, the intervention was illegal according to various articles of the U.N. Charter, but that it was morally legitimate. This was the finding of the U.N. Kosovo Commission, many members of which do not share the same view of the Iraq war (IICK 2000).[2] My position, though, is that the Iraq war can be seen in much the same way as the war in Kosovo, albeit with some important modifications, and a conscious recognition that the central motivation for the war by those who waged it does not appear to have been humanitarian in nature. The question of moral legitimacy must, in my view, be measured not only in terms of intent, but also in consideration of the moral and ethical consequences of armed intervention.

However, moral judgments of war cannot be based on considerations of intent and motives alone. In contrast, I would argue that *motive* is actually not the most important factor to consider in assessing the justness or unjustness of any human action, even war. While this may be the most important factor in jurisprudence, especially with regard to crimes such as genocide (as, for example, the requirement of *dolus specialis*, or special intent), legal criteria are not the only ones that can be used for assessing the justice or injustice of human action. It is just as important to consider the moral and ethical *consequences* of war as we consider the overall question of whether a war can be considered just or not. There are quite a number of historical situations in which the ethical motivations of humanitarian interventions on the part of states were questionable, but the consequences of such interventions were rather positive. The abolition of the British slave trade, for instance, was not carried out because the British Parliament itself came to its ethical senses. Rather, it was primarily a result of ethically motivated activists who organized the anti-slavery movement and pressured their leaders to abolish slavery. The consequence – the abolition of slavery in the British Empire – was surely a positive ethical consequence that no one would seriously deny, and which can, in its moral qualities, be considered quite outside of the intentions of the agents who brought it about.

---

[2] Justice Richard Goldstone, the head of the Commission, summarized the findings as follows: "[The Commission] concluded that, in the absence of United Nations Security Council authorization, the NATO military response violated international law but was nonetheless politically and morally legitimate. The illegality lay in NATO's decision to avoid the Security Council and certain Chinese and Russian vetoes. The legitimacy arose from the egregious oppression and violations of the human rights of the Kosovar Albanians by their Serb rulers" (Goldstone 2002: 143).

In this sense, the central argument of the chapter rests on a consideration of the war from the standpoint of *consequentialist ethics* in moral philosophy. My purpose is not to defend the use of force and the violation of international law generally as the preferred means for advancing human rights. This would be a disaster, to be sure, as many critics of the war have pointed out. My view is rather more like Kant's in *Perpetual Peace*, in which he argued that if wars were to occur they should be used as opportunities for the reform of the situations that caused them to happen.[3] And as Kant's major modern interpreter John Rawls has argued, there are situations in which gross violations of human rights by "outlaw states" warrant armed intervention.[4] War, in this sense, is not an absolute evil; just war theorists in the Augustinian tradition have long pointed out, it is actually the lesser evil in some cases, and I hold that this is true in the case of the war in Iraq. My attempt here is not to persuade those who opposed the war to change their minds and suddenly decide that the war was actually a great victory for human rights. Rather, my position is that the Iraqi people, who were subjected to tyranny, had the right of revolution against it, and lacking the ability to mount such a revolution, had the right to assistance and that this assistance can be described as a type of humanitarian intervention.

My own support, indeed, was very ambivalent, yet always measured by my insuperable belief that to stand against the war would be to participate in an act of unjust appeasement of a brutal tyrant and an act of abandonment of the victims of his brutal regime, most of whom, as I shall stress later, were supportive of the war as a means to their liberation. I denied myself the possibility of standing against them. The view I offer here is meant to provide a case for the war that challenges the dominant anti-war orthodoxies of the humanitarian and legal communities, and illustrates the necessity to force debate on the current disjuncture between ethics and international law – a disjuncture that cannot in any way be seen as a positive development for the advancement of human rights.

---

[3] Kant argues in *Perpetual Peace*, in his section "On the guarantee of perpetual peace," that Perpetual Peace is guaranteed by complying with the three definitive articles (republican government, confederation, and cosmopolitan right to short visit) out of respect for a "duty of reason," and that having experienced many times the horrors of war and realized that Perpetual Peace is in its best interest, war might be said to contribute to the future removal of war ([1795] 1983: 120–5). I am indebted to Nicolas de Warren for this interpretation of Kant.

[4] See, for instance, Rawls 1999. Rawls is maddeningly unclear as to what specific conditions would justify humanitarian intervention outside of the framework of the law, noting only that, ". . . war is no longer an admissible means of government policy and is justified only in self-defense, or in grave cases of intervention to protect human rights." (1999: 79).

One of the problems with the human rights argument for intervention is that it can be seen as absolutist: in any case where we see violations of human rights, we are obligated to stand against them. In no way do I want to make this absolutist claim – and take great heed of those who have argued that such interventions could unleash a virtually boundless future of human rights crusades.[5] I make no claim that it is right in all cases for a state to intervene unilaterally on absolutist grounds of human rights. Rather, intervention on the grounds of rights is acceptable to the degree to which agents who are subjected to human rights abuses desire intervention and see the intervening power as a force that they wish to act on their behalf because they do not have the ability to do so themselves. Legal philosopher Fernando Tesón articulates this perspective of humanitarian intervention succinctly:

> The recognition of the right to resist tyranny is extremely important in international law. Beyond the consequences for the law of international human rights itself, it has consequences for the theory of humanitarian intervention. If citizens did not have a right to revolt against their tyrants, foreigners a fortiori would not have a right to help them, even by non-coercive measures, in the struggle against despotism. Humanitarian intervention can be defended as a corollary to the right to revolution: victims of serious human rights deprivations, who have rationally decided to revolt against their oppressors, have a right to receive proportionate transboundary assistance, including forcible help. (1998: 6)

In addition, it must be possible for the intervening power to act where it is possible to do so without creating more widespread global conflicts. Thus, it would be entirely ethical for a state to intervene in, say, Tibet, because the abuses of the Chinese government there are so palpable, and the majority of Tibetans would support such an intervention. Yet, because China, as a world power with nuclear weapons and formidable armies, could be expected to retaliate forcefully, this would not be pragmatically possible. The ethical argument for intervention is not an absolute one, but tempered by a consideration of the realities of power in the world. An ethical case for war does not have to proceed without any consideration of pragmatic consequences.

---

[5] One eloquent elaboration of this argument can be found in Chesterman's *Just War or Just Peace: Humanitarian Intervention and International Law* (2001). Chesterman argues that "unilateral enforcement is not a substitute for but the opposite of collective action. Though often presented as the only alternative to inaction, incorporating a 'right' of intervention would lead only to more such interventions being undertaken in bad faith, it would be incoherent as a principle, and it would be inimical to the emergence of an international rule of law" (2001: 6). Whether or not the Iraq war will lead to these things is an empirical question, rather than something that should be accepted on the basis of Chesterman's prognosis.

Intervention must depend upon both the reasonable assumption, or empirical verification, of a widespread desire for rescue on the part of those subjects who are denied their sovereignty, and a subsequent willingness of the people in need to bear the costs of war – destruction of civilian life, property, infrastructure, and social disorganization – in order to achieve a greater benefit. Furthermore, the intervening power must execute the war according to strict *jus in bello* criteria, and seek to minimize the threat to all those entities that are not direct objects of military action. Finally, the victorious power is strictly obligated to engage in a process of social reconstruction, in order to ensure that the outlaw state is transformed into a liberal republic. Gary Alan Bass has recently referred to this as "*jus post bellum*," and argued that the overall justness of a war is dependent on whether or not the conquering state fulfills its duties after the war (2004: 386).[6] This process entails the provision of all the material resources necessary for such an accomplishment: including the presence of the military, to provide security and safety, and the establishment of democratic political structures. I see nothing inconsistent with basic liberal principles in a position of support of the war in Iraq – indeed, on the grounds already mentioned, it is questionable whether those who were against the war were, in fact, truly liberal ... but that is a question for another day. Suffice it to say that those of us liberals who have tried to offer liberal justifications for the war have experienced no small amount of frustration that our liberal colleagues have not even been willing to listen to the arguments, much less change their positions.

For purposes of this chapter, I would like to set aside the arguments about the ways in which the Bush Administration mishandled the justification or prosecution of the war. These debates will rage on; my preferred approach is to simply acknowledge that each side in the debate has valid, principled points of view, and to present what might be called a "third view" – the human rights case – which has seldom been presented in the polarized discourse on the war.[7] Critics will immediately argue that these considerations cannot be set aside, since they are central to their opposition: if there were no WMDs, or if Saddam and bin Laden had no objective relationship, then the war could not have been an act of anticipatory self-defense. Perhaps this may be true; my reason for setting aside this argument, however, is to focus on articulating a humanitarian case for the war that stands over and above not only "Bush's war," but also the "anti-war proponents' war." What I am asking, plainly and

---

[6] An eloquent argument for the ethical and moral obligations of the United States and the international community in post-war Iraq can also be found in Feldman 2004.

[7] For a more detailed discussion of this "third view" and the positions of other liberal supporters of the war, see Cushman 2005.

simply, is for those of us who share a commitment to the advancement of human rights to at least consider whether there is a legitimate human rights case for the war to be made. There is a distinct advantage to engaging specifically with other human rights thinkers on this question, because it is probably pointless to convince, say, George W. Bush, Jacques Chirac, Noam Chomsky, Howard Zinn, or Michael Moore of the human rights case. Rather, I want to foster a discourse among those who consider themselves to be humanitarians; in this case, I present my argument for the war as one humanitarian to others who also consider themselves to be humanitarians, but who may not agree with my view.

The Humanitarian Case Against the War

For purposes of this chapter, I would like to begin by considering, in detail, the case of one extended argument *against* seeing the Iraq war as a humanitarian war. In Chapter 6, "War in Iraq: Not a Humanitarian Intervention," Kenneth Roth, the director of Human Rights Watch, puts forth a strong argument against viewing the conflict as a humanitarian intervention. Indeed, he finds such arguments dangerous, and even subversive of the more general cause of humanitarian rescue in the future. In making the case against the human rights argument, Roth reproduces several aspects of the currently accepted logic regarding what constitutes legitimate humanitarian intervention. Thus, I shall use Roth's own arguments about the specific case of Iraq to raise more general points, which I consider to be problematic in thinking about humanitarian intervention. Following this critical appraisal of Roth's views, I shall provide my own view of the human rights case, which is grounded, in part, on a concrete sociological appraisal of the war's consequences for the Iraqi people, and, also in part, on an application of consequentialist ethics to the case of Iraq.

Whether or not we see the Iraq war as a humanitarian intervention depends upon how one defines the term "humanitarian intervention." In general, based on the literature on the subject, there are at least five factors that must be present in order to consider an act of aggression as a humanitarian intervention:

1) There must be a recognition of some imminent threat by an organized group of perpetrators to some group of people who are imagined as victims. These victims must be considered to be in need of rescue; and all other – pacific – efforts to rescue them must have been attempted and failed, so that the use of military force, then, necessarily represents a last resort.

2) In general, humanitarian intervention ought to be welcomed by the subjects of gross violations of human rights and is not dependent on the consent of rulers who are the source of their peoples' suffering (Kolb 2003: 119).[8]

3) The intent of the rescuers must be moral and ethical in nature, and may neither be based on self-interest (i.e., the acquisition of territory or resources), nor national interest exclusively. The war must be publicly acknowledged as a humanitarian intervention, and the humanitarian goals must be specified (Lang 2003).[9]

4) Such humanitarian interventions must be approved by the U.N. Security Council and, thereby, have the sanction of international law (Chesterman 2001: 236).

5) The basic humanitarian goals must have a reasonable chance of success and once accomplished, the intervention must not mutate into something else – such as the destruction of the sovereignty of the state and its leaders, the acquisition of material resources, or the implementation of a program of nation-building (Cook 2003: 153).

Based on these criteria, humanitarian interventions – generally speaking – are not transformative events, but "reactive" ones. They do not aim to eradicate the social-structural sources that give rise to crises and violations of human rights, but, instead, are meant to alleviate the latter. They are essentially conservative, in the sense that they conserve the status quo formations; the criteria for humanitarian intervention are so rigidly specified that a good number of the worst violations of human rights are tolerated and allowed to occur. This was the case in Iraq, and has been the case in many other situations of great social suffering in the modern world.

In his very title – "War in Iraq: Not A Humanitarian War" – Roth wants to be perfectly clear about establishing the ontological reality of the war: it is not a humanitarian war. The central criterion that he appears to adopt as the basis for his classification is that the aim and intent of the war were not to prevent genocide, which, for him, is the principle determining factor for what constitutes a legitimate humanitarian intervention. Roth notes (presumably speaking as the director of Human Rights Watch for the entire organization):

> In our view, as a threshold matter, humanitarian intervention that occurs without the consent of the relevant government can be justified only in the face of

---

[8] Humanitarian intervention of a non-military aid, such as the provision of food, medicine, or other forms of assistance, can be by invitation of rulers (Kolb 2003: 119).

[9] Lang does note that intent alone is not a necessary condition, but, rather: "a mix of motives, means, and outcomes must all play a role in determining if an intervention is humanitarian or not" (2003: 3).

ongoing or imminent genocide, or comparable mass slaughter or loss of life. To state the obvious, war is dangerous. In theory it can be surgical, but the reality is often highly destructive, with a risk of enormous bloodshed. Only large-scale murder, we believe, can justify the death, destruction, and disorder that so often are inherent in war and its aftermath. Other forms of tyranny are deplorable and worth working intensively to end, but they do not in our view rise to the level that would justify the extraordinary response of military force. Only mass slaughter might permit the deliberate taking of life involved in using military force for humanitarian purposes.

Roth, thus, sets the threshold for humanitarian intervention as "genocide prevention" – and only that. States and international organizations may only engage in humanitarian intervention reactively, when there is a distinct threat of genocide, or when genocide is actually occurring. What this means is that humanitarian intervention can *never* be justified except in cases of actual or impending genocide. This is an unnecessarily restrictive view of humanitarian intervention. Even though genocide is "the crime of crimes," is it really the case that humanitarian intervention ought to be reserved only for this crime against humanity and this crime alone?

Let us imagine, for a moment, that in the year 1995 Saddam Hussein had decided that each day he would publicly torture fifty children of suspected dissidents, and, afterwards, televise the beheading of ten women suspected of prostitution. Further, let us imagine that in the same year, the world community finally came to a firm determination about what exactly constitutes genocide (there is, of course, no consensus at present), and established a threshold that, if met, would lead to swift and severe humanitarian intervention to stop it. Imagine that, soon after this, Saddam Hussein began a program of mass killing that approached that threshold, but intentionally fell short of it in order to escape the sanction of "humanitarian intervention."

Thus, if genocide prevention were regarded the only acceptable criterion for humanitarian intervention, then whole classes of human rights abuses would be relegated to the margins of concern: the systematic torture and killing of people would be allowable and acceptable, and could proceed without sanction. Even worse, if rulers such as Saddam Hussein were to know what demarcates the threshold of genocide, they would be further emboldened to engage in genocidal actions that approach that threshold, but never actually meet it. Such rulers, who always operate referentially and reflexively in assessing what they think other parties will or will not do in response to their behavior, would know fully that they would be safe from outside intervention – so long as they managed their atrocities within the established parameters of what is acceptable. If Roth's view firmly establishes the principle that only genocide prevention is an acceptable rationale for humanitarian intervention, then it leaves open the possibility – a possibility that is, actually, all too real in the modern world – for despots and tyrants to violate human rights in any way, shape, or form, as long as they remain under the threshold for humanitarian intervention: rather than acting as an impediment to human rights abuses, such a threshold would actually embolden human rights violators to further violate human rights with impunity.

There is another issue, alluded to above, related to the problematic question of how genocide is defined by the international community. There is clearly no consensus on the issue, but one thing that is clear is that the international community has had a very difficult time defining genocide with enough clarity so that resolute action against it can proceed. The lack of humanitarian intervention in Bosnia and Rwanda was, in large part, a result of the fact that the United Nations – as well as those states that had the power to intervene – could not come to an agreement as to whether these situations were, in fact, instances of genocide. While foreign powers were deciding on this issue – and, for practical reasons, specifically avoiding the use of the term "genocide" whilst doing so – the mass killing continued unabated. In the cases of both Bosnia and Rwanda, this was something of a "green light" to those who were planning to commit genocide, as they recognized that Western hesitation would not lead to intervention. Roth argues that there was no evidence that Saddam Hussein was planning another genocide; this may or may not be true. In 1988, the regime of Saddam Hussein waged the Anfal campaign against the Kurds in Northern Iraq, a planned and systematic program of mass murder, torture, deportation, and cultural destruction. This campaign constituted genocide in the view of Human Rights Watch.[10] After the Gulf War in 1991 and throughout the 1990s, the Iraqi regime engaged in an all-out campaign of devastation against the Ma'dan, or Marsh Arabs, Shi'a Muslims who inhabited the marshlands of Southern Iraq. This campaign was characterized by mass executions, widespread imprisonment, torture, and forced migrations; Human Rights Watch estimates that from an original population of 250,000 in 1991, the population of Ma'dan in their ancestral homelands was reduced to 40,000 by 2003 (HRW 2003). This certainly constitutes a mass crime against humanity, if not, according to standard sociological definitions, a genocidal campaign. So the fact of the matter is that Saddam Hussein perpetrated at least one genocide and another campaign that was, at the very least, genocidal. In his chapter, Roth allows for the possibility that humanitarian intervention might be justified if there were an impending genocide, as was

---

[10]   See HRW 1993 for full report on the Anfal campaign.

the reasoning in considering Kosovo to be a humanitarian intervention (it appeared that Milosevic was planning a repeat of the Bosnian genocide in the fields of Kosovo). I would like to leave open the question of whether human-itarian intervention could be justified, based on a reasonable suspicion that it might occur again. But on the other hand, it seems reasonable, in thinking about whether or not humanitarian intervention is justifiable, to consider that those who have already committed genocide – not once but twice – ought to be considered at danger to commit it again. When coupled with other considerations of gross violations of human rights, this possibility must fig-ure into the equation that assesses the potential for genocide. Another way of putting this might be: why would anyone seriously committed to human rights and genocide prevention want to give a potential *genocidaire* with a track record in committing the crime the benefit of the doubt? Roth's views, in this regard, are very little different than many opponents of the war, who continually gave Saddam Hussein the benefit of the doubt, in spite of his outra-geous violations of human rights, acts of genocide, and over-flaunting of U.N. resolutions.

In any case, even if we suspend the question of what constitutes a threat to commit genocide, we are still left with the central question of whether or not humanitarian intervention can be justified in cases of non-genocidal gross violations of human rights.

Roth himself seems aware of the contentions of those who argued that there could be positive human rights consequences to war beyond simply stopping mass killing. He notes:

> Because the Iraq war was not mainly about saving the Iraqi people from mass slaughter, and because no such slaughter was then ongoing or imminent, Human Rights Watch at the time took no position for or against the war. A humanitarian rationale was occasionally offered for the war, but it was so plainly subsidiary to other reasons that we felt no need to address it. Indeed, if Saddam Hussein had been overthrown and the issue of weapons of mass destruction reliably dealt with, there clearly would have been no war, even if the successor government were just as repressive. *Some argued that Human Rights Watch should support a war launched on other grounds if it would arguably lead to significant human rights improvements. But the substantial risk that wars guided by non-humanitarian goals will endanger human rights keeps us from adopting that position.* (Emphasis added)

Roth's argument that other humanitarian rationales were simply not even worthy of addressing is truly remarkable, given the fact that Human Rights Watch has done more than any other international non-governmental organi-zation(NGO) to document the gross violations of human rights in Iraq. Does it seem too much to ask the very organization that made us aware of such gross violations in Iraq to at least consider other rationales for the war, rather than dismissing them out of hand? Also odd is Roth's concern about the "risk that wars guided by non-humanitarian goals will endanger human rights." It is hard to imagine how leaving Saddam Hussein in power (and substantially emboldened by the appeasement of institutions of global governance, just as he was after the first Gulf War) could in any way not "endanger human rights." And in spite of the fact that the war in Iraq has many negative consequences, it is still hard to imagine that the war has "endangered human rights" more than Saddam Hussein. Perhaps it is the case that, given the chaos of post-war Iraq, Roth could be said to have been astute in his predictions; however, ultimately, this question must be considered from a consequentialist standpoint and can be stated quite simply: is Iraq better off now than it was under Saddam Hussein? Those who argue that it is better off now bear the burden of having to justify their view in light of the physical and human costs of the war and the current problems in post-war Iraq. Those who argue that it was better off under Saddam must bear the burden (and moral consequences) of arguing that any population could be better off under a regime that was, arguably, one of the greatest violators of human rights in modern times.

Putting aside the issue of Roth's dismissal of any humanitarian rationales for a moment, a more central question becomes: why was it the case that the war could never be seen by Roth, or others, as having any positive consequences for human rights? Many in the human rights community were not even willing to entertain the thought. It ought to have been obvious that the most immediate consequence of the war would be the removal of Saddam Hussein and his regime – the central sources of human rights violations; thus, it is hard to imagine that Human Rights Watch, which has probably compiled more damning information on Saddam's crimes than any other organization, could not have recognized this act alone as an ontological improvement in the situation of the Iraqi people. To be fair, Roth and others were most likely concerned about the unpredictable consequences and outcomes of such a war: it would, indeed, cause a degree of chaos and ontological insecurity in Iraqi society, which would lead to negative outcomes.

However, it is seldom the case in revolutions that aim to depose tyranny that a clear vision of the future is articulated at the same time that the fight for liberation is proceeding. The radical British political philosopher Norman Geras has termed the overthrow of Saddam Hussein a revolution; and I substantially agree with his assessment, while stressing that it was a revolution that only could have occurred with decisive intervention by powers greater than those of Saddam Hussein (Geras 2005). It seems, though, as if Roth was looking well beyond the deposing of the tyrant, and seeing Thermidor, when I would argue that in situations in which the imperative to overthrow a tyranny is as clear as it was in Iraq, the decision not to support the revolution because you see only Thermidor is a mistake. And while opponents of the war would now like to paint a picture of post-war Iraq as Thermidor, it is, in fact, a far cry from that.

Roth notes that he does not mean to ignore the plight of the Iraqi people, in spite of his denial that they ought to be aided:

> In stating that the killing in Iraq did not rise to a level that justified humanitarian intervention, we are not insensitive to the awful plight of the Iraqi people. We are aware that summary executions occurred with disturbing frequency in Iraq up to the end of Saddam Hussein's rule, as did torture and other brutality. Such atrocities should be met with public, diplomatic, and economic pressure, as well as prosecution. But before taking the substantial risk to life that is inherent in any war, mass slaughter should be taking place or imminent. That was not the case in Saddam Hussein's Iraq in March 2003.

But this raises exactly a point that neither Roth nor other opponents of the war have ever really considered: how is it that Saddam Hussein could have been stopped with "public, diplomatic, and economic pressure, as well as prosecution"? The entire history of his regime is, in some ways, a story of victory against such pacific and well-intentioned means. Indeed, he even survived a multilateral war against him in 1991, and further intensified his genocidal policies and gross violations of human rights after his military defeat. The idea that, somehow, Saddam Hussein could be indicted or prosecuted by anybody in the world, all the while enjoying full member status in the U.N. while being treated as a negotiating partner with U.N. bodies and other states, while enjoying the fiscal and material support of powerful U.N. Security Council members such as France and Germany, seems fantastical. Even more fantastical is the idea – very often taken as a matter of faith in the international community – that, somehow, the indictment and/or prosecution of Saddam Hussein by some international tribunal while he was still in power, and being treated as a *bona fide* member of the Society of Peoples, would have any practical positive consequences for human rights at all. Prosecutions do not stop human rights violations; human rights violations are stopped by interventions. Moreover, Roth seems to accept, a priori, that war would have a far worse consequence than allowing Saddam Hussein to remain in power. He argues:

> Another factor for assessing the humanitarian nature of an intervention is whether it is reasonably calculated to make things better rather than worse

in the country invaded. One is tempted to say that anything is better than living under the tyranny of Saddam Hussein, but unfortunately, it is possible to
imagine scenarios that are even worse. Vicious as his rule was, chaos or abusive
civil war might well become even deadlier, and it is too early to say whether such
violence might still emerge in Iraq.

On this view, the immediate consequence of removing one of the most
heinous violators of human rights from power is subordinated to some greater
concern that the situation might worsen after his removal. To some extent,
Roth's logic is vindicated by some of the negative outcomes since the war:
Islamist fundamentalist resistance, the rise of factionalism, and the fractious
nature of emergent politics. But of course, these outcomes – which are very
real, and, which were to be expected – must be offset by considering some of
the positive outcomes of the war, outcomes that are seldom acknowledged by
critics who wish to see the war in the most negative terms possible in order
to vindicate their original position against it. In any case, it can by no means
be ascertained now that chaos or abusive civil war has been the dominant
result of the war, even though we are disposed by negative media coverage
to see it that way. The mishandlings of the post-war situation by the Bush
Administration were many: too few soldiers were used, there was no plan for
winning the peace, that policing was carried out by soldiers who were not
trained as policemen. The latter, though, were not in any way determined to
happen – but, to the detriment of the Iraqi people, they did; while they have
watered down some of the more idealistic expectations of Iraqis, they have
not extinguished them.

Finally, in his chapter, Roth holds to the conventional wisdom of the international community (and of the human rights community as well) that, somehow, international law is the best hope for the protection of human rights.
Clearly, this is neither a view that the majority of Bosnian Muslims, Rwandan
Tutsi, Kosovar Albanians, or Afghanis under the Taliban (or numerous other
people in other extreme situations of danger who require rescue) would have
taken at the time when they were subjected to crimes against them, nor is it a
position that survivors would take now. In each of these cases, those who were
victims of genocide and gross violations of human rights begged for deliverance from the institutions of global governance, and, to this day, resent that
it was not provided for them. (Indeed, as I have discovered in Bosnia, much
of the post-conflict resentment is directed not only towards perpetrators, but
also towards those who knew what was going on and did nothing to stop it:
a phenomenon that I refer to as "nested resentments.") For it was precisely
under the cover of international law that many of the gross violations of the
human rights of these peoples were allowed to occur.

The very fact that so many people found some justification for the interventions in Bosnia and Kosovo – even though they were technically outside of the bounds of international law – means that we ought to apply the same logic to the Iraq war. As mentioned, the argument that motive and intent are the most important criteria for considering whether a war is humanitarian is not valid. Rather, some consideration of the moral and ethical consequences of the war must also figure into the equation. For many of those who supported the war on human rights grounds (an admittedly small group), the rationales provided by the Bush Administration were deeply problematic, and, in fact, made support of the war (in any form) a difficult choice to make. But one common thread that united such people was the ability to see that, beyond the failures of ideological justifications, and beyond the failures of institutions of global governance and international law, one had to consider the likely positive consequences of the war; and upon such balance, many of those who supported the war felt that the positive consequences and benefits for the Iraqi people potentially outweighed the negative costs. Even more importantly, many of those who supported the war on these terms did so with conscious recognition that it was not they alone who were making the cost-benefit determination, but the Iraqi people. We who supported the war were, first and foremost, ethnographers of the conscience and desire of the Iraqi people, as well.

The Human Rights Case for the War in Iraq: A Consequentialist-Sociological View

In what follows, I would like to offer something of a phenomenological journey, which gives those who might be puzzled by the strange and dissident view of the human rights case for the war some sense of what we who made this case felt and experienced as we faced the impending war and eventually made our stand in support of it. For those of us liberals who supported the war in Iraq, one of the principal reasons for doing so was to express solidarity with the Iraqi people. On the eve of the war, it was clear to many of us – mostly through networks of displaced Iraqis and other information emanating from Iraq, as well as site visits to various places in Iraq and extended conversations with Iraqis – that the majority of Iraqi people wanted to see Saddam Hussein deposed, and were quite open about the means by which to achieve that end.[11] In short, it seemed to us that the principal ethnographic reality was that most

[11] Two clear examples of this solidarity can be found in Faber 2005 and Clwyd 2005.

Table 3.1.

From today's perspective and all things considered, was it absolutely right, somewhat right, somewhat wrong, or absolutely wrong that the US-led coalition forces invaded Iraq in Spring 2003?

	Count	%	Combined %
Absolutely right	520	22.5	
Somewhat right	759	32.8	55.2
Somewhat wrong	343	14.8	
Absolutely wrong	694	30.0	44.8
TOTAL	2316	100.0	100.0

Source: Oxford Research International, February 2004.

of the Iraqi people supported the war as a means of liberation from tyranny. In the years before the war, it had been very difficult to get any valid or reliable surveys of opinion from Iraq; so, ethnographic sensibilities were extremely important, if not somewhat tentative and risky.

Yet, in the months following the war, new survey research seemed to confirm on a more general level, the supposition that most Iraqis supported the war and wished to see Saddam Hussein deposed, according to Oxford Research International, which has commissioned and carried out five waves of systematic social research on the opinions and attitudes of the Iraq people in the post-war situation. The results of this survey, overall, show that that, in spite of the costs of the war, problems with insurgencies, and the humiliating experience of occupation, a majority of surveyed Iraqis supported the war.[12]

As Table 3.1 shows, in February of 2004, almost one year after the war and occupation, 55.2 percent of Iraqis felt that the war was absolutely right or somewhat right, while 44.8 percent felt that it was somewhat wrong or absolutely wrong. In addition, in contrast to the negative imagery that was the mainstay of the Western press regarding Iraq, in February 2004, there was

[12] All of the data presented in this chapter in the form of tables are taken from Oxford Research International's National Surveys of Iraq in February and June of 2004. These full reports, as well as the results of surveys prior to February and ongoing future reports of successive waves of research can be found at: http://www.oxfordresearch.com/publications.html. These reports are rich with data about all aspects of Iraqis' lives, and I have drawn selectively from them to illustrate patterns of public opinion that favor a humanitarian argument for the war and the results that I present here must be compared with ongoing events in Iraq and future surveys that will have been published by the time of this chapter appearing in print. I gratefully acknowledge the work of Oxford International Research, and permission to use their data in this chapter.

Table 3.2.

Overall, how would you say things are going in your life
these days – very good, quite good, quite bad, or very bad?

	Count	%	Combined %
Very good	355	13.5	
Quite good	1501	57.2	70.7
Quite bad	376	14.3	
Very bad	392	15.0	29.3
TOTAL	2624	100.0	100.0

Source: Oxford Research International, February 2004.

a rather remarkable optimism about the present and future among Iraqis. Table 3.2 indicates that 71 percent of Iraqis felt that their lives at the time were very good or quite good, as opposed to 29 percent of Iraqis who felt that things were quite bad or very bad.

Table 3.3 shows that, in comparison with their lives a year before the war, 57 percent of Iraqis felt that things were much better or somewhat better overall in their lives, 24 percent felt that things were about the same and only 19 percent felt that things were somewhat worse or much worse.

And what is most striking is the overwhelming sense of optimism expressed by Iraqis about the future. As Table 3.4 indicates, a huge majority of Iraqis, 82 percent, felt that things overall in their lives would be much better or somewhat better a year from February 2004. It is vital to stress that these measures of optimism occur in a post-war, occupation situation, rife with violence,

Table 3.3.

Compared to a year ago, I mean before the war in Spring 2003,
are things overall in your life much better now, somewhat
better, about the same, somewhat worse, or much worse?

	Count	%	Combined %
Much better now	581	22.3	
Somewhat better	917	35.1	57.4
About the same	618	23.7	23.7
Somewhat worse	338	12.9	
Much worse	156	6.0	18.9
TOTAL	2609	100.0	100.0

Source: Oxford Research International, February 2004.

Table 3.4.

	Count	%	Combined %
Much better	975	42.2	
Somewhat better	911	39.4	81.5
About the same	250	10.8	10.8
Somewhat worse	86	3.7	
Much worse	91	3.9	7.7
TOTAL	2312	100.0	100.0

What is your expectation for how things overall in your life will be in a year from now? Will they be much better, somewhat better, about the same, somewhat worse, or much worse?

Source: Oxford Research International, February 2004.

social, political and economic problems, and are even more astounding in that light.

A few months later, in April of 2004, the Roper Center for Public Opinion Research surveyed Iraqis and found that more than a year after the war and occupation, 61 percent of Iraqis said that in spite of the hardships they had endured under war and occupation, ousting Saddam Hussein was worth it, while only 28 percent felt that it was not. As Table 3.5 shows, there are regional and religious variations, but still a quite sizeable majority, even in the face of the hardships of war, felt that the removal of Saddam was a positive event (and this view did not change hardly at all in Baghdad from April 2003 to April 2004).

Another fascinating finding of the February 2004 survey by Oxford International Research, shown below in Table 3.6, is that about half of Iraqis felt that the U.S.-led coalition force liberated Iraq, while about half felt it humiliated Iraq.

Table 3.5.

Thinking about the hardships you might have suffered since the invasion, do you think ousting Saddam Hussein was worth it?

	All(%)	Baghdad	Baghdad 2003	Shiite Areas
Yes, was worth it	61	57	62	74
No, was not worth it	28	38	30	17

Source: CNN?USA Today/Gallup Poll, provided by the Center for Public Opinion Research, April 2004.

Table 3.6.

Apart from right and wrong, do you feel the US-led coalition force invasion:		
	Count	%
Humiliated Iraq	1093	49.7
Liberated Iraq	1109	50.3
TOTAL	2202	100.0

Source: Oxford Research International, February 2004.

It is important to note that many Iraqis are of two minds about the war: they see it, simultaneously, as an act of liberation and – especially in the occupation phase – of humiliation. Most observers of the war have not been able to grasp the fact that these two feelings of the war could coexist; but in each case, the existence of the two attitudes is explainable in relation to the social-structural sources that have given rise to them: gratitude for relief from totalitarian domination in the case of the experience of liberation, and suspicion and resentment about the imposition of a new regime of occupation over which the average person had little control.

Although there is no systematic data before the war, or immediately after, one might hypothesize that these numbers of supporters and those who experienced the war as liberation might have been even higher. In any case, such survey results have not enjoyed wide attention in Western publics, and contradict the narrative of negativity about the war and the views of the Iraqi people, which was a convenient narrative for those who were against the war in seeking to delegitimate it.

Lest I paint too optimistic a scenario, though, it is important to note that as the post-war situation deteriorated, mostly due to the violence of the insurgency and the lack of security, the views of Iraqis changed considerably by June 2004, which is the latest survey research published by Oxford Research International by the time of this writing. The views of Iraqis began to become increasingly negative. Table 3.7 indicates that only four months later, 41 percent of Iraqis felt that the war was absolutely right or somewhat right, while 59 percent felt that it was somewhat wrong or absolutely wrong.

Still, Iraqis maintained a clear sense that things were still going well for them and expressed a rather strong degree of optimism about the future. Table 3.8 shows that 55 percent of Iraqis still felt that their lives were very good or quite good (and the majority of 43 percent still perceive life as "quite good"), while 45 percent felt that things were quite bad or very bad.

Table 3.7.

From today's perspective and all things considered, was it absolutely right, somewhat right, somewhat wrong, or absolutely wrong that the US-led coalition forces invaded Iraq in Spring 2003?

	Count	%	Combined %
Absolutely right	373	13.2	
Somewhat right	782	27.6	40.8
Somewhat wrong	728	25.7	
Absolutely wrong	947	33.5	59.2
TOTAL	2830	100	100.0

Source: Oxford Research International, June 2004.

Table 3.9 shows a decline in well-being in comparison with one year before, with 44 percent of Iraqis feeling that they were better off, 32 percent felt that things were about the same, and 25 percent indicated that things were somewhat worse or much worse.

Finally, Table 3.10 indicates a persistent optimism among the Iraqi people: 64 percent of them had the expectation that things overall in their lives would be much better or somewhat better, 18 percent expected that they would be about the same, and 19 percent felt that things would be somewhat worse or much worse.

So there is clearly some decline in Iraqis' perceptions of the war and their lives, but nonetheless, the data indicate overall that many Iraqi people express positive opinions about their lives and futures, even in the midst of the chaos of the post-war period. The decline from February to June is mostly due to concerns about security and the coalition forces' sometimes gross

Table 3.8.

Overall, how would you say things are going in your life these days – very good, quite good, quite bad, or very bad?

	Count	%	Combined %
Very good	373	12.5	
Quite good	1281	42.8	55.3
Quite bad	866	28.9	
Very bad	472	15.8	44.7
TOTAL	2993	100.0	100.0

Source: Oxford Research International, June 2004.

Table 3.9.

Compared to a year ago, I mean before the war in Spring 2003, are things overall in your life much better now, much worse, somewhat better, about the same, somewhat worse, or much worse?

	Count	%	Combined %
Much better now	347	11.8	
Somewhat better	933	31.8	43.6
About the same	922	31.5	31.5
Somewhat worse	538	18.4	
Much worse	190	6.5	24.9
TOTAL	2931	100.0	100.0

Source: Oxford Research International, June 2004.

mismanagement of the occupation. Such events as the Abu Ghraib prison abuses could only work against the view of the war as a humanitarian venture. In the June survey of public opinion, 67 percent of Iraqis were surprised by the revelations of human rights abuses at Abu Ghraib, while 33 percent were not surprised. Nonetheless, most Iraqis do not feel that this was a matter of systematic policy of the U.S. government, nor do they think that it is at all morally comparable to the practices of Saddam's regime; 54 percent of Iraqis felt that the abuse of prisoners at Abu Ghraib were carried out by fewer than 100 people, while only 26 percent felt that more people were involved, and a scant 20 percent thought that the behavior of soldiers at the prison indicated that the entire United States was like this (ORI 2004: 31). The majority of

Table 3.10.

What is your expectation for how things overall in your life will be in a year from now? Will they be much better, somewhat better, about the same, somewhat worse, or much worse?

	Count	%	Combined %
Much better	724	27.4	
Somewhat better	967	36.6	64.0
About the same	463	17.5	17.5
Somewhat worse	335	12.7	
Much worse	155	5.9	18.6
TOTAL	2664	100.0	100.0

Source: Oxford Research International, June 2004.

Iraqis do not think that the Abu Ghraib scandal was a systematic policy of the U.S. administration, even though Abu Ghraib has been cited extensively by anti-war opponents as a violation of *jus post bellum* ethics, which they call upon to question the *just ad bellum* justifications for the war. Unlike most opponents of the war, an overwhelming 76 percent of Iraqis felt that the human rights abuses at Abu Ghraib would make no difference to the future of Iraq, except to increase hatred and negative perceptions of Americans (ORI 2004: 32).

It is clear from survey results that many Iraqis would like the occupation to end and for coalition forces to leave. In June 2004, 34 percent felt they should leave now, although most felt that they should stay for varying time periods, with 28 percent believing they should not leave until a permanent government is in place (ORI 2004: 34). Even so, this desire does not mitigate a desire for democracy on and to take control of their own destiny: a sentiment which is entirely in keeping with the human rights case for the war – a case which has never been about imposing a regime of rights on the Iraqi people, but which has always valued the restoration of their sovereignty, agency, and right to self-determination.

In the wake of the war – with rising discontent about the war and increasing resistance – it is clear that public opinion in Iraq in favor of the war began to change. Yet, from the existing survey data that we have – which, though quite substantial, is seldom referred to in discussions of the war – we can discern that this was consequential to the failures in administration and management of the occupation, rather than attributable to a fundamental realignment of an original position of moral support for the war.

These facts about public opinion confirm, for me, the rightness of my initial stance of support for the war as an act of solidarity with the majority of the Iraqi people. One of the most troubling aspects of the response to the war, however, is that many people who were against the war simply ignored such public opinion, or – even worse – distorted it to serve their own anti-war positions. The dominant concern, at least of the more pacifistic anti-war forces, was for the number of civilians who would be killed in the war. Although this is a legitimate concern, it was often expressed without consideration of the actual wishes and desires of the majority of the Iraqi people: their collective public opinion has indicated that they were willing to suffer a certain degree of short-term pain for the more pleasurable outcome of liberation from over thirty years of despotism, and the more enduring prospect of achieving some measure of collective happiness from a democratic future. In short, a determination of whether the war was just has been based not on a sterile, utilitarian calculus made from the outside, but a consideration of the moral calculus used by the Iraqi people themselves, which has been made apprehensible through the tools of social-scientific research.

This positive public opinion of the Iraqi people toward the war was a kind of moral capital of which the Bush Administration – in offering its rationales for the war – never failed to squander. It is, indeed, one of the great failures of the administration of the post-war occupation. For if it could be ascertained and documented that the Iraqi people were in favor of the war, and this fact had been stressed by the Bush Administration, it would have made the case all the more compelling from a human rights perspective. The result, in my opinion, is that more liberals, who were generally against the war, might have been inclined to support it on traditional liberal internationalist grounds. In my experience, liberal-humanitarians are united by a strong sense of solidarity with the weak. While many of us did not expect George W. Bush to take a strong stand on human rights, many of us felt disillusioned by the fact that our left-liberal colleagues not only did not stand in solidarity with the Iraqi people against Saddam, but also turned steadfastly against the war and left the Iraqi people to the vicissitudes of their dictator and the ethically challenged system of international law. Left-liberals who had so long championed resistance to tyranny and fascism in, say, Latin America, South Africa, and elsewhere, as well as resistance to imperialism throughout the twentieth century, suddenly found themselves enthralled with the empire of international law, the neo-imperial machinations of France and Germany, and the inclination to reduce the entire war to a reductive Marxist scheme of "blood for oil" or the "quest for American empire." The result was a distantiation from the very ethical principles that are the core of liberal internationalism: solidarity with the weak, anti-fascism, anti-totalitarianism, and the fundamental principles of human rights. Only a small handful of liberals were making the argument that we ought to consider the public opinion and desires of Iraqis as a central aspect of our positions on the war. The imperative of solidarity with the weak became invisible, masked by concerns about international law, the motivations of George W. Bush, and the fear of American empire – anything else but the elemental sense of solidarity with the oppressed, which, for me, is the defining characteristic of liberal conscience.

A human rights case for the war has depended, fundamentally, on imagining both the consequences of not going to war, and of the war itself. The consequence of not going to war would have been the appeasement of Saddam Hussein and a toleration of brutality of his regime. The consequence of not going to war would have been to allow international law to become a tool of tyrants who have a keen sense of how to manipulate the Western (and, especially, the European) desire for peace at all costs. The consequence of not going to war was to seriously jeopardize the legitimacy of the United Nations and its central decision-making apparatus, the Security Council. The consequence of not going to war would have been to confirm the very fact that the ethical basis of the entire global order – the U.N. Declaration of Human Rights – was, for the Iraqi people, a meaningless rhetorical charade.

This does not mean that most of those who supported the war on the liberal grounds, which I have laid out here, made this decision lightly. As I have noted, the decision to support the war – at least in my case – was made with the conscious knowledge that the Iraqi people were looking to the West for deliverance and that – flawed though war is as a means to this end – a war promised them that, at least in the short run. Let us imagine for a moment that the Iraqi people are agents who desire to make a revolution against their dictator. Furthermore, as educated people, they are fully aware that many people in the rest of the world enjoy human rights and freedoms, which they have been denied. These agents are also fully aware that many of the world's most powerful states have previously aligned themselves – for *realpolitik* reasons – with their oppressors, while at the same time continuing to hold onto the possibility that it will not always be that way. Now, let us imagine that these very same people get wind of the fact that the American president, with several key allies, is now set to depose their dictator: that is, is willing to assist them in their revolution. They also recognize that various other powerful states, such as France and Germany, are allied against the American president, and, therefore, against them. They have little or no faith in a system of international law that, although promising them great things, has never actually delivered them much of anything, except toleration of their oppression, and economic sanctions, which hurt them, but, actually, empowered their oppressor both financially and politically. In this scenario, the American president and his allies are really the only means by which these oppressed people can reclaim their agency and the ability to reclaim their own sovereignty. They would like to do it another way, but they have no other choice. They realize that war will bring with it the dissolution of a certain way of life, ontological insecurity, the deaths of innocents, the destruction of economic and material infrastructure, in short, a degree of certain pain. But, at the same time, these people have already experienced a level of pain accrued from living for over thirty years in a totalitarian regime that had few equals in history. They imagine a future, even an imperfect one, in which they are liberated from their oppression and empowered as agents to choose their own destiny. They are not specifically asking to be given a specific set of rights, or a particular kind of political or economic system, but to be given the possibility to act as autonomous agents to choose their own destiny and self-determination – a possibility that had previously been denied them. They do not want to become America, or a colony of America, but a free Iraq.

In this situation, there can be no legitimate reason to deny these people the right to assistance and rescue, and by way of that, the right to claim their human status as free and autonomous agents. In his recent work on human rights, Michael Ignatieff makes an important reformulation of what he had considered to be the central goal of the human rights movement. He notes that fostering human rights is not so much the act of giving specific rights, but allowing people the agency to claim those rights that they desire. Ignatieff notes:

> Human rights matter because they help people to help themselves. They protect their agency. By agency, I mean more or less what Isaiah Berlin meant by "negative liberty," the capacity to achieve rational intentions without let or hindrance ... Human rights is a language of individual empowerment, and empowerment for individuals is desirable because when individuals have agency they can protect themselves against injustice. Equally, when human beings have agency, they can define for themselves what they wish to live and die for. In this sense, to emphasize agency is to empower individuals, but also to impose limits on human rights claims themselves. To protect human agency necessarily requires us to protect all individuals' right to choose the life they see fit to lead. . . . In this way of thinking, human rights are only a systematic agenda of "negative liberty," a tool kit against oppression, a tool kit that individual agents must be free to use as they see fit within the broader frame of cultural and religious beliefs that they live by. (Ignatieff 2001: 57)

Ignatieff's view of "human rights as agency" is an important amendment to the usual view of human rights as a kind of "gift" given by the strong to the weak. Its importance lies in the fact that it tames the missionary zeal that characterizes so much of the human rights movement, and, which has caused people, at various times and places, to insist that people be given rights, regardless of whether they – *as agents* – actually desire them. Ignatieff is perfectly clear that in some cases – in traditional Muslim societies, for example – the ideal of the total equality of women and men is something that the vast majority of people in such societies do not want. Any attempt to give them such rights over and against their wishes is a form of "human rights imperialism," better, to be sure, than other forms of more retrograde imperialism, but imperialism all the same. Rather, what is given to them is the agency to choose for themselves, even if this choice means that they do not choose the entire panoply of rights at their disposal. In this sense, humanitarian intervention, far from being a simple reaction to managing the consequences of tyranny, is a more proactive exercise in "negative liberty," an act, even, of what might be called "negative liberation" in the service of human agency.

Ignatieff's view is important for making the human rights case for the war in Iraq, because, in this case, it was clear that the majority of the Iraqi population 1. wanted to be free of Saddam's tyranny and 2. remain committed to the project of liberation and self-determination and 3. wanted to claim certain human rights as free agents but 4. were denied that agency by various forces, among them: Saddam's own repression; the mechanisms of international law, which denied intervention except on grounds of genocide; and the *realpolitik* machinations of certain great powers – France, Germany, Russia, for instance – that had much to lose if Saddam were to be deposed. The current scandal about the U.N. Food-for-Oil program and the material interests of several nations that opposed the war is something that must also be considered as a factor in our consideration as to whether the Iraqi people were better off consequentially under a regime of international organization or as a result of unilateral intervention. These various structural forces directly repressed the autonomy of the Iraqi people as agents who could claim the rights entitled to them, in principle, by the U.N. Declaration of Human Rights. In this respect, the war was justifiable on the simple grounds that it opposed the internal and external sources of constraint that affected the ability of the Iraqi people to act as agents. The war is then not so much about giving the Iraqi people specific rights, but allowing them as agents to construct a situation in which they can claim those rights that they freely choose as a democratic society. Of course, according to this view, if we see the war in Iraq more centrally – as the provision of agency to the Iraq people – then we must, necessarily, allow them to choose their own destiny, even if that destiny is not entirely in keeping with the vision of what the "victorious power" would like to see. The American-led coalition is an occupying force, which has led some to make the charge that it is an imperial venture. Yet, at the same time, the restoration of sovereignty and the provision of security whilst Iraq forges out something resembling a democracy, surely indicates that, unlike the empires of old, the current venture is more in keeping with the principle of self-determination and the allowance for a collective expression of the agency of the Iraqi people than it is the strict imposition of an imperial design. To the extent that the occupation is anything more than that, it is not a success as a "humanitarian intervention" as I have redescribed that phenomenon here. In sympathy with those who still oppose the war on the grounds that it does not really establish true agency and autonomy to the Iraqi people, I would myself want to keep a close eye on events, all the while keeping alive a spirit of liberal hope that the history of Iraq over the next few years should show those suspicions to be without merit.

Concluding Remarks

Having made this elemental human rights case for the war, it is necessary to self-critically point out the shortcomings of it, as a way of further engaging with those who might not agree with it. In this case, there may be some common issues of concern to share with those who are critical of my arguments. I end by raising a series of questions and providing some commentary.

Are war and violence the best means by which to promote solidarity with oppressed peoples? No. The decision to go to war, as Kant himself noted, means that the structural processes, which have developed in the "civilized world" to avert war, are flawed and in need of correction. Those who share a concern for the illegality of the war according to international law, or who fear the idea of preemptive war, are legitimately committed to the Kantian idea of reason in global affairs. Yet, at the same time, they have failed to understand the limits of their own rationality as a means to counter the irrationality and persistent tenacity of human right abuses in the modern world. The question that the war raises for the future of global governance is quite simple: does the political will exist at the United Nations to seriously take on and address human rights issues, despotism, and tyranny in ways that will avert future wars? Those hold their faith in the United Nations as the "last best hope of mankind" must ask themselves that question in light of some of the arguments presented in this chapter. One positive consequence of the war in Iraq, which would have significance, more generally, for the future of global governance, is that it forced a consideration of reforms in international law and international institutions, which might mitigate future possibilities of such events occurring again. Whether there is any optimism about that possibility is a matter for further discussion.

Does the decision to label the Iraq war a humanitarian war on consequential grounds jeopardize future humanitarian interventions, which are more in line with the conventional wisdom of humanitarian intervention as rescue from genocide? No, because it is quite conceivable that the institutions of global governance could be highly successful in the future in intervening to prevent genocide, without any reference at all to the case of Iraq. The case of genocide in Darfur, Sudan, offers some hope that some consensus on the reality of genocide there can be forged while the genocide is actually going on, rather than in an ex post facto way that leaves thousands of people dead and generates the weak and self-serving apologies rendered by those who failed to act. It is quite conceivable that the world community, working through the United Nations, could multilaterally decide to intervene in Sudan to stop the mass killing there, although at the time of this writing, it appears that the same old pattern of avoidance, negotiation, and considerations of *realpolitik* will win the day and we will find ourselves, in five years' time, asking the same question that we ended up asking about Bosnia or Rwanda: how did we let it happen? There is a time when the rhetoric of "never again" becomes tiresome in light of the failure of any appreciable social-structural changes to redress the fact that – over and over again – the institutions that are designed to protect and foster human rights have failed in the worst ways imaginable.

Does the decision to go to war in contravention of international law mean that a plethora of similar "humanitarian interventions" of a bogus nature will be unleashed by powerful actors who claim to be acting in the interests of humanity, but actually have imperial or other less idealistic ambitions? Possibly. But, not necessarily. The possibility of this happening ought to be seen in light of an actual consideration of the historical record and there is no evidence that would warrant making the determination that any unilateral intervention, including that in Iraq, has or will lead to the increased incidence of bogus humanitarian wars. Of course, because I do not consider the claim that the Iraq war was a bogus humanitarian war to be valid, I do not see it as a threat in this sense.

Finally, one might raise the question: if the threshold for humanitarian intervention is lowered from the conservative principle of "genocide prevention only," who is to decide what that threshold is? And where to apply it? To be sure, it is worrisome to imagine that the threshold for humanitarian intervention could become entirely subjective and, perhaps, a product of the caprice of powerful states. In the case of Saddam Hussein's Iraq, those of an authentic liberal-humanitarian disposition ought to argue, in the face of more than thirty years of brutal repression, crimes against humanity, and genocide in Iraq that the regime deserved more than a response of willful indifference, capitulation, and appeasement on the part of the liberal-humanitarian community.

REFERENCES

Bass, G. A. (2004). 'Jus post bellum'. *Philosophy and Public Affairs*, vol. 32.
Chesterman, S. (2001). *Just War or Just Peace: Humanitarian Intervention and International Law*. Oxford: Oxford University Press.
Clwyd, A. (2005). 'Why did it take you so long to get here?' In T. Cushman (Ed.), *A Matter of Principle*. Berkeley, CA: University of California Press.
Cushman, T. (Ed.). (2005). *A Matter of Principle: Humanitarian Arguments for the War in Iraq*. Berkeley and London: University of California Press.
Cook, M. L. (2003). 'Immaculate War: Constraints on Humanitarian Intervention'. In A. Lang (Ed.), *Just Intervention*, p. 153. Washington, DC: Georgetown University Press.

Faber, M. J. (2005). 'Peace, human rights, and the moral choices of the churches'. In T. Cushman (Ed.), *A Matter of Principle*. Berkeley, CA: University of California Press.

Feldman, N. (2004). *What We Owe Iraq*. Princeton and Oxford: Princeton University Press.

Geras, N. (2005). 'Notes from a Journal of Commentary'. In T. Cushman (Ed.), *A Matter of Principle*. Berkeley, CA: University of California Press.

Goldstone, R. J. (2002, April). 'Wither Kosovo? Whither Democracy?' *Global Governance*, vol. 8, no. 2: 143–7.

Human Rights Watch (HRW) (2003). *The Iraqi Government Assault on the Marsh Arabs*. Retrieved from http://www.hrw.org/backgrounder/mena/marsharabs1.htm.

_____. (1993). *Genocide in Iraq: The Anfal Campaign Against the Kurds*. Available at: http://www.hrw.org/reports/1993/iraqanfal/.

Ignatieff, M. (2001). *Human Rights as Politics and Idolatry*. Princeton: Princeton University Press.

Independent International Commission on Kosovo (IICK). (2000). *Kosovo Report: Conflict, International Response, Lessons Learned*. Oxford: Oxford University Press.

Kant, I. ([1795] 1983). *Perpetual Peace*. Indianapolis, IN: Hackett.

Kolb, R. (2003). 'Note on humanitarian intervention'. *International Review of the Red Cross*, no. 849, pp. 119–34.

Lang, A. (2003). 'Introduction'. In A. Lang (Ed.), *Just Intervention*, p. 3. Washington, DC: Georgetown University Press.

Oxford Research International (ORI) (2004, June). *National Survey of Iraq, June 2004*. Retrieved from http://www.oxfordresearch.com/Iraq%20June%202004%20Frequency%2 0Tables.PDF.

Rawls, J. (1999). *The Law of Peoples; with "The Idea of Public Reason Revisited."* Cambridge, MA: Harvard University Press.

Tesón, F. (1998). *A Philosophy of International Law*. Boulder, CO.: Westview Press.

4. Human Rights as an Ethics of Power

JOHN R. WALLACH

From the time of their association with natural rights in eighteenth-century America and France to their encoding by the United Nations in the Universal Declaration of Human Rights (UDHR) in 1948, the idea and practice of human rights have possessed constitutively ambiguous and paradoxical – if not contradictory – political features. On the one hand, they would constrain the actions of institutional political actors within a universal ethical framework that coincides with international law. In this vein, they presumptively operate outside of both domestic and international politics. On the other hand, the actualization of human rights amounts to a comprehensive moral charge for social change, which requires political action by individuals and institutions. This suggests that human rights can be powerful and legitimate but only when they are enforced by an invisible hand – a political *deux ex machina*. In other words, the practical integrity of human rights depends on their being simultaneously political and non-political, a sign of immutable morality and a practical tool of particular political actors.

This constitutive political ambiguity of human rights has belonged to the discourse of human rights since its origins, but only recently has "human rights" factored seriously in the justification of political action by powerful states. Since the end of the Cold War in 1989, the emergence of the European Union as a political actor, and the consolidation of the global hegemony of the United States – the discourse of human rights has become dramatically more significant in the language of international relations and the politics of states.[1] Previously functioning as a powerless, moral conscience haunting international politics, it has now become a tool of the powerful as well. This

---

[1] For empirical confirmation of the increased salience of "human rights" in the news, see Ron & Ramos 2004. It documents the approximately three-fold increase in coverage of human rights issues from 1990 to 2000 in *The Economist* and *Newsweek* magazines.

fact of contemporary political life has created distinctive issues for the ever-problematic nature of human rights as an ethics of power.[2]

The newfound practical relevance of human rights has not eliminated the political ambiguity of its discourse or practice. Indeed, the decade-long nightmare of the former Yugoslavia, the Rwandan genocide, and the American-led war against Iraq has featured the use – or failure to use – human rights as a justification for military interventions and invasions. Recent acts of Congress along with the rhetoric of the Bush Administration have officially associated "human rights" with American foreign policy, while the 1998 Human Rights Act of the United Kingdom integrates the language of the [European] Convention for the Protection of Human Rights and Fundamental Freedoms with the broad goals of British public policy.[3] The increasingly official language of human rights has highlighted self-serving patterns of human rights enforcement by their would-be governmental champions and problematic professional advocacy by financially constrained human rights non-governmental organizations (Kennedy 2004). Previously confident assertions of a single, coherent, "human rights culture" sound like echoes from a long-gone era.[4]

The increasing practical importance *and* ambiguity of human rights have led to greater efforts by scholars and public intellectuals to define human rights discourse in a way that makes it politically relevant to questions of power while preserving its distinctive conceptual identity. But rather than resolving its constitutive ambiguity, these recent developments in politics and discourse have too often just exacerbated it. The explanation for this situation stems from the failure to recognize both the constitutively political nature of human rights and the need to promote it by enhancing the democratic agency of ordinary human beings. In what follows, I chart a path that would lead us out of this conceptual and political confusion. Part I provides critical

---

[2] The paradoxical nature of human rights discourse has been noted previously and significantly in several scholarly pieces written from various intellectual perspectives. See Arendt [1951] 1973; Hunt 2000; Asad 2003: 129.

[3] The Human Rights and Security Assistance Act, 22 U.S.C.A. section 2304 makes "human rights" an official condition of American foreign aid and an official goal of American foreign policy. For full citations, see Weissbrodt 2001. This rhetorical fact has been publicized in the official papers on National Security Strategy produced by the administrations of Bill Clinton in 1996 and 1997 and George W. Bush in 2002. For a critical review of the current fate of the Human Rights Act in the United Kingdom, see Campbell, Ewing & Tomkins 2001.

[4] See Rorty 1993: 111–34, in which he borrowed the notion of a "human rights culture" articulated by the Argentinian jurist Eduardo Rabossi to designate a summary of intuitions in "our own culture." Ironically, Michael Ignatieff reflected this era in a much more effusive endorsement of human rights and the existence of "a single human rights culture," in his essay, "Human Rights" (1999: 318).

background with a brief theoretical analysis of "ethics" and "power" and some historical notes about sources of the contemporary problematic. In light of this perspective, Part II critically appraises contemporary perspectives on human rights in relation to ethics and power – namely, those of human rights "negativists" who only sanction rights that protect "negative freedom" and human rights "normativists" who embrace human rights as a regulative ethic for political power. I argue that neither forthrightly recognizes the nature of human rights as an ethics of power. In the third and final part, I articulate a constructive account of human rights as an ethic of democratic agency for ordinary citizens – a political ethics of the governed – arguing that it helpfully (1) distances the political significance of human rights discourse from both the self-interested policies of contemporary states and parochial associations with Western liberalism, and (2) renders human rights proper as an agent of egalitarian democracy. Such an ethic offers the best possible account for human rights as an ethics of power and source of contemporary justice.

I. A Critical Background

Theoretical discussions of human rights often uncritically signify conventional political ideas and understandings of the world. For example, they typically presuppose that discourses of ethics and power operate as isolated phenomena or that the history of human rights offers a transparent story of progress. Neither of these conventional views is warranted. A brief analysis of "ethics" and "power" as analytical terms of art reveals how they implicate each other, while a brief account of the history of human rights discourse indicates the ambiguity of that tradition.

A. A Brief Analysis of Power and Ethics for a Discourse of Human Rights

Power. The English word "power" derives from the Latin *potere*, which means *to be able* but particularly *to be able to exercise power over another*.[5] As such, it signifies the two principal meanings of "power," namely (1) the capacity to accomplish something – sometimes signified as "power to," and (2) the capacity to effect a change in the environment, often despite resistance from nature or persons – which amounts to "power over." The exercise of power in these modes also implies a *relationship* of sorts between the agent of power and

---

[5] See *Oxford English Dictionary* and the *Oxford Dictionary of English Etymology* under the entries for "power."

its object.[6] *Political* power exhibits these meanings of power, in the context of agents exercising power *either* within a political community or state – as members or representatives of it, in relation to itself or external political entities – *or* more indeterminately across multiple borders in transnational or global settings. This exercise of political power may be short-lived or long-lasting. Whether genuine, sustainable political power results from its exercise as persuasion *or* force is a matter of considerable debate among political thinkers and actors – a debate that carries over into discussions about the "power" of human rights. But every exercise of *political* power entails two elements. First, it presupposes the need to overcome an extant social conflict or difficulty facing human beings and citizens. As such, the exercise of political power is essentially contested. Second, a purpose always informs the exercise of political power, and that purpose signifies a relationship to an ideal or real community. While the purpose for which power is exercised does not inherently belong to the fact of its exercise, power without a purpose is sheer force. Insofar as the purpose of power is justified as a social practice, that purpose comprises an "ethics." Thus does power involves ethics? Indeed, "politics" as a discursive activity entails conflicting accounts of the ethical use of power.

Ethics. The English word "ethics" derives from the Greek *ethos*, which signifies a practical habit or disposition of persons concerning the purpose of their way of life (Liddell, Scott & Jones 1968). An "ethics" may be encapsulated in a monolithic set of principles, in which case it could amount to a "morality," but that narrows the domain of ethics and typically privileges the authority of abstract, neo-Kantian principles *over* particular personal and social practices – an authority that has been critically undermined (as well as practically ignored) (see, for example, Williams 1985). Unlike "morality," ethics concerns the practical realization of human purposes. As such, it essentially involves power and politics. Indeed, in ancient Greek political thought, all ethics were political. Since the institutionalization of monotheistic religions

---

[6] The numerous studies of the concept of power play on these two basic meanings and its relational identity. How this play is performed depends on the theoretical framework that embeds the concept. Thus, "power" means different things to a "liberal," for whom it is basically "constraint"; a Marxist, for whom it is basically economic and class-based; an Arendtian or Habermasian, for whom it depends on authoritative, shared discourse; or a Foucauldian, for whom it implies a kind of productive disciplinarity that lacks an authoritative, responsible agent. For a useful discussion of the literature, see Oksenberg 1992; Ball 1992. The so-called "faces" of power are (1) causal-mechanical-effective; (2) taken-for-granted domination; (3) the exercise of force or influence contrary to its subject's interests. For a post-structuralist reading of power as ability, see Dyrberg 1997.

and the development of the powerful, coercive legitimacy of the modern state, not all ethics are *inherently* political. Ethics would shape, direct, or impart purpose to the exercise of politics and power. Moreover, the integrity of ethics depends on it not being reducible to or merely a function of power. But many aspects of ethics still have political dimensions. In this vein, those who minimize the significance of ethics for politics still have an "ethics," and that ethics has distinctive political features.

From this simple account of power and ethics in language and social realities – and without retreating behind the protective shield of religious and psychological faith – one ought to recognize the interdependence of ethics and power and the artificiality of intellectual genres that treat them as isolated phenomena. Yet the discourse of human rights has often bracketed the implications of their connection. "Human rights" implies a "universal" ethics, but it only can be effective in particular, irregular contexts constituted by the exercise of power – whether they are legal, moral, cultural, economic, political, etc. This theoretical truth indicates the ultimate futility for the "universality" versus "relativism" debate – a claim that recent political developments have validated.[7] While the forces of globalization have obliterated the insular identity of cultures, the actions of terrorists and their state-sponsored opponents have undermined the legitimacy and efficacy of the "international community" of powerful states and inter-governmental institutions that heretofore sponsored an unambiguous global role for human rights. As a result, we can expect to find conceptual lacunae in efforts by *either* human rights normativists to assert the moral uncontestability of human rights *or* human rights negativists who dismiss the political relevance of human rights.

B. Historical Notes on Human Rights Discourse. Only when the UDHR encoded specifically "human" rights did a discourse of specifically "human" rights officially signify a moral obligation for political powers. But its meaning was inherently ambiguous on two levels. First, the Preamble of the UDHR

---

[7] Much previous debate about the ethics of human rights nonetheless presupposed dichotomous options of universality or relativity. If human rights were to be conceptually meaningful, they needed to validate their claims in universal terms. Noting the powerful role of social contexts in defining the practical efficacy of human rights seemed to invalidate the discourse as a whole. But this misleading dichotomy has become less prominent of late, amid increasingly porous spatial and disciplinary boundaries created by our contemporary era of economic, cultural, and political globalization. A number of recent studies by anthropologists and political theorists have been particularly important in casting doubt on the utility of the "universalism-relativism" debate for understanding human rights. See Wilson 1997; Sarat & Kearns 2001; Cowan, Dembour & Wilson 2001; Wilson & Mitchell 2003. Cf. Baehr 1999.

refers to the "human rights" subsequently enumerated *not* as enforceable obligations *but* "as a *common standard of achievement* [my italics] for all peoples and nations." In this regard, the UDHR operates as an affirmation rather than an argument – in the manner of "we hold these truths to be self-evident, that all men are created equal . . ." – despite the transformation of the language of the UDHR into binding covenants. Moreover, the agents of enforcement are the very states that often are the objects of its critical scrutiny. Second, its language affirms the significance of *preexisting* "human rights" that have been contemptuously disregarded in "barbarous acts which have outraged the conscience of mankind." Yet a brief review of the history of human rights discourse does not tell a story of transparent neglect for humanly held rights but a contested drama that continuously redefines the notion of what is both "human" and worthy of political respect.

The historical roots of the human rights in the UDHR derives primarily – though not exclusively – from the Western natural rights tradition.[8] A crucial element of the Western tradition stems from ancient Greece, the cultural heritage of which was absorbed by non-Western as well as Western societies, and the ancient Greeks lacked any clear notion of "rights" or "human rights" (Burnyeat 1994). In ancient Greek political discourse, political life essentially constituted the ethical value of a human being; only "citizens" (all of whom were Greek) were regarded as fully human.[9] Insofar as practical standards of political treatment governed the status of Athenian citizens, for example, they belonged to privileges of political power rather than a legally protected domain secured from the effects of political deliberation. The great Greek political theorists reflected this relationship in their works: Plato's perfectly just man was a perfectly just philosopher-ruler; Aristotle's most virtuous man was a citizen-statesman.

While ancient Greek thought did not have a notion of "rights," its writers did articulate a concept of a "law of nature" (*nomos tou phusei*) that was later transformed. Working out of the Greek philosophical tradition, Romans such as Cicero developed the idea of "natural law." And the tradition of Roman law

---

[8] For a guide to sources of human rights discourse that lie outside the Western tradition or anterior to the natural rights tradition, see Ishay 2004: 15–69. An argument for the contribution of non-Western traditions to the UDHR appears in Glendon 2001. For a brief overview of the connections and differences between "natural rights" and "human rights," see Pennock 1981: 1–7. For accounts of the history of natural rights discourse, see Tuck 1979; Tierney 1997. For a recent synopsis of approaches to the idea of human rights, emphasizing its position at the interface of ethical and social scientific inquiry and including historical perspectives, see Freeman 2002.

[9] See Plato, *Apology of Socrates, Crito,* and *Republic,* along with Aristotle, *Politics,* Bk. I.

so important for the history of Western states broke new ground by enunciating a notion of individual "rights." The liberty associated with such "rights," however, was constituted by the Roman state or commonwealth (*civitas* or *res publica*); individuals could not claim it as an independent protection from a duty-bound state. That development, which marked the emergence of "natural rights" – initially as moral rights backed by religion and then as the basis for political rights designed to limit the powers of the state – was a decidedly "modern" invention of the seventeenth century. While such "rights" became informally respected in England as a result of political uprisings during the seventeenth century, they only became positive rights of individuals enforced by a legal system and independent judiciary in the 1790s, with the passage of the American Bill of Rights and the judicial enforcement of the French *Declarations* [sic] *of the Rights of Man*. Subsequently, "rights" traditions became important in the political systems of France, the United Kingdom, and the United States, albeit in significantly different dialects.[10]

The early modern liberal revolutions of the mid-late seventeenth and late eighteenth centuries only provided local, national support for a new discourse of rights that nonetheless rhetorically applied to all human beings. In so doing, they continued the ancient tradition of blurring the distinction between human rights and political recognition. But they also placed that ambiguity on different ethical and political foundations. Each imbued generically identified human beings (practically defined as white men) with "natural rights" and associated assertive political agency with these rights. Practically speaking, this had two effects: first, the political reality of protected "human" rights was guaranteed only for particular citizenries, and, secondly, the practice of such rights depended on guarantees provided by the formal, legal entity of the nation-state – which guaranteed little actual power for individual human beings and citizens.[11]

From the beginning of the nineteenth century to the end of World War I, "human" rights did not play a significant role in political discourse – even if a "humanistic" or "humanitarian" sensibility began to emerge (Bender

---

[10] For an overview of these differences between the rights traditions of the United States, France, and the United Kingdom, and their bearing on conceptualizations of human rights, see Claude 1976.

[11] Relevant to this discussion is Marx's analysis in his 1843 essay, "On the Jewish Question," of the political character of "human rights." There, he defined "human rights" as a "right of separation," rather than a "right of connection." In this respect, he anticipated Arendt's critique of early twentieth-century "human rights" as paradigmatic signs of rightlessness. Marx also went on to criticize human rights discourse because it was practically defined by egoistic, privatistic values of bourgeois civil society, rather than the political, emancipatory values of "species-being." However, "human rights" has not been conceptually or practically defined solely in the dismal terms he assigned to it in the 1840s. See O'Malley 1994: 43–7.

1992). The primary political struggles of these times attempted to impart substance to constitutional guarantees for *all* adults *within* particular states, and involved social conflict if not civil wars on behalf of the formal political equality of women and the elimination of slavery. While the anti-slavery and suffragette movements justified their rights claims as universal moral entitlements, they still could acquire those rights only within a discursive and practical framework recognized by particular states. The emergence of a specific discourse of *human* rights on the global stage only occurred after World War I, in the era of the League of Nations and the phenomena of millions of new refugees produced by the war's human and political destruction. But even here, the ambiguity and ambivalence of the history of human rights discourse remained. Hannah Arendt noted that human rights in this era had become the quintessential sign of politically *rightless* individuals ([1951] 1973).[12]

In the wake of World War II and the Holocaust of European Jewry in particular, the United Nations designated a committee to draft a universal declaration of human rights. The subsequent UDHR was designed to provide universal protection for human beings where the League of Nations and politics of states more generally had not. Resulting from negotiations conducted by a committee established by the United Nations, the UDHR was ultimately approved in the third General Assembly of the United Nations on December 10, 1948, by a vote of 48-0, with eight abstentions (six Communist nations, Saudi Arabia, and South Africa). It incorporated many features of the French and American declarations of rights but also drew from the more substantive economic and social rights traditions of Latin American socialism.[13] These differences and similarities between the UDHR and the earlier *Declarations* constitute current understandings of human rights and their political deployment.

Two of its current political features stand out – one practical, one conceptual. Notwithstanding the international covenants implementing the UDHR that many countries have signed, the activities of the United Nations' Human Rights Committee, and the newly established International Criminal Court, no governmental entity has a generally recognized authority to enforce the

---

[12] Arendt's critical views about human rights, however, do not mean that she wholly rejected their value or political potential.

[13] Articles 1–21 reflect the traditional civil and political rights of modern liberal states and protect international freedom of political movement (Articles 13–14). The article on the equal right to marry without regard to religion led to Saudi Arabia's abstention. Articles 22–27 declare economic, social, and cultural rights not found, e.g., in the American Constitution. Articles 28–30 promote these rights as the foundations for an international political order that is compatible with the welfare of democratic societies and the authority of the United Nations. For good accounts of the genealogy, composition, and character of the *Universal Declaration of Human Rights*, see Morsink 1999; Glendon 2001.

UDHR and its attending covenants and conventions. Moreover, the legitimacy of the UDHR is attached to that of the United Nations, which can authorize force only if the odd company of the five permanent members of the Security Council agree. These morally compromised agents for the practical implementation of human rights renders suspect its cogency as a universal standard. Second, the ambit of the human rights signified in the UDHR transcend the protective language of liberal rights. More than the liberal rights protected by Western states, which rights of individuals secured in *past* political struggles that are to regulate future politics, human rights would be foundations for *future* political progress in economic, social, and cultural domains.

These features of today's common understanding of international human rights did not initially generate much consternation – but only because international human rights in the immediate aftermath of 1948 were politically insignificant. Although the signatures of both the United States and the U.S.S.R. helped to launch the UDHR in 1948, the world-historical conflict of the Cold War then emerging reduced the resonance of any presumptively international moral language for politics. Each "superpower" emphasized different parts of the document, and neither sought to negotiate their differences – at least until the Helsinki Final Act of 1975.[14] In the late 1970s, Jimmy Carter introduced the language of human rights as an important element of United States foreign policy in Latin America. This development paralleled the more extensive usage of human rights discourse by Latin American and Eastern European activists, which catalyzed its usage by academics and non-governmental organizations (NGOs). But the discourse of human rights on the whole remained politically marginal in international relations until the end of the Cold War. Then, "an international human rights regime" and "international human rights community" began to assume more significant institutional and semantic careers. When they did, they only highlighted the distinctively ambiguous political character of contemporary codes of international human rights – which reflect the informality of any international consensus about basic human entitlements, the fitful character of practical efforts for bettering the lives of the vast majority of the human race, and the contested political history of the discourse of human rights.

---

[14] Recently, the political significance of the Helsinki Final Act has been much touted (see Thomas 2001). The Act surely had identifiable influence – especially to eastern European dissidents and the formation of Western non-governmental organizations (NGOs) – particularly Human Rights Watch. But precisely how much it factored in the delegitimation and ultimate disintegration of Warsaw Pact – an overdetermined albeit mostly unforeseen historical event – is difficult to assess with any degree of precision.

II. Contemporary Perspectives on Human Rights as an Ethics of Power

The ambiguities that have accompanied the historical emergence of human rights as a political language for all peoples have compromised its allure. Although the international human rights regime was in its infancy when Arendt claimed that it ultimately signified political impotence and moral hypocrisy, recent writers echo her charge.[15] Indeed, "human rights" and "human rights abuses" appear in public discourse mostly to mark occasions when nation-states have reneged on their basic obligations under "the international human rights regime" – when they have exercised their sovereignty as an *exception* to political power authorized by the consent of the people, without international legal constraint or deference to the people for whom the UDHR was written. Yet the UDHR was written to assist those people – to protect and promote their well-being, not as a presupposition of their extant well-being. So the language of human rights has politically proliferated, and its character as an ethics of power is increasingly addressed by professional scholars and public intellectuals – often in relation to the rhetorically loaded and comparably contestable concept of democracy. But we shall see how these authors perpetuate deficient conceptions of human rights as an ethics of power, and the effect undermines the intellectual and practical value of human rights as an agent of human well-being.

Whether they seek to minimize or maximize the authority of human rights as a guidepost for the contemporary exercise of political power, prominent exponents of human rights discourse root it in the moorings of Western liberalism. This notion of human rights is fundamentally a right of individuals to freely express their moral agency, unconstrained by coercive political power. As such, it presupposes the analytical, linguistic, and practical isolation of the ethics and power. Its paradigmatic exposition appears in the work of Isaiah Berlin. In an essay of the late 1950s, entitled "Two Concepts of Liberty," Berlin articulated the fundamental value of "negative freedom" or "negative liberty" as a basic human right of *personal* autonomy.[16] Berlin's rationale for this belief is that human beings have conflicting goals or purposes for themselves

---

[15] Giorgio Agamben has identified the politically powerless and anonymous refugee as emblematic of most persons' experience of contemporary political life (see [1995]1998; [1996] 2000). In producing this analysis, Agamben explicitly draws on the work of Arendt, as well as that of Carl Schmitt's theory of sovereignty, Martin Heidegger's interpretation of *Dasein*, and Michel Foucault's account of the dispersed, anonymous character of modern forms of political domination.

[16] For Berlin's concept of "negative liberty" or "negative freedom," see his essay, "Two Concepts of Liberty" (1969: 122–31). Berlin only approved of the exercise of "positive liberty" or "positive freedom" – i.e., the ability to actualize one's goals of personal and political development –

and their political communities; politically enforcing any one of these goals or purposes invariably results in coercion. While Berlin accepts the political necessity of coercion, he justifies it only to preserve negative freedom and the "moral flourishing" that he believes results from its protected preservation. Because the political life of society naturally favors the pursuit of some goals over others, the sanctity of negative liberty depends on enforcement of a "rule of law" that regulates and constrains the arena of legitimate politics. Making negative liberty the primary political value presupposes a practically valid judicial system that can prevent society's politics from inequitably constraining personal freedom.

Since its presentation in 1958, Berlin's essay has provided a textual foundation for liberal ethics and a philosophical defense of the sanctity of individual rights to security and relative autonomy. When contemporary writers seek to reduce the corpus of the UDHR to "basic rights" "core human rights," or "personal rights" whose violation is then regarded as a "gross human rights abuse," the rights implied are those whose exercise amounts to the performance of "negative" liberty or freedom. In addition, such conceptions of human rights typically appeal to international law and international tribunals as the ultimate sources of political protection. They would enforce "the rule of law" as an international standard and thereby practically defend "basic human rights." But the unique ethical and practical identity of *human rights* as opposed to efforts by global powers simply to extend the protection of *liberal rights* thereby becomes suspect – opening defenders of human rights to the charge that espouse intellectually incoherent ideas or that they have simply provided rhetorical cover for Western economic and political power.

The first charge has been leveled by Raymond Geuss, who addresses human rights through the lens of "negative freedom" and rejects any logical attempt to extend human rights discourse beyond its liberal roots (2002).[17] Geuss associates "the doctrine of human rights" with an updated version of natural law theory, now applied to political subjects but without the contextual backing of a generally accepted religion. Thus, for his purposes, he assumes that "a 'human right' is an individual, subjective right each human has simply by virtue of being human" (2001: 140). But the discourse of human rights

---

if its pursuit serves the preservation of negative liberty. For Berlin's definition of "positive liberty" or "positive freedom," see Ibid. at 131–4.

[17] One of Geuss's recent books offers a vigorous critique of rights discourse in general, on both philosophical and political grounds, and the discourse of human rights in particular – claiming at one point that "to speak of 'human rights' is a kind of puffery or white magic." He does not think that the concept is salvageable in any other form than its "ideologically advantageous property of being elusively polymorphous" (2001: 144, 152).

suffers the limits of all rights discourse, namely an incapacity to link its moral ideals coherently and consistently to their likely usage in practical, political contexts. "Human rights" cannot provide ethical foundations for politics or a sufficient basic guide to moral political action. Ultimately, Geuss argues that the discourse of human rights amounts to "an inconvenient fiction [because] thinking about the social and political world in terms of rights encourages illusory assumptions of stability and predictability" (Ibid. at 147).[18] Indeed, Geuss's criticism reaches the distinctive core of human rights discourse insofar as the latter's most innovative features extend the domain of rights discourse beyond its liberal origins to include more generic notions of human dignity and the conditions of its realization (see Glendon 2001: 69). Lacking any mechanism of universal *political* enforcement – the United Nations can hardly fit the bill – the language of human rights becomes a measure of conceptual confusion in politics or a disingenuous feature of political rhetoric used by groups that do have the power of enforcement. Geuss's response to this situation is to say to those who use the language of human rights as political tools, "drop it."

But this response does not address the realities of contemporary political discourse. The language of human rights is now a tool of states and individuals; it has roots in international covenants; it is used (along with "democracy") as the moral currency of global politics.[19] Further, a system of international criminal law has been established to try military commanders and heads of state for genocide, torture, and other "crimes against humanity" and to imprison those found guilty. This system is weak and selective, but only the United States has seriously questioned its integrity and its authority is expected to grow. "Human rights" need not assume a "foundational" status

---

[18] Just as worrisome is his point that making human rights less like "white magic" will only increase our dependence on "bureaucrats, administrators, and lawyers" (2001: 152). Geuss argues that conflict, rather than agreement, is the hallmark of politics and that "rights discourse" provides inappropriate barriers for the consideration of how best to resolve these conflicts. Indeed, he has embraced four traditional critiques of rights discourse as either overly individualistic and rigid or conceptually confused: (1) the Burkean criticism of rights language as deaf to the social practices and traditions that make it politically meaningful, (2) the Benthamite criticism that views it as useless without predictable social sanctions for non-compliance, and (3) the Marxian criticism that views it as so anti-socially individualistic that it becomes a rhetorical cover for the untrammeled economic and political power of the bourgeoisie. He has linked these to (4) the Deweyan criticism that any effort to extend human rights language beyond its subjective and individualist roots in the natural rights tradition or the positive security rights enforced by states (Ibid. at 132, 146, 154–6). For anticipations of some of these criticisms, see Waldron 1987.

[19] For a good account of how international human rights norms have been incorporated in the rulings of domestic judiciaries, see Amit 2003.

for contemporary morality or politics, and it need not pretend to be a sufficient first principle of good reasons for social action. If we can find an appropriate political lens for viewing human rights as an ethics of power, Geuss's criticisms become moot.

Rather than condemning human rights discourse as inherently incoherent, other human rights advocates have tried to adapt it to the language of contemporary power politics. This has been notably done by Michael Ignatieff – a student of Isaiah Berlin, journalist, public intellectual, and Director of the Carr Institute for Human Rights Policy at Harvard University's John F. Kennedy School of Government.[20] He explicitly rejects the human rights skepticism articulated by Geuss, insofar as he embraces the "moral standard" upheld by the UDHR as a genuine advance in political discourse. But Ignatieff (like Berlin and Geuss) only finds the liberal core of human rights discourse worthy of political respect. Insofar as liberalism and many advocates of human rights do not directly address the issue of how to exercise political power apart from observance of the rule of law, Ignatieff has sought to supplement these limitations by stitching his moral defense of human rights to a sympathetic view of the burdens of global governance. This political perspective is best understood as "liberal realism," but it also iterates a kind of "human rights negativism," for he maintains a basic devotion to Berlin's notion of "negative liberty" but then adapts to his version of the "realities" of contemporary political power.[21] Faced with the realities of massive killing of civilians, a weak United Nations, and the military and economic ascendancy of the United States, Ignatieff's explicit aim in two books about human rights and public policy is to salvage the moral relevance of human rights discourse for the exercise of political power (2001; 2004).

The first book stems from lectures given at Princeton University in April 2000. It seeks to bring political coherence to the utilization of human rights discourse. The initial conceptual means for doing so, Ignatieff argues,

---

[20] Ignatieff's style of discourse operates on the margins of both political theory and public policy. At the same time, he is well-respected in the academy and commands a wide audience outside it by means of his employment by *The New York Times*. He is a regular contributor to *The New York Times Magazine* and has authored more cover articles for that publication over the past two years than any other individual. See Ignatieff 2000; 2002a; 2003a; 2003b; 2003c; 2004b; 2004c; 2004d; 2004e.

[21] The popular label for this political posture is that of "liberal hawks." It is used to designate liberal opponents of the Bush Administration's Republicanism who nonetheless support an aggressive American policy on behalf of democracy and human rights. Those who fall into this category include Paul Berman, Thomas Friedman, and Kenneth Pollack. For a reprise of the positions of some well-known "liberal hawks," see Packer 2002. I prefer to encapsulate their position as that of "liberal realism."

is to separate the practical from the impractical features of the UDHR as a guide for international politics. The impractical features are associated with economic, social, and cultural rights, whose links to the vagaries of democratic politics make them unreliable as clear benchmarks of human rights. For Ignatieff, there is a genuine "core" of human rights; they crucially protect the "moral agency" for individuals in any and all cultures to participate as deliberative agents able to protect themselves from the "injustice" of political, cultural, and religious "oppression" fostered by "family, the state, and the church" (2001: 57, 66). Aware that such vague terms need more concrete definition, he ultimately emphasizes the "defensible core of rights . . . that are necessary to the enjoyment of any life whatever," which turn out to be the traditional civil and political liberties whose exercise materializes Berlin's notion of "negative freedom" – in the language of international human rights law, those human rights stated in the International Covenant on Civil and Political Rights rather than the International Covenant on Economic, Social, and Cultural Rights.[22]

Ignatieff recognizes that his view of liberalism seeks to constitute political power by restricting its reach. As a result, protecting liberal rights provides little guidance for a foreign policy that would benefit his core human rights. To the contrary, in this pre-9/11 book, he asserts that the political instability of weak states accounts for the chief threats to core human rights, and he identifies that weakness as a manifestation of the Hobbesian view of the political state of nature – not only anarchic but also "nasty, brutish, short." As a result, the minimal liberal rights that define Ignatieff's "core human rights" now appear as correlates of "stability," and stability becomes the key to coherent human rights policy (Ignatieff 2002a; 2002b). The practical interests of foreign policy "realists" now find common ground with the moral values of human rights advocates such as Ignatieff who define their conceptions of human rights in terms of "negative liberty." No longer troubled by the tragic dilemma he once formulated, where " 'interests' say 'Stay Out' [while] values cry 'Go in,' " Ignatieff has elided any critical distance between the defense of human rights and the offensive, imperial deployment of American power (2001: 41). In so doing, he has inverted the traditional association of human rights with opposition to the use of military force. Much like Samuel Huntington, who long ago argued that freedom came in the wake of the use of American military power, Michael Ignatieff now sees American military power producing respect for human rights (Huntington 1981: 246–59). Because the United States is more

---

[22] The United States has ratified the ICCPR but not the ICESCR.

able to create or impose political stability by the use of force than any other state, Ignatieff has supported the global use of American military power on behalf of human rights – even as he complains about its incoherence. Thus, he supported the American invasion of Iraq as an imperfect but necessary enterprise on behalf of human rights.[23] Indeed, one might say that Ignatieff's combination of liberalism and realism explains the unseemly deference by prominent American media to the Bush Administration's justification of war against Iraq from August, 2002 to March, 2003.

In his post-9/11 book, based on lectures given at the University of Edinburgh in January, 2003, Ignatieff seeks to articulate a "political ethics" that embraces his devotion to both human rights principles and the immediate, political conditions that can sustain them in practice. More particularly, he argues on behalf of a political ethics for "democracies" adjusted to the exigencies of the current "age of terror." References to human rights become marginal in this book, as he believes they provide no political compass for moral action. But his previous "liberal realism" that unites "human rights negativism" with a political preference for the stability of existing Western regimes continues to inform his argument. Indeed, Ignatieff has articulated human rights as an "ethics of power" in his most recent book, but it is one that will be practiced at the expense of much democracy and many human rights.

The primary title of Ignatieff's book – *The Lesser Evil* – aptly labels his political ethics. It combines moralistic, higher-law, rights-based language – hence the reliance on "evil" as a political category – and consequentialist, utilitarian reasoning – hence, the comparative term "lesser." But his general outlook presupposes a particular conception of democracy as liberal democracy, one that he outlines in the book's opening chapter, "Democracy and the Lesser Evil."[24] It is more accurately identified as "liberal republicanism." This feature of his political perspective appears when he cites his favored political theorists. He explicitly roots his argument in a passage from James Madison's *The Federalist No. 51*. In a previous installment of *The Federalist, No. 10*, Madison defined his favored form of government as a "republic." Indeed, its virtues stemmed from its ability to do what "democracy" could not, namely "cure the ills" or "control the effects" of faction. "Democracy" had no cure for

---

[23] Now, with the lack of evidence of Saddam Hussein's possession of any weapons of mass destruction, Ignatieff retrospectively criticizes the Bush Administration for acting too hastily. But he has not retracted his earlier support of the invasion.

[24] Unfortunately, Ignatieff opens his book with a tendentious translation. He mentions "the old Roman adage – the safety of the people is the first law," when that adage – *Salus Populi Suprema Lex* – is better translated as "the health [or well-being] of the people is the supreme law," the connotations of which are far different.

these ills, because it sanctioned the political activity of ordinary citizens who were, he claimed, naturally short-sighted, relatively ignorant and morally limited by their dominating self-interest. Large-scale republics could cure these ills by constitutionally empowering putatively enlightened, virtuous political representatives. *Their* potential for arrogant, factional behavior was to be controlled by cross-cutting geographical and interests in civil society that disaggregated their popular base, along with checks and balances among the branches of government.

Taking his bearing from Madison, Ignatieff believes that a "democratic system" can resolve its conflicts through elite political processes of "deliberation" and "adversarial justification" (2004: 24, 36). His updated Madisonianism combines what he calls two conceptions of democracy, the "moral," which involves respect for individual dignity as a basic right, and the "pragmatic," which attends to collective self-preservation.[25] Because Ignatieff believes that "majority rights" often endanger minorities, democracies are "moral" only when they are ruled by wise minorities – in other words, when their politics are advanced by the few not the many. Indeed, apart from its legitimating function for the elites who run the adversarial system of checks and balances, the main political virtue of democracy for Ignatieff is amoral and dangerous, namely its "ruthless" ability to generate militant popular energy: "the great strength of democracies [is] its capacity to mobilize the allegiance and self-sacrifice of its citizens" (Ignatieff 2004: 57).[26] For Ignatieff, "democracy" does not signify a political system that sanctions the power of the *demos* or promotes its well-being.

The problem he addresses is how a "liberal democracy" that prizes the protection of civil liberties ought to deal with political exigencies or "necessities" that "threaten" the existence of the state, how to reconcile "political necessity"

---

[25] Ignatieff takes these ideal-typical formulations of democratic principle from Ronald Dworkin and Richard Posner and combines them with notions of "formal" and "substantive" democracy articulated by the Israeli jurist, Aharon Barak (2004: 5–6). Ironically, Judge Barak has been at the forefront of efforts to limit the Israeli government's exclusive ability to define the meaning of security for its citizens. See Barak 2004; *Beit Sourik Village Council v. The Government of Israel* (HCJ2056/04) (2004), "The Fence Case."

[26] Although there is some evidence for this claim, Ignatieff does not provide it. He cites the firemen and policemen who ran up the Twin Towers of the World Trade Center, and failed to mention the Bush Administration's refusal to ask for any *economic* sacrifice for fighting terrorism (e.g., in the form of taxes to pay for the "war against terrorism") but only *political* sacrifice of their civil rights (in the form of the USA PATRIOT Act and suspension of *habeas corpus* for terrorist suspects). Moreover, later in the book he *minimizes* the loss of political freedom for the political *majority* in the wake of September 11 – regarding it rather as a loss of rights for *minorities*.

and "moral principle" (Ignatieff 2004: 1–2).[27] At times, these "necessities" assume the form of "emergencies"; at others, they define an entire – that is, our current, post-9/11 – political "era." In any event, their essential source is no longer "political instability" but "terrorism." On the one hand, Ignatieff believes that "democracies" – by which he clearly designates contemporary states such as the United States and the United Kingdom – naturally possess the answers to this challenge. In response to "a terrorist emergency . . . democracy's institutions provide a resolution, through a system of checks and balances, to ensure that no government's answer has the power to lead us either straight to anarchy or to tyranny" (Ibid. at 2–3).[28] On the other hand, democracies facing such emergencies are encumbered by their two basic principles – the promotion of majority rule or popular sovereignty and the protection of minority rights. The former allows for tyranny while the latter could encourage anarchy.

Given Ignatieff's not very latent suspicions of democracy, it is not surprising that, in order to ward off "evil" in the "age of terrorism," he justifies compromises by political leaders of *both* democratic principles as "the lesser evil." Done well, such statecraft can apply Ignatieff's "ethics of emergency" and "dissolve the morally problematic character of necessary measures" (Ibid. at 8). To articulate how a democratic political ethic entails certain support for "the lesser evil," Ignatieff draws support from Machiavelli's princely *virtu* (as interpreted by Isaiah Berlin) for the consequentialist component and Berlin for the priority of individual rights to "negative liberty" over democratic purposes (Ibid. at 15).[29] In other words, the *majoritarian* component of Ignatieff's political ethics derives from Machiavelli's defense of the prerogatives of the ruler's judgment of the requirements of public security, while the individual or *minority*-rights component derives from a moralistic suspicion of democratic politics. Ignatieff's democratic political ethics of "the

---

[27] Throughout the book, Ignatieff slides between "democracy" and "liberal democracy," suggesting that the latter is the only legitimate version of the former.

[28] For the closing sentence of the book's opening chapter, Ignatieff makes the rhetorically meaningful but illogical statement, "It is . . . in the nature of democracy that it prevails against its enemies precisely because it does" (2004: 24). But later, perhaps to remind the democratic reader to be anxious, he says that in the face of "terrorism that deploys weapons of mass destruction . . . we *could* lose" (Ibid. at 153). This train of thought naturally justifies the Bush Administration's association of Saddam Hussein, terrorism, the threat of weapons of mass destruction in irresponsible hands, increased legal constraints on the exercise of civil liberties, and preventive war as the best way to protect democracy and human rights.

[29] Oddly, Ignatieff later cites a passage from Machiavelli's *Discourses* – though the textual source is not cited – that defends the rule of law against extra-constitutional measures whose significance he then proceeds to minimize (2004: 25).

lesser evil" radically limits the power of ordinary citizens, and his elevation of "security" to the principal political problem implicitly endorses the discretionary judgment of rulers. To be sure, Ignatieff maintains distance between his endorsement of discretionary political authority from that of the anti-liberal (and proto-Nazi) theorist Carl Schmitt by maintaining that leaders must ground their legitimacy on "the consent of the people." But Ignatieff typically does not regard the people as informed, and he emphasizes how the character of the terrorist threat is only intelligible by leaders who can quickly exercise executive authority. In the "age of terror," ordinary citizens lack an authoritative basis for political judgment, and he gives political leaders the benefit of our doubt. For if leaders err, that often results from them having to make risky decisions for the sake of National Security while maintaining support from risk-averse citizens.

Having eviscerated the moral authority and political agency of the exercise of ordinary democratic citizenship, Ignatieff turns his attention to "human rights." As in his previous book, he immediately reduces the relevant political content of the human rights corpus. After acknowledging how the human rights corpus is officially indivisible and does not establish a hierarchy among rights, he proceeds to justify a hierarchy of rights, dismissing those of the ICESCR as politically arbitrary and unenforceable. Core "human rights" are clearly liberal rights. But they are liberal rights with a utilitarian bent. For Ignatieff, they operate much like the rights symbolized by Jon Elster as the "pre-commitment" of Odysseus to having his sailors bind him to their ship's mast in order to avoid the temptations of the Sirens. If such "binding" does not contribute to collective security, it loses its justification. Thus, when Ignatieff adapts his concept of human rights to an ethics of power, he differentiates "derogable" from "non-derogable" rights – as is done in the International Covenant of Civil and Political Rights. But in the grip of "the age of terror," the only right not subject to derogation is torture. (But even here he grants politicians considerable wiggle room in defining what counts as torture) (Ignatieff 2004: 136–41).[30] In a piece written not long after September 11,

---

[30] While he differs with Alan Dershowitz's more expansive acceptance of duly "regulated" torture, he accepts the "coercion" if not "torture" of terrorist suspects, and his definition of tolerable "coercion" includes tactics that could be reasonably interpreted as "torture" under Part I, Article I of the United Nations *Convention Against Torture* – which was approved by the United States but only with reservations that limited its reach to agreement with the standing authority of the United States Constitution (see Weissbrodt 2001: 77–8, 282–3). For Ignatieff, torture at times seems necessary, albeit only as a last resort and done "for the sake of law" (2004: 145). Moreover, he justifies "preemptive military action" that violates international law as long as it is done judiciously and wisely. While Ignatieff criticizes the

2001, Ignatieff seemed to regret somewhat the passing of "the human rights era" of the 1990s. But insofar as we are now in "the age of terror," he seems to have said good riddance, for the ethics of human rights must defer to the ethics of power as exercised by elites of security-conscious states that are more likely to honor the rhetoric than the reality of democracy.

Other contemporary advocates of human rights as an ethics of power adopt a more positive view of its political potential. They may be categorized as human rights "normativists" (rather than human rights "negativists"), as they have made their notion of basic or core human rights the main anchor for a twenty-first-century political ethics. Although indebted to the liberalism of Berlin, they have crafted their views of human rights by means of philosophically constructivist accounts of Kantian moral principles (John Rawls), neo-Aristotelian notions of human development (Amartya Sen), or politically constructivist accounts of international human rights law and the "norms" of the international human rights regime (CHS 2003). Despite their differences from human rights negativists about the political role to be played by human rights in global affairs, the practical effects positions taken by human rights normativists are similar: the elevation of individual, political rights and international norms of law and security as basic political values – which effectively reduces the scope of human rights and democracy as critical perspectives on the contemporary exercise of political power.

Insofar as the work of Rawls and Sen has received much critical attention already, I shall more directly consider the work of those who would directly dispute Ignatieff by advocating the practical political relevance of human rights "norms" for the conduct of international relations (IR).[31] Calling themselves "constructivists," they have theoretically and empirically identified "human rights norms" as an institutional practice that defies the presuppositions of foreign policy "realists" who dismiss the political significance of human rights. A standard definition of "norms" for IR constructivists is the "collective expectation of appropriate conduct for a given identity"

---

actual deceit of the Bush Administration in marshaling support for the conquest of Iraq in practice, he theoretically endorses the principles they employed. Indeed, the manner in which the ethics of power sanctioned by liberal realism focuses negatively on threats to security and the evil of potential enemies while minimizing the political significance of human rights and the political virtue of democracy encourages the kind of deference to rulers that made such deceit successful.

[31] The idea of "norms" for politics is alien to the tradition of political theory, but it is used by post-war analytical philosophers of political ethics and more recent "constructivist" theorists of international relations who question the theoretical and practical adequacy of "realist" or "neo-realist" accounts of international politics that focus on material and coercive political power and dismiss the significance of "values," "political identity," and "norms."

in particular contexts. They may be "constitutive" norms that directly exercise causal effects or "regulative" norms that effectively precondition legitimate action on behalf of practical interests (Jepperson, Wendt & Katzenstein 1996).[32] Such norms resemble traditional understandings of virtues and the ethics that justify them. Many IR constructivists who invoke the political significance of norms see their enterprise as empirical as realists but they also regard "political identity" as well as entities known as "the international human rights regime" and "the international human rights community" as coherent political agents. In any event, they assert the realistic effect on individual interests of social, institutional, and ideational constraints (see Risse & Sikkink 1999).

By arguing for the past effectiveness and future political promise of "human rights norms," these IR constructivists amount to human rights "normativists" who emphasize the collective and institutional dimension of human rights as effective constraints on the power of states. They affirm a notion of human rights that is not solely rooted in the protection of human rights as individual rights to equal respect and human dignity, but their views of the political substance of human rights complement those of human rights negativists. For human rights normativists regard human rights "norms" as typically exemplified by "liberal democratic states" – a reified, institutionalized, collective embodiment of the discourse and politics of "liberal democracy" promoted by Ignatieff. And like human rights "negativists," human rights "normativists" such as Risse and Sikkink in their study of "the power of human rights" chose to focus on "a central core of rights" that signify "rights of the person." These "basic" rights "have been most accepted as universal rights, and not simply rights associated with a particular political ideology or system" – although human rights norms require of *all* political systems the establishment of "the rule of law" (Risse & Sikkink 1999: 2–3).[33]

Like human rights "negativists," human rights "normativists" understand power as either an artificially regulative or ethically natural feature of the human condition – rather than as potentiating, productive, and contested phenomenon. As a result, an incomplete or poorly etched picture emerges of the relationship between the exercise of power and the protection or

---

[32] These attributions of the empirical effectiveness of norms resemble the authoritative constraint of political languages on political action highlighted in the intellectual histories of J. G. A. Pocock and Quentin Skinner. But IR normativists do not confine themselves to studying the effects of discourse.

[33] For a critique of "humanitarian law" as a theoretical framework for understanding contemporary politics, see Teitel 2002.

promotion of human rights. "Human rights norms" function as abstract legal standards that constitute judgments of "abuses" of power that violate the exercise of liberal rights. The radar screen of this perspective will pick up gross human rights abuses by poorly trained armed agents of the state; thus, the focus will be post-colonial and economically underdeveloped states. Human rights scholars interested in studying the impact of "human rights norms" embodied in various international organizations or treaties to which these states are parties then attempt to verify the impact of obligations to such organizations on human rights abuses, often as efforts to determine the causal relationship between "globalization" and human rights. But the array of causal factors at work on the protection or promotion of human rights in the country are typically decontextualized and limited. Not surprisingly, the evidence provided by these studies conflicts (see Freeman 2002:148–66).

A similar phenomenon occurs with the notion of "democracy" used by human rights normativists. The default definition is another name for the formal institutions of electoral accountability that operate in economically developed, Western liberal-capitalist democracies or a vague aspiration for equal dignity for all human beings.[34] Human rights normativists tend to overlook the *manner* in which power is exercised or its relationship to more substantive understandings of democracy as a political system that sanctions an equitable distribution of political power and agency. They do not see or do not adequately account for the significance for human rights of many of the injustices tolerated by nominal democracies. Their overarching political value is respect for human rights norms instantiated in international law. To be sure, the political virtue of "the rule of law" is demonstrable; its authority is the first casualty of fascism. But its interpretation remains principally within the hands of judicial authorities who focus on violations of individual rights and whose legitimacy also requires that they remain above the substantive goals of democratic politics. As a result, human rights normativists – like human rights negativists – could well defer to political judgments and actions based on interpretations of political "necessity" offered by the political leaders of these states. Such a result diminishes the critical substance of human rights as an ethics of power.

---

[34] This notion appears in the compatibility of human rights and democracy voiced by advocates of the UDHR who root it in a Catholic natural law tradition, such as Mary Ann Glendon, and Amartya Sen's more thickly articulated account of democracy as a value of universal culture. See Glendon 2001: 223–7; Sen 1999: 3–17; and "The Content of Democracy," lecture delivered at The New School University in New York City, April 22, 2004.

III. Human Rights as a Political Ethics for the Governed

The most prominent current versions of human rights as an ethics of power *either* diminish the ethical significance of human rights and so privilege the discretionary judgments of contemporary managers of the power of liberal states *or* make that significance primary without recognizing the role of practical politics in actualizing that significance. Neither appreciates the pivotal role of the democratic agency of ordinary citizens in making practical the ethics of human rights. In other words, neither appreciates the necessary link between human rights as an ethics of power and a political ethics for the governed. Ultimately, the explanation for this deficiency lies in overarching assumptions about the political world that inform the theoretical framework of both human rights negativists and normativists. They stem from the post-World War II mindset that encouraged both the political priority of "negative liberty" and the UDHR as a bulwark against the totalitarianism of states. Insofar as totalitarianism was regarded as totalizing political power, rather than negating it, democracy became regarded as a potential incubator of totalitarian tendencies. Its power was read as an unstable source of state power and required severe limitations. This justified the radical subordination of democratic authority to the sanctity of individual rights and the belief that the democratic exercise of such rights was adequately guaranteed by domestic constitutionalism and a presumed harmony between sovereign states and international law.

With the end of World War II and the Cold War, the threat of state-sanctioned totalitarianism has sharply diminished. Political power that threatens human rights assumes different guises. Some of these include terrorism, but terrorism certainly does not exhaust the range of threats to the actualization of human rights – even if it is the most dramatic and photogenic. One might argue that it is political inequality understood as institutionalized inequalities of power, both between groups and classes within states and between states and cultures. These problems cannot be remedied by a politics of security that seeks to reinforce extant political institutions. Yet political arguments that take their bearings primarily from the ethics of liberal rights and the international law of human rights will fail to attend to problems of political inequality. For the primary political impulse that remains faithful to post-war conceptions of liberal rights (such as that of human rights negativists) or post-war conceptions of human rights as ethical aspirations potentially enforceable by international law and institutions (such as that of human rights positivists) is logically *security* rather than *democracy*. And *security*, as Hobbes taught us long ago, is best guaranteed by a strong state – not a democratic congerie of citizens.[35] As long as the current political era is dominated by discourse that interprets its political character primarily as an age of terror, contemporary justifications of human rights as an ethics of power will directly or indirectly promote the power of states whose often demagogic politicians maintain their privileges at the expense of the political agency of ordinary citizens. The illusory post-war belief in the virtually automatic complementarity of human rights and democracy can be readily achieved in an age whose principal political foe is "terrorism" and principal political need is "security" only by minimizing the political exercise and egalitarian achievement of both human rights and democracy.

Aligning human rights as an ethics of power with a democratic political ethics of the governed does not reject traditional justifications for the unique value of human rights. For democracy to function successfully as a system of power, it must possess a complementary ethics. Such an ethics must include human rights, and many of its important features are noted by human rights negativists and normativists. The ethics of human rights negativists constitute democratic value because they secure the legal value of political agency – against the threats of both state-sanctioned and transnational terrorists. The ethics of human rights normativists promote an ethical universality that can address the global requirements of democracy, which need to respond not only to the global network of anti-institutional terrorists but also to the inegalitarian and anti-democratic effects of globalized capitalism. Moreover, democracies need good political leaders and responsible judges who can reconcile differences among individuals and groups as well as exhibit fidelity to the rule of law. But if democracy is to benefit the citizens who nominally constitute it, its character must be more firmly rooted in the political agency of ordinary human beings rather than in the language or international institutions of human rights.[36] Here, the importance of social movements for human rights cannot be underestimated, for they regularly challenge the consolidation of human rights into tokens of institutional mechanisms of governance (see Stammers 1999). The political significance of such movements is one of the casualties of an era that focuses on terrorism as the primary vehicle of political disturbance.

---

[35] This argument does not bode well for the effectiveness of recent efforts of international intellectuals to outflank the hegemonic claims of dominant states as the guarantors of security by merging notions of *protection* and *empowerment* in the language of "human security" (see CHS 2003).

[36] For an optimistic attempt to spell out such a notion of democracy in a globalized world, correcting for the vagaries and formalisms of Dewey and Habermas, see Brunkhorst 2002.

This alternative notion of human rights as an ethics of power cannot prevent the political abuse of the rhetoric of human rights and democracy. It will continue to be used by political antagonists. This paradoxical situation will continue for the foreseeable future, as it derives from the inherently ambiguous language of human rights as an ethics of power and the nature of "democracy" as the rhetorical term of choice to legitimate particular forms of contemporary state power. Moreover, the argument of this chapter does not aspire to establish a new discursive paradigm that reduces the need for dialectical exchanges among critics and agents of democracy.[37] But if the benefits of the discourse of human rights are to be meaningful to the vast majority of humanity, it must reduce its association with the political perspectives of human rights negativists and normativists. For they employ incompletely integrated conceptions of ethics and power along with thin conceptions of human rights and democracy that are too readily co-opted by jealous guardians of economic and political privilege.

Part of the problem stems from reliance of advocates of human rights on a discourse of rights that trades on its liberal origins even as it would transcend them. The theoretical problem has been spelled out by Geuss, but the political problem is more urgent in a world that will not abandon the language of human rights and it is this: rights discourse grounded primarily in the liberal tradition that would promote more than negative liberty and state-sponsored security becomes ineffective in the face of governmental policies that benefit from the politics of insecurity. As a result, the associations of human rights with liberal rights, the conceptual amalgam of the UDHR, or legalistic interpretations of human rights norms can no longer assume primacy for human rights as an ethics of power. Insofar as the meaning of human rights can still make good on the promise of the UDHR for a new political order, it must extend beyond standard liberal rights guaranteed by security-conscious states partnered to global capitalism. This is not because of some unavoidable trade-off between "rights" and "security." The possession of "rights" presumptively entails security of the person. But in a political climate where terror is the primary nemesis, the meaning of security tends to be defined by those able to fight it – and governments are much better suited to do that than ordinary citizens. Citizens then become dependent on the government for the provision of their security, and power flows away from

---

[37] That effort has been nobly but vainly pursued by Jurgen Habermas, who has formulated a critical theory that harmonizes human rights, the rule of law, and democracy by imputing authority to discursive and procedural norms. For a useful, recent account of the current status of the Habermasian project, see Scheuerman 2006 (forthcoming).

ordinary citizens and towards authorities in established religious, economic, and political institutions. When the political world is understood in this way, both human rights and democracy suffer, sacrificed on the altar of national security. But we have seen that defining our political age in these terms plays to the advantage of the politically powerful and is contestable.

Understanding human rights as a political ethics of the governed not only has the benefit of providing a better account of its potential political meaning. It also shifts our view of what counts as criteria for political well-being to the actual lives and prospects of most human beings; it defines human rights through a political lens that identifies local and social conditions that promote democracy. Human rights advocates need to subordinate their strategies to a political ethics of the governed that highlights democratic political agency as the principal vehicle of contemporary justice. In this way, the "human" in "human rights" will preserve its political and critical content, always exceeding its practical realization in imperfect institutions, while the "rights" of human rights preserves the necessary connection between "the common standard of achievement for all peoples and nations" and actual legal institutions – thereby restraining political leaders who would make "human rights" instrumental to their vision of power. *This* understanding of human rights as an ethics of power does not presume its transparency as a political ideal or its value as a rhetorical asset of rulers. Instead, it confirms the inherently paradoxical character of human rights while practically promoting the well-being of those for whom the language of human rights was coined.

Human rights as an ethics of power defined more by democratic citizens than its institutional leaders is not immediately transparent or efficacious. Human rights "abuses" in this perspective are not readily captured in photographs or remedied in criminal courts. Remedying them requires fostering effective democratic politics by ordinary citizens – a long-term process in a world that prizes short attention spans. Indeed, we do not fully understand what is required for an ethics of equality and power in a world of globalized politics – a pluralized discourse and practice of democratic virtue. Traditionally, "virtue" and "democracy" have not been conceptually or practically reconciled. The result has been overly monistic conceptions of the nature of democracy and the meaning of virtue, along with insufficient critical attention to formulating ethical guidelines for democracy that benefit democracy itself. This rhetorical gap has been filled by political elites from the time of the French Revolution to the current era of American domination who protect individual rights at the expense of democracy and effect a concept of democracy aligned to state power that cares little for the political agency of the *demos*. To be sure, the meaning and practice of that agency are elusive.

Defining and fostering that agency amid economic insecurity, cultural diversity, political anxiety, and globalized contexts for the social exercise of power comprises a daunting task. Yet one might entertain some hope that the threats to both human rights and democracy generated by the activities of terrorists and the responses of powerful states will promote newfound attention to a linkage of human rights and democracy that relies less on the prerogatives of institutional leaders than a practical political ethics of, by, and for the governed.

REFERENCES

Agamben, G. ([1995] 1998). *Homo Sacer: Sovereign Power and Bare Life* (D. Heller Hoazen, Trans.). Stanford: Stanford University Press.

―――. ([1996] 2000). *Means Without End: Notes on Politics (Theory Out of Bounds, V. 20)*, (V. Binetti and C. Casarino, Trans.). Minneapolis: University of Minnesota Press.

Amit, R. (2003). 'Justices Without Borders'. Doctoral dissertation, University of Washington, 2003.

Arendt, H. ([1951]1973). 'The Decline of the Nation-State and the End of the Rights of Man'. In *The Origins of Totalitarianism* (new edition), pp. 267–302. New York: Harcourt Brace Jovanovich.

Asad, T. (2003). 'Redeeming the "Human" Through Human Rights'. In *Formations of the Secular*, p. 129. Stanford: Stanford University Press.

Baehr, P. R. (1999). *Human Rights: Universality in Practice*. New York: St. Martin's Press.

Ball, T. (1992). 'New Faces of Power'. In T. Wartenberg (Ed.), *Rethinking Power*, pp. 14–31. Albany: State University of New York Press.

Barak, A. (2004). 'The Supreme Court and the Problem of Terrorism'. In *Judgments of the Israel Supreme Court: Fighting Terrorism within the Law*, pp. 9–23. Available at: http://www.mfa.gov.il/MFA/Government/Law/Legal+Issues+and+Rulings/Fighting+Terrorism+within+the+Law+2-Jan-2005.htm.

Beit Sourik Village Council v. The Government of Israel (HCJ2056/04) (2004), "The Fence Case." In *Judgments of the Israel Supreme Court: Fighting Terrorism within the Law*, pp. 208–10.

Bender, T. (Ed.). (1992). *The Antislavery Debate: Capitalism and Abolitionism as a Problem in Historical Interpretation*. Berkeley: University of California Press.

Berlin, I. (1969). 'Two Concepts of Liberty'. In *Four Essays on Liberty*. London: Oxford University Press.

Brunkhorst, H. (2002). 'Globalising Democracy Without a State: Weak Public, Strong Public, Global Constitutionalism'. *Millennium: Journal of International Studies*, vol. 31, no. 3, pp. 675–90.

Burnyeat, M. (1994). 'Did the ancient Greeks have the concept of human rights?' *Polis*, vol. 13, nos. 1 & 2, pp. 1–11.

Campbell, T., Ewing, K. D. & Tomkins, A. (2001). *Sceptical Essays on Human Rights*. Oxford: Oxford University Press.

Claude, R. P. (1976). 'The Classical Model of Human Rights Development'. In R. P. Claude (Ed.), *Comparative Human Rights*, pp. 6–50. Baltimore: Johns Hopkins University Press.

Commission on Human Security (CHS). (2003). *Human Security Now*. New York. Available at: http://www.humansecurity-chs.org/finalreport/index.html.

Cowan, J. K., Dembour, M. B. & Wilson, R. A. (Eds.). (2001). *Culture and Rights: Anthropological Perspectives*. Cambridge: Cambridge University Press.

Dyrberg, T. B. (1997). *The Circular Structure of Power: Politics, Identity, Community*. London: Verso.

Freeman, M. (2002). *Human Rights: An Interdisciplinary Approach*. Cambridge: Polity Press.

Geuss, R. (2001). *History and Illusion in Politics*. Cambridge: Cambridge University Press.

———. (2002, June). 'Liberalism and Its Discontents'. In *Political Theory*, vol. 30, no. 3, pp. 320–38.

Glendon, M. A. (2001). *A World Made New: Eleanor Roosevelt and the Universal Declaration of Human Rights*. New York: Random House.

Hunt, L. (2000). 'The Paradoxical Origins of Human Rights'. In J. N. Wasserstrom, L. Hunt, and M. B. Young (Eds.), *Human Rights and Revolutions*, pp. 3–17. Lanham, MD: Rowman & Littlefield.

Human Rights and Security Assistance Act. 22 U.S.C.A. § 2304 (West. WESTLAW through P.L. 109-10 (excluding P.L. 109.8, P.L. 109.9) approved Apr. 29, 2005).

Huntington, S. P. (1981). *American Politics: The Promise of Disharmony*. Cambridge, MA: Harvard University Press.

Ignatieff, M. (1999). 'Human Rights'. In C. Hesse and R. Post (Eds.), *Human Rights in Political Transitions*, pp. 313–25. New York: Zone Books.

———. (2000, February 13). 'The Next President's Duty to Intervene'. *New York Times*, Op-Ed, Late Edition – Section 4, Page 17, Column 2.

———. (2002a, February 5). 'Is the Human Rights Era Ending?' *New York Times*, Op-Ed, Late Edition – Section A, Page 25, Column 2.

———. (2003a, January 5). 'The American Empire; The Burden'. *New York Times Magazine*, Late Edition – Section 6, Page 22, Column 1.

———. (2003b, March 23). 'I am Iraq'. *New York Times Magazine*, Late Edition – Section 6, Page 13, Column 3 (THE WAY WE LIVE NOW: 3-23-03).

———. (2003c, September 7). 'Why Are We in Iraq? (and Liberia? and Afghanistan?)'. *New York Times Magazine*, Section 6, Page 38, Column 1.

———. (2004b, March 14). 'The Year of Living Dangerously'. *New York Times Magazine*, Late Edition – Section 6, Page 13, Column 3 (THE WAY WE LIVE NOW: 3-14-04).

———. (2004c, May 2). 'Lesser Evils'. *New York Times Magazine*, Late Edition – Section 6, Page 46, Column 1.

———. (2004d, November 14). 'The Terrorist as Auteur'. *New York Times Magazine*, Late Edition – Section 6, Page 50, Column 1 (THE WAY WE LIVE NOW: 11-14-04: PHENOMENON).

———. (2004e, December 12). 'Democratic Providentialism'. *New York Times Magazine*, Late Edition – Section 6, page 29, Column 3 (THE WAY WE LIVE NOW: 12-12-04).

———. (2001). *Human Rights as Politics and Idolatry*. A. Gutmann (Ed.), with commentary by K. A. Appiah, D. A. Hollinger, T. W. Laqueur, and D. F. Orentlicher. Princeton: Princeton University Press.

———. (2002b). 'Intervention and State Failure'. *Dissent*, Winter, vol. 49, no. 1, pp. 114–23.

———. (2002c). 'Human Rights, the Laws of War, and Terrorism'. *Social Research*, Winter, vol. 69, no. 4, pp. 1137–58.

———. (2004a). *The Lesser Evil: Political Ethics in an Age of Terror*. Princeton: Princeton University Press.

Ishay, M. R. (2004). *The History of Human Rights: From Ancient Times to the Globalization Era*. Berkeley: University of California Press.

Jepperson, R. L., Wendt, A. & Katzenstein, P. J. (1996). 'Norms, Identity, and Culture in National Security'. In P. J. Katzenstein (Ed.), *The Culture of National Security: Norms and Identity in World Politics*, p. 54. New York: Columbia University Press.

Kennedy, D. (2004). *The Dark Sides of Virtue: Reassessing International Humanitarianism*. Princeton: Princeton University Press.

Liddell, H. G., Scott, R. & Jones, H. (1968). *Greek-English Lexicon*. Oxford: Clarendon Press.

Morsink, J. (1999). *The Universal Declaration of Human Rights: Origins, Drafting, and Intent*. Philadelphia: University of Pennsylvania Press.

Oksenberg, A. (1992). 'Power and Powers: A Dialogue Between Buff and Rebuff'. In T. Wartenberg (Ed.), *Rethinking Power*, pp. 1–13. Albany: State University of New York Press.

O'Malley, J. (Ed.). (1994). *Marx: Early Political Writings*. Cambridge: Cambridge University Press.

Packer, G. (2002, December 8). 'The Liberal Quandary Over Iraq'. *The New York Times Magazine*.

Pennock, J. R. (1981). 'Rights, Natural Rights, and Human Rights – A General View'. In J. R. Pennock and J. W. Chapman (Eds.), *Human Rights – NOMOS XXIII*, pp. 1–7. New York: New York University Press.

Risse, T. & Sikkink, K. (1999). 'The Socialization of Human Rights Norms'. In T. Risse, S. C. Ropp, and K. Sikkink (Eds.), *The Power of Human Rights: International Norms and Domestic Change*, pp. 1–38. Cambridge: Cambridge University Press.

Ron, J. & Ramos, H. (2004). 'The Global Human Rights Agenda'. Working Paper, McGill University Research Group in Conflict and Human Rights. Montreal.

Rorty, R. (1993). 'Human Rights, Rationality, and Sentimentality'. In S. Shute and S. Hurley (Eds.), *On Human Rights: The Oxford Amnesty Lectures, 1993*. New York: Basic Books.

Sarat, A. & Kearns, T. R. (Eds.). (2001). *Human Rights: Concepts, Contests, Contingencies*. Ann Arbor: University of Michigan Press.

Scheuerman, W. E. (2006, forthcoming). 'Critical Theory Beyond Habermas'. In John Dryzek, Bonnie Honig and Anne Phillips, eds., *The Oxford Handbook of Political Theory*. Oxford: Oxford University Press.

Sen, A. (1999). 'Democracy as a Universal Value'. *Journal of Democracy*, vol. 10, no. 3, pp. 3–17.

Stammers, N. (1999). 'Social Movements and the Social Construction of Human Rights'. *Human Rights Quarterly*, vol. 21, no. 4, pp. 980–1008.

Teitel, R. (2002, Fall). 'Humanity's Law: Rule of Law for the New Global Politics'. *Cornell International Law Journal*, vol. 35, pp. 355–87.

Thomas, D.C. (2001). *The Helsinki Effect: International Norms, Human Rights, and the Demise of Communism*. Princeton: Princeton University Press.

Tierney, B. (1997). *The Idea of Natural Rights*. Atlanta: Scholars Press.

Tuck, R. (1979). *Natural Rights Theories: Their Origins and Development*. Cambridge: Cambridge University Press.

Waldron, J. (Ed.). (1987). *Nonsense Upon Stilts: Bentham, Burke, and Marx on the Rights of Man*. London: Methuen.

Weissbrodt, D., et al. (2001). *Selected International Human Rights Instruments* (3rd ed). Cincinnati: Anderson Publishing Co.

Williams, B. (1985). *Ethics and the Limits of Philosophy*. Cambridge: Cambridge University Press.

Wilson, R. A. (Ed.). (1997). *Human Rights, Culture & Context: Anthropological Perspectives*. London: Pluto Press.

Wilson, R. A. & Mitchell, J. P. (Eds.). (2003). *Human Rights in Global Perspective: Anthropological Studies of Rights, Claims and Entitlements*. London: Routledge.

5. How Not to Promote Democracy and Human Rights

ARYEH NEIER

This chapter addresses the policies of the Bush Administration, and the damage that it has done to the cause of democracy and human rights worldwide. But I have to start out by saying that, in certain respects, the Bush Administration's record of attempting to promote human rights is very good. That is, the Bush Administration has been as outspoken as any previous administration in championing human rights in different parts of the world. It has been willing to take quite strong action in efforts to promote human rights. We have the example in 2004 of Secretary of State Colin Powell's decision to label what is taking place in Darfur in the Sudan as "genocide," which implies a responsibility under the Genocide Convention to prevent genocide and to punish those who are responsible for genocide.

It contrasts with the Clinton Administration's stand a decade earlier in Rwanda, where the Administration danced around but refused to use the label genocide in a much clearer case than the case in the Sudan. Also, of course the Clinton Administration led the effort in the United Nations Security Council to withdraw United Nations troops from Rwanda – troops who, according to the commander, General Romeo Dallaire, probably could have stopped the genocide from taking place. In the Bush Administration, the State Department's Bureau of Human Rights under its recently departed Director, Lorne Kraner, has been very vigorous worldwide in protesting abuses of human rights, not only in countries considered antagonistic to the United States, but also in countries that are allies of the United States. We might consider a couple of examples: the Bush Administration's decision to deny certification to Uzbekistan, one of the countries that played a very important role as a staging ground for the war in Afghanistan, and the Bush Administration's decision at a certain point to threaten to withhold about 135 million dollars in aid to Egypt, unless a notable democracy and human rights campaigner, Saad Eddin Ibrahim, was released from prison.

The Bush Administration has also been outspoken in a rhetorical commitment to human rights, as evidenced in the National Security Strategy of the United States of America, which was issued on September 17, 2002. I am going to come back to this document, because it is of seminal significance in understanding the policies of the Bush Administration. Page 4 of the National Security Strategy of the United States of America (2002) says:

> We will speak out honestly about violations of the non-negotiable demands of human dignity, using our voice and vote in international institutions to advance freedom; use our foreign aid to promote freedom and support those who have struggled nonviolently for it, ensuring that nations moving towards democracy are rewarded for the steps they take; make freedom and the development of democratic institutions key themes in our bilateral relations, seeking solidarity and cooperation from other democracies while we press governments that deny human rights to move to a better future; take special efforts to promote freedom of religion and conscience, and defend it from encroachments by repressive governments. We will champion the cause of human dignity and oppose those who resist it.

I do not think any human rights organization could do better in articulating a policy.

So, how is it that a government that is both rhetorically committed to human rights and that has taken systematic action to try to promote human rights has done damage to the human rights cause? There are three reasons that it has done damage, and I will consider each of those reasons in turn. One has to do with the war in Iraq and the projection of American military force. President Bush has repeatedly said that promoting freedom and democracy in the Middle East is essential for America's security. In the wake of the collapse of the argument for going into Iraq because of weapons of mass destruction, and given the Bush Administration's concession – not always including such a concession by Vice President Cheney but at least by President Bush himself – that there is not a connection between Iraq and Al Qaeda, increasingly the administration has relied on the argument that it went into Iraq to promote human rights. That is, it acted to remove a tyrant who oppressed his people. The president has argued, and members of his administration have argued, that it is essential for the United States to promote democracy and human rights throughout the Middle East to ensure America's security. The willingness to use American force to try to impose democracy and human rights has aroused great antagonism in the Middle East, as well as in other parts of the world, particularly in parts of Asia. It has resulted in what President Mubarak of Egypt has termed a level of anti-Americanism that is unprecedented worldwide. One of the consequences of this is that proponents of democracy and human rights in the Middle East, but also in various parts of Asia, have found themselves on the defensive because they are seen as promoting the American cause. It is increasingly difficult for them to articulate concern with democracy and human rights.

There is an interesting controversy taking place that involves the United Nations Development Program, which illustrates this point. In 2002, the United Nations Development Program (UNDP) and the Regional Bureau for Arab States (RBAS) issued what is called the "Arab Human Development Report 2002: Creating Opportunities for Future Generations." This report is a book-length document produced by Arab intellectuals. It identifies what are considered three deficits in development in the Arab countries. One is the knowledge deficit; the second is the deficit in the engagement of women in various aspects of society; the third deficit is identified as the democracy deficit (UNDP & RBAS, 2002). The report was very well done and became a rallying point for Arab intellectuals who saw a United Nations document as something they could unite behind, and in that way, avoid identification with the American project of promoting democracy and human rights in the Middle East by military means.

The United Nations Development Program followed this up with another volume in 2003 titled "The Arab Human Development Report 2003: Building a Knowledgeable Society." The 2003 volume addressed the "knowledge deficit," pointing out for example, that there are many times the number of books translated into Greek, a language spoken by about 10 million people, as translated into Arabic, a language spoken by about 200 million people (UNDP & RBAS, 2003: 67). The volume gave many other examples of this knowledge deficit. There was to be another report issued that would go into greater detail about the democracy deficit. Yet the work on that report has resulted in turmoil. Whether the report on the democracy deficit will be produced is now unclear, because the Arab intellectuals who are associated with the project want to include lengthy denunciations of United States policy in the report, and a United Nations agency does not want to be the sponsor of a document that include denunciations of United States policy.

From the standpoint of the Arab intellectuals, they feel they have to separate themselves from United States policy in order to have credibility in their region. So, when the United States speaks in the name of democracy and human rights in justifying its policy in the Middle East, Arab intellectuals who are themselves committed to democracy and human rights run away as fast as they can. It tarnishes their effort. That is, I believe, one of the consequences of American military policy that is proving very destructive. The very terms democracy and human rights are increasingly associated in many parts of the world with American willingness to impose our government's will by its superior force, and to act in a way that seems to disregard all international agreements and international conventions in the process of imposing its will.

A second way that the Bush Administration's policies have helped to give human rights a bad name has to do with our own practices since September 11, 2001. The United States always had something of a checkered record in promoting human rights internationally. There were parts of the world where we were very vigorous in promoting human rights, and there were parts of the world where we were allies of those who were abusing human rights. On balance, however, the United States was a force worldwide for the human rights cause, and part of that had to do with our own reputation as a government that was respectful of human rights. The United States' own practices were widely admired worldwide, and those who criticized United States policy complained that we were willing to ally ourselves with governments that were not similarly respectful of human rights. The chapters in this volume by Carol Greenhouse and Neil Hicks expand on this point.

What has happened since September 11, 2001, is that the image of the United States worldwide is now the image of a human rights violator, rather than the image of a respecter of human rights. Everywhere in the world people know about Guantanamo Bay, and Guatanamo has become a symbol of American policy. The idea that the United States would arbitrarily hold a large number of people in a legal black hole for a period of years with no access to attorneys, no access to families, and no charges, was beyond anything that anyone could have expected. Several other democratic countries have had terrorist problems. Britain has had the IRA, Spain has had the ETA, India has had terrorism related to Kashmir, Israel has had suicide bombing and other forms of terrorism. None of the democratic countries elsewhere in the world that have experienced terrorism did anything that is comparable to Guantanamo in the manner that they dealt with terrorism. There were delays in bringing detainees before judges in various places, and periods of time when they did not have access to lawyers and families, but Guantanamo exceeded what any other democratic government has done in dealing with those persons it accused of terrorism. Though the U.S. Supreme Court's 2004 decisions in *Padilla* and *Hamdi* have now limited, to some degree, the extent of the arbitrariness with which the United States may hold prisoners at Guantanamo, most of the detainees there have not yet seen a lawyer, nor have they yet had contact with members of their families. The prolongation of detention without charges is likely to be a factor for a good while to come.

In addition, of course, the Abu Ghraib scandal and the images that went around the world of American soldiers engaged in the intentional humiliation and torture of detainees is another part of America's new image. The consequence is that when the United States now attempts to lecture other governments about human rights, the images that come to mind worldwide are the images from Abu Ghraib and the images from Guantanamo. The United States is seen as hypocritical in its advocacy of human rights. That perception of hypocrisy is another factor that tends to give the human rights cause, as espoused by the United States, a bad name.

The third factor that has tended to give the human rights cause a bad name is the way that it is linked, in the strictures of the Bush Administration to various other governments, to free trade. I traveled to Mexico in 2004, and one of the things you hear when you talk to Latin Americans is that the Bush Administration takes the position, in dealing with their countries, that the freedom of capital movement is a basic human right. In the U.S. National Security Strategy of September 2002 that I mentioned previously, free trade is referred to as "a moral principle" (p. 18). This is immensely damaging. I am not a partisan of the view that it is possible to deal with what are labeled as economic and social rights as matters of rights. Those are matters that have to be dealt with through the political process, not through assertions of rights. The same has to hold for economic rights when articulated in terms of free trade.

In Latin America today, only one country, Cuba, is an out and out dictatorship. Democracy, sometimes in a somewhat authoritarian mode, prevails everywhere else in Latin America. Yet, if you study surveys of public opinion in Latin America, you will see that substantial numbers of people throughout the western hemisphere think that democracy has not achieved much for them. Many throughout the region would prefer a return to military regimes or some other form of authoritarian rule, because they are so disappointed with democracy. A major reason is that democracy has been unable to deliver for them economically. They tend to see the free trade policies, or the manner in which the United States espouses free trade policies and labels them as fundamental human rights, as part of the problem with democracy. This has caused a popular disenchantment with democracy and human rights in Latin America. While this is less true in other parts of the world that have not been such significant targets of free trade agreements, it is the case with much of Latin America.

These are the three factors that, in combination, are doing a disservice to the human rights cause internationally. Unfortunately the United States looms so large in world affairs, that having the United States and its policies on the one hand associated with the promotion of democracy and human rights, and on the other hand arousing antagonism in many parts of the world, is very bad for the human rights cause.

I recall that when we launched Human Rights Watch a little more than a quarter of a century ago, a significant component of our strategy was to leverage the power, purse, and influence of the United States to promote human rights more systematically around the world. From the standpoint of those who are trying to promote human rights today, it is necessary to pursue the opposite course. One has to put as much distance as one can between one's own efforts and the efforts of the United States government.

Whether the situation is subject to repair, if there were to be a change of administration, I do not know. The damage has been done for a very long time to come.

I cannot think of any ready substitute for the influence that the United States previously could bring to bear to promote human rights. Unfortunately, even at a time when good faith efforts are made by the United States, as indeed I think many of the efforts of the Bush Administration have been, the effect is very often counterproductive. This is one of the collateral consequences of 9/11 and the manner in which the United States responded to it, especially in the case of the nexus that the Bush Administration established between its use of military force and the human rights cause, and in the degree to which its abuses of human rights at Guantanamo and Abu Ghraib made the United States seem hypocritical in claiming to stand for human rights. September 11, 2001, was, of course, a disaster. Yet I wonder if even the perpetrators of 9/11 could have imagined all the collateral disasters that have followed in its wake.

REFERENCES

Hamdi v. Rumsfeld, 124 S. Ct. 2633, 159 L. Ed.2d 578, 72 N.S.L.W. 4607 (2004).
Rumsfeld v. Padilla, 124 S. Ct. 2711, 159, L. Ed.2d 513, 72 N.S.L.W. 4584 (2004).
The National Security Strategy of the United States of America. (2002, September). Retrieved from http://www.whitehouse.gov/nsc/nss.pdf.
United Nations Development Programme (UNDP) & Regional Bureau for Arab States (RBAS). (2002). *The Arab Human Development Report 2003: Creating Opportunities for Future Generations.* New York: United Nations Publications.
_____. (2003). *The Arab Human Development Report 2003: Building a Knowledgeable Society.* New York: United Nations Publications.

6. War in Iraq: Not a Humanitarian Intervention

KENNETH ROTH

Humanitarian intervention was supposed to have gone the way of the 1990s. The use of military force across borders to stop mass killing was seen as a luxury of an era in which national security concerns among the major powers were less pressing and problems of human security could come to the fore. Somalia, Haiti, Bosnia, Kosovo, East Timor, Sierra Leone – these interventions, to varying degrees justified in humanitarian terms, were dismissed as products of an unusual interlude between the tensions of the Cold War and the growing threat of terrorism. September 11, 2001, was said to have changed all that, signaling a return to more immediate security challenges. Yet surprisingly, with the campaign against terrorism in full swing, recently there have been four military interventions that are described by their instigators, in whole or in part, as humanitarian.

In principle, one can only welcome this renewed concern with the fate of faraway victims. What could be more virtuous than to risk life and limb to save distant people from slaughter? But the common use of the humanitarian label masks significant differences among these interventions. The French intervention in the Democratic Republic of Congo, later backed by a rein-forced U.N. peacekeeping presence, was most clearly motivated by a desire to stop ongoing slaughter. In Liberia and Côte d'Ivoire, West African and French forces intervened to enforce a peace plan but also played important humanitarian roles. (The United States briefly participated in the Liberian intervention, but the handful of troops it deployed had little effect.) All of these African interventions were initially or ultimately approved by the U.N. Security Council. Indeed, in each case the recognized local government con-sented to the intervention, though under varying degrees of pressure.

By contrast, the U.S.-led coalition forces justified the invasion of Iraq on a variety of grounds, only one of which – a comparatively minor one – was humanitarian. The Security Council did not approve the invasion, and the

Iraqi government, its existence on the line, violently opposed it. Moreover, while the African interventions were modest affairs, the Iraq war was massive, involving an extensive bombing campaign and some 150,000 ground troops.

The sheer size of the invasion of Iraq, the central involvement of the world's superpower, and the enormous controversy surrounding the war meant that the Iraqi conflict overshadowed the other military actions. For better or for worse, that prominence gave it greater power to shape public perceptions of armed interventions said by their proponents to be justified on humanitarian grounds. The result is that at a time of renewed interest in humanitarian intervention, the Iraq war and the effort to justify it even in part in humanitarian terms risk giving humanitarian intervention a bad name. If that breeds cynicism about the use of military force for humanitarian purposes, it could be devastating for people in need of future rescue.

Human Rights Watch ordinarily takes no position on whether a state should go to war. The issues involved usually extend beyond our mandate, and a position of neutrality maximizes our ability to press all parties to a conflict to avoid harming noncombatants. The sole exception we make is in extreme situations requiring humanitarian intervention.

Because the Iraq war was not mainly about saving the Iraqi people from mass slaughter, and because no such slaughter was then ongoing or imminent, Human Rights Watch at the time took no position for or against the war. A humanitarian rationale was occasionally offered for the war, but it was so plainly subsidiary to other reasons that we felt no need to address it. Indeed, if Saddam Hussein had been overthrown and the issue of weapons of mass destruction reliably dealt with, there clearly would have been no war, even if the successor government were just as repressive. Some argued that Human Rights Watch should support a war launched on other grounds if it would arguably lead to significant human rights improvements. But the substantial risk that wars guided by non-humanitarian goals will endanger human rights keeps us from adopting that position.

Over time, the principal justifications originally given for the Iraq war lost much of their force. After the declared end of major hostilities, weapons of mass destruction have not been found. No significant prewar link between Saddam Hussein and international terrorism has been discovered. The difficulty of establishing stable institutions in Iraq is making the country an increasingly unlikely staging ground for promoting democracy in the Middle East. As time elapses, the Bush administration's dominant remaining justification for the war is that Saddam Hussein was a tyrant who deserved to be overthrown – an argument of humanitarian intervention. The administration is now citing this rationale not simply as a side benefit of the war but also as a prime justification for it. Other reasons are still regularly mentioned, but the humanitarian one has gained prominence.

Does that claim hold up to scrutiny? The question is not simply whether Saddam Hussein was a ruthless leader; he most certainly was. Rather, the question is whether the conditions were present that would justify humanitarian intervention – conditions that look at more than the level of repression. If so, honesty would require conceding as much, despite the war's global unpopularity. If not, it is important to say so as well, because allowing the arguments of humanitarian intervention to serve as a pretext for war fought mainly on other grounds risks tainting a principle whose viability might be essential to save countless lives.

In examining whether the invasion of Iraq could properly be understood as a humanitarian intervention, our purpose is not to say whether the U.S.-led coalition should have gone to war for other reasons. That, as noted, involves judgments beyond our mandate. Rather, now that the war's proponents are relying so significantly on a humanitarian rationale for the war, the need to assess this claim has grown in importance. We conclude that, despite the horrors of Saddam Hussein's rule, the invasion of Iraq cannot be justified as a humanitarian intervention.

The Standards for Humanitarian Intervention

Unusual among human rights groups, Human Rights Watch has a long-standing policy on humanitarian intervention. War often carries enormous human costs, but we recognize that the imperative of stopping or preventing genocide or other systematic slaughter can sometimes justify the use of military force. For that reason, Human Rights Watch has on rare occasion advocated humanitarian intervention – for example, to stop ongoing genocide in Rwanda and Bosnia.

Yet military action should not be taken lightly, even for humanitarian purposes. One might use military force more readily when a government facing serious abuses on its territory invites military assistance from others – as in the cases of the three recent African interventions. But military intervention on asserted humanitarian grounds without the government's consent should be used with extreme caution. In arriving at the standards that we believe should govern such nonconsensual military action, we draw on the principles underlying our own policy on humanitarian intervention and on our experiences in applying them. We also take into account other relevant literature, including the report of the Canadian government-sponsored International Commission on Intervention and State Sovereignty.

In our view, as a threshold matter, humanitarian intervention that occurs without the consent of the relevant government can be justified only in the face of ongoing or imminent genocide, or comparable mass slaughter or loss of life. To state the obvious, war is dangerous. In theory it can be surgical, but the reality is often highly destructive, with a risk of enormous bloodshed. Only large-scale murder, we believe, can justify the death, destruction, and disorder that so often are inherent in war and its aftermath. Other forms of tyranny are deplorable and worth working intensively to end, but they do not in our view rise to the level that would justify the extraordinary response of military force. Only mass slaughter might permit the deliberate taking of life involved in using military force for humanitarian purposes.

In addition, the capacity to use military force is finite. Encouraging military action to meet lesser abuses may mean a lack of capacity to intervene when atrocities are most severe. The invasion of a country, especially without the approval of the U.N. Security Council, also damages the international legal order which itself is important to protect rights. For these reasons, we believe that humanitarian intervention should be reserved for situations involving mass killing.

We understand that "mass" killing is a subjective term, allowing for varying interpretations, and we do not propose a single quantitative measure. We also recognize that the level of killing that we as a human rights organization would see as justifying humanitarian intervention might well be different from the level that a government might set. However, in either circumstance, because of the substantial risks inherent in the use of military force, humanitarian intervention should be exceptional – reserved for the most dire circumstances.

If this high threshold is met, we then look to five other factors to determine whether the use of military force can be characterized as humanitarian. First, military action must be the last reasonable option to halt or prevent slaughter; military force should not be used for humanitarian purposes if effective alternatives are available. Second, the intervention must be guided primarily by a humanitarian purpose; we do not expect purity of motive, but humanitarianism should be the dominant reason for military action. Third, every effort should be made to ensure that the means used to intervene themselves respect international human rights and humanitarian law; we do not subscribe to the view that some abuses can be countenanced in the name of stopping others. Fourth, it must be reasonably likely that military action will do more good than harm; humanitarian intervention should not be tried if it seems likely to produce a wider conflagration or significantly more suffering. Finally, we prefer endorsement of humanitarian intervention by the U.N. Security Council or other bodies with significant multilateral authority.

However, in light of the imperfect nature of international governance today, we would not require multilateral approval in an emergency context.

Two Irrelevant Considerations

Before applying these criteria to Iraq, it is worth noting two factors that we do not consider relevant in assessing whether an intervention can be justified as humanitarian. First, we are aware of, but reject, the argument that humanitarian intervention cannot be justified if other equally or more needy places are ignored. Iraqi repression was severe, but the case might be made that repression elsewhere was worse. For example, an estimated three million or more have lost their lives to violence, disease, and exposure in recent years during the conflict in the eastern Democratic Republic of Congo (DRC), yet intervention in the DRC was late and, compared to Iraq, modest. However, if the killing in Iraq warranted military intervention, it would be callous to disregard the plight of these victims simply because other victims were being neglected. In that case, intervention should be encouraged in both places, not rejected in one because it was weak or nonexistent in the other.

Second, we are aware of, but reject, the argument that past U.S. complicity in Iraqi repression should preclude U.S. intervention in Iraq on humanitarian grounds. This argument is built on the U.S. government's sordid record in Iraq in the 1980s and early 1990s. When the Iraqi government was using chemical weapons against Iranian troops in the 1980s, the Reagan administration was giving it intelligence information. After the *Anfal* genocide against Iraqi Kurds in 1988, the Reagan and first Bush administrations gave Baghdad billions of dollars in commodity credits and import loan guarantees. The Iraqi government's ruthless suppression of the 1991 uprising was facilitated by the first Bush administration's agreement to Iraq's use of helicopters – permission made all the more callous because then-President Bush had encouraged the uprising in the first place. In each of these cases, Washington deemed it more important to defeat Iran or avoid Iranian influence in a potentially destabilized Iraq than to discourage or prevent large-scale slaughter. We condemn such calculations. However, we would not deny relief to, say, the potential victims of genocide simply because the proposed intervener had dirty hands in the past.

The Level of Killing

In considering the criteria that would justify humanitarian intervention, the most important, as noted, is the level of killing: was genocide or comparable mass slaughter underway or imminent? Brutal as Saddam Hussein's reign had been, the scope of the Iraqi government's killing in March 2003 was not of the exceptional and dire magnitude that would justify humanitarian intervention. We have no illusions about Saddam Hussein's vicious inhumanity. Having devoted extensive time and effort to documenting his atrocities, we estimate that in the last twenty-five years of Ba'th Party rule, the Iraqi government murdered or "disappeared" some quarter of a million Iraqis, if not more. In addition, one must consider such abuses as Iraq's use of chemical weapons against Iranian soldiers. However, by the time of the March 2003 invasion, Saddam Hussein's killing had ebbed.

There were times in the past when the killing was so intense that humanitarian intervention would have been justified – for example, during the 1988 *Anfal* genocide, in which the Iraqi government slaughtered some 100,000 Kurds. Indeed, Human Rights Watch, though still in its infancy and not yet working in the Middle East in 1988, did advocate a form of military intervention in 1991 after we had begun addressing Iraq. As Iraqi Kurds fleeing Saddam Hussein's brutal repression of the post-Gulf War uprising were stranded and dying in harsh winter weather on Turkey's mountainous border, we advocated the creation of a no-fly zone in northern Iraq so they could return home without facing renewed genocide. There were other moments of intense killing as well, such as the suppression of the uprisings in 1991. But on the eve of the latest Iraq war, no one contends that the Iraqi government was engaged in killing of anywhere near this magnitude, or had been for some time. "Better late than never" is not a justification for humanitarian intervention, which should be countenanced only to stop mass murder, not to punish its perpetrators, desirable as punishment is in such circumstances.

But if Saddam Hussein committed mass atrocities in the past, wasn't his overthrow justified to prevent his resumption of such atrocities in the future? No. Human Rights Watch accepts that military intervention may be necessary not only to stop ongoing slaughter but also to prevent future slaughter, but the future slaughter must be imminent. To justify the extraordinary remedy of military force for preventive humanitarian purposes, there must be evidence that large-scale slaughter is in preparation and about to begin unless militarily stopped. But no one seriously claimed before the war that the Saddam Hussein government was planning imminent mass killing, and no evidence has emerged that it was. There were claims that Saddam Hussein, with a history of gassing Iranian soldiers and Iraqi Kurds, was planning to deliver weapons of mass destruction through terrorist networks, but these allegations were entirely speculative; no substantial evidence has yet emerged. There were also fears that the Iraqi government might respond to an invasion with the use of chemical or biological weapons, perhaps even against its own people, but no one seriously suggested such use as an imminent possibility in the absence of an invasion.

That does not mean that past atrocities should be ignored. Rather, their perpetrators should be prosecuted. Human Rights Watch has devoted enormous efforts to investigating and documenting the Iraqi government's atrocities, particularly the *Anfal* genocide against Iraqi Kurds. We have interviewed witnesses and survivors, exhumed mass graves, taken soil samples to demonstrate the use of chemical weapons, and combed through literally tons of Iraqi secret police documents. We have circled the globe trying to convince some government – any government – to institute legal proceedings against Iraq for genocide. No one would. In the mid-1990s, when our efforts were most intense, governments feared that charging Iraq with genocide would be too provocative – that it would undermine future commercial deals with Iraq, squander influence in the Middle East, invite terrorist retaliation, or simply cost too much money.

But to urge justice or even criminal prosecution is not to justify humanitarian intervention. Indictments should be issued, and suspects should be arrested if they dare to venture abroad, but the extraordinary remedy of humanitarian intervention should not be used simply to secure justice for past crimes. This extreme step, as noted, should be taken only to stop current or imminent slaughter, not to punish past abuse.

In stating that the killing in Iraq did not rise to a level that justified humanitarian intervention, we are not insensitive to the awful plight of the Iraqi people. We are aware that summary executions occurred with disturbing frequency in Iraq up to the end of Saddam Hussein's rule, as did torture and other brutality. Such atrocities should be met with public, diplomatic, and economic pressure, as well as prosecution. But before taking the substantial risk to life that is inherent in any war, mass slaughter should be taking place or imminent. That was not the case in Saddam Hussein's Iraq in March 2003.

The Last Reasonable Option

The lack of ongoing or imminent mass slaughter was itself sufficient to disqualify the invasion of Iraq as a humanitarian intervention. Nonetheless, particularly in light of the ruthlessness of Saddam Hussein's rule, it is useful to examine the other criteria for humanitarian intervention. For the most part, these too were not met.

As noted, because of the substantial risks involved, an invasion should qualify as a humanitarian intervention only if it is the last reasonable option to stop mass killings. Because there were no ongoing mass killings in Iraq in early 2003, this issue technically did not arise. But it is useful to explore whether military intervention was the last reasonable option to stop what Iraqi abuses were ongoing.

It was not. If the purpose of the intervention was primarily humanitarian, then at least one other option should have been tried long before resorting to the extreme step of military invasion – criminal prosecution. There is no guarantee that prosecution would have worked, and one might have justified skipping it had large-scale slaughter been underway. But in the face of the Iraqi government's more routine abuses, this alternative to military action should have been tried.

An indictment, of course, is not the same as arrest, trial, and punishment. A mere piece of paper will not stop mass slaughter. But as a long-term approach to Iraq, justice held some promise. The experiences of former Yugoslav President Slobodan Milosevic and former Liberian President Charles Taylor suggest that an international indictment profoundly discredits even a ruthless, dictatorial leader. That enormous stigma tends to undermine support for the leader, both at home and abroad, often in unexpected ways. By allowing Saddam Hussein to rule without the stigma of an indictment for genocide and crimes against humanity, the international community never tried a step that might have contributed to his removal and a parallel reduction in government abuses.

In noting that prosecution was not tried before war, we recognize that the U.N. Security Council had never availed itself of this option in more than a decade of attention to Iraq. The Council's April 1991 resolution on Iraq (resolution 688), in condemning "the repression of the Iraqi civilian population in many parts of Iraq," broke new ground at the time as the first council resolution to treat such repression as a threat to international peace and security. But the Council never followed up by deploying the obvious tool of prosecution to curtail that repression. Yet if the U.S. government had devoted anywhere near the attention to justice as it did to pressing for war, the chances are at least reasonable that the Council would have been responsive.

Humanitarian Purpose

Any humanitarian intervention should be conducted with the aim of maximizing humanitarian results. We recognize that an intervention motivated by purely humanitarian concerns probably cannot be found. Governments that intervene to stop mass slaughter inevitably have other reasons as well, so we do not insist on purity of motive. But a dominant humanitarian motive is important because it affects numerous decisions made in the course of an intervention and its aftermath that can determine its success in saving people from harm.

Humanitarianism, even understood broadly as concern for the welfare of the Iraqi people, was at best a subsidiary motive for the invasion of Iraq. The principal justifications offered in the prelude to the invasion were the Iraqi government's alleged possession of weapons of mass destruction, its alleged failure to account for them as prescribed by numerous U.N. Security Council resolutions, and its alleged connection with terrorist networks. U.S. officials also spoke of a democratic Iraq transforming the Middle East. In this tangle of motives, Saddam Hussein's cruelty toward his own people was mentioned – sometimes prominently – but, in the prewar period, it was never the dominant factor. This is not simply an academic point; it affected the way the invasion was carried out, to the detriment of the Iraqi people.

To begin with, if invading forces had been determined to maximize the humanitarian impact of an intervention, they would have been better prepared to fill the security vacuum that predictably was created by the toppling of the Iraqi government. It was entirely foreseeable that Saddam Hussein's downfall would lead to civil disorder. The 1991 uprisings in Iraq were marked by large-scale summary executions. The government's Arabization policy raised the prospect of clashes between displaced Kurds seeking to reclaim their old homes and Arabs who had moved into them. Other sudden changes of regime, such as the Bosnian Serb withdrawal from the Sarajevo suburbs in 1996, have been marked by widespread violence, looting, and arson.

In part to prevent violence and disorder, the U.S. army chief of staff before the war, General Eric K. Shinseki, predicted that "several" hundreds of thousands of troops would be required. But the civilian leaders of the Pentagon dismissed this assessment and launched the war with considerably fewer combat troops – some 150,000. The reasons for this decision are unclear, but they seem due to some combination of the U.S. government's faith in high-tech weaponry, its distaste for nation-building, its disinclination to take the time to deploy additional troops as summer's heat rose in Iraq and the political heat of opposition to the war mounted around the world, and its excessive reliance on wishful thinking and best-case scenarios. The result is that coalition troops were quickly overwhelmed by the enormity of the task of maintaining public order in Iraq. Looting was pervasive. Arms caches were raided and emptied. Violence was rampant.

The problem of understaffing was only compounded by the failure to deploy an adequate number of troops trained in policing. Regular troops are trained to fight – to meet threats with lethal force. But that presumptive resort to lethal force is inappropriate and unlawful when it comes to policing an occupied nation. The consequence was a steady stream of civilians killed when coalition troops – on edge in the face of regular resistance attacks, many perfidious – mistakenly fired on civilians. That only increased resentment among Iraqis and fueled further attacks. Troops trained in policing – that is, trained to use lethal force as a last resort – would have been better suited to conduct occupation duties humanely. But the Pentagon has not made a priority of developing policing skills among its troops, leaving relatively few to be deployed in Iraq.

To top it all off, L. Paul Bremer III, the U.S. administrator in Iraq, disbanded the entire Iraqi army and police force. That left the occupying authorities without a large pool of indigenous forces that could have helped to establish the rule of law. We recognize that security forces or intelligence agencies that had played a lead role in atrocities, such as the Special Republican Guard or the Mukhabarat, should have been disbanded and their members prosecuted. Some members of the Iraqi army and police were also complicit in atrocities, but the average member had significantly less culpability; there was no penal justification for disbanding these forces en masse rather than pursuing the guilty on an individual basis. The blanket dismissal took a toll on Iraqi security.

The lack of an overriding humanitarian purpose also affected Washington's attitude toward the system of justice to be used to try Iraqi officials' human rights crimes. The Bush administration, like many other people, clearly would like to see those responsible for atrocities in Iraq brought to justice, but its greater distaste for the International Criminal Court (ICC) has prevented it from recommending the justice mechanism that is most likely to succeed. The administration has insisted that accused Iraqi officials be tried before an "Iraqi-led process." In theory, it is certainly preferable for Iraq to try its own offenders. But after three-and-a-half decades of Ba'th Party rule, the Iraqi judicial system has neither a tradition of respect for due process nor the capacity to organize and try a complex case of genocide or crimes against humanity. Were such prosecutions to proceed in Iraqi courts, there is much reason to believe that they would be show trials.

The obvious solution to this problem is to establish an international criminal tribunal for Iraq – either a fully international one such as those established for Rwanda and former Yugoslavia, or an internationally led tribunal with local participation such as the special court created for Sierra Leone. Although the Bush administration has supported these pre-existing tribunals, it adamantly opposes an international tribunal for Iraq. The reason appears to lie in the ICC. The ICC itself would be largely irrelevant for this task since its jurisdiction would begin at the earliest in July 2002, when the treaty establishing it took effect. Most crimes of the Saddam Hussein government were committed before that. But the administration so detests the ICC that it opposes the creation of any international tribunal for Iraq, apparently out of fear that such a new tribunal would lend credibility to the entire project of international justice and thus indirectly bolster the ICC. An overriding concern with the best interests of the Iraqi people would have made it less likely that this ideological position prevailed.

Compliance with Humanitarian Law

Every effort should be made to ensure that a humanitarian intervention is carried out in strict compliance with international human rights and humanitarian law. Compliance is required in all conflicts – no less for an intervention that is justified on humanitarian grounds. The invasion of Iraq largely met this requirement, but not entirely. Coalition forces took extraordinary care to avoid harming civilians when attacking fixed, pre-selected targets. But their record in attacking mobile targets of opportunity was mixed.

As Human Rights Watch reported in detail in its December 2003 report on the war, U.S. efforts to bomb leadership targets were an abysmal failure. The 0-for-50 record reflected a targeting method that bordered on indiscriminate, allowing bombs to be dropped on the basis of evidence suggesting little more than that the leader was somewhere in a community. Substantial civilian casualties were the predictable result.

U.S. ground forces, particularly the Army, also used cluster munitions near populated areas, with predictable loss of civilian life. After roughly a quarter of the civilian deaths in the 1999 NATO bombing of Yugoslavia were caused by the use of cluster bombs in populated areas, the U.S. Air Force substantially curtailed the practice. But the U.S. Army apparently never absorbed this lesson. In responding to Iraqi attacks as they advanced through Iraq, Army troops regularly used cluster munitions in populated areas, causing substantial loss of life. Such disregard for civilian life is incompatible with a genuinely humanitarian intervention.

Better Rather than Worse

Another factor for assessing the humanitarian nature of an intervention is whether it is reasonably calculated to make things better rather than worse in the country invaded. One is tempted to say that anything is better than living under the tyranny of Saddam Hussein, but unfortunately, it is possible to imagine scenarios that are even worse. Vicious as his rule was, chaos or abusive civil war might well become even deadlier, and it is too early to say whether such violence might still emerge in Iraq.

Still, in March 2003, when the war was launched, the U.S. and U.K. governments clearly hoped that the Iraqi government would topple quickly and that the Iraqi nation would soon be on the path to democracy. Their failure to equip themselves with the troops needed to stabilize post-war Iraq diminished the likelihood of this rosy scenario coming to pass. However, the balance of considerations just before the war probably supported the assessment that Iraq would be better off if Saddam Hussein's ruthless reign were ended. But that one factor, in light of the failure to meet the other criteria, does not make the intervention humanitarian.

U.N. Approval

There is considerable value in receiving the endorsement of the U.N. Security Council or another major multilateral body before launching a humanitarian intervention. The need to convince others of the appropriateness of a proposed intervention is a good way to guard against pretextual or unjustified action. An international commitment to an intervention also increases the likelihood that adequate personnel and resources will be devoted to the intervention and its aftermath. And approval by the Security Council, in particular, ends the debate about the legality of an intervention.

However, in extreme situations, Human Rights Watch does not insist on Security Council approval. The council in its current state is simply too imperfect to make it the sole mechanism for legitimizing humanitarian intervention. Its permanent membership is a relic of the post-World War II era, and its veto system allows those members to block the rescue of people facing slaughter for the most parochial of reasons. In light of these faults, one's patience with the Council's approval process would understandably diminish if large-scale slaughter were underway. However, because there was no such urgency in early 2003 for Iraq, the failure to win Council approval, let alone the endorsement of any other multilateral body, weighs heavily in assessing the intervenors' claim to humanitarianism.

We recognize, of course, that the Security Council was never asked to consider a purely humanitarian intervention in Iraq. The principal case presented to it was built on the Iraqi government's alleged possession of and failure to account for weapons of mass destruction. Even so, approval might have ameliorated at least some of the factors that stood in the way of the invasion being genuinely humanitarian. Most significantly, a Council-approved invasion is likely to have yielded more troops to join the predominantly American and

British forces, meaning that preparation for the post-war chaos might have been better.

Conclusion

In sum, the invasion of Iraq failed to meet the test for a humanitarian intervention. Most important, the killing in Iraq at the time was not of the exceptional nature that would justify such intervention. In addition, intervention was not the last reasonable option to stop Iraqi atrocities. Intervention was not motivated primarily by humanitarian concerns. It was not conducted in a way that maximized compliance with international humanitarian law. It was not approved by the Security Council. And while at the time it was launched it was reasonable to believe that the Iraqi people would be better off, it was not designed or carried out with the needs of Iraqis foremost in mind.

In opening this chapter, we noted that the controversial invasion of Iraq stood in contrast to the three African interventions. In making that point, we do not suggest that the African interventions were without problems. All suffered to one degree or another from a mixture of motives, inadequate staffing, insufficient efforts to disarm and demobilize abusive forces, and little attention to securing justice and the rule of law. All of the African interventions, however, ultimately confronted ongoing slaughter, were motivated in significant part by humanitarian concerns, were conducted with apparent respect for international humanitarian law, arguably left the country somewhat better off, and received the approval of the U.N. Security Council. Significantly, all were welcomed by the relevant government, meaning that the standards for assessing them are more permissive than for a nonconsensual intervention.

However, even in light of the problems of the African interventions, the extraordinarily high profile of the Iraq war gives it far more potential to affect the public view of future interventions. If its defenders continue to try to justify it as humanitarian when it was not, they risk undermining an institution that, despite all odds, has managed to maintain its viability in this new century as a tool for rescuing people from slaughter.

The Iraq war highlights the need for a better understanding of when military intervention can be justified in humanitarian terms. The above-noted International Commission on Intervention and State Sovereignty was one important effort to define these parameters. Human Rights Watch has periodically contributed to this debate as well, including with this essay, and various academic writers have offered their own views. But no intergovernmental body has put forth criteria for humanitarian intervention.

This official reticence is not surprising because governments do not like to contemplate uninvited intrusions in their country. But humanitarian intervention appears to be here to stay – an important and appropriate response to people facing mass slaughter. In the absence of international consensus on the conditions for such intervention, governments inevitably are going to abuse the concept, as the United States has done in its after-the-fact efforts to justify the Iraq war. Human Rights Watch calls on intergovernmental organizations, particularly the political bodies of the United Nations, to end the taboo on discussing the conditions for humanitarian intervention. Some consensus on these conditions, in addition to promoting appropriate use of humanitarian intervention, would help deter abuse of the concept and thus assist in preserving a tool that some of the world's most vulnerable victims need.

7. The Tension between Combating Terrorism and Protecting Civil Liberties

RICHARD GOLDSTONE

Introduction

The tragic and previously unimaginable events of 9/11 have changed the United States and indeed the world in ways that are still emerging and difficult to comprehend. Leaders in many countries are struggling to find appropriate policies to deal with the new reality that this level of terrorism presents.

This is not a new problem and has been a challenge in many countries for many years. Governments combating terrorism in democracies have an additional burden. They are required to balance efficient law enforcement with respect for the civil liberties of their citizens. There is a consensus that all lawful means must be used to prevent such terrible crimes. The problem relates to the legitimacy, and sometimes the lawfulness, of those means. In particular, to what extent can civil liberties be curtailed and normal legal processes circumvented?

I do not share the pessimism of some human rights activists who suggest that the age of human rights has come and gone. Too much momentum has been gathered during the past sixty years to allow the recognition and implementation of human rights to be derailed. At the same time there is danger in complacency, and the setbacks to the human rights movement since 9/11 must be acknowledged and recognised as a challenge.

The Development of Human Rights since 1945

It is as well to consider briefly the huge advances made in the area of human rights and humanitarian law since the end of World War II. I will devote disproportionate attention to the role of the United States, as it was crucial to these advances. It is ironic that the greatest threats to further advances are those emanating from this country.

Prior to World War II, the way in which citizens were treated by their respective governments was an internal affair and not the business of other governments or the international community. That changed in consequence of the horrors of the Holocaust that so shocked the conscience of all decent people worldwide.

The changes that occurred, for the most part, were inspired by leaders in the United States. The first was the decision, initially opposed by Winston Churchill, to put the Nazi leaders on trial. It was in consequence of the strong views of Henry Stimson, the Secretary for Defence, that President Truman convinced the leaders of the other three victorious powers that it would be inappropriate to summarily execute those leaders whose guilt was assumed. The consequence was the London Agreement, which set out the basis upon which the Nuremberg Trials were conducted.

International law at the end of World War II did not contemplate crimes of the magnitude of those that had been perpetrated. The result was that new crimes were defined. One was crimes against humanity – serious offences committed against a civilian population. The idea was that such egregious crimes offended not only the people who were directly affected by them, but were truly crimes committed against the whole of humankind. The corollary was that the persons who committed such crimes were to be amenable to the jurisdiction of courts in any nation, and not only those where the crimes were committed or the victims were to be found. This effectively extended the concept of universal criminal jurisdiction which until then applied only to the crime of piracy.

In effect, universal jurisdiction was a genie released from the bottle. It found its way into the new Geneva Conventions of 1949, which recognised it for 'grave breaches' of those conventions. In 1973, such jurisdiction was conferred upon all national courts of any nation in respect of the crime of Apartheid. It also declared Apartheid to be a crime against humanity. It was included in the Torture Convention of 1984. Universal jurisdiction was conferred on all courts by the series of international conventions, which began in the 1970s and were designed to combat terrorism.

The Genocide Convention of 1948 did not provide for universal jurisdiction. Instead, it explicitly assumed that genocide would be amenable to an international criminal court. That no such court was established for almost half a century would have surprised and disappointed the drafters of that Convention. It is accepted today that customary international law recognises universal jurisdiction for the crime of genocide.

In the last decade, a number of nations, especially in Western Europe, began to confer universal jurisdiction upon their domestic courts in respect of crimes such as genocide and other serious war crimes. This trend has accelerated in light of the complimentarily provisions of the Rome Statute that established the International Criminal Court.

When the United Nations Security Council established the ad hoc criminal tribunals for the former Yugoslavia and Rwanda, it conferred jurisdiction on those courts on the basis that the crimes amenable to their jurisdiction were international crimes that attracted universal jurisdiction.

With regard to these developments, the United States played a contradictory role. Generally, the Congress and successive presidents supported the recognition of universal jurisdiction for such shocking crimes. At the same time they objected to United States citizens, and especially members of the military, becoming amenable to foreign or international courts. This approach is demonstrated by the United States opposition to the International Criminal Court, the Kyoto Protocol on global warming and the Protocol to the Torture Convention which seeks to make prisons subject to international inspection.

At the same time, the United States was instrumental in persuading the Security Council to establish the ad hoc criminal tribunals. And, having been established, they would not have got off the ground without the diplomatic and financial support they received from Washington. And, again, it was the crucial support from the United States that led to the use of military force to end the ethnic cleansing of the Albanian population of Kosovo in 1998. The United States played a key role in encouraging the Secretary-General of the United Nations to call the diplomatic conference in Rome, in June 1998, that gave birth to the International Criminal Court[1]. It is that Court that has become such anathema to the Bush Administration.

From this brief sketch of developments since 1945, it is apparent that human rights and humanitarian law have grown and developed in an impressive fashion. It is against that background that we must examine the current debate in this and many other countries with regard to the tension between respecting and protecting civil liberties and combating terrorism.

Human Rights During War

In secure times civil liberties, generally speaking, are not in much danger. It is in times of threat and fear that governments tend to take actions subversive of human rights. Democracies have not done too well in this area. In this country there was the shameful treatment of Japanese Americans during World War II.

---

[1] As of November 11, 2004, ninety-seven countries have ratified the Treaty.

Some 126,000 were interned. Of those, over 70,000 were American-born citizens. No single act of sabotage or espionage after Pearl Harbour was ever uncovered. A FBI Report of May 1942 stated as follows:

> We have not, however, uncovered through these searches any dangerous persons that we could not otherwise know about. We have not found among all the sticks of dynamite and gun powder any evidence that any of it was to be used in bombs. We have not found a single machine gun nor have we found any gun in any circumstances indicating that it was to be used in a manner helpful to our enemies. We have not found a camera which we have reason to believe was for use in espionage.

Nearly three years later, in December 1944, the Supreme Court upheld the constitutionality of that mass evacuation of Japanese Americans. In the test case of *Korematsu v. United States*, 323 U.S. 214, 223–4 (1944), the Supreme Court concluded:

> Korematsu was not excluded from the Military Area because of hostility to him or his race. He was excluded because we are at war with the Japanese Empire, because the properly constituted military authorities feared an invasion of our West Coast and felt constrained to take proper security measures, because they decided that the military urgency of the situation demanded that all citizens of Japanese ancestry be segregated from the West Coast temporarily, and finally, because Congress, reposing its confidence in this time of war in our military leaders – as inevitably it must – determined that they should have the power to do just this. There was evidence of disloyalty on the part of some, the military authorities considered that the need for action was great, and time was short. We cannot – by availing ourselves of the calm perspective of hindsight – now say that these actions were unjustified.

That decision of the Supreme Court is today generally recognised as a low watermark of the jurisprudence of the Court in the area of human rights. Many years later in 1988, the first President Bush apologised for that action and offered reparations to the survivors.

Overreacting to war-time danger and fears is by no means peculiar to the United States and similar actions have been taken in other major democracies. In England, the House of Lords deferred ingloriously to the Executive in *Liversage v Anderson*, [1942] A.C. 206. Defence Regulation 18B provided that the Home Secretary might order a person to be detained if 'he has reasonable cause to believe [the] person to be of hostile origin or associations' (Ibid. at 207). Four of the five Law Lords held that it was sufficient for the Home Secretary to 'think' he had good cause (Ibid. at 225). The decision was wholly subjective and therefore not capable of judicial review. Lord Atkin dissented holding that, on a proper interpretation of the statute, the Home Secretary was required to have reasonable grounds for detention (Ibid. at 226). He said that 'amid the clash of arms the laws are not silent' (Ibid. at 244). He added that judges should not 'when face to face with claims involving the liberty of the subject show themselves more executive minded than the executive' (Ibid.). In later years, Lord Atkin's view prevailed[2]. The position was succinctly articulated by Lord Steyn, a member of the Judicial Committee of the House of Lords[3]:

> The theory that courts must always defer to elected representatives on matters of security is seductive. But there is a different view, namely that while courts must take into account the relative constitutional competence of branches of government to decide particular issues they must never, on constitutional grounds, surrender the constitutional duties placed on them.

That is the approach which the United States Supreme Court has now adopted in response to the efforts of the Bush Administration to place itself above the law and indeed the Constitution.

The Rule of Law

I turn now to consider more directly the effects of combating terrorism in this and other democracies. In this debate, it has become a kind of mantra to express support for the duty on governments to take every reasonable step to protect the lives of their citizens and to prevent and punish human rights abuses both by domestic criminals and by non-state actors and especially terrorists.

The tension between protecting the state and upholding civil liberties is nothing new and this and many other states have had to grapple with it over the centuries. It is no problem for oppressive societies which, by definition, do not respect the civil rights of their citizens. They have all the machinery they might need to put down attacks from within and outside their borders. The problem is peculiarly one for democratic states.

The issue is the extent to which the rule of law is to be respected and allowed to protect people from arbitrary power. According to Professor Archibold Cox, it was 'the genius of American constitutionalism, which supports the Rule of Law' (1987: 27).

One principle of the Rule of Law has become universally accepted since it was first enunciated by Professor A. V. Dicey in 1885: "A man may with us

---

[2] *Nakkuda Ali v. Jayaratne*, [1951]AC 66.
[3] The Twenty-Seventh F. A. Mann Lecture delivered at Lincoln's Inn Old Hall on November 25, 2003.

be punished for a breach of the law but he can be punished for nothing else" ([1885] 1973: 202).

No less controversial is the presumption of innocence in all criminal prosecutions. Guilt by association and collective guilt are inconsistent with a free and democratic society. So, too, the right of trial before an independent court. To the extent that these rights need to be limited during times of war, if at all, the limitation should be only to extent absolutely necessary to achieve a legitimate government interest.

The important provisions of the 1966 International Covenant on Civil and Political Rights came into effect in 1976. In the following year, President Carter requested the Senate to ratify the Convention. A statement by Robert Owen, the legal advisor in the State Department read in part as follows:

> ... the primary objective in the fostering of international commitments to erect and observe a minimum standard of rights for the individual as set forth by the treaties. This standard is met by our domestic system in practice, although not in precisely the same way that the treaties envision. By ratification we would commit ourselves to maintain the level of respect we already pay to the human rights of our people; we would commit ourselves not to backslide, and we would be subjecting this commitment to and our human rights performance as a whole to international scrutiny.

The Senate did not agree to ratify the Convention. It was only in 1991, at the request of the Administration of the first President Bush, that the United States ratified the Convention. When he submitted the Convention for advice and consent, President Bush stated:

> The end of the Cold War offers great opportunities for the forces of democracy and the rule of law throughout the world. I believe that the United States has a special responsibility to assist those in other countries who are now working to make the transition to pluralist democracies ... United States ratification of the Covenant on Civil and Political Rights at this moment in history would underscore our natural commitment to fostering democratic values through international law ... U.S. ratification would also strengthen our ability to influence the development of appropriate human rights principles in the international community (International Legal Materials 1991).

Another United States president said this:

> America will always stand firm for the non-negotiable demands of human dignity: the rule of law; limits on the power of the state; and respect for women; private property; free speech; equal justice; and religious tolerance.

That was President George W. Bush in his 2002 State of the Union Address[4].

---

[4] Delivered January 29, 2002. Available at: http://www.state.gov/r/pa/ei/wh/rem/7672.htm.

The ambiguity in the policy and practice of the United States with regard to the protection of civil liberties, both in times of peace and war, must be acknowledged. There is a common tendency in human rights circles to concentrate only on the negative aspect of this policy. This is neither fair nor productive.

On the other side there have been disturbing developments inconsistent with these clear expressions of principle. The most worrying developments concern the extent to which the present Administration is acting and being allowed by Congress to act in ways quite inconsistent with the Rule of Law:

a) Keeping detainees indefinitely on Guantanamo Bay;
b) Indefinite detention of illegal immigrants;
c) Secret deportation hearings;
d) Denial of legal representation to two American citizens being held on capital crimes;
e) Special 'military commissions';
f) Broad-based wire tapping powers;
g) Violating the privilege between attorney and client;
h) The serious abuse of prisoners in both Afghanistan and Iraq; and
i) 'Ghost' detainees held in United States prisons abroad.

Until the recent decisions of the United States Supreme Court, the response from the federal judiciary has been anything but reassuring. Some of their decisions have echoes of the *Korematsu* decision more than fifty years earlier. To all those around the world who traditionally look to the United States as the leader of the free world, it came as a great relief that the Supreme Court refused to allow the Bush Administration to proceed in the way it chose.

The despair of democrats around the world was demonstrated in the unusually strong criticism which came from Lord Steyn:

> The purpose of holding the prisoners at Guantanamo Bay was and is to put them beyond the rule of law, beyond the protection of any courts, and at the mercy of the victors. The procedural rules do not prohibit the use of force to coerce prisoners to confess. On the contrary, the rules expressly provide that statements made by a prisoner under physical or mental distress are admissible 'if the evidence would have value to a reasonable person', i.e. military officers trying enemy soldiers (Presidential Military Order of November 13, 2001, s. 4(3)). At present we are not meant to know what is happening at Guantanamo Bay. But history will not be neutered. What takes place there today in the name of the United States will assuredly, in due course, be judged at the bar of informed international opinion[5].

---

[5] See note 3.

We should also bear in mind the approach of the President of the Israeli Supreme Court, Aharon Barak, when violent interrogation was declared to be unlawful even if its use might save lives by preventing acts of terrorism. He said:

> We are aware that this decision does not make it easier to deal with the reality. This is the fate of democracy, as not all means are acceptable to it, and not all methods employed by its enemies are open to it. Sometimes, a democracy must fight with one hand tied behind its back. Nonetheless, it has the upper hand. Preserving the rule of law and recognition of individual liberties constitute an important component of its understanding of security. At the end of the day, they strengthen its spirit and strength and allow it to overcome its difficulties (2002: 148).

The Geneva Conventions

It is also disturbing that the manner in which persons detained on the battlefield are being held in violation of the Third Geneva Convention. This Convention, to which the United States is a party, provides that such persons are deemed to be prisoners of war. If that status is questioned by the detaining power, the presumption continues to operate until a 'competent tribunal' has determined their status. No such determination was made in respect of anyone held at Guantanamo Bay and all have been denied the status of prisoner of war. Notwithstanding the decision of the Supreme Court that all the detainees are entitled to question their detention before a competent court, there is doubt as to whether the tribunals chosen by the Administration are consistent with the order of the Justices.

What is of particular concern is that this violation of international law, binding on the United States, might well weaken the Geneva Conventions and be used to justify similar violations by other countries. Indeed, it might well return to haunt the United States if a *tu quoque* argument is used to justify similar treatment for captured members of the United States Army.

Is It Appropriate to Wage a 'War' against Terrorism?

The Supreme Court has also ruled that the Administration has acted in violation of the United States Constitution by holding United States citizens without trial and without access to a lawyer. In the recent past such conduct by other governments has earned the strongest condemnation from the government of the United States.

Part of the problem is the approach by the Bush Administration in using the analogy of 'war' in combating terrorism. Terrorism is not new and it is not a 'war' in the conventional understanding of that word. Terrorism is unlikely ever to end, and formulating a policy based upon a model of 'war' is only calculated to allow the government to regard anyone who opposes undemocratic means as unpatriotic. If the government fails to act within the law, it undermines its democratic legitimacy, forfeits public confidence, and damages respect for the criminal justice system.

The Effects of 9/11 in Other Democracies

Repressive actions by governments have been taken in other democracies. Prior to 9/11, the United Kingdom had enacted wide-ranging measures to counter terrorism. It did so predominantly in the face of the Irish Republican Army terrorist activities in London. After 9/11, a new anti-terrorism statute was enacted. Its most controversial provision provides for the internment, without trial, of a 'suspected international terrorist' if the Home Secretary reasonably believes that such person's presence in the United Kingdom is a risk to national security, and suspects that such person is a terrorist. If the person is not a United Kingdom citizen, he or she may be detained for an unspecified period of time without charge or trial. There is no appeal to the ordinary courts but only to a government-appointed commission. It was this provision that led the United Kingdom to derogate from the human rights provisions of the European Convention on Human Rights.

Similarly, the Indian legislation passed in the aftermath of 9/11 substantially invaded the rights of privacy and allowed for the detention of suspected terrorists without trial for periods of up to ninety days. When, a few months ago, a new legislature and executive were voted into power, the whole enactment was repealed by Parliament.

Post-9/11 draft South African legislation also made provision for detention without trial for periods of ninety days. After protests from leading politicians who had themselves been held under such provisions by the Apartheid authorities, the Parliamentary Committee on Justice caused these provisions to be removed.

Since 9/11, in a number of democracies, racial profiling and the detention of illegal immigrants from Muslim countries has become a common occurrence. This cannot be justified unless there is a factual basis that makes it both effective and proportionate to the perceived danger.

Disproportionate invasions of civil liberties, especially in the United States, are causing an unfortunate domino effect in other nations. It is being used to justify far more repressive actions. President Mugabe of Zimbabwe and Charles Taylor, the former head of state of Liberia, both relied on the United

States' classification of 'unlawful combatant' to justify wholly oppressive actions against journalists critical of their leadership. Leaders in Indonesia have talked about establishing their own 'Guantanamo Bay'.

The United Nations Security Council was also tardy in making an appropriate effort to ensure respect for civil liberties in legislation that member states were peremptorily required by Resolution 1373 to enact. Initially the attitude of the Counter Terrorism Committee was that human rights were not the concern of the Security Council.

The Future

When he addressed the Counter Terrorism Committee, the late High Commissioner for Human Rights Sergio Vieira de Mello said that:

> [Such] measures must be taken in transparency, they must be of short duration, and must respect the fundamental non-derogable rights embodied in our human rights norms. They must take place within the framework of the law. Without that, the terrorists will ultimately win and we will ultimately lose – as we would have allowed them to destroy the very foundation of our modern human civilization.

A United States commission of inquiry recommended, to no avail, that a non-partisan committee of Congress should monitor the invasion of civil liberties by the executive branch of government. I would suggest that all democratic nations should take precisely that kind of initiative. Such a committee should report on violations of their own constitutional guarantees and of provisions of international conventions to which their nation is a party. That kind of public oversight would unquestionably act as an effective brake on excessive and unjustified encroachments upon civil liberties. The fact of oversight is in effect the best deterrent against disproportionate and inappropriate invasions of human rights.

Politicians, by the nature of their occupation, are concerned to be seen taking action that is likely to be popular with their electorate. In that context, it is deemed to be preferable to take inappropriate or excessive action rather than none at all. And the greater the public fear, the greater the temptation to been seen to be active in defence of the people.

If citizens are vigilant, they can act as an effective brake against disproportionate and unnecessary invasions of civil liberties. A striking illustration of this is to be found with regard to the rules published in the Presidential Military Order of November 13, 2001. They provided for secret hearings by military judges who could, by a majority vote, impose the death sentence.

There was no provision for independent defence counsel and no appeal to the ordinary courts. They provoked widespread criticism and especially from the leaders of the legal profession and from human rights organisations. The result was that in March 2002, the rules were drastically amended and some of the worst features were abandoned.

Those who value the protection of human rights and the dignity of all people should remain vigilant in these difficult and worrisome times. They should assist those in authority who hold a balance between the necessity of protecting the lives of citizens, on the one hand, and protecting their fundamental civil liberties on the other. They must ensure that governments and their officials do not rely on repressive measures for no reason other than to placate the fears of popular prejudice.

There is reason for optimism. It is to be found in the reaction of the Supreme Court of the United States to the unmeritorious claim of the Bush Administration that in a time of war the president's actions remain beyond the reach of the courts. It is to be found in the widespread criticisms of the military in reaction to the photographs that came out of Abu Ghraib Prison in Iraq. It is to be found in the responses from some members of Congress to those events and the refusal to allow the blame to be laid at the door only of the lower ranks who are made scapegoats. Importantly, it is to be found in the opposition to these actions from within the United States military itself. I refer in this regard especially to the courageous and professional defences that have been pursued by military lawyers in cases against Guantanamo defendants.

There is similar reason for hope in the courageous decision of the Israel Supreme Court that found the separation wall in some parts of the Occupied Territory to be unlawful because of its devastating effects on Palestinians in the areas concerned.

There is reason for hope in the victory of the anti-Apartheid campaign that was instrumental in bringing down the unlawful white minority government in my country.

I would suggest that the post-9/11 setbacks for human rights will be seen by historians as an unfortunate detour and not a roadblock. The United States, as the sole superpower, has a special responsibility for shaping the world in the twenty-first century. It can only hope to establish an international rule of law and to encourage democratic forms of government if it sets a good example at home.

The United States has traditionally been perceived as the leader of the free and democratic world. That perception has become tarnished in the days since 9/11. This country has sought to lead by dint of its power alone. My fervent hope and wish is that it will regain its position of pre-eminence in the democratic world by leading by its traditional values and not by power alone.

REFERENCES

Barak, A. (2002, November). 'A Judge on Judging: The Role of a Supreme Court in a Democracy'. *Harvard Law Review*, 116(1), pp. 19–162.

Bush, George W. (2002, January 29). State of the Union Address. Available at: http://www.state.gov/r/pa/ei/wh/rem/7672.htm.

Cox, A. (1987). *The Court and the Constitution*. Boston: Houghton Mifflin.

Dicey, A. V. ([1885] 1973). *Introduction to the Study of the Law of the Constitution* (10th ed.). London: Macmillan.

International Legal Materials 660 (1991).

Korematsu v. United States, 323 U.S. 214, 223–4 (1944).

Liversage v. Anderson, [1942] A. C. 206.

Nakkuda Ali v. Jayaratne, [1951] AC 66.

Presidential Military Order of November 13, 2001: 'Detention, Treatment, and Trial of Certain Non-Citizens in the War Against Terrorism'. *Federal Register*, Vol. 66, No. 222, section 4(3). Available at: http://www.cnss.org/milorder.pdf.

8. Fair Trials for Terrorists?

GEOFFREY ROBERTSON

The title of this chapter, 'Fair Trials for Terrorists?', is oxymoronic. The trial of anyone already labelled a terrorist cannot, by definition, be fair. But the first casualty of war is always logic. The Pentagon's original brand name for its bombing of Afghanistan was 'Operation Infinite Justice', which makes no sense because human justice is both finite and fallible. It has to be fair, of course, otherwise it is not justice; and it has to be expeditious (see Magna Carta) and it should be effective, even if that today increasingly means 'cost effective'. This chapter argues that the justice we dispense to alleged terrorists cannot be exquisitely fair, but need not be rough. Above all, it must be justice that conforms to the definition our inherited Anglo-American traditions have provided; essentially, a genuine adversary process determined by judges who are independent of the prosecuting authority.

The acute problem we face is how to achieve fair trials for men and women who are demonized by the society from which their judges and jurors are drawn. In the United Kingdom, we have been trying terrorists unfairly for centuries, but at least they have been tried in courts. Whatever label is given to the proceedings in Guantanamo Bay, before 'special military commissions', they do not appear to be taking place in a forum that satisfies the generally agreed definition of a court, although they are proceedings of an adversary nature and are thus far being held in public. They are being heard by men who, for all their personal wish to be fair, are not judges with that quality of independence established by Parliament – yours and ours – in 1641. Until then, judges held office at the King's pleasure; now, the Guantanamo judges hold office at Donald Rumsfeld's.

Special military commissions are preferable, of course, to shooting captured enemy leaders on sight, or making them victim of what Cordell

169

Hull, the wartime U.S. Secretary of State, described as the 'historic accident'[1]. Just suppose that tomorrow, a mosque near Peshawer is surrounded by Pakistani and U.S. troops, and out of it walks Osama Bin Laden – with his hands up. The soldier who develops a sudden uncontrollable itch in his trigger finger causes an 'historic accident'. He will face a court martial at which he will be acquitted, and the world will breathe a sigh of relief. An execution without trial, of course, but can a fair trial for Osama Bin Laden be a prospect any reasonable person could relish?

There can never be a warrant for the cold-blooded execution of a surrendered terrorist. 'If you wish to teach the people to reverence human life', as John Bright said in 1850, 'you must first show that you reverence it yourself' (Robertson 1999: 103). Terrorism succeeds if it tempts us to abandon the core values of democratic society, such as due process and rights to a fair trial. But it is vital to understand the arguments in favour of 'historic accidents' and non-curial experiments like special military commissions, because they challenge us to provide a form of justice that can live up to that name but which is also workable, expeditious and effective. The Anglo-American system does not have a good record in trying alleged terrorists, be they Sacco and Vanzetti or the 'Birmingham Six', and some features from the developing international criminal justice systems might be borrowed to improve on that record. We may have to reconsider a few of our cherished rights, such as trial by jury. But whatever we do, we must try to try alleged terrorists fairly, simply because the alternatives are impossible to contemplate for any society committed to the rule of law.

The United States and the United Kingdom have a long history of trying terrorists, and some of it is a shared history. I make no apologies for going back to the seventeenth century, because that is where the Supreme Court's majority, in *Rasul v. Bush* (2004), found the map for *habeas corpus* to travel to the limbo island of Guantanamo. The 1600s began with Jesuit religious terrorism – those Catholic fundamentalists who tried to blow up Parliament. If you want to know how they were treated, go to the Tower of London today and see the racks on which they were stretched until they confessed. You can view Guy Fawkes' signature on his deposition before and after he was put on the rack, and you will notice how the handwriting trails away – at the end, he hardly had the strength to hold the pen.

---

[1] Hull said, 'If I had my way, I would take Hitler and Mussolini and Tojo and their accomplices and bring them before a drumhead court martial, and at sunrise the following morning there would occur an historic accident'. Minutes of Moscow Conference, November 1943, quoted by Hartley Shawcross, *Tribute to Justice Jackson* (New York Bar, 1969).

The Star Chamber of the Stuart Kings was too much for a new breed of religious fundamentalists, the Puritans. They left England for New England in their tens of thousands, in search of Winthrop's 'city on a hill'. Many came back in the 1640s to fight the civil war, not only for democracy and the rights of Parliament, but also for an end to prerogative courts like the Star Chamber and an end to the appointment of judges 'at the King's pleasure'. They won, and then they lost, and come the Restoration in 1660, the Puritan leaders were put on trial as terrorist fanatics at the Old Bailey for a crime in 1649 that had much the same emotional impact on Britain as September 11 had on the United States – the execution of Charles I, when 'the world turned upside down'[2]. This crime, said Charles II's Attorney-General, prosecuting at the Old Bailey, was hatched by fundamentalist Puritan preachers in Massachusetts, who sent over to England to carry it out men such as Sir Harry Vane, the state's first governor, and the Rev. Hugh Peters, a founder of Harvard University ('Account' 1660: 153).

Vane and Peters were convicted and publicly disembowelled. That was the penalty for terrorism, or treason as it was called then, but their courage in facing the ordeal was such that public sympathy started to swing behind them. The government's prisons were full of other republicans that it dared not put on trial. So what to do with them? They could not be detained in prison in England indefinitely, because of *habeas corpus*. So some smart but devious lawyer said, 'Why not put them on an offshore island, where *habeas corpus* won't reach?', and so they were imprisoned in Castle Orgueil in Jersey and on other island prisons. Thus Charles II provided George Bush II with the precedent for Guantanamo Bay, but as Justice Stevens explains in *Rasul*, it was such a deplorable precedent at the time that Parliament passed the Habeas Corpus Act of 1679 to endow the great writ with extraterritorial effect, and it applies today to provide the Guantanamo detainees with due process.

What is also important about this period in shared U.S./U.K. history is that during those eleven astonishing years when England was actually a republic, the basic rights of fair trial in the Anglo-American system were established. We owe many of them to a charismatic but incorrigible seditionist called John Lilburne, 'Freeborn John' as he was known and loved by the mob (Gregg 1961). He was the Michael Moore of his day and he provoked every government beyond endurance. He was first imprisoned by the Star Chamber for refusing to answer its questions, so when the Puritans abolished it, he appealed to the House of Lords which ruled that everyone had the 'right to silence' – he created

---

[2] The story is told in detail in: Geoffrey Robertson, *The Tyrannicide Brief* (Knopf, 2005).

the rule against self-incrimination. In due course he attacked Cromwell, who had him tried for treason, for the first time before a bench of independent judges and a jury of his peers. In that trial, he established the right to a public hearing – the open justice principle. He then insisted on his right to have the indictment translated into a language he could understand (English, because at that time indictments were in Latin). He then insisted that the prosecution provided him with particulars of the charge and an adjournment to study them. He stopped the practice of prosecutors conferring privately with the judges. He established the right of the defendants to be treated with some respect, to have pen and paper, to sit rather than to stand at the bar, even to relieve themselves when they had to – a chamber pot was brought to him in court for this purpose, and he shared it with his jury.

Above all, his acquittal by the jury, a rare event in treason trials, established in the popular mind, in England and in its colonies, an invincible and almost superstitious belief in the rightness of trial by jury. So much so that when the Stuarts returned with a vengeance in 1660 to disembowel these terrorist fanatics from New England, they could not bring back the Star Chamber, and they could not use Cromwell's special military commissions; instead, they had to afford all defendants trial by jury. For this reason, they had to work out how to rig the trials to ensure convictions, and they hit upon vetting the jury panel for loyalty to the King. They denied lawyers to the accused, they arranged for secret meetings between prosecution and judges, and they devised methods for judicial control of the jury, such as 'summing up' the evidence, that is, saying to the jury, 'well if that isn't treason then I don't know what is'.

The reason I have gone back to this time of a shared Anglo-American legal heritage is twofold. Firstly, as a reminder of the origins of certain of these non-negotiable fundamentals of a fair trial – for everyone, and especially for terrorists: open justice, judges independent of the prosecuting authority, equality of arms, right to understand the particulars of the charge, and so forth. (Later centuries add rights to counsel, to have the prosecution prove the charge beyond reasonable doubt and refinements of due process). Secondly, to show that certain rights have been entrenched for reasons that were not necessarily rational.

The rule against self-incrimination is one example. This rule is very valuable in protecting discombobulated defendants from being forced to talk to police immediately on arrest or during long periods of pre-trial detention. But where the prosecution has made out a *prima facie* case of mass murder, I have never understood why a court cannot draw a commonsensical inference, if the defendant declines to offer any explanation. It seems to me that the rights of victims, which have for so long been overlooked in our criminal law, in fact demand that anyone credibly accused of murder, and *a fortiori* mass murder or crimes against humanity – should either explain the evidence away or run the risk of an adverse inference being drawn.

As for jury trial, it does not feature in any human rights treaty, and indeed there are some European lawyers who believe that anyone sentenced to life imprisonment has the right to have a reasoned judgement, rather than the one word verdict of 'guilty' from the jury foreman. In Anglo-American jurisprudence and in rhetoric, we salute the jury as the lamp that shows that freedom lives, but for every Lilburne and Zenger and Wilkes there are a legion of dissidents who have been convicted by prejudiced and pressured juries. During the nineteenth century, English juries always convicted in blasphemy trials and usually in sedition and treason trials – the British jury has a very poor record in protecting free speech. In terrorist trials in Britain, indeed in any trial where public prejudice runs strongly against a defendant, its record is not good. After 1973, when the IRA bombs in Birmingham took thirty young lives, the United Kingdom lived through twenty-five years of terrorism; thousands of lives were lost in Northern Ireland or the mainland. In Northern Ireland, where terrorists came from all sides of the community, juries were simply impractical. In England, where alleged terrorists were always put on jury trial, there were some very wrongful convictions. This had nothing to do with procedures – all the fair trial conventions were maintained, although there was some 'noble cause corruption' by overzealous policemen who doctored the evidence against those they believed (but could not prove) to be guilty. As a defence counsel in some of those trials, it always seemed that what was critical to wrongful outcomes was jury prejudice, against Irish defendants who sympathised with the republican cause. Together, of course, with the whole atmosphere of a so-called 'terrorist' trial, with police dogs in the court precincts, sharpshooters visible to the jurors on the roof as they go into court, the security checks and so on, all screaming out: 'these defendants are guilty, they must be guilty because this is a *terrorist* trial'. The point is that if you are accused of terrorism, your right to trial by a frightened and prejudiced jury may not be of overriding value.

Grand juries in New York have been handing down various indictments against Osama Bin Laden and his lieutenants, but imagine the international objections were he ever captured and put on trial here. A New York jury, literally twelve angry men, would be too emotionally involved in September 11 to consider the evidence dispassionately. Even if the trial were moved to Denver like Timothy McVeigh's, the events of 9/11 were so traumatic for American society that it must be doubted whether an impartial jury could be empanelled anywhere to deal with anyone accused of masterminding it. The verdict of conviction simply would not carry conviction in those remarkably many places where the opinion of the Saudi Home Affairs Minister, that 9/11 was some sort of Israeli conspiracy, is still credited. What is required in such cases is a carefully reasoned judgement, setting out incontrovertibly the evidence for guilt. Just as the judgement at Nuremburg confounded Holocaust deniers ever after, so the judgement on Al Qaeda and Taliban leaders already denounced and demonized by the Western media must be unimpeachable.

Then, inevitably, comes the problem of the death penalty, perhaps voted by a jury majority of 7–5, as in the Oklahoma bombing case. The spectacle of Bin Laden, spot-lit on a gurney, lethally injected in some amphitheatre large enough to hold the relatives of his victims who are entitled to be present, let alone all his own relatives, is almost too grotesque to contemplate. Executing Islamic jihadists provides the sentencing paradox of all times, because it gives them exactly what they want and most devoutly wish – in their belief system, a direct passport to paradise. The last thing they want is to end their life in a banal and uneventful manner on a prison farm in upstate New York. Besides, the death penalty has been firmly eschewed by most of America's main allies, and these countries simply will not extradite alleged terrorists for trial in the United States without firm undertakings that if convicted, they will not be executed.

For all the problems of jury trial, however, at least it is a true adversary procedure. There is an alternative procedure, announced in November 2001 by Vice President Cheney in respect of combatants captured in Afghanistan. 'They don't deserve to be treated as prisoners of war, they don't deserve the same safeguards as a normal American citizen going through the judicial process', he said. If convicted, 'They deserve to be executed in relatively rapid order, like the German saboteurs dispatched in World War II by a special military commission'. This model, the special military commission, had not been used since 1945, when General Yamashita was convicted, one of the few Japanese generals whom historians now tell us was innocent of the war crimes alleged against him (Robertson 2001: 502). It was a model rejected by Truman and Jackson for Nuremburg, and rejected by the United Kingdom when it was suggested for the Libyans suspected of the Lockerbie bombing. Today, there is a commission in session in Guantanamo Bay.

These commissions have been much vilified – described by the *New York Times* and other commentators as 'Kangaroo courts'. This is a description I dislike, perhaps because I am an Australian who grew up with these lovable marsupials and cannot imagine how their name ever came to be associated with instruments of injustice. But my real objection is that they are not courts at all. They are an extension of the executive power, a prerogative body as unacceptable today as the Star Chamber of the Stuart Kings was unacceptable, in the dawn of modern democracy, to Pym and Hampden and the Long Parliament. Although the procedures of the special military commission have been much improved since that original executive order of November 2001, the basic objection remains – it is not a court, it is a panel of five military officers, employees of the same authority that detains and prosecutes the defendants. It is now apparent, after the Commission's first hearings at Guantanamo[3], that only one member – the presiding officer, Colonel Brownback – is legally qualified. How did he get the job? Because, he explained, he is a close friend of the Major-General who is supervising the whole tribunal and who is head of the appointing authority that appoints the prosecutor as well. They are such close friends that they roasted each other at their retirement parties. Colonel Brownback, on whose legal ruling the fate of these defendants depends, admitted in answer to defence questions that he had let his law license lapse and he would need to take some continuing education courses before he could recommence practice.

Colonel Brownback is to be saluted for his candour. But he combines the role of judge and juror. He makes the legal rulings, then he participates with the other four officers in deciding the facts and bringing down the verdict, like a judge who retires with the jury. One of his four officer/jurors admitted at those hearings that he had been in charge of the logistics of bringing the detainees from Afghanistan to Guantanamo – rather like the prison guard who escorts the prisoners to the court, then takes a seat in the jury box. Another of these officer/jurors was the senior intelligence officer in Afghanistan, rather like an FBI agent who sits as a juror on a case brought by the FBI, having helped to generate the intelligence that led to the arrest.

These commissioners may lack the *appearance* of impartiality, but more importantly they lack independence. The appointing authority is a department of the Defense Department, which is responsible for selecting the prosecution charges and is supervised by the Defense Secretary. So, in effect, the Guantanamo panels are emanations of the Defense Department, the same Department which employs the prosecutors and the lead defence attorneys, all of whom are military officers and who have been imposed on the defendants, who will not, it seems, be allowed to defend themselves. They will be permitted to hire at their own expense private attorneys to assist those army lawyers imposed upon them, so long as those attorneys pass a security

---

[3] The following quotations are taken from Jess Bravin's coverage of the first week of hearings of the Special Military Commission which sat at Guantanamo Bay. See *Wall Street Journal*, 25 August 2004, and the following articles on 26, 27 and 30 August 2004.

clearance. Most unacceptably, communications between defendants and counsel will be monitored, so there is no attorney-client privilege. The prosecution can withhold evidence – even 'potentially exculpatory' evidence – from the lead defence counsel, even though he or she will be an army officer. At least there is the possibility of review by four respected civilian lawyers, but they do not form a court of appeal, and they are not required to hold hearings.

These commissions do not satisfy the fair trial standards in the Geneva Conventions and in other human rights instruments, and they will not be perceived by the rest of the world as satisfying those standards. A proper trial for the Guantanamo detainees is imperative, and it is regrettable that the decision has been made to put them through a process which is neither a court martial nor a jury trial. It is regrettable because it would have been so easy to call upon real and independent judges to do the job, much more expeditiously and effectively than military officers who for all their wish to be fair, cannot disentangle themselves or their appointments from the U.S. military authority that brings the prosecution.

In devising an acceptable model for a tribunal in which alleged terrorists can be tried, as fairly as possible in the circumstances, we can now draw on the experience of the war crimes courts which have been established over the last decade and which have been developing the new legal discipline of international criminal justice. A justice dispensed for political and military leaders accused of war crimes, usually in the form of state terrorism unleashed against their own people. These international criminal courts have shown that procedures can be devised to protect witnesses and to protect intelligence information whilst also allowing reasonable defence challenge. They have demonstrated that acceptable verdicts can be reached by international judges, some of whom are from Muslim countries, on men charged with mass murder and mass torture.

International criminal law is now dispensed by a number of ad hoc tribunals, made up of international judges, prosecutors and defence counsel. There is the ICTY in the Hague (for dealing with crimes against humanity committed in former Yugoslavia), and the ICTR in Arusha, Tanzania (for the Rwandan genocide). A somewhat different model, the Special Court for Sierra Leone, on which I sit as an appeal judge, has a minority of judges and lawyers appointed by the country's government, working together with a majority appointed by the United Nations: it is tasked with bringing to justice those who bear the greatest responsibility for the atrocious ten-year war which ended in 2002. The Khmer Rouge genocide in Cambodia may soon be subject to a similar retributive process – a quarter century too late, but better late than never. The International Criminal Court is now up and running.

There is no reason to be starry-eyed about the justice these courts are dispensing: it is excruciatingly slow and unacceptably expensive and there have been examples of serious inefficiency and even corruption. The U.S. government's refusal to contemplate an international tribunal or indeed any court at all, for the Guantanamo detainees and the "playing card suspects" in Iraq, is understandable on these grounds, which are infuriating to supporters of international criminal justice as well. But the reasons for these failures are being addressed: commentators have variously attributed them to diplomatic hostility, to U.N. bureaucracy, to nepotistic appointment systems, to some judges who are too slow or simply want to stay in office for as long as possible; to overzealous prosecutors who overload indictments; to defence lawyers who spin out trials and 'fee split' with defendants and their families; to non-governmental organizations (NGOs) which insist on elaborate and unnecessary protections for the accused. Such issues can, where appropriate, be dealt with, although international sensitivities must be overcome.

What needs to be emphasised is just how new the experiment is. Nuremburg was a 'one off': the twenty-three defendants were charged, tried and convicted within a year, because Germany was under allied occupation and the German people had turned against the Nazis – the three acquitted defendants could not be released for fear that they would be lynched. Moreover, as Justice Jackson explained, the trial owed its success to the ready availability of incriminating documentary evidence, as a result of 'the teutonic habit of writing everything down'. There are no 'night and fog decrees' printed in Sierra Leone or Kosovo or East Timor – evidence comes much more painstakingly there, through informers and inferences from mass graves.

Individual criminal responsibility is new and its exponents must be given time to sort themselves out. A good job is being done so far with the jurisprudence but much less so with court management. And there are serious problems with procedure, as the Milosevic trial has so painfully demonstrated. What has to be remembered is that in national courts, persons accused of crime – and they are very often criminals – will accept the court and play the justice game in the hope of a legitimate acquittal because their lawyer establishes, for example, that the prosecution has failed to discharge the burden of proof. In war crimes cases, however, some defendants will depict themselves as victims of 'victor's justice' and will want nothing more than to destroy the court or at very least to conduct propaganda for their cause from the dock – the danger Winston Churchill feared from putting Hitler on trial. Judges, programmed to give fair trial to defendants who play by the rules of the game, can be bemused when confronted with defendants who do not believe that the game should be played at all and whose agendas will be – sometimes openly, sometimes not – to sabotage the playing field.

How do you give fair trial to a person who does not accept your right to try him? That has been a problem every since our republican ancestors brought Charles I to trial on charges of tyranny – in effect, the charge against Saddam Hussein. They set up a special court, but the King refused to recognise it: 'By what authority am I called hither?' He would not put up a defence or even enter a plea – so they convicted him according to the law of the time and made him a martyr who returned, in the form of his son, to have the judges disembowelled eleven years later. At Nuremburg, Herman Goering at first decided to follow the King Charles gambit: he called all the defendants together and instructed them to say only three words to the court – a catch cry of one of Goethe's warrior heroes, loosely translated as 'kiss my ass'. It was probably the prospect of seizing the opportunity to make their excuses to posterity that changed the defendants' minds: they played the adversary game, attracted by the fairness of its rules (at least, by comparison with those applied in Nazi courts) and by so doing gave the Nuremberg trial its enduring credibility as a justice procedure.

Milosevic, however, has tried to have it both ways: he denounces the court as having no authority over him, yet instead of staying in his cell and confining his appearances to contesting the jurisdiction (the tactic of King Charles) he struts and frets his hour – regrettably, his years – upon the stage. The court has bent over backwards to be fair to him – by providing no less than three distinguished *amici* to take all available points, as well as permitting him to self-defend at inordinate length. Despite his high blood pressure, this defendant has insisted upon his right of self-defence, a course which has – as he must have known – aggravated his medical condition such that the court has lost sixty-six full hearing days and has had numerous early adjournments, even before it had to resort to a three-day trial week and then allow six months to elapse after the close of the prosecution case so that the defendant could rest before his opening statement.

In hindsight, it may be thought that the court has been overindulgent to this defendant – certainly it has allowed him to dictate delays that would never be tolerated in a national court. With hindsight, again, the court may have been mistaken to combine the three indictments, relating to his command responsibility for ethnic cleansing respectively in Kosovo, Croatia and Bosnia – into one big indictment, which means the trial may last for five years. Certainly it was a mistake, for a trial of even half this length, not to make provision for an alternate judge (there were four of them at Nuremburg) in case one of the three trial judges became incapacitated. Sadly, the presiding judge, Richard May, died in mid-trial and was replaced by a jurist who had to read up on the past two years of prosecution evidence from the transcript – an obviously unsatisfactory expedient, but preferable to starting the trial all over again.

Milosevic's health problems were so disruptive that the court eventually imposed counsel upon him, directing one of the *amici* to take that position, against the defendant's wishes and without the defendant's instructions or cooperation. The Appeals Chamber endorsed the defendant's right to represent himself, but as a qualified right which should not be permitted persistently to obstruct the proper and expeditious conduct of the trial. The trial chamber order had relegated Milosevic to a subsidiary role but the Appeals Chamber insisted that he must be permitted to take the lead in presenting his case, for example, by questioning witnesses and making any motions he wished, relying on imposed counsel only to avoid unnecessary delays (ICTY 2004). Whether this compromise will work, in the case of a defendant who has exercised his right of self-defence with such damage both to himself and to the trial process, remains to be seen.

These problems with the Milosevic trial do not show that fair trials for state terrorists are impossible, but rather that international justice is in its very early and rudimentary stages. That trial is part of a learning process and we still have to learn how to respond to the defiant gage thrown down by Charles I. In the case of non-cooperative defendants, and/or those whose agenda is to destroy the whole process, fairness has its limits – or rather must be balanced by fairness to the victims of the alleged crimes who have rights as well, and by the imperative of upholding the rule of law. My own view is that persons who are indicted for crimes against humanity by independent prosecutors and who are committed for trial by independent judges must be required to take that trial unless they are terminally ill or utterly incapable of giving instructions. If they refuse to acknowledge the court or to plead or to participate, then they should forfeit the right to adversary proceedings and should be tried by an inquisitorial process used in many continental countries and throughout South America, where a judge conducts an investigation irrespective of the cooperation of the defendant and reports to a trial court at which the conclusions may be challenged (or not) by the defendant. If a defendant accepts an adversary trial he is entitled to defend himself, but if by so doing the consequence is persistent delay and disruption, the court should have the power (subject to appeal court direction) to turn itself into an inquisitorial bench of 'examining justices' to investigate whether the defendant is guilty and to present a report on that question to another trial chamber.

This is not a perfect solution and the 'inquisitorial' or public enquiry alternative would need to be carefully worked out, but it would ensure that defendants do not hold the court hostage by refusing to cooperate or by insisting on self-defence in circumstances where they put their health at risk and disrupt the proceedings in consequence. It would also end the professionally unpalatable position of counsel forced to represent someone who does not want to be represented – by them or by anyone else. The approach is essentially that of carrot and stick: the adversary trial procedure as developed by Anglo-American jurisprudence offers the best guarantees for the rights of defendants but only if they accept that jurisdiction and the rules of the court. If they refuse all cooperation or offer it in a form which entails persistent disruption, they will be made subject to an inquisitorial process whether they like it or not – a process which passes the fairness muster in many countries of the world and which does not depend on the defendant's involvement (although obviously benefits from it). Making these two quite different models alternatives, rather than merging them discordantly as the ICC system tries to do – for example, by involving judges in approving investigations and by allowing counsel to appear for victims – may well be the best way forward.

Whatever happens to the ongoing trial of Slobodan Milosevic, it is the trial of Saddam Hussein that the world awaits. That is particularly an American responsibility, shared to a lesser extent with the United Kingdom, but it is crucial to get it right. There is not much chance of it happening while Iraq remains in a state of civil war, but there are fifty defendants charged with international crimes, to be put through a process which must satisfy international standards. The simplest way of doing that is to involve international judges and prosecutors and defence lawyers, working alongside their Iraqi counterparts – a court modelled on the Sierra Leone tribunal, perhaps. At any event, it will be crucial to support this process: whether you agree with the Iraq invasion or not, you must surely support a fair and effective trial for members of a regime widely accused of genocide and terrorism against ethnic groups like the Kurds and the marsh Arabs. Genocide has, more recently, raised its intolerable head in Darfur. There is a court established by the United Nations to deal with such cases and the ICC is ready to do so now the Security Council has made a reference. The mass killings in Darfur have been described by both Congress and Colin Powell as genocide, and that engages an obligation under the Genocide Convention (ratified post-Bitburg by President Reagan) to punish them. It is pleasing that U.S. hostility to the ICC was not allowed to frustrate international efforts to bring justice to the Sudan, given the lack of any other available tribunal.

In prognosticating the future, I do not see their hostility as permanent although it will only materially melt once international trial processes show themselves to be capable of dealing with defendants effectively and cost effectively. That will take some more years of (quite literally) trials and errors, with attention focused on streamlining procedures – a somewhat complex subject – and improving the quality and mindset of lawyers involved in those procedures – a delicate and embarrassing task which has yet to be squarely confronted. It may perhaps be said – I hope not too optimistically – that the case for international justice has been conclusively established and there has been a momentum to the jurisprudence which has now settled the core elements of international crimes. What must next be done, and it will be a long slog, is to reform the delivery systems, the procedures and personnel, so that future trials of political and military leaders who have deliberately breached international law may be confidently expected. There is nothing wrong with 'victor's justice' so long as it means bringing victors to justice if they have committed atrocities, as well as their defeated enemies.

As long ago as 1937, the League of Nations proposed an international criminal court for terrorist offences. Now we have one, but it is a court to which the U.S. administration seems implacably opposed, although to its credit it has been very supportive of ad hoc courts like the ICTY and the Special Court for Sierra Leone. I do not want to revisit the debate over the ICC, but rather pose these questions: Given that ad hoc tribunals are acceptable to try political leaders for international crimes of mass murder, why are they not acceptable to try international terrorists on the same charge? For the Guantanamo Bay detainees, why not opt for a tribunal that the countries where they come from – including the United Kingdom and Australia – can accept? What is *lost* by having an independent tribunal rather than a special military commission? What makes anyone think that the verdicts are going to be different, in any significant respect? Is the bottom line answer that the military wants a panel that it can control and which will convict everyone it wants convicted, and fears that an independent court may acquit a few of those people because of lack of evidence? If that is what it all boils down to, what sort of example is being set for respecting the rule of law?

I raise these questions with some diffidence. It has become evident that in Guantanamo, the commissioners, as well as the prosecution and defence lawyers, are making the best of a difficult brief. Moreover, special commissions are at least a form of adversary process. There are many who would deny any process at all to those believed to be major terrorist operatives. Bill Clinton claims to have authorised, secretly, a CIA assassination of Bin Laden after the Embassy bombings in Nairobi in 1998. No doubt such authorisation is still in force, and it might perhaps be justified in the case of hot pursuit, but not in the event of surrender or capture. The case for executing captured enemy leaders was made memorably by Winston Churchill, in his argument with Roosevelt and Truman over whether the Nazi commanders should be put on trial at Nuremberg. Churchill was implacably opposed to this trial, and argued that the top seventy-five Nazi leaders should be treated as outlaws, and face a firing squad as soon as they were captured. To give them a trial, he argued, would allow them to turn the dock into a soapbox, to justify their policies and to blame the allies. This was a historic debate between the British, who opposed any kind of trial, and the Americans who argued for due process. It was a deadlock, broken by the casting vote of Joseph Stalin, who loved show trials so long as everyone got shot in the end. He voted for the American position, and so Nuremberg came to pass (Robertson 2001: 228).

There are those who regard the Milosevic trial as partly vindicating Churchill's fear, and argue that Saddam Hussein and Osama Bin Laden should not be given the oxygen of publicity from an open process. But this ignores the fact that the nature of that process tends to demystify dictators and terrorists, by confronting them with evidence of the moral squalor in which they have operated, of their hypocrisies and cruelties, and of the barbarous results of their rhetoric and theology. Any cult status they may have acquired will dissipate over months of evidence about their *mens rea* for the commission of crimes against humanity. Far better, I think, to reduce their status in the dock, as they are seen listening to evidence of how they have engineered the killing of innocent civilians, rather than to leave the world with the last picture of their martyred body stretched like that of Che Guevara's on a mortuary table. Trials can have a cathartic impact in demystifying defendants who have appeared heroic to their followers, and in helping to deprogramme the deluded – although logic obviously has its limits in persuading religious zealots. But by exposing the inhumanity of terrorist leaders through a process which accords them the fundamental human rights that they denied to their victims, a standard may be set which will emphasize that international justice is truly international.

For that reason and even for the alleged mastermind of September 11, I would not balk at the prospect of giving as fair a trial as security considerations would permit. The best argument for that course is still to be found in the philosophy of Jackson and Truman, in their dispute with the British over the fate of the Nazi leaders:

> To free them without trial would mock the dead and make cynics of the living. On the other hand, we could execute them or otherwise punish them without a hearing. But undiscriminating executions or punishments without definite findings of guilt, fairly arrived at, would violate pledges repeatedly given, and not sit easily on the American conscience or be remembered by our children with pride. The only other course is to determine the innocence or guilt of the accused after a hearing as dispassionate as the times and horrors we dealt with will permit, and upon a record that will leave our reasons and our motives clear (Tusa & Tusa 1983: 66).

REFERENCES

'An Exact and Most Impartial Account of the Indictment, Arraignment Trial and Judgement of Nine and Twenty Regicides' (herein 'Account'). (1660, October 31). Trial of Hugh Peters, p. 153.

Gregg, P. (1961). *Freeborn John – The Biography of John Lilburne*. London: Dent.

ICTY Appeals Chamber. (2004, November 1). 'Decision on the assignment of defence counsel'.

Rasul v. Bush, 124 S. Ct. 2686, 159 L. Ed. 2d 548, 72 U.S.L.W. 4596, 2004 U.S. LEXIS 4760 (2004).

Robertson, G. (2001). *Crimes Against Humanity*. New York: New Press.

———. (2005). *The Tyrannicide Brief*. Chatto & Windus: London; Knopf: New York.

———. (1999). *The Justice Game*. London: Vintage.

Tusa, J. & Tusa, A. (1983). *The Nuremberg Trial*. London: Macmillan. Report, 1 June 1945, Jackson to Truman.

Wall Street Journal. 'As War Talks Opens, Legality Is Challenged'. 25 August 2004.

9. Nationalizing the Local: Comparative Notes on the Recent Restructuring of Political Space

CAROL J. GREENHOUSE

In the United States, in the aftermath of the attacks of September 11, 2001, the tensions between *security* and *civil liberties* have become iconic of the new state of affairs. At the same time, that very state of affairs, like the claim that "everything changed after 9/11" (as one often hears), is both a cause and effect of the normalization of the opposition between the competing demands of security and civil liberties. The normalizing element that is the main focus of this chapter is the oft-heard premise that the opposition between security and civil liberty runs to the very core of democracy – as if order and disorder were competing *interests*. The connection to interests hints at the more fundamental context of the discourse of democracy's trade-offs, and that is the conditions of executive power in the midst of globalization. Security and civil liberties are not inevitably opposed in themselves. Rather, their state of tension refers to the state of play among the institutional arenas associated with them: *security* stands in for executive power at the national level, and *civil liberties* stands in for the political grassroots. In this chapter, I suggest that the problem for democracy implied by the contradictions drawn between security and civil liberties is not first a question of values conflict, but of political conflict between national and local forums over the future of neoliberal reform.

In the United States, debates over the USA PATRIOT Act, military tribunals, Guantánamo, and Abu Ghraib, among other things, have conditioned us to assaying new federal powers, especially executive powers, against previous benchmarks of civil liberties guarantees. As already mentioned, that security and civil rights are necessarily at odds is in itself an arguable assumption, but in what follows, I am mainly concerned with what goes without saying in that framing. The discussions about trade-offs always start with September 11, 2001, and reach the issue of individual rights only indirectly, after "the terrorist" has been imagined as a personalized vehicle of a global threat. They inevitably end in a calculus stymied by the unknowns on the security side of the brief. Without gainsaying the reality of insecurity, I want to suggest that the political question is not how to leverage security against civil liberties (that question is one that responders and their supervisors must face, as a practical and immediate choice) – but rather in how the unknowns in the security scenario are politicized. Once the discourse of trading off is in play, the trade-off is always one way – strengthening executive power at the national level at the expense of local level political organizations.

For this reason, I leave to one side the question of *necessary* trade-offs, and instead focus on the contexts in which national leaders pose the question of trade-offs, and also on what they do with their widened powers *after* the trades. By a variety of channels and rationales, specific powers instituted as elements of the global counterterrorism tactics quickly normalize in other, wholly domestic, political currencies. Taking these effects into account both broadens and alters the context in which we might think about these issues not as "trade-offs" but as substantially different visions of democracy's futures.

This chapter involves three case studies developed around recent events in and between three members of the coalition: Spain, Italy, and the United States. As we shall see in each case, trading off meant trading *up*, in highly specific and often very concrete ways. These concrete realities look quite different than the usual abstraction with which the security/civil liberty question tends to be debated – but they have several points in common. In each case: (1) the war on terror has widened the democracy deficit already associated with globalization and neoliberalism (Aman 2004). (2) The iconic trade-off between security and civil liberties is the linchpin of a political realignment both within and across the main coalition countries – initially, at least, to the great advantage of the party in power. (3) The sharpest opposition to those new developments has come from the local level, rather than opposition parties within the national government. (4) Trade-offs are not limited to revisions of police tactics or criminal prosecution, but quickly reach more fundamental issues of national and transnational governance.

In what follows, I develop the country situations as a series of case studies, based primarily on my review of press reports from the United States, Spain, and Italy, since November 13, 2001 – the day of President Bush's order establishing military tribunals for non-citizen detainees in the war on terrorism. Taken together, the patterns in this real-time archive suggest that when we talk about trade-offs between security and civil liberties, we are in practice talking about the widening distance between national government and local political life. Trade-offs, once made, are consistently to the disadvantage of local arenas of political expression. In this sense, trade-offs cannot be recalled, even if specific orders are reversed or repealed. The very claims to novelty and globality that – almost by definition – characterize evocations of the post-9/11 milieu are in fact integral to the rhetoric that supports subsequent political restructurings. These dynamics are of concern in relation to this edited volume, because they both curtail people's access to institutionalized forms of redress, relief, and reform, and increase the risk of violence and other forms of disorder.

In the United States and the other main coalition partner countries, the most visible profile of change was a new degree (and in some cases new forms) of executive authority relative to broad legal developments that reshaped the political space. Yet, in the United States as well as in Spain and Italy, new powers acquired in the international security context were quickly put to use in the domestic context, primarily to promote a neoliberal social agenda and to contain grassroots opposition. In Spain, the war on terror crossed domestic terrain in a way that precipitated (but did not in itself cause) the banning of an opposition political party, with the resulting isolation of legitimate local political institutions. In Italy, the war on terror redounded negatively for unions and workers' rights. In the United States, containing opposition at municipal and state levels, as well as striking a blow to unions, have also been elements of the new context.[1]

Indeed, it is easier to see the war against terror as integral to what came before in light of its administrative and political aspects rather than as a military or policing operation.[2] The politics of the war on terror in the United States as well as (differently) in other coalition countries involve a range of contests along familiar fronts. In the United States, the lines of contention are drawn along older lines of debate over federalism, separation of powers,

---

[1] For example, during this period, the administration was implicated in the Texas redistricting controversy (see below) and in the 2003 mayoral election in Philadelphia – where an FBI "bug" was discovered in the office of incumbent Democratic Mayor John Street within a month of the election. Against FBI and Justice Department refusals to clarify Street's relevance to what they acknowledged as an ongoing investigation, voters returned Street to office – a result locally interpreted as a racially unifying backlash against what was perceived as Bush Administration attempts to co-opt a local election. See, for example, Acel Moore, "What the bug did for Street," Philly.com, November 6, 2003. http://www.philly.com/mld/inquirer/news. For details, see daily reporting in the *Philadelphia Inquirer* from the time the device was discovered (on October 7, 2003) through November 6, 2003.

[2] In the four main coalition countries (including the United Kingdom), immigration has also been intensively (and negatively) politicized, with obvious potential for human rights concerns. I set that issue aside, because my own main concern in this chapter is less with the human rights issues involved in a state of emergency, than with the potential for crisis as situations of emergency are selectively normalized.

sovereignty, and globalization. In Spain and Italy, too, it has produced conditions under which grassroots democratic organizations – local political parties, unions, as well as spontaneous citizen action – face new challenges from "above."

As suggested above, the war on terror both depends on and intensifies the democracy deficit in globalization and – in specific ways in the European context – in relation to European government. By "democracy deficit," I mean the unmooring of national executive leadership from grassroots political organizations such as local parties, unions, and citizens' movements. The war on terror depends on the democracy deficit in the sense that the popular opposition to the war in Iraq would have precluded the international effort if the leaderships in the main coalition partner countries had been held fully to account politically for their positions in support of President Bush. Yet we certainly cannot say that the war on terror has caused the democracy deficit. In each country, certain political organizations associated with opposition (whether parties, unions, or citizens' movements) were already under intense pressure from the national administration's party. This dimension is most readily visible in the case of Spain.

Spain

A week or so after President Bush's Military Order, Judge Baltasar Garzón (in the Ministry of Justice) announced that Spain would not extradite its eight detainees suspected of aiding the attacks of September 11, 2001. Most EU countries do not extradite to the United States without assurances that prosecutors will not seek the death penalty, but in this case, the bar to extradition was the military tribunal – "special courts" being constitutionally barred in Spain (see Bumiller 2001; Dillon 2001; Dillon & McNeil 2001; Stout 2001; Vitzthum & Shishkin 2001). The United States had not made an extradition request, but the announcement drew attention in the United States as offering the makings of a diplomatic contretemps over the president's preemption of jurisdiction (and judicial powers) over detainees. Within a few days, President Aznar visited President Bush in Washington, D.C., where the news coverage focused on their mutual expressions of admiration and support, and their cooperation in the war on terrorism. President Aznar, responding to questions, gave assurances that an extradition request would be considered, and that both countries looked forward to cooperation along this and other lines. The most public first result of this pledge seemed to come on January 16, in Aznar's inaugural address to the European Parliament as president of the EU. To a lukewarm reception, Aznar urged the body to put the war against terrorism at the top of its agenda, offering numerous proposals, including closer coordination with the United States and Russia (Yarnoz 2002).

The Spanish government's position on the prosecution of terrorists had been honed in the course of years of effort to bring an end to the activities of the ETA, the militant Basque separatist group. In that context, the issue of jurisdiction over detainees between the governments of Spain or the Basque Country is strongly contested with respect to Basque prisoners held in the Canary Islands and other locations far from the Basque Country. Families of those detainees have long protested their separation, demanding repatriation and local trials. The block to U.S. extradition can be read alongside this longer story of struggle over jurisdiction.

But the physical location of prisoners is only one element in that story. The larger strategy on the part of the Aznar administration involved pressing the Basque political parties to break with the Batasuna (formerly Herri Batasuna), the political arm of the ETA – and in the process, co-opting the local Basque parties so as to align them with the parties of the national government. (The Basque Country is an autonomous region with its own parliament and political parties.) In this sense, the story begins not in September, 2001, but in August, 2000, when the ETA broke its cease-fire and resumed a campaign of terror in the Basque Country, Barcelona, and Madrid. Since that time, the moderate Basque nationalist parties – Basque Nationalist Party and the Basque Country Socialist Party – have been under intense pressure by Spain's national parties to condemn the ETA, even while they make their own efforts in increasing isolation to support the nationalist cause on democratic grounds while bringing an end to the violence (*Le Monde* 8 June 2002).

The local parties cast the government's strategy as opportunism – a tactic for dividing the Basque left and for sweeping the fragments of the regional parties into the national parties. But at least initially, Aznar's campaign was highly popular nationally. The national government's moves against Batasuna became progressively more concrete. On November 18, 2001, the ruling party (PP) and the major opposition party (PSOE) agreed to keep Batasuna off the European list of terrorists pending a domestic constitutional process banning the party (Aizpeolea 2001). This concession to the PSOE, which had insisted on the priority of a domestic constitutional process, did not prevent President Aznar from personally internationalizing the case against ETA and Batasuna. In an interview marking his Spain's EU presidency, President Aznar said that there was "no difference between the ETA and Osama Bin Laden" (Decamps & Leparmentier 2002). After the congress of the ruling party in early 2002, the PP was said never to have been more solid, disciplined, and powerful (Casqueiro & Ordaz 2002).

Parliamentary action led to passage of new legislation, the *Ley de partidos politicos*, in May, 2002, opening the way to the judicial process that culminated in a ban on August 26, 2002 (Daly 2002a).[3] Almost immediately, in a joint operation between Spanish and Basque Country police units – the joint operation being highly symbolic in itself – raided clubs, bars, and union halls held to be gathering places for ETA and Batasuna in the Basque Country and shut them down (see *El Pais* 28 August 2002, 'Auto de choque', 'El Gobierno de EE UU muestra su 'comprensión ante la medida'', and 'La policía vasca desaloga por la fuerza las sedes de Batasuna'; *Le Monde* 28 August 2002).

While the parliamentary vote was nearly unanimous (295–10) and the ban had widespread popular support, at least one major issue at the core of the debate was not settled by the outcome – and that was the character of the ban. While the PP and the PSOE united in their support of the legislation, they divided over its implications for democracy. On the one hand, President Aznar, like other leading members of his party, held that it was a moral question, outside of politics. "There is no political dimension," he said, "simply a need to crush the terrorists of ETA" (Daly 2002a). On the other hand, socialist members referred to the ban as "one more tool" (Aizpeolea 2002). But there were far more than two sides to this debate. For the new president of the *Audiencia Nacional*, magistrate Carlos Dívar, the criminal code would have been sufficient for dealing with terrorists and their allies (*El Pais* 5 December 2001).[4] The Basque *lehendakari*, Juan José Ibarretxe, held to the view that Basque nationalism is a political issue that transcends Spain, proposing to appeal to the European Commission to establish the Basque Country as an "independent associated state" (*El Pais* 11 October 2002).[5] In this context, the national government categorically rejected European involvement, and Juan Rodriguez Zapatero – praised by editorialists for his effective diplomacy early in the renewed Basque crisis of 2000 (*El Pais* 2 August 2000) – pursuaded Ibarretxe to stand down (see *El Pais* 28 August 2002, 'El Gobierno de EE UU . . . ').

---

[3] The ruling allowed elected Batasuna representatives and local councillors to finish their terms of office. Moderate Basque parties opposed the measure; communists and representatives of small parties abstained. The Galician nationalist party and members of the United Left (Communist) expressed concern over the prospects for deepening violence, while Aznar's party maintained that the party ban was a "moral obligation" (*Le Monde* 28 August 2002). On the Ley de Partidos Politicos, see http://www.elpais.es/temas/dossieres/leydepartidos/inex.html.

[4] The *Audiencia Nacional* is Spain's national criminal court; its jurisdiction includes all cases of terrorism.

[5] Separatists had long cast the Basque question as a transnational issue (see Gastaminza 2000).

At the same time, Aznar maintained an international campaign of his own against the ETA and Batasuna, through the European Parliament as well as in his dealings with President Bush (see Yarnoz 2002, January 17; Bumiller 2003, May 8; *New York Times* 24 May 2003). State Department spokesman Richard Boucher expressed support for the Batasuna ban in August, 2002, as evidence of a strong stand against terrorism: "This action was not directed against legitimate political activity or freedom of expression, but against the demonstrated ties that Batasuna maintained with the terrorist group ETA" (*El Pais* 28 August 2002, 'El Gobierno de EE UU . . . '). In May, 2003, at Aznar's request, the White House added Batasuna to the State Department's list of international terrorist organizations, and moved to cut off funds for Batasuna (see Yarnoz 2002; Bumiller 2003; *New York Times* 24 May 2003). Otherwise, international reaction was mixed. *Le Monde* and *The Guardian* were critical of the ban on democratic grounds; former Italian president Francesco Cossiga, pleading for a peaceful solution, condemned the action. Batasuna's lawyer and a member of parliament, Jone Goirizelaia, compared the ban to Turkey's 1993 banning of the Kurdish People's Labour Party for its support of the militant separatist group, PKK – an action that incurred censure by the European Court on Human Rights in April, 2002 (and thence reweaving into the scenario of U.S.-Turkey-EU negotiations in 2002) (*El Pais* 28 August 2002, 'Cerco judicial . . . ', 28 August 2002, 'El Gobierno de EE UU . . . '; *Reuters* 28 August 2002).

Writing for the *New York Times*, Tim Golden observed that the ban "mark[ed] an end to the policy of accommodation with more moderate Basque nationalists that Spanish leaders have generally followed since democracy was restored" after Franco's death. The ban radicalized the moderate nationalists who control the Basque parliament, and who now considered "seizing new administrative powers from the Spanish government, including control over prisons and social security" (Golden 2002). Critics' fears of deepening antagonisms seemed to be confirmed by the growing scale of public demonstrations against the ban, in the Basque Country and in Madrid – some protesters carrying signs in English and Euskera (*El Pais* 1 September 2002; Daly 2002b).

Meanwhile, the national campaign against the Basques continued along a broad front. In February, 2003, the government shut down a Basque newspaper alleged to be supporting Batasuna (Daly 2003a). In May, 2003, the Constitutional Court struck down 241 lists of candidates in the Basque Country, a total of some 1,500 politicians (*New York Times* 10 May 2003). In June, 2003, the Supreme Court dissolved Sozialista Abertzaleak – alleged to be the successor to Batasuna – freezing its assets, withdrawing public funds, and barring its representatives from parliament (Daly 2003d). Then, in July, 2003, in a dramatic play of the security trump card, Aznar sent the first of Spain's soldiers to Iraq without parliamentary debate, over the protests of the Socialist Party and some 80 percent of Spaniards polled (*New York Times* 12 July 2003).[6]

President Aznar and his party enjoyed very strong popular support in the year and a half after the break in the cease-fire with the ETA, but on the eve of the next round of local and municipal elections in 2003, his approval ratings had plummeted to 31 percent; 41 percent of Spaniards polled said their vote would be affected by the government's policy on the war (*New York Times* 24 May 2003). While the election might have appeared to be a referendum on the war, especially to outsiders (as will be discussed below), the Aznar administration had by then faced significant political crises on the domestic front – arising from an abortive attempt at legislating new immigration restrictions as well as policies against workers' rights, the latter precipitating a general strike in May, 2003. In the hindsight of this later context, the Batasuna ban and, perhaps even more so, the administration's lumping Batasuna with moderates (effectively withholding recognition of the main Basque Country political institutions) and the ETA with Al Qaeda came to be seen widely as signs of a failed anti-democratic policy (Grimond 2004: 5–7).

Taking into account the broader intersection of the war against terror and the Aznar administration's agenda in Spain and beyond, the outcome of that election accords with the dramatic expansion of popular opposition to the government's attempts to set the Basque issue outside of a domestic political framework – an attempt that proved to be a template for Aznar's commitment of Spanish troops and resources to the war in Iraq. It was precisely this attempt in parallel that the Bush Administration endorsed, and continues to support, in representing the Spanish electorate as having yielded to terrorism (discussed below). Such an interpretation misses the fact that since the earliest days of the crisis (in August and September, 2000), Juan Rodriguez Zapatero, as head of the PSOE, was a spokesman for ongoing discussion and open political debate. At critical junctures he moved effectively to support the local socialists as well as the moderate nationalist parties in the Basque Country, working to prevent the isolation of the PNV (the leading moderate party and the administration's main target). By May, 2003, the socialists led the PP in polls for the first time since 1996, thereafter winning a plurality in the regional and municipal elections (Daly 2003c; see also Henneberger 2001).

---

6 President Aznar and President Bush had implied that the U.S. moves against Batasuna were reciprocity for Spain's support of the U.S.-led war in Iraq (Bumiller 2003; Daly 2003b).

On March 14, 2004, PSOE regained the national government. Three days earlier, Al Qaeda had attacked the commuter rail lines of Madrid, resulting in massive casualties. Some analysts ascribe the PP's defeat to Aznar's aggressive efforts to pin the attack on the ETA in the hours immediately following the attacks. The Bush Administration put its own "spin" on the Madrid attacks, primarily by ascribing the election outcome to the attacks themselves, rather than to Aznar's immediate politicization of them. (For discussion of the latter, see Grimond 2004: 5–7). We return to this episode below, in connection with the U.S. presidential campaign of 2004.

Italy

The Military Order of November 13 joined a different chain of events in Italy. Europe had responded to the attacks on the United States with a proposal for a European arrest warrant. Meanwhile, Judge Baltasar Garzón – the Spanish judge who opposed extradition of Spanish detainees for trial by military tribunal – demanded the extradition of Silvio Berlusconi, Italy's prime minister, on tax evasion charges in 2001. Italy refused to sign onto the arrest warrant (Henneberger 2001). This situation precipitated a crisis.

The arrest warrant – conceived as a key weapon in the war against terrorism and pushed forward on an accelerated deadline – grants signatories powers of arrest in the other countries, obviating requests for extradition within Europe. Berlusconi's Justice and Interior Ministers objected to the list of crimes – which included (among other things) corruption, fraud, nuclear traffic and traffic in human tissue, and falsification of documents (*Corriere della Sera* 17 November 2001). Also at issue was a phase-in process that would have been retroactive, making Berlusconi himself vulnerable to arrest. The statute of limitations was ultimately renegotiated and, under pressure from the other fourteen countries, Italy signed the agreement in late November, 2001 (*Economist* 15 December 2001).

The crisis over the arrest warrant was a transitory conflict between Italy and Europe, but it was also part of a longer and deeper conflict within the government between Berlusconi and his Minister of Foreign Affairs, Renato Ruggiero, over Europe's role in Italian affairs. Ruggiero had actively supported the arrest warrant and other European projects, including the euro and the Airbus – both of which Berlusconi and others among his ministers resisted (and in the case of the Airbus, rejected) (Henneberger 2002a; 2002b). Berlusconi asked Ruggiero to resign on January 5, 2002, taking the vacant post himself – initially on a short-term basis and then more formally for a projected six months, to give himself time (he said) to accomplish his goal of reorganizing the ministry and reorienting Italy's relationship to Europe. He eventually served for eleven months, nominating Franco Frattini to the post on November 14, 2002 (*New York Times* 13 November 2002).

In his newly expanded role, Berlusconi announced a new national priority on small business within Italy, while retaining defense and foreign policy ties with Europe. A recent poll had shown Ruggiero to be the government's "most popular official," and the Italian electorate showed "overwhelming support for a strong Europe" (Henneberger 2002c). Initially conciliatory toward pro-Europe constituencies in the days following Ruggiero's departure, Berlusconi's tone quickly sharpened. "Nobody, I repeat nobody, can think they can put us under their control or worse still, treat us as a subject with limited sovereignty," he said in a speech to Parliament a week later (Henneberger 2002d).

As the war in Afghanistan yielded to the build-up to war in Iraq, and Secretary of Defense Rumsfeld chastised the "old Europe," Berlusconi compared Italy's position on Europe to that of the United Kingdom, "heavily promoting the idea of British-Italian-Spanish counterweight to Germany and France" (Henneberger 2002e). Two of his cabinet ministers took up this theme, referring to Italy, Spain, and the United Kingdom as a "counterweight" to France and Germany in the management of European affairs – and to Italy's determination to see fundamental reformulation of the European Union for the sake of greater national autonomy. In an interview, Berlusconi's Minister of European Union Policy compared his (Berlusconi's) defense of Italy's interests within Europe as the equivalent of President Bush's military defense of the United States (Ibid.). Berlusconi remained a strong advocate for the Bush Administration's preemption doctrine, suggesting that "a change in international law" might be necessary so as to facilitate future intervention "as exporters of democracy and freedom in the whole world" (Bruni 2003b).[7]

The crisis over the arrest warrant widened a gap within Europe as well as within Italy's political field. The rhetoric of the war on terror was useful as an idiom of personal leadership that appears to have suited Berlusconi's situation. But it is also the case that his opposition was in a greatly weakened condition due to internal divisions in the aftermath of Berlusconi's election in June, 2001, and this, too, gave Berlusconi increased room for maneuver (Heuze 2002; see also Tagliabue 2002). His first major policy initiative was a move to reform Italy's labor law so as to facilitate firings, to which anti-globalization groups and trade unions responded with strong opposition. In the midst of the controversy, on March 19, 2002, the ministry adviser who

---

[7] On the administration's position, see Slaughter 2003.

had drafted the new law was murdered. Police and press reports called the killing a political assassination, and a group affiliated with the Red Brigades claimed responsibility. Members of Berlusconi's governing coalition, however, blamed the unions for the killing, precipitating a massive demonstration against terrorism and the new reforms. A few weeks later, the leader of that demonstration, Sergio Cofferati, called for a general strike – Italy's first in over twenty years – on April 16, 2002 (Henneberger 2002f; 2002g; Tagliabue 2002; Szymanski 2002).

Throughout Berlusconi's tenure to date, his leadership has been dogged – but not damaged – by a series of criminal charges of corruption, litigation, and a series of legislative and executive maneuvers transparently aimed at protecting his ownership interests in Italian media as well as his other personal and family financial interests (Henneberger 2002c).[8] He apparently relished his role as president of the European Council as a vindication of his leadership and stature as a world leader, although he was unsuccessful in his attempts to broker compromise on a European Constitution (Bruni 2003a; Quinn 2003; *Economist* 2 August 2003; see also *New York Times* 6 April 2003). He made himself a vocal advocate of U.S. interests in the coalition against Iraq, including taking up the Administration's support of Turkey's bid for admission to the European Union (Henneberger 2002f; 2002g; Tagliabue 2002; Szymanski 2002). But above all, he has managed to maintain himself in office as Italy's wealthiest man while on trial for corruption, and his combination of anti-Europe, anti-union positions have so far kept the political field open between the anti-globalization left and the nationalist (anti-immigrant) right (Heuze 2002). His endorsements of the Bush Administration have been most robust at the junctures of maximum contradiction amidst these circumstances: the crisis over the arrest warrant, labor reforms, and the criticism over his term as EU president. Local and provincial elections in May, 2003, gave Rome to the opposition, but otherwise his governing coalition remained secure (Flamini 2003).

In short, in Italy, too, developments since November, 2001, show how new executive powers arise from both the institutions and rhetoric of the war on terror (most visibly the doubling of Berlusconi's roles as prime minister and minister of foreign affairs). This concentrated expansion of powers at the national level effectively widens the gap between national policy and public opinion as expressed through grassroots political organizations (in this case, opposition parties and unions). As in Spain, the United Kingdom, and the

---

[8] On Italy's response to the arrest warrant, see Fuchs 2003; see also *Corriere della Sera* 17 November 2001; *El Pais* 7 December 2001; Henneberger 2002a.

United States, this "space" – as mapped by public opinion polls and electoral results – enlarges the scope for personal authority (charismatic authority, in Weber's sense of the term) on the part of individual leaders, and opens the way to other structural changes in the political field in at least two ways. First, as we have seen, in some cases, opposition groups may come under direct attack under the rhetorical shield of the need for national unity in the interests of national security. Second, the new executive authority tends to divide (and benefit from the division of) opposition. In the United Kingdom, Spain, and Italy, the alliance with the Bush Administration has created a zone where government is both anti-Europe *and* aligned with globalization; internationalist *and* nationalist – and where inconsistency may be a political necessity. Similar labor reforms are contentious elsewhere, too, but in the absence of a connection to the war on terror, the political options for national leaders are substantially different.[9] Let us now turn to the United States, where broadly parallel dynamics played out within the government itself, and in relation to the presidential campaign of 2004.

The United States

In all of the major coalition countries – the United States, United Kingdom, Spain, and Italy – the administrative side of the war on terror extended and deepened what was already a marked evolution toward the concentration of executive power. The main effects in this regard include the enhancement of the personal power of the incumbent as well as the restructuring critical elements of the political field. Bush, Blair, Aznar, and Berlusconi gained new levels of executive authority in the security context, and – as in the war against terror generally – their programs projected "security" onto a broad horizon of economic and social interests. The coalition was – is – less a transnational partnership than a bundle of bilateral partnerships. This choreography allows leaders to portray themselves simultaneously as nationalists and internationalists – trumping (if temporarily) certain anti-globalization left and conservative right nationalist elements on their respective domestic political spectrums.

On the domestic front in the United States, the declared "state of war" (Military Order of November 13, 2001) has been consistently invoked by the Bush Administration as the grounds for new presidential powers (Heyman 2002: 1). But viewed from a wider context, the new levels of presidential

---

[9] For example, most recently, in Germany, where 70,000 demonstrators protested nationwide against cuts in unemployment benefits, on August 23, 2004 (Edmondson 2004).

discretion can be seen as continuing – and accelerating – the effects of dereg-
ulation and globalization that already tend to favor the executive branch (see
Aman 2004). As the United States pressed the leaders of the main coalition
countries to resist majority opinion at home in the build-up to the war in Iraq,
the breaks in those countries came along fault lines already carved by domestic partisan opposition over immigration, labor rights, and European Union.
While the specifics in each case are different, the patterns are similar. Italy and
Spain saw their first general strikes in over twenty years, as well as unprece-
dentedly large street demonstrations against the war. In the United States,
too, national security became the basis on which the administration barred
unions from certain areas of federal employment, and persuaded Congress to
grant advance authorization for the president to use military force in Iraq –
to cite just two examples.[10]

As for the connection between expanding executive powers and the
extended state of post-9/11 emergency, we shall see that in important respects
the institutionalization of the war on terror does not represent a new state of
affairs, but rather an intensification of specific effects of globalization on the
administrative state.[11] A decade ago, Martin Flaherty observed that "never
has the executive branch been more powerful, nor more dominant over its
two counterparts, than since the New Deal" (1996: 1727). This is the context
in which the new security scenario is now constructed as requiring yet further
executive powers (e.g., jurisdiction over the trials of detainees through military tribunals) and restrictions on civil liberties. The Bush Administration's
international campaign highlights the distinction between internationalism
and transnationalism, strong and weak states, states and non-states, as well as
the interpenetration of the public and private sectors, especially in contexts
where private entities carry out public functions (technical and quartermaster

---

[10] On unions, see Greenhouse 2002. On the Department of Homeland Security, see Fox News
     26 July 2002. Conflicts over collective bargaining continued, see Sullivan 2004. The president's
     interventions were not wholly anti-union. He intervened in the longshoremen's strike in
     Seattle, requiring employers to end a lock-out when contract negotiations failed in October,
     2002, on grounds of military necessity (Sanger & Greenhouse 2002). On presidential powers,
     see Fuchs 2003.

[11] For analyses of the effects of globalization on U.S. executive power since the New Deal
     era, see Aman 2004. Flaherty (1996) links the rise of executive power to the expansion of
     specific areas under executive branch control – the "colossal array of agencies" and the
     military – as well as an increasing tendency on the part of the Supreme Court to defer to
     presidential power, sometimes at the relative expense of Congressional power. Saskia Sassen
     develops a related thesis in more schematic terms – linking globalization to what she calls
     "de-nationalization." She emphasizes that denationalization does not signal the decline of
     "the national state *tout court*" (1999: 8), because some sectors of government are actually
     strengthened by globalization (Ibid. at 10).

services for troops, interrogations of detainees, security services for oil wells and pipelines, federalization of airport security in the United States, and so forth).

The militarized elements of the war against terrorism tend to overshadow the extent to which military and economic strategies are in fact deeply inter-twined – for example, in the National Security Strategy of 2002 and the Millennium Challenge Accounts, as well as in the mobilization of the coali-tion in the immediate build-up to the Iraq war (see, for example, Fuchs 2003). The Bush Administration's courtship of Turkey in the months leading up to the war on Iraq was perhaps the most explicit instance of the inter-play between economic, political, and military interests – as the United States coupled increasingly generous offers of aid with a bid to the EU in support of Turkey's petition for admission (among other things), in return for U.S. military bases on Turkish soil.[12] That effort – ultimately thwarted by critical opposition to various elements of the package by all three sides – also demon-strates the extent to new developments unfold along well-worn lines of inter- and intranational tension, as well as partisan debate in multiple national and local arenas. The failure of the Bush Administration to win Turkey's support for U.S. bases intersected with the paths by which the Erdogan and the Bush Administration came to power – but that is another story.

In short, while many American commentators seem to subscribe to the axiom that "everything changed" on September 11, 2001, it is increasingly clear that some things remained ongoing throughout the crisis. For the pur-poses of this cited collection, there is perhaps fresh insight to be gained in considering the war against terror less as a new state of affairs than as one ele-ment in a wider context in which the tensions between states and non-states, and between internationalism and transnationalism, were already significant political issues with far-reaching implications and pragmatic consequences. Indeed, from this standpoint, in all three cases, the war on terror did not intro-duce new conditions or consequences *sui generis*, but new political opportu-nities for dealing with essentially normal conditions. The new opportunities essentially involved a new discursive link between domestic and international political institutions, adding to what globalization had already revealed to be "multiple relations between territory and institutional encasement" (Sassen 1999: 2).

In the United States, further areas in which the war on terror can be fitted to a larger (and longer) context of partisan debate include the selective executive

---

[12] For a timeline of the negotiations anticipating the war in Iraq, see 'Chronology of U.S.-Turkish Relations: July 2002–January 2004' at http://www.washingtoninstitute.org./

preemption of judicial and legislative powers,[13] suspension of certain rights (habeas corpus, legal representation) associated with the criminal trial process for detainees designated "enemy combatants" (Weiser 2003; *New York Times* 8 January 2003),[14] federal authority over states, municipalities, and private entities,[15] as well as formal and informal checks on political opposition (see, for example, Wald & Schwartz 2004; Lithwick 2004; Shaffer 2004; Lichtblau 2003). While these developments are legally grounded in the war on terror, they may also be seen as political trump cards in relation to older, ongoing lines of partisan contest with respect to police powers and the rights of criminal defendants, federalism, and civil liberties. In the United States, an additional element of the backdrop is the ongoing project of redistricting to enhance Republican control of state legislatures, most famously but not only in Texas (Halbfinger 2003).[16] Here as elsewhere, then, the war on terror crisscrosses business as usual, making any question of its parameters and required trade-offs – not to speak of the institutional locations where such questions might be addressed – both pressing and elusive. In the United States, as in Spain and Italy, the sharpest opposition to the administration has not come from within the national government, but from local constituencies, "third party" political organizations, and grassroots movements.

This is the context in which I read the official U.S. "spin" on the Spanish elections as a partisan political intervention. Indeed, in the security scenarios I am describing, there can be no politically neutral interpretation of security risk, given the strong association claimed by incumbents between their administration's prosecution of the war on terror – and a corresponding assessment of terrorists' interests in removing the administration from power. The evolution of this claim into a totalizing logic of threat and counter-threat bears closer examination.

The Bush Administration's claim regarding terrorists' interests in the outcome of the U.S. presidential election of 2004 was made most explicitly, initially, in relation to Spain. In an interview just two days after Spain's election,

---

[13] The Military Order of November 13, 2001, gave the executive branch judicial powers. Congressional legislation on October 11, 2002, gave the president power to use "all means he determines to be appropriate" – including military action – against Saddam Hussein (Purdum & Bumiller 2002).

[14] For comprehensive summary of these and related legal developments, see Lewis 2004.

[15] Most notably in enforcement of the provisions of the USA PATRIOT Act, as well as in implementation of terror alerts (which involve mandates on state and local police departments, among other things). On local resistance to the USA PATRIOT Act, see Egan 2004. On terror alert status, see Shenon 2003.

[16] For details of the Texas controversy in October 2003, see *New York Times* 8 October 2003; Blumenthal 2003a; *New York Times* 12 October 2003; Blumenthal 2003b.

and only five days after the Madrid bombings, Deputy Defense Secretary Paul
Wolfowitz connected the two events:

> I just hope when the dust settles in the cool light of day that the Spaniards,
> who after all have a long record of courage, this is the land of bullfighters and
> matadors, that they will recognize that it would be a terrible mistake to reward
> terrorism. The terrorists went after Spain – I shouldn't say this, I mean assuming
> it's the al Qaida people, we read in their documents that they believe that by
> targeting Spain they would break up the coalition (CBS Radio 2004, March 16).

Speaking for President Bush the same day, Scott McClellan also referred to
the electoral outcome as reflecting the terrorists' intentions – though without the bullfighting caricature (Press Briefing 2004, March 16). The next day,
Vice-President Cheney, too, described the elections as a test of Spain's resolve
against terrorists (Cheney 2004). Editorialists took up the association (for
example, see Masterson 2004). In April, National Security Adviser Condoleeza
Rice took this association as a premise in her comments on the necessity
to brace for attempts by terrorists to influence U.S. elections – an opportunity "too good to pass up for them" (CNN interview 19 April 2004). On
May 28, 2004, Homeland Security Secretary Tom Ridge and Attorney General
John Ashcroft issued a joint statement, opening with the same premised link
between the Bush Administration's war on terror and a terrorist counterattack
in the form of a Democratic victory – the implied parallel to the situation in
Spain ('Joint Statement'). In early July, a background briefing by an anonymous "Senior Intelligence Official" sharpened the point: "Al Qaeda remains
committed to carrying out a full-on attack, series of attacks, in the homeland.
And recent and credible information indicates that Al Qaeda is determined
to carry out these attacks to disrupt our democratic processes" ('Background
Briefing' 8 July 2004). An unnamed questioner pressed the official for specifics
regarding the time and place of maximum threat, ultimately asking: "How do
you protect the polling stations?" (Ibid.). Responding, the official accepted
the premise that there would be threats against polling places, drawing the
connection between the United States and Spain (however, failing to note
that Spain's polling places were not targets). A questioner then introduced
the possibility of postponing elections for reasons of security: "Would you
postpone voting?"[17] Response: "That's a speculative question that I'm not
prepared to answer . . . And by the way, when you're talking about securing
an event that occurs on one day, very inappropriate for us to talk about the

---

[17] Earlier, Prime Minister Tony Blair was said to have decided to cancel the 2005 election in the
United Kingdom (Gilfeather 2004).

detail of that" (Ibid.). Asked whether the briefing was itself in response to new threats, the official seemed to back away, stating that "there has been a growing body of intelligence over the past several years...," but stopping short of claiming current threat data pointing toward the conventions or the elections (Ibid.).

This briefing appears to have precipitated a double-stranded news cycle for approximately one week (July 8–16, 2004), focusing on both the prospect of a new policy that would allow a federal agency to postpone the national elections, and the imminence of a security threat (presented as a newly informed reading of old information). On July 8, White House spokesman Scott McClellan was careful to distinguish between threat information and "our" growing understanding:

> Q: You said there is specific information but, in fact, when Ridge was asked about this today –
>
> MR. McCLELLAN: Not as to place, time, or location. But the intelligence that we are receiving is credible information that points to what Governor Ridge said, which was that we know that credible reporting now indicates that al Qaeda is moving forward with its plans to carry out a large-scale attack in the United States in an effort to disrupt our democratic process (Press Briefing 2004).

The briefing then moved on to other matters, but near the close of the session, a journalist returned to the question of election security: "Can the President today guarantee Americans that no terrorist attack can upset the U.S. elections this November, that they will go ahead as planned?" McClellan's response – "I don't think anyone can make guarantees" – made headlines the same day (Ibid.). A few days later, DeForest Soaries, Junior, head of the newly created U.S. Election Assistance Commission, publicly advocated a federal policy on electoral postponement, a proposal put forward in the form of a letter to Homeland Security Secretary Tom Ridge – said by *Newsweek* to have been forwarded to the Department of Justice (Isikoff 2004; see also *Reuters* 11 July 2004; *USA Today* 12 July 2004). Meanwhile, Homeland Security detailed its preparations for security at the Democratic Convention. The discussion of Spain and the news cycle on electoral security came to a sudden end on July 16, with the announcement by the Department of Justice that it had "no plans to examine federal laws or legal precedents to determine whether the Nov. 2 presidential election might be rescheduled because of the threat of a terrorist attack" (Johnston 2004). Condoleeza Rice denied that this had ever been an idea of the Administration's; moreover, Justice denied having received the letter Ridge claimed to have sent. "No one is thinking of postponing the elections," Rice said ('Background Briefing' 8 July 2004). Shortly thereafter, Secretary Ridge issued a heightened security alert, based on new readings of old intelligence, involving potential threats to New York City and northern New Jersey. This spin cycle drew to a close, subsequently morphing into debate over security issues in the campaign itself; however, by that time, "security" had been thoroughly politicized by the discursive maneuvers in the course of the spring and summer.

Conclusions

I draw five main conclusions from these case studies:

First, they confirm the insight of Cowan, Dembour, and Wilson: "Empirical studies offer [an] ... opportunity of exploring the ways that rights struggles ... involve political and legal institutions at different levels – local, regional, national, and international" (2001: 21). I take this to mean that human rights depend on the viability of political institutions at all levels of society, through which people are guaranteed access to both a diversity of responsive forums and meaningful political participation. The vulnerability of such oppositional grassroots institutions to the restructuring of executive power in the context of the war on terror is of primary relevance to the pragmatics of human rights, even where there has been no civic emergency, no terrorist attack, and no overt political instability. "Democracy," Julia Paley writes, "is not a single condition that countries do or do not have, but rather a set of processes unevenly enacted over time" (2002: 479).

Second, the case studies show that transnationalism is mediated and refracted by the politics *inside government* at the country level, as well as within countries more generally (e.g., as attitudes of Europeans toward the EU) and between them. In each case reviewed here, national leaders voiced heightened demands for sovereignty and transnational cooperation simultaneously, intensifying the domestic political focus on their personal leadership – and, for at least the first year of the coalition – keeping their opposition and smaller marginal parties off-footed. Each country is a distinct context in this regard, but in each case the gap left by the paralysis or fracturing of opposition yielded a new concentration of executive power, tending toward a restructuring of democracy: in Spain through the Batasuna ban and the delegitimation of the Basque Country's governing institutions; in Italy through the Berlusconi's multiple roles as prime minister, media mogul and minister of foreign affairs; and in the United States through the military tribunals, the preemption doctrine, and a tightening of vertical political alignments by a state-level redistricting campaign that long preceded 9/11.

Third, to the extent that human rights regimes tend to be imagined as supranational and extraterritorial, the case studies suggest that this view is not altogether accurate. The close-ups of how transnationalism "works" in domestic politics show that transnationalism is not necessarily an external intrusion into the space of the nation, but can also derive from entirely domestic origins, or be successfully domesticated within the domestic political space. In the contexts of these case studies, one striking point in common is the compression and reconstitution of national and transnational interests (and indeed, of the very categories "foreign" and "domestic"). In the examples we have considered, the issue is less one of how citizens and foreigners are treated relative to each other, than of how domestic circumstances may turn citizens into outsiders in the process of leaders' promotion of whatever interests they put forward as national imperatives.

In our cases, the main sites of compression appear to be at the zones where domestic political fields are divided over issues of transnational integration more or less across the left-right spectrum (as is the case in Italy and somewhat less so in Spain) (van der Eijk & Franklin 2004: 38, 44). Thus, Basques become outlaws and opponents of Berlusconi's labor reforms become "anti-European"[18] at the junctures where there are domestic political gains for Aznar and Berlusconi in their respective alliances with George W. Bush – effectively rearticulating their neoliberalism as anti-European, that is, co-opting the anti-Europe elements of the left.[19]

A further point along these same lines is that from a practical standpoint, transnational and domestic regimes are not separate (Sassen 1999); however, they may be metaphorically or symbolically (or even legally) rendered separate. A transnational human rights regime is no more "outside" the domestic political space than Europe is "outside" of Italy or Spain – or than globalization is "outside" Washington, D.C. The question would seem to be rather how domestic political contests work through the different registers afforded by these different institutions – and how politicians choreograph the symbolic line between the inside and the outside. The war on terror – given the emotional immediacy and physicality of terrorist threat – appears to have widened politicians' room for maneuver in this regard, against their political opponents at the grass roots.[20]

---

[18] The quotation is from an opinion piece by Berlusconi's labor reform adviser, Marco Biaggi, published shortly before his murder, quoted in Henneberger 2002f.

[19] How domestic political contests become arenas for addressing supranational issues or vice versa is not a well-understood aspect of European integration, in part because attitudes for or against integration do not correlate neatly along a right-left spectrum or in relation to specific interests or issues (Marks & Steenbergen 2004).

[20] A negative example of this scenario illuminates its fundamental structural dynamics: in the early weeks of the war on terror, high Macedonian officials kidnapped and killed several Albanian men, staging the murders as the deaths of captured Al Qaeda

Fourth, vulnerability to human rights crisis may arise from within a stable political process and within the democratic rule of law. In the contexts we have considered in this chapter, the loss of democratic access was produced by legitimate constitutional processes – while adding to both the risk and the actual quotient of violence.

Fifth, such destructurations of political access in and of themselves have the capacity to produce identities, cast them as marginal, and vest difference with political negativity (Comaroff 1996). The war on terror lent credence to the Aznar Administration's exclusion of Basque political parties (and the banning of Batasuna), and to Berlusconi's campaign to debilitate labor. Though they write in a somewhat different context, Cowan, Dembour, and Wilson's suggestion applies to these situations – to the effect that "legal regimes, including the human rights regime, dictate the contours and content of claims and even of identities" (2001:11). Processes of political compression and decompression are integral to constitution of collective identities, including cultural identities. If for this reason alone, "culture" should not be imagined theoretically as inherently opposed to state or transnational legalities (including human rights law). In many circumstances, state institutions are deeply involved in making the conditions that account for antagonisms between cultural or ethnic groups and the state. To the extent that cultural relativism "burdens" discussion of human rights (Messer 1993: 224), a closer examination of state processes, and in particular their articulation with local institutions, might be productive in illuminating how cultural opposition is overdetermined by fractures such as the ones we have been discussing, along the vertical dimension of political space. Anthropology's traditional reserve in human rights discussions (Ibid. at 221) is entirely consistent with its traditional lack of attention to states (including the role of non-state actors in governing processes).

The case studies show how vulnerability can be produced out of security, as well as how anti-politics can emerge from the midst of constitutionalism – in these cases, effects of globalization and neoliberal governmentality that are accelerated by the war on terror.[21] In sum, the case studies show where there is room to question the axiomatic assumption that civil liberties involve a necessary trade-off against security, because in each of the cases considered

---

"mujahedeen" – hoping to draw the West into giving it a "free hand" against Muslim Albanians living in Macedonia (Wood 2004). Elsewhere, too, the war on terror has become a means of settling old political scores.

[21] "Anti-politics" is Ferguson's (1994) term for the effects of international development programs on local systems of authority – borrowed here to refer to the dampening effects of the imbrication of national and transnational institutions (essentially involving the executive branch and non-state actors) on domestic political debate.

here, the new executive powers were not restricted to the security context, but relatively soon put to use for older and more familiar purposes – that is, the concentration of executive power and party political contestation at the national level. In practice, the tensions between liberty and security emerge not because they are inherently at odds, but because those terms encode an ongoing competition between central government and ground-level opposition. In Spain and Italy, and increasingly in the United States, political opposition is not over tensions between security and civil liberties, but rather over the preemption of the political process itself by the party in power when it equates political opposition with support for terrorism, turning it into grounds for disqualification.

REFERENCES

Aizpeolea, L. R. (2001, November 19). 'El Gobierno y el PSOE pactan no incluir aun a Batasuna en la lista terrorista de la UE'. *El Pais*.

———. (2002, May 23). 'PP y PSOE admiten que ignoran las consecuencias de ilegalizar a Batasuna'. *El Pais*.

Aman, A. C. (2004). *The Democracy Deficit: Taming Globalization with Law Reform*. New York: New York University Press.

'Background Briefing by Senior Intelligence Officials'. 8 July 2004. http://www. dhs.gov/dhspublic/interapp/press_release/press_release_0458. xml.

Blumenthal, R. (2003a, October 9). 'Texas Republicans Report a Deal on Hotly Disputed Redistricting'. *New York Times*. Late Edition – Section A, Page 24, Column 1.

———. (2003b, October 13). 'After Bitter Fight, Texas Senate Redraws Congressional Districts'. *New York Times*. Late Edition – Section A, Page 1, Column 4.

Bruni, F. (2003a, June 30). 'For Berlusconi, a fickle political sky suddenly turns rosy'. *New York Times*, p. A2.

———. (2003b, December 5). 'Berlusconi urges support for U.S. on Iraq'. *New York Times*. Late Edition – Section A, Page 18, Column 4.

Bumiller, E. (2001, November 29). 'Spain to Study U.S. Requests to Extradite Terror Suspects'. *New York Times*. Late Edition – Section B, Page 4, Column 1.

———. (2003, May 8). 'Spanish leader visits Bush, who delivers on a promise'. *New York Times*. Late Edition – Section A, Page 18, Column 1.

Casqueiro, J. & Ordaz, P. (2002). 'El momento del PP'. *El Pais*, n.d.

CBS Radio. (2004, March 16). Regional Radio Interview with Deputy Secretary of Defense Paul Wolfowitz. Retrieved from http://www.defenselink.mil/transcripts/ 2004/tr20040316-depsecdef0547.html.

Cheney, D. (2004, March 17). Remarks by the Vice President at the Ronald Reagan Presidential Library. Retrieved from http://www.whitehouse.gov/news/releases/ 2004/03/20040317-3.html.

CNN interview. (2004, April 19). 'Rice: Terrorists hope to influence election'. Retrieved from http://www.cnn.com/2004/ALLPOLITICS/04/19/monday/index.html.

Comaroff, J. L. (1996). 'Ethnicity, nationalism, and the politics of difference in an age of revolution'. In E. Wilmsen and P. McAllister (Eds.), *The Politics of Difference: Ethnic Premises in a World of Power*, pp. 162–83. Chicago: University of Chicago Press.

Corriere della Sera. 17 November 2001, p. 10.

Cowan, J., Dembour, M.-B., & Wilson, R. A. (2001). 'Introduction'. In J. Cowan, M.-B. Dembour, & R. A. Wilson (Eds.), *Culture and Human Rights: Anthropological Perspectives*, pp. 1–26. Cambridge: Cambridge University Press.

Daly, E. (2002a, August 27). 'Judge bans Basque party, linking it to terrorists'. *New York Times*. Late Edition – Section A, Page 4, Column 3.

———. (2002b, September 9). 'Basque March Reflects Gains in Anti-Madrid Separatism'. *New York Times*. Late Edition – Section A, Page 3, Column 1.

———. (2003a, February 21). 'Spain shuts a Basque newspaper, accusing it of aiding separatists'. *New York Times*. Late Edition – Section A, Page 11, Column 1.

———. (2003b, May 8). 'Writers Sign Statement Denouncing Basque Nationalist Violence'. *New York Times*. Late Edition – Section A, Page 11, Column 1.

———. (2003c, May 26). 'Aznar's party keeps hold on Madrid in vote'. *New York Times*. Late Edition – Section A, Page 2, Column 4.

———. (2003d, June 19). 'Judges Move on Basque Party'. *New York Times*, p. A10 (World Briefing: Europe: Spain).

Decamps, M. C. & Leparmentier, A. (2002, January 17). 'ETA y Bin Laden son lo mismo'. *El Pais*.

Dillon, S. (2001, November 14). 'U.S. and Spain Swap Notes'. *New York Times*.

Dillon, S. & McNeil, D. G., Jr. (2001, November 24). 'Spain sets hurdle for extraditions'. *New York Times*. Retrieved from http://www.criminology.fsu.edu/transcrime/articles/Spain%20Sets%20Hur dle%20for%20Extraditions.htm.

Economist. 15 December 2001, 362(8252), p. 45.

———. 'Answers, please: An open letter to Silvio Berlusconi'. 2 August 2003, 386(8335), p. 23.

Edmondson, G. (2004, September 6). 'Commentary: Schröder needs to help business create jobs, not just slash the dole'. *Business Week*. http://www.businessweek.com/magazine/content/04_36/b3898092_mz054.htm. (Retrieved 3 October 2004).

Egan, T. (2004, August 8). 'Sensing the Eyes of Big Brother, and Pushing Back'. *New York Times*, p. 16.

El Pais. 'PP y PSOE frente a ETA'. 2 August 2000. (Editorial).

———. 'El presidente de la Audiencia apunta que no es necesario ilegalizar Batasuna'. 5 December 2001.

———. 'Italia renueva su negativa a la 'euroorden' a pesar de los contactos de última hora'. 7 December 2001.

———. 'Auto de choque'. 28 August 2002.

———. 'Cerco judicial: Editorialies internacionales sobre la ilegalización de Batasuna'. 28 August 2002.

———. 'El Gobierno de EE UU muestra su 'comprensión ante la medida''. 28 August 2002.

———. 'El Gobierno vasco acusa a PP y PSOE de romper el entendimiento entre los demócratas'. 28 August 2002.

———. 'La policía vasca desaloga por la fuerza las sedes de Batasuna'. 28 August 2002.

———. 'Incidentes tras la manifestación de Batasuna en San Sebastián'. 1 September 2002.

———. 'Zapatero exige a Ibarretxe que acabe 'cuanto antes' sus contactos y rectifique 'a fondo''. 11 October 2002.

Ferguson, J. (1994). *The Anti-Politics Machine*. Minneapolis: University of Minnesota Press.

Flaherty, M. S. (1996). 'The Most Dangerous Branch'. *Yale Law Journal* 105(7), pp. 1725–839.

Flamini, R. (2003, May 28). 'Vote losses in Spain, Italy blamed on Iraq'. *Washington Times*.

Fox News. 'Bush threatens veto of Homeland Security Bill'. 26 July 2002. http://www.foxnews.com/printer_friendly_story/0,3566,58748,00.html (Retrieved 23 September 2004).

Fuchs, D. (2003, November 6). 'Spain is told its help in Iraq will pay off'. *New York Times*. Late Edition – Section W, Page 1, Column 6.

Gastaminza, G. (2000, October 13). 'El PNV pide a los dirigentes de la UE que intervengan para solucionar el conflicto vasco'. *El Pais*.

Gilfeather, P. (2004, June 20). 'Blair Set to Cancel 2005 Election'. http://www.sundaymirror.co.uk/news/news/tm_objectid=14349008%26method=full%26siteid=106694-name_page.html.

Golden, T. (2002, August 29). 'Buoyed by world's focus on terror, Spain cracks down in Basque region'. *New York Times*, p. A8.

Greenhouse, S. (2002, January 16). 'Bush, Citing Security, Bans Some Unions at Justice Department'. *New York Times*, p. A14.

Grimond, J. (2004). 'From A to Z' in 'Special Section: A Survey of Spain'. *The Economist*, 371(8381), pp. 5–7. (26 June–2 July).

Halbfinger, D. M. (2003, July 1) 'Across U.S., Redistricting as a Never-Ending Battle'. *New York Times*, p. 1.

Henneberger, M. (2001, December 11). 'Italy's Leader Raises Storm by Opposing European Warrant Plan'. *New York Times*. Late Edition – Section A, Page 7, Column 1.

———. (2002a, January 6). 'After Clashes, Minister Quits His Post in Italy'. *New York Times*. Late Edition – Section 1, Page 10, Column 6.

———. (2002b, January 7). 'Italian Leader Takes Over Ministry'. *New York Times*, p. A7.

———. (2002c, January 14). 'For premier of Italy, mud doesn't seem to be sticking'. *New York Times*, p. A4.

———. (2002d, January 15). 'Berlusconi says Italy won't take Europe's orders'. *New York Times*, p. A6.

———. (2002e, February 17). 'Italy Cooling on Europe, and 2 Aides Explain Why'. *New York Times*, p. A13.

———. (2002f, March 20). 'Adviser for Italian labor reform is killed'. *New York Times*. Late Edition – Section A, Page 6, Column 4.

———. (2002g, March 21). 'Official sees links to Italian leftists in adviser's killing'. *New York Times*. Late Edition – Section A, Page 10, Column 3.

Heuze, R. (2002, February 1). 'La gauche italienne au bord de l'implosion'. *Le Figaro*.

Heyman, P. B. (2002). 'Civil liberties and human rights in the aftermath of Stepember 11'. *25 Harvard Journal of Law and Public Policy* 440. http://www.ca3.uscourts.gov/conf2003/HarvJL%26Pparticle.pdf.

Isikoff, M. (2004, July 19). 'Exclusive: Election Day Worries'. *Newsweek*. http://www.msnbc.msn.com/id/5411741/site/newsweek.

Johnston, D. (2004, July 17). 'Justice Dept. Says Threat Is Not Issue for Election'. *New York Times*. Late Edition – Section A, Page 10, Column 6.

'Joint Statement of Homeland Security Secretary Tom Ridge and Attorney General John Ashcroft'. 28 May 2004. Retrieved from http://www.dhs.gov/dhspublic/display?content=3654.

Le Monde. 'Les nationalistes basques critiquent José Maria Aznar'. 8 June 2002.

_____. 'La police regionale basque et la police espagnole ferment les permanences de Batasuna'. 28 August 2002.

Lewis, A. (2004, July 15). 'Making Torture Legal'. *New York Review of Books* 51(12), pp. 4–8.

Lichtblau, E. (2003, September 27). 'U.S. Uses Terror Law to Pursue Crimes from Drugs to Swindling'. *New York Times*.

Lithwick, D. (2004, August 12). 'Tyranny in the Name of Freedom'. *New York Times*, p. A27.

Marks, G. & Steenbergen, M. R. (2004). 'Introduction: Models of political conflict in the European Union'. In G. Marks & M. R. Steenbergen (Eds.), *European Integration and Political Conflict*, pp. 1–10. Cambridge: Cambridge University Press.

Masterson, W. V., Jr. (2004, March 21). 'Spain's Zapatero: The Cowardly Bull'. Available at: http://www.enquirer.com/editions/2004/03/21/editorial_ed2v.html.

Messer, E. (1993). 'Anthropology and human rights'. *Annual Review of Anthropology* 22, pp. 221–49.

New York Times. 'Italian Cabinet Decision' [unsigned]. 13 November 2002, p. A5.

_____. 'Court Rules U.S. Can Hold Citizens as "Enemy Combatants"'. 8 January 2003. Associated Press.

_____. 'Italian Leader Faces Dissent over Control of the Media'. 6 April 2003, p. A4, col. 1.

_____. 'Election Ban on Radical Basque Parties'. 10 May 2003 (World Briefing: Europe: Spain).

_____. 'Spanish leader stumps in local elections'. 24 May 2003. Associated Press.

_____. 'Spaniards on Way to Back U.S. in Iraq'. 12 July 2003, p. A5.

_____. 'Texas Lawmakers Reach Tentative Agreement on Redistricting'. 8 October 2003. Associated Press.

_____. 'Democrats in Texas House Stage Another Walkout Over Remap'. 12 October 2003. Associated Press.

Paley, J. (2002). 'Toward an Anthropology of Democracy'. *Annual Review of Anthropology* 31, pp. 469–96.

Press Briefing by Scott McClellan. (16 March 2004). Office of the Press Secretary. Retrieved from http://www.whitehouse.gov/news/releases/2004/03/20040316-6.html.

_____. (8 July 2004). Office of the Press Secretary. Retrieved from http://www.whitehouse.gov/news/releases/2004/07/20040708-15.html.

Purdum, T. S. & Bumiller, E. (2002, September 20). 'Bush to Seek Power to Use "All Means to Oust Hussein" '. *New York Times*, p. 1.

Quinn, P. (2003, July 1). 'Europe's media lashes Berlusconi as Italy takes over EU presidency'. *Associated Press*. http://www.sfgate.com/cgi-bin/article.cgi?f=/news/archive/2003/07/01/international0813EDT0529.DTL.

Reuters. (28 August 2002). 'Party or No Party, Radical Basques Vow to Fight On'. *New York Times*.

———. (11 July 2004). 'U.S. Mulling How to Delay Nov. Vote in Case of Attack'. http://www.commondreams.org/headlines04/0711-07.htm.

Sanger, D. E. & Greenhouse, S. (2002, October 9). 'President Invokes Taft-Hartley Act to Open 29 Ports'. *New York Times*, p. 1.

Sassen, S. (1999). 'De-nationalization: Some conceptual and empirical elements: APLA Distinguished Lecture, 1998'. *Political and Legal Anthropology Review* 22(2), pp. 1–16.

Shaffer, G. (2004, August 2). 'Treating Protesters Like Terrorists: Force Multiplier'. *The New Republic*, vol. 231, issue 4672, pp. 19–21.

Shenon, P. (2003, September 13). 'High Alerts for Terror Get Harder to Impose'. *New York Times*. Late Edition – Section A, Page 9, Column 6.

Slaughter, A.-M. (2003, March 18). 'Good reasons for going around the U. N.' *New York Times*, p. A33, column 1.

Stout, D. (2001, November 28). 'Spain pledges support to U.S. on Terrorism'. *New York Times*.

Sullivan, E. (2004, August 30). 'Unions denounce meetings on Homeland personnel system'. *Federal Times*.

Szymanski, T. (2002, April 30). 'Italy Strikes Again'. *World Press Review*.

Tagliabue, J. (2002, March 29). 'Italy's Unions Seem Ready for Battle'. *New York Times*, p. A16.

USA Today. 'Counterterrorism officials look to postpone elections'. 12 July 2004. Retrieved from http://www.usatoday.com/news/politicselections/nation/president/2004-07-12-postpone-elections_x.htm.

van der Eijk, C. & Franklin, M. N. (2004). Potential for contestation on European matters at national elections in Europe. In Gary Marks and Marco R. Steenbergen, (Eds.), *European Integration and Political Conflict*, pp. 32–50. Cambridge: Cambridge University Press.

Vitzthum, C. & Shishkin, P. (2001, November 29). 'Spain seeks to bridge key U.S.-EU divide'. *The Wall Street Journal*.

Wald, M. L. & Schwartz, J. (2004, September 19). 'Screening Plans Went Beyond Terrorism'. *New York Times*, p. 35, col. 1.

Weiser, B. (2003, January 10). 'U.S. Asks Judge to Deny Terror Suspect Access to Lawyer, Saying It Could Harm Investigation'. *New York Times*. Late Edition – Section A, Page 11, Column 1.

Wood, N. (2004, May 14). 'Macedonia officials suspected of faking terror plot'. *New York Times*, p. A3.

Yarnoz, C. (2002, January 17). 'Aznar pide a la UE que acabe con los santuarious del terror'. *El Pais*.

10. The Impact of Counter Terror on the Promotion and Protection of Human Rights: A Global Perspective

NEIL HICKS

Human rights activists in many parts of the world share a sense of alarm about the new challenges of promoting human rights in the context of heightened global concern about the threat of terrorism.[1] Pre-existing conflicts in different parts of the globe have been sustained and exacerbated by being characterized as fronts in the global war on terrorism – a designation that governments appear to believe gives them greater latitude to disregard the constraints of international human rights law and humanitarian law. Previously peaceful countries have seen tractable, if difficult, political problems escalate into violence as governments have resorted to military force as a preferred method in confronting a terrorist threat.

Everywhere human rights activists are confronting a sea-change in what might be called the presumptive norm in international affairs that prior to September 11, 2001, saw adherence (or at least the pretense of adherence) to international human rights standards as generally desirable. The adoption by the United Nations General Assembly of the Declaration on Human Rights Defenders in 1998 was an important indication of this growing international consensus. The Declaration codified the right to promote and protect human rights as a normative standard. Through voting for its adoption, states took on obligations to ensure that individuals would have the "effectively guaranteed" right "individually and in association with others, to promote and to strive for the protection and realization of human rights and fundamental freedoms at the national and international levels" (Declaration 1998: Article 1).

In contrast, today the primacy of respect for international human rights standards, and the legitimacy of striving for their realization and protection, is routinely challenged and questioned in word and deed by governments of

---

[1] See, for example, The Atlanta Declaration 2003, which provides a concise expression of the concerns of leading human rights defenders from forty-three countries.

all kinds, democratic and undemocratic alike. Because the rights of human rights defenders have been and are being violated, we are all less safe.

The post-9/11 world has thrown up obstacles to the promotion and protection of human rights, often in the name of enhancing security, that paradoxically risk having the opposite effect. At the time of its adoption U.N. Secretary-General Kofi Annan noted, "The Declaration rests on a basic premise: that when the rights of human rights defenders are violated, all our rights are put in jeopardy and all of us are made less safe" (1998). The idea that upholding human rights contributes to peace and security is literally a fundamental principle of the contemporary human rights regime. The preamble to the Universal Declaration of Human Rights declares that "disregard and contempt for human rights have resulted in barbarous acts which have outraged the conscience of mankind." It proclaims that human rights are "the foundation of freedom, justice and peace in the world" (UDHR 1948: Preamble). This chapter argues that the obstacles to human rights promotion and protection it describes contradict the basic premises and assumptions on which international human rights standards rest, and represent a setback to the objective of enhancing human security that security measures are ostensibly designed to promote.

New legislation, policies, and practices have proliferated in the name of increased security. Even as some strong voices have spoken out on the need to hold those who wage terror against civilians accountable under international law, many governments have seized upon the war against terrorism to turn their backs on international standards and to turn back the clock of human rights protection.

Human rights promotion has been impeded by a variety of negative developments. Among those that have been the most widespread and have had the broadest deleterious impact are the following:

1) Human Rights Defenders Increasingly Equated with Terrorists

Efforts of human rights defenders have been denigrated as being supportive of terrorism and insufficiently attentive to the imperatives of national security threats. Human rights defenders who speak out against repression as a response to the threat of terrorism have themselves been subjected to attack for their criticisms.

Defaming human rights defenders as terrorist sympathizers is an old device. The post-September 11 global emphasis on the primacy of counterterrorism gave new potency to such criticisms and gave them a veneer of international respectability. Even leaders of democratic governments have stooped to seeking to stifle open debate on proposed counterterrorism measures by accusing their critics of aiding terrorists. For example:

- Former Indian Deputy Prime Minister L. K. Advani, in November 2001, called for the passage of a new Prevention of Terrorism Act that would curtail numerous previously protected rights and freedoms. He stated: "If the opposition opposes the ordinance they will be wittingly or unwittingly helping terrorists" (Tully 2002).
- In the United States, Attorney General John Ashcroft, in testimony before the Senate Judiciary Committee on December 7, 2001, said: "To those who scare peace-loving people with phantoms of lost liberty, my message is this: Your tactics only aid terrorists for they erode our national unity and diminish our resolve . . . They give ammunition to America's enemies and pause to America's friends. They encourage people of good will to remain silent in the face of evil" (CNN.com 2001).
- In Colombia, the government of President Alvaro Uribe, which came to power in May 2002, has stated that its struggle against guerrilla forces is "working to the same ends" as the U.S.-led global war on terrorism. It has stepped up its military campaign against insurgents and has frequently accused human rights defenders of "serving terrorism and hiding in a cowardly manner behind the human rights flag," to use the president's own words (*Semana* 13 September 2003).

Contrary to these slanders, human rights defenders are among those speaking out for an effective response to the threat of terrorism. Human rights leaders have been emphatic on the need to confront the menace of terrorism. For example, the U.N. Special Representative on Human Rights Defenders, prominent Pakistani lawyer Hina Jilani, said: ". . . we are not denying the menace of terrorism. We were the first ones to experience the threats and the violence of these terrorists. This was much before 9/11 . . . I come from a part of the world where there is no denying the problem of terrorism" (Carter Center Report 2004: 26). But for Jilani and other human rights leaders there should be no contradiction between counterterrorism measures and human rights, and when such measures undermine human rights they become counterproductive.[2]

Steps taken to silence the voices of human rights defenders in a context of heightened concern about the threat of terrorism include broad controls on

---

[2] Opening remarks of Ms. Hina Jilani, United Nations Special Representative of the Secretary General on Human Rights Defenders, at the "Human Rights Defenders on the Frontlines of Freedom" conference, November 11–12, 2003 (see Carter Center Report 2004).

freedom of expression, association, and movement, and measures to intimidate, demonize, brutalize, imprison, exile, or murder the individuals who
stand up for human rights. These measures affect basic freedoms for all but
often have a particular impact on human rights defenders – in some cases
leading to threats to their lives and liberty and in all cases constraining their
ability to protect the rights of others.

2) The Intensification of Civil Conflicts: Giving Precedence to Military Means to Resolve Political Conflicts

The context of the global war against terrorism has intensified extreme nationalist and sectarian sentiment in many countries, building added pressures to
curtail rights protections, particularly of minority communities, on grounds
of national security. The often long-standing tensions between governments
and their opponents, particularly in situations involving violent separatist or
nationalist movements, have intensified with new emphasis given to responding militarily to pre-existing challenges repackaged as terrorist threats. Violence has intensified in the Philippines, Russia, Thailand, and India, and
minority Muslim communities have suffered disproportionately from violence and deprivations of rights that have been justified by governments as a
legitimate response to the threat of terrorism.

In Russia, a report by the International Helsinki Federation for Human
Rights indicates that attacks on human rights defenders have escalated since
the outbreak of the Second Chechen War in 1999, and that violent attacks on
human rights defenders, most of them perpetrated by state agents, increased
sharply in 2003 and 2004 (IHF 2004: 27).

Other long-standing internal conflicts, that are not primarily influenced
by religious sectarianism, in countries like Colombia, Indonesia, and Nepal,
have also been recast as fronts in the war against terrorism since September
2001. Indonesia faces a real and serious threat from a regional network of
terrorists, some of whom are thought to be linked to al-Qaeda. The police
have been praised for their investigative work, particularly after the 2002 Bali
bombing, and there is undoubtedly a need for an effective intelligence network to identify attacks before they occur. However, the specter of terrorism
has also been used to target human rights defenders, who report an increase
in intimidation and attacks in recent years. In May 2004, Indonesian intelligence chief Hendropriyono told the House of Representatives that twenty
local and foreign non-governmental organizations (NGOs) were a threat to
security in the run-up to the July 5 presidential elections. He warned that

the country might need to return to "old measures" against people who "sell out their country." Soon after, Sidney Jones, a leading Indonesia analyst and regional director of the International Crisis Group, was forced to leave the country. Such comments coming from a powerful former military leader are, in themselves, intimidatory. Any escalation in violence in simmering internal conflicts in Indonesia would inevitably lead to severe violations of human rights and would endanger Indonesia's fragile transition to democracy.

An internal conflict involving the Muslim Uighur minority in northwestern China has been portrayed by the Chinese government as its front in the global war against terrorism. The post-September 11 climate has aided the Chinese government's long-standing suppression of internal political dissent throughout the country, including its intolerance of independent human rights activists.

Mainstream politicians and media in countries like Israel and Russia have discussed positions previously considered extreme and unreasonable, like population transfers of minority ethnic and religious groups. With public fear heightened by political leaders emphasizing national vulnerabilities, it becomes increasingly difficult for activists to promote a human rights agenda.

The example of Thailand is particularly striking. For decades Thailand has distinguished itself from other countries in Asia by the ability of those in power to find peaceful solutions to problems that in other countries have provoked full-fledged civil wars (Sagar 2004). In the four southern states of Songkhla, Pattani, Yala, and Narathiwat, a resurgence of the long-simmering unrest among Thailand's Muslim minority has been met with a harsh military response, including the imposition of martial law, inflaming and injecting an unprecedented level of violence into the troubled relations between the government and the small Muslim minority in southern Thailand. After a lull in separatist activity since the late 1980s, a new wave of violence began with a January 4, 2004, attack on an army depot. On April 28, 2004, the Thai security forces massacred 107 young Muslims armed with only machetes who had attempted to raid a police station. Security forces, which by many accounts had advance knowledge of the attacks, suffered five fatalities themselves.

On October 25, 2004, at a mass protest against the detention of six local men outside a police station in Narathiwat province, soldiers firing into the crowd killed six and wounded at least twenty, while more than 1,000 people were arrested under martial law provisions. The next day, authorities reported that seventy-eight detainees died of suffocation while packed into trucks on the five-hour drive to Pattani. Thai Prime Minister Thaksin Shinawatra commented, "This is typical. It's about bodies made weak from fasting. Nobody hurt them," provoking widespread condemnation from neighboring Muslim countries and even a rebuke from the King of Thailand (Mydans 2004).

This incident brought the total to more than 400 people killed during or after clashes in southern Thailand since the beginning of the year. The Thai authorities have characterized the worsening conflict in southern Thailand as a product of either criminal gangs or terrorism, and have justified their actions as legitimate counterterrorism measures. Human rights activists who have sought to defend apparent victims of governmental repression have been criticized as terrorist sympathizers. Denigration of human rights defenders makes their work more dangerous. For example, prominent defense lawyer Somchai Neelaphaijit, who had been threatened because of his activities defending Muslim activists, disappeared on March 12, 2004. Witnesses saw him being led away from his car by masked armed men who appear to have been members of the security forces (HRF 2004).

The January attack was followed by the announcement of martial law in the four southern states and a corresponding wave of arrests, including the detainees who became Mr. Somchai's clients. In the court papers filed just prior to the lawyer's disappearance, these detainees allege that they confessed as a result of extensive torture. The Thai National Human Rights Commission also found evidence of torture and detention without access to lawyers or family members. In August 2003, the Thai government adopted counterterrorism decrees that broadened the scope for the use of protracted detention without charge or trial. Such measures violate Thailand's obligations under the International Covenant on Civil and Political Rights.

After each violent incident the government has claimed a victory against terrorists and Muslim opposition groups in Thailand and surrounding countries issued violent threats of revenge attacks against Thai civilians and tourists. There is a real danger that the heavy-handed response to discontent in the south is only exacerbating the separatist feelings in the region and fueling more violence.

3) The Weakening of State-to-State Peer Pressure

At the interstate level, governments have shown greater deference towards other states implicated in violations of human rights, if they justify their conduct by reference to counterterrorism. For example, Australian Foreign Minister Alexander Downer declared in June 2003 that the military crackdown in Aceh by the government of Indonesia was "justified," despite the resultant suffering of the civilian population in the region, and the reports of widespread violations of human rights (*Sydney Morning Herald* 19 June 2003).

State-to-state peer pressure as a factor in human rights promotion and protection has been greatly weakened, thus undermining one of the most important techniques available to human rights activists for bringing pressure to bear on human rights violators. For example, in May 2002, prior to a meeting between former Malaysian Prime Minister Mahatir and President Bush, then Malaysian Minister of Justice, Dr. Rais Yatim met with U.S. Attorney General Ashcroft and discussed national security measures employed by both countries to combat terrorism. The United States government had previously criticized the Malaysian Internal Security Act (ISA), which among other things, permits protracted detention without charge or trial. Minister Yatim remarked:

> I believe that after the meeting there will be no more basis to criticize each other's systems, specifically the ISA, because if they do that, then the Patriot Act, which is quite similar in nature to the ISA, could come into a position of jeopardy itself: Ashcroft seemed to understand the existence, need, and the future of the ISA in as much as we understand the Patriot Act. (*Sunday Star* 12 May 2002)

The minister was correct in his prediction. At the subsequent meeting between President Bush and the Malaysian Prime Minister, there was no public criticism by the United States of the ISA.

Governments that were previously criticized for human rights violations that occurred during counterinsurgency campaigns have felt vindicated by the newly permissive attitude towards departures from international human rights standards in the name of security. For example, President Kumaratunga of Sri Lanka remarked: "When countries like Sri Lanka fought against terrorists, developed nations worried only about the human rights of terrorist organizations" (*Global News Wire* 18 September 2001). The government in Colombia also pointed to what it saw as a double standard in Western attitudes. Referring to antiterrorism measures passed in the United States, United Kingdom, France, and Spain, it stated: "For these countries, [the measures] are to defend democracy, liberty, and the citizens' rights, but in our country they are called authoritarian measures that violate human rights treaties, when we are clearly working towards the same ends" (*Semana* 12 December 2003).

In Russia, the government's brutal tactics in Chechnya had become a target of growing national and international criticism by 2001. After September 11, the Russian government has increasingly sought to justify its harsh military actions in Chechnya as a response to the Chechens' ties to al-Qaeda and global Islamic terrorism. No resolution criticizing Russian practices in Chechnya has been presented to the United Nations Human Rights Commission since 2002, in contrast to previous years.

Human rights defenders were weaker and more vulnerable to attack because of this erosion of international disapproval of human rights violations for whatever pretext.

4) The Proliferation of Exceptional Laws that Violate Human Rights Standards

Many states have either implemented new national security laws or found new validation for pre-existing emergency legislation by claiming to be responding to the threat of terrorism.[3] These laws tend to undermine human rights protections. Because definitions of terrorism employed by these laws are often both vague and sweeping, their effect is to substantially increase unchecked executive power. In some countries, the U.S.-led war on terrorism has had a direct impact on domestic human rights conditions. Elsewhere, domestic factors have provided the primary motive for worsening human rights conditions. Often, nonetheless, states invoke the U.S. example to mask or justify violations.

Authoritarian governments felt emboldened to declare that U.S. departures from international human rights norms showed that their own methods of addressing security threats had been right all along. President Mubarak of Egypt, for example, declared that the new U.S. policies proved "that we were right from the beginning in using all means, including military tribunals, to combat terrorism . . . " (Stork: 6).

Counterterrorism measures have been used as a justification for noncompliance with international human rights standards – and domestic law – by a wide variety of governments. For example, former President of Georgia Eduard Shevardnadze stated in December 2002, after coming under criticism for colluding with Russia in the violation of the human rights of Chechens, that "international human rights commitments might become pale in comparison with the importance of the anti-terrorist campaign" (IHF 2003).

Human rights defenders who spoke out against repression as a response to the threat of terrorism have themselves been subjected to attack for their criticisms. For example, in the Russian province of Krasnodar, the regional authorities used the new Law on Extremist Activities, passed in July 2002, to order the summary closure for six months of the Krasnodar Human Rights Center, an organization that had monitored violations occurring in Chechnya and the North Caucasus.

---

[3] For extensive information on new counterterrorism laws and their impact on human rights conditions, see ICJ 2004.

Prior to the passage of the new law, the organization would have been able to contest the closure order in court while continuing with its work, but the new law left it with no legal redress. The law includes only a vague definition of extremist activities. The broad language of the new law has been criticized by authoritative international bodies like the U.N. Human Rights Committee and the U.N. Committee on the Elimination of Racial Discrimination.

It is a matter of particular concern that the law allows a prosecutor to suspend the work of organizations before a judge has considered the basis or motivation for the complaint. When a prosecutor claims that an organization is "extremist" under the 2002 law, the organization's activities can be suspended by the prosecutor if the prosecutor's complaint alleges a threat of damage by the organization. Whether or not the allegations of extremism or damage are found to be true by the court, the organization cannot function legally for up to six months. If the court finds that the organization's activities fit the broad definition of "extremist," the organization will be liquidated. Subjecting human rights organizations to this law violates their right to freedom of association.

The Russian authorities have used this law repeatedly to silence human rights organizations reporting on violations in Chechnya and the North Caucasus. In August 2004, the prosecutor's office of Ingushetia accused the Chechen Committee of National Salvation (CCNS), a prominent human rights organization based in Nazran, Ingushetia, of disseminating information of an extremist character. The prosecutor's office alleged that CCNS press releases about human rights abuses allegedly committed by Russian armed forces constituted extremist speech under the Law on Countering Extremist Activities.

5) Mixed Messages from the United States Government on Human Rights

There was a pronounced shift in the global discourse about human rights after September 11. It was a shift brought about because of the perception that when challenged by the threat of terrorism, the most powerful country in the world violated human rights in the name of upholding national security.

Since September 11, 2001, the international community's progress toward protecting human rights for all has suffered a setback – not least because the leaders of the United States government itself appear to have lost confidence in the very framework of law the United States has been so instrumental in developing.

The relationship between the U.S. government and the people it serves has changed; this "new normal" of U.S. governance is defined by the loss of particular freedoms for some, and, worse, a detachment from the rule of law as a whole.[4]

The undermining of U.S. compliance with fundamental human rights standards has serious implications for human rights norms in scores of other countries. The consequences of changing U.S. policy have been more serious where partner governments, confident that they are needed for the global "war against terrorism," feel new liberty to violate human rights.

There is a widespread belief among human rights activists in many parts of the world that U.S. disregard for international human rights principles has set a negative global pattern. The arguments for this view are compelling. The views and actions of the United States carry great influence in all parts of the world. Moreover, the United States has been a leading member of the contemporary international human rights system from its inception in 1948. Since the presidency of Jimmy Carter in 1976, human rights have played an increasingly prominent part in U.S. foreign policy under both Democratic and Republican administrations. Therefore, it is only natural that governments around the world should look closely at U.S. practice and rhetoric as a guide to their own compliance with international standards.

This is not to say that the United States is responsible for human rights violations committed by other governments. It is not. Each government is obliged to abide by the international human rights treaties it has ratified. Human rights violations were widespread prior to September 11, 2001, and they continued to be so afterwards, often for many of the same reasons.

Nevertheless, for decades the United States has been a leading voice for human rights around the world and a linchpin of the international system of human rights protection. This multilateral system functions imperfectly without U.S. participation and leadership. At the present time, there is a case to be made that the United States is pulling in the opposite direction, undermining the multilateral system for human rights promotion and protection that has been painstakingly constructed over more than fifty years.

U.S. policy, both when it has been supportive of human rights and when it has disregarded or undermined them, has been troubling to human rights activists because of its inconsistency, which leaves the U.S. open to criticism

---

[4] For an overview of Human Rights First's work on human rights conditions in the United States post-September 11, 2001, see LCHR 2003. The website of the U.S. Law and Security Program of Human Rights First contains regular updates on these concerns: http://www.humanrightsfirst.org/us_law/us_law.htm.

of hypocrisy and double standards, and because of the disconnect between statements and actions. The prominent Egyptian human rights activist Saad Eddin Ibrahim observed in 2003:

> Every dictator in the world is using what the United States has done under the Patriot Act and other derivative measures to justify their past violations of human rights, as well as declaring a license to continue to abuse human rights at present and in the future. (Carter Center Report 2004: 29)[5]

In a deeply polarized global political environment, where many U.S. policies are controversial, human rights defenders with any perceived or actual association with the United States now face added threats and pressures. This is a particular problem for human rights advocates in the Middle East and the broader Muslim world, a vast region spanning from Indonesia to West Africa that has been repeatedly identified by the Bush administration as the target of a "forward strategy for freedom." In this region, U.S. support for the principles of human rights and democracy has tended to reflect negatively on local activists who are ostensibly pursuing some of the same objectives. The U.S. government is, if anything, placing more emphasis on this aspect of its counterterrorism policy. For example, on February 5, 2004, President Bush compared the war on terror to the challenges confronting Winston Churchill during the Second World War. He told an audience at the Library of Congress in Washington, D.C.:

> Our great challenge (i)s support the momentum of freedom in the greater Middle East. The stakes could not be higher. As long as that region is a place of tyranny and despair and anger, it will produce men and movements that threaten the safety of Americans and our friends. We seek the advance of democracy for the most practical of reasons: because democracies do not support terrorists or threaten the world with weapons of mass murder.
>
> America is pursuing a forward strategy of freedom in the Middle East. We're challenging the enemies of reform, confronting the allies of terror, and expecting a higher standard from our friends.

In recent years, the U.S. government has become publicly identified in this region with many of the issues of democratization, good governance, promotion of the rule of law, and human rights that are the core concerns of human rights activists in the region. Attention to serious problems in these areas may be considered progress after decades of apparent indifference. However, regional governments and their supporters, who have reason to feel

---

[5] Opening remarks by Professor Saad Eddin Ibrahim at the "Human Rights Defenders on the Frontlines of Freedom" conference, November 11–12, 2003.

threatened by the types of reforms promoted by the United States, have found it easy to criticize the U.S. proposals and brand local human rights activists as tools of broader U.S. policies. They focus on what is widely viewed as hypocrisy in U.S. policy: where the United States is curtailing rights protections at home while promoting human rights and the rule of law abroad. In this context, many critics view U.S. human rights initiatives as cynical tools aimed at reinforcing U.S. political domination throughout the world. Some criticism goes so far as to say that U.S. actions after September 11 have demonstrated that Western championing of human rights was "never more than thinly disguised self-interest," and that, "the United States has given up all credibility as a critic of other states' human rights practices" (Mahbubani 2003).

Another aspect of U.S. policy that has proved problematic to U.S. credibility as a global force for good in the field of human rights is the embrace of states notorious for their poor human rights practices and disregard of democratic principles as allies in the war on terrorism. In such countries, apparently unqualified U.S. support and aid have continued despite continuing violations.

Colombia, Indonesia, Pakistan, the Philippines, and Uzbekistan have all received a substantial increase in U.S. foreign assistance since September 11, some of it direct military assistance, as well as closer formal military cooperation, especially in the field of counterterrorism. Pakistan was designated a Major Non-NATO Ally (MNNA) of the United States in May 2004, despite a lack of progress towards democracy by President Musharraf. Observers have noted that: "The major non-NATO ally declaration may serve to embolden the Pakistan government, and reinforce the notion that it may continue along its current path without undertaking democratic reforms" (Prosser 2004). When the President of Pakistan visited the White House in 2002, President Bush remarked: "President Musharraf is a leader with great courage, and his nation is a key partner in the global coalition against terror" (The White House 2002). President Bush did not voice concern about the Pakistani government's human rights record during his public remarks.

Even when the United States has criticized human rights violations in these countries, as it has continued to do in the annual *Country Reports on Human Rights Practices* and elsewhere, the governments concerned have been able to weigh that against the practical cooperation and material assistance they have continued to receive. In such circumstances, the strength of the verbal reprimands in official human rights statements is diminished.

Skepticism about U.S. motives and actions has created a paradoxical situation. The United States cannot be seen as a human rights violator that flouts international legality and as a friend of anti-democratic leaders who disparage human rights if, at the same time, it wishes to be taken seriously as the promoter of liberty and democracy in the greater Middle East or elsewhere in the world.

Human Rights and Security as Complementary Concepts

The idea of human rights and security being antithetical or linked in negative correlation – a reversal of the logic of the drafters of the Universal Declaration of Human Rights, and a consequence of short memories and political opportunism – is profoundly damaging to the work of human rights defenders. Within such an intellectual construct those promoting human rights are characterized as obstacles to security, if not supporters of terrorism.

U.N. Secretary General Kofi Annan has set out an alternative vision of the complementarity of human rights and counterterrorism:

> Our responses to terrorism, as well as our efforts to thwart it and prevent it, should uphold the human rights that terrorists aim to destroy. Respect for human rights, fundamental freedoms, and the rule of law are essential tools in the effort to combat terrorism – not privileges to be sacrificed at a time of tension. (Annan 2003)

Perhaps the greatest damage done to the international human rights system, with human rights defenders on the front line, has been the erosion of state respect for human rights, fundamental freedoms, and the rule of law. The pretext of counterterrorism has sparked a race to the bottom in compliance by states with their human rights obligations.

Weakening the international standards and mechanisms for human rights promotion and protection, or shaking the international consensus on human rights, has no connection to implementing effective policies against terrorism. In this regard it is worth reflecting on the experiences of states that endured internal armed conflict including violence directed against civilians and other acts of terrorism. Years and sometimes decades later, in countries and territories as varied as Peru, Guatemala, Sri Lanka, Turkey, and Northern Ireland, governments and societies are struggling to overcome the destabilizing legacy of conflicts that were, in their time, pursued as struggles against a terrorist enemy in which the rule of law and respect for human rights were seen as a dispensable luxury, or even as an obstacle to the imperative defeating terrorism. After long years of death and destruction, efforts toward reconstruction and reconciliation are moving forward, in some cases precariously, on the basis of a renewed commitment to justice and equality rooted in respect for human rights principles.

Building conditions within states where human rights defenders operate freely, and where they can effectively carry out their function of promoting and protecting human rights, helps to create an environment where terrorism does not prevail. All governments should reaffirm their commitment to support the essential work of human rights defenders.

There are perhaps reasons to be hopeful that the international mood among nations on the need to satisfy both rights and security concerns in counter-terrorism policy has subtly shifted in the past year. Today some governments and many civil society organizations are increasingly emphasizing the need to more scrupulously protect human rights in times of crisis and not least in the fight against terrorism. This is argued on its own merits – and as an important contribution to halting lawless attacks on civilian lives and property in the long term. The reaction of much of the world to the terrible attack on a school in Beslan, Russia, in September 2004, the new Indian government's repeal of that country's hastily imposed Prevention of Terrorism Act, and the recommendations of the bi-partisan 9/11 Commission in the United States[6] are all indicators of growing support for human rights promotion to be an integral part of effective counterterrorism measures.

Respect for human rights, democracy, and the rule of law is an essential antidote to the conditions that give rise to terrorism. In contrast, the abuse of basic rights in the course of efforts to combat terrorism can ultimately be self-defeating – blurring the distinction between those who stand for the rule of law and those who defy it.

REFERENCES

The 9/11 Commission Report: Final Report of the National Commission on Terrorist Attacks Upon the United States. (2004). Authorized Edition. New York: W. W. Norton.

Annan, K. (1998, September 14). Address to the Fifty-First Annual DPI/NGO Conference, United Nations Headquarters, New York.

————. (2003, March 6). Statement to a special meeting of the Security Council's Counter-Terrorism Committee with International, Regional, and Sub-Regional Organizations, New York. Available at: http://www.unhchr.ch/terrorism/.

The Atlanta Declaration (2003, November 12). A Consensus Document from "Human Rights Defenders on the Frontlines of Freedom," The Carter Center,

---

[6] For example, the 9/11 commissioners recommend: "One of the lessons of the long Cold War was that short-term gains in cooperating with the most repressive and brutal governments were too often outweighed by long-term setbacks for America's stature and interests" (2004: 376).

Atlanta, GA. Available at: http://www.cartercenter.org/documents/nondatabase/atlantadeclaration.pdf.

CNN.com (2001, December 7). 'Ashcroft: Critics of new terror measures undermine efforts'. Available at: http://archives.cnn.com/2001/US/12/06/inv.ashcroft.hearing/.

Declaration on the Right and Responsibility of Individuals, Groups and Organs of Society to Promote and Protect Universally Recognized Human Rights and Fundamental Freedoms (herein "Declaration") (1998). Adopted by the United Nations General Assembly, December 9, 1998. Retrieved from http://www.ohchr.org/english/law/freedom.htm.

Global News Wire. 'Sri Lanka rebukes West for Double Standards'. 18 September 2001.

Human Rights Defenders on the Frontlines of Freedom: Protecting Human Rights in the Context of the War on Terror – Conference Report (herein "Carter Center Report") (2004, May). The Carter Center, Atlanta, GA. Available at: http://cartercenter.org/documents/1682.pdf.

Human Rights First (HRF) (2004, October 28). 'Demand an Independent Inquiry into the Disappearance of Prominent Thai Lawyer'. Available at: http://www.humanrightsfirst.org/defenders/hrd_thailand/alert102804_Neel aphaijit.htm.

International Commission of Jurists (ICJ) (2004, August). 'ICJ E-Bulletin on Counterterrorism and Human Rights'. Available at: http://www.icj.org/article.php3?id_article=3494&id_rubrique=37?=en.

International Helsinki Federation for Human Rights (IHF) (2004, September 15). 'The Silencing of Human Rights Defenders in Chechnya and Ingushetia'. Vienna, Austria. Available at http://www.ihf-hr.org/documents/doc_summary.php?sec_id=3&d_id=3965.

———. (2003, December 23). 'Violations of the Rights of Chechens in Georgia'.

Lawyers Committee for Human Rights (LCHR) (2003). *Assessing the New Normal: Liberty and Security for the Post-September 11 United States*. New York. Available at: http://www.humanrightsfirst.org/pubs/descriptions/Assessing/AssessingtheNewNormal.pdf.

Mahbubani, K. (2003, November 7). Remarks by the Permanent Representative of Singapore to the United Nations at New York, during an international conference organized by the International Peace Academy, New York.

Mydans, S. (2004, November 2). 'Thai King Urges Premier to be More Lenient in the Muslim South'. *New York Times*, p. A3.

'President Bush Discusses Importance of Democracy in Middle East: Remarks by the President on Winston Churchill and the War on Terror'. (2004, February 5). Library of Congress, Washington, D.C. Available at:http://www.whitehouse.gov/news/releases/2004/02/20040204-4.html.

Prosser, A. (2004, May 3). 'U.S. Arms Transfers to America's Newest "Major Non-NATO Ally"'. Center for Defense Information. Available at: http://www.cdi.org/program/document.cfm?documentid=2443&programID=73&from_page=. ./friendlyversion/printversion.cfm.

Sagar, S. (2004, June). 'The War on Terror Comes to Thailand'. *Just Commentary*, vol. 4, no. 6. International Movement for a Just World, Malaysia.

Semana. 'Derechos Humanos: La ira presidencial'. 13 September 2003, ed. 1115, sec. Nacion.

———. 'Legislacion: Arma de doblo filo'. 12 December 2003, ed. 1128, sec. Nacion.

Stork, J. 'The Human Rights Crisis in the Middle East in the Aftermath of September 11'. Cairo Institute for Human Rights Studies. Available at: http://www.cihrs.org/conference/storkpaper_e.htm.

Sunday Star. 'U.S. Endorses ISA'. 12 May 2002.

Sydney Morning Herald/ The Age. 'Aceh Crackdown Justified, says Downer'. 19 June 2003.

Tully, M. (2002, March 21). 'Politics key to India's anti-terror moves'. CNN.com. Available at: http://archives.cnn.com/2002/WORLD/asiapcf/south/03/21/tully.terror/.

Universal Declaration of Human Rights (UDHR) (1948). Adopted by the United Nations General Assembly resolution 217 A (III) on 10 December 1948. Available at: http://www.un.org/Overview/rights.html.

The White House (2002, February 13). 'U.S.–Pakistan Affirm Commitment Against Terrorism'. Available at: http://www.whitehouse.gov/news/releases/2002/02/20020213-3.html.

11. Human Rights: A Descending Spiral

RICHARD FALK

Scope of Inquiry

My chapter is written in the context of discussion within the United States, but seeks to be sensitive to what might be described as "a global perspective." In this regard, the central point is the degree to which much of the rest of the world, especially at the level of civil society, has grown over time more disturbed by the American response to the September 11 attacks than by the attacks themselves, and the continuing threat posed by such forms of non-state political violence. In this regard, the impact of September 11 on adherence to human rights standards and on American foreign policy is different than in any other country, including the main American ally, Britain. In one sense, this uneven response is a natural reflection of the degree to which the United States, its people, and interests around the world are the main target of Al Qaeda-type political violence. But in another more important sense, this unevenness expresses a critical attitude toward the American response as exaggerated, motivated by a geopolitical project to achieve global domination, and a related manipulation of the terrorist threat to inhibit dissent within the United States by inducing fear among the citizenry. By adopting a global perspective on these issues, this chapter embodies this critical attitude.

Given this outlook, it seems worth questioning whether the label of "Age of Terror," so widely used in American discussions of world order since September 11, including as the subtitle of Michael Ignatieff's widely discussed *A Lesser Evil* (2004), is a helpful reminder that there has occurred a shift in focus from globalization to terrorism or is an example of a misleading label.[1]

---

[1] The full title is *The Lesser Evil: Political Ethics in an Age of Terror*; a similar title appears in an outstanding volume: *Philosophy in a Time of Terror: Dialogues with Jürgen Habermas and Jacques Derrida* (Borradori 2003).

I take the latter view that to describe the global setting in this period as "an age of terror" tends to bias discussion by adopting the rhetorical stance of the U.S. government, which tends to validate the mobilization for an anti-terrorist war of ill-defined scope and indefinite duration. Against this background of skepticism about such a centering of terrorism on the global policy agenda, the chapter goes on to consider the general adverse effects on the protection of international human rights of the September 11 attacks and the American response. This discussion is followed by some brief consideration of specific adverse effects on American behavior at home and in the course of the conduct of its self-proclaimed generalized war against terrorism.[2] A concluding section discusses three alternative response patterns: the Turkish exception; the Spanish response to the Madrid train attacks of March 11, 2004; and an enhanced law enforcement model.

An "Age of Terror"?

I find it important to clarify what is achieved by an acceptance of the label an "Age of Terror" as the defining dimension of our historical moment. If it is intended to refer only to anti-state political violence, then I find the use of the word "terror" not only misleading, but also regressive. It is further misleading if anti-state political violence that is directed at military or government targets is described, as routinely occurs in the mainstream media, as terrorism. Terrorism, a slippery term at best, seems polemical unless it consistently refers to state and anti-state political violence directed against civilians, that is, in a broad sense political violence against "innocence." Of course, problems remain, and it is not just an American problem. The character of innocence is contested, manipulated, and far from transparent. Are armed settlers living in West Bank settlements innocent in relation to Palestinian resistance? In Iraq, Turkey, Israel, India, and elsewhere, those who attack soldiers are generally characterized by the media and government officials as "terrorists," thereby helping to construct a political and moral climate that denies to such individuals, and their political organizations, normal rights as civilians, combatants, and as political actors.

The issues here are far more important and complex than matters of semantics, and pre-date the September 11 preoccupations with "terrorism." By describing all Palestinian or Kurdish political violence as "terrorism" the official authorities both sanitize their own violence as well as invalidate *any* form of armed struggle in settings of resistance to an oppressive occupation or

---

[2] Such a perspective is given its most expansive expression by Norman Podhoretz in an article insisting that the American response to September 11 be treated as World War IV (2004).

in relation to efforts by dissatisfied "captive nations" to exercise their right of self-determination.[3] Of course, the opposite point of sanitizing all non-state violence undertaken in a resistance mode by claiming an unrestricted "right of self-determination" or a legal exemption for "a war of national liberation" is certainly not intended.[4] Assuming the retention of terrorism as a descriptive term, *some* anti-state political violence is properly described as terrorism, as, for instance, suicide bombing of civilian targets. And certainly not all state political violence directed at non-state opposition is terrorism, if resulting from isolated instances of excessive police violence or if military and para-military is directed in a proportional and discriminate manner at anti-state combatants actively engaged in armed struggle that amounts to an insurgency. These definitional concerns have never been trivial, and the varying approaches to "terrorism" even at the level of state policy has been so great as to prevent an agreed definition that could underpin a global anti-terrorist treaty. But certainly it is true that such concerns have grown in magnitude since September 11, not least because of an extremely unpopular American diplomacy around the world that insists that those who do not side with the United States in its global "anti-terrorist policies" will be treated as siding with "the terrorists."[5]

This emphasis on terminology has assumed a more significant form since September 11. American leaders immediately declared war on "terrorism" in general, which was meant to encompass both anti-state violence and state support for only such violence.[6] This unspecified American mandate was immediately seized upon to validate escalating violence by the Russian and Israeli governments against longtime internal adversaries under the banner of anti-terrorism. These practices raise a fundamental point. The attacks of

---

[3] It is useful to recall the evolution of the term terrorism, which has had its origins in the use of state terrorism in the Thermidor stage of the French Revolution, perhaps most memorably described by Crane Brinton in his influential book *The Anatomy of Revolution* (New York: Vintage, 1957, originally published in 1952). It has been a successful statist campaign to engineer this shift in word usage, restricting the word terrorism to anti-state violence, and extending its usage even to political violence that occurs in the course of a legitimate political struggle against oppressive rule and is directed at military and governmental targets.

[4] I have tried to reconstruct a more satisfactory pattern of usage for the terminology of terrorism, considering its usage in some form as unavoidable. See Falk 1998, 2003a.

[5] An argument cogently presented by Zbigniew Brzezinski (2004: 24–36).

[6] This failure to restrict the objective of the American response to September 11 has been a consistent feature of official statements, starting with President Bush's Address to a Joint Session of Congress on September 20, 2001. It became a issue on a global level particularly after the U.S. government kept extending its militarist responses, first verbally by its designation of states as forming an "axis of evil" and then by initiating a non-defensive war against a member of the axis, Iraq, without any prior authorization by the United Nations Security Council.

September 11 involved a novel challenge to world order, raising issues of the severity, scale of harm, as well as the apocalyptic methods and goals of Al Qaeda. To merge this threat with the many pre-existing issues of unresolved resistance and self-determination struggles is to denigrate the character of these anti-state movements and, at the same time, to encourage states to resolve such conflicts by indiscriminate violence. This issue of merger has also been posed by the American encounters with armed resistance in Afghanistan and Iraq. It is possible to draw some distinctions, including the plausibility of treating Al Qaeda fighters and jihadist operatives as "terrorists." At the same time, to brand organized movements of resistance, especially in Iraq as inherently "terrorist" even when the main targets of this political violence are occupying soldiers who invaded the country in a manner contrary to international law and in violation of the United Nations Charter is to do violence to language and politics alike.[7] To the extent that either side targets civilians in Iraq, it is appropriate to regard such political violence as terrorism, but to single out the resistance fighters and their tactics is to mislead and distort perceptions of the conflict.

With these considerations in mind, is it still clarifying to speak of this epoch as an "Age of Terrorism"? Such a question hovers over any deliberation as to the effect of September 11 in an ambiguous manner.[8] It is true that the declared *American* preoccupation since September 11 has been officially focused on restoring global security by destroying Al Qaeda. At the same time, many critics here and abroad challenge this official version of American policy, and are far less concerned with the Al Qaeda threat to world order than with the American project, which is most often discussed under the rubric of "empire," making "Age of Empire" a more fitting sequel to the 1990s, which was widely regarded as the "Age of Globalization."[9] From this perspective, to accept blandly the designation of an Age of Terror is to allow Washington to frame and so manipulate the historical moment, especially if terrorism is limited in its usage, as has been the case in official usage, to anti-state violence by non-state political actors.[10]

---

[7] The emergence of a consensus among international law specialists as to the illegality of the Iraq invasion and subsequent occupation was evident at a plenary panel of the 2004 Annual Meeting of the American Society of International Law. See "Iraq, One Year Later," Proceedings of the 98th Annual Meeting, March 31–April 3, 2004, Washington, D.C., 261–73.

[8] Such a discussion is imaginatively present in the Borradori volume (2003).

[9] There is a vast literature on this theme of empire. See the following for the most notable works: Hardt & Negri 2000; Joxe 2002; Bacevich 2002; Harvey 2003; Mann 2003.

[10] For background on state terrorism in an Asian setting, but also useful for its conceptual understanding, see Selden & So 2004; on a more general level, see the older but still useful collection of essays in George 1991.

It is my view that we cannot properly assess the human rights impacts of September 11 without taking a position on these broad contextual matters. For purposes of the discussion in this chapter only, I accept provisionally, and with the serious qualifications noted, the American insistence that the defining idea of our present era is terror, and that we are thus justified in reaching a conclusion that we are living in an Age of Terror, rather than, say, the Age of Empire or the Age of Globality.[11] As argued, my discomfort would be greatly reduced if the Age of Terror was generally understood as an acknowledgment of the salience of indiscriminate political violence, including the continuing retention and development of weapons of mass destruction, particularly nuclear weapons. Yet it is here that labeling is subject to political control, reflecting the capacity of the American government, as well as its supporters in conservative think tanks and the media, to restrict unacceptably the general comprehension of the terrorist discourse to the enemies of the United States. For this reason, in part, I do not believe that the label will travel well beyond the territorial confines of the United States even if it is understood in the more critical fashion being proposed here. It will also not travel well because for most other parts of the world "terror" in either the narrow or broad sense is not the primary preoccupation of most of the peoples in the world and their leaders.

This consideration of labels also bears on the perspective taken on human rights. By highlighting "terrorism" there is an almost unavoidable tendency to perceive issues through the lens of the September 11 attacks, and to downplay such other issues as are associated with the inequities arising from the operation of the world economy or with the practices that produce environmental decay. In these respects from the perspective of human rights' priorities, the highlighting of the security agenda inevitably leads to a downplaying of economic and social rights, the right of self-determination, health issues, and rights associated with environmental protection. It is to be expected that academic discussions of security would take different forms in other parts of the world, that the American context of discussion is in this respect rather the exception than the rule.

Overall Adverse Effects of September 11

Even assuming a prudent and ethically sensitive American response to September 11, which by now is a non-sustainable position, some serious

---

[11] With some hesitation I have earlier made the argument that labeling the 1990s as the era of globalization was justified (Falk 1999).

adverse effects would have inevitably occurred in any country experiencing such severe and unexpected attacks. First of all, the severity, shock, and fears associated with the attacks would have induced *any* American leadership immediately to put the security of the society at the center of its political agenda, and by so doing, diminish the attention and priority accorded to the protection of international human rights as matters of national policy. This generalized impact was reinforced by the realization that "sleeper cells" of terrorists likely exist within American borders and that high-profile soft targets abound in the country. For these reasons, it was reasonable to expect greater security precautions impinging on human rights in America, especially as associated with air travel and access to high-value soft targets. In this regard, it was reasonable to expect enhanced efforts to keep dangerous individuals from entering the country or operating freely within it. This inevitable impact of September 11 was soon made unacceptable from a human rights perspective, however, by the gratuitously abusive treatment of individuals, especially of Islamic males, detained on the basis of scant suspicion or deported for trivial technical infractions of immigration regulations. This flagrant series of failures to show minimum respect for the rights of individuals was deeply disturbing, especially as this governmental behavior seemed to flow from the highest levels of authority and could not be convincingly rationalized as necessary for "security," even taking into account the anxieties associated with the post-attack atmosphere in America, which included the anticipation of further attacks.

Also, given the leading position of the United States both as political actor and as promoter of human rights, its new preoccupation with security would diminish the emphasis previously accorded to human rights in American foreign policy, most notably during the 1990s.[12] The emphasis by Washington on its security agenda, including the significance given to the acquisition of allies in its "war on terror" inevitably meant turning a blind eye toward oppressive practices of countries that were acting under the banner of anti-terror. This was the case with respect to countries with serious ongoing self-determination struggles, but also such newly found strategic partners as Uzbekistan and Pakistan, both with very poor human rights records.[13] In effect, American foreign policy in the period since September 11 has reverted to a cold war strategic outlook in which *geopolitical* considerations have taken consistent

---

[12] For consideration of what I have called "the normative revolution" of the 1990s, with its emphasis on a global justice agenda that accented the role of human rights, see Falk 2004.
[13] See the Neil Hicks chapter in this volume.

and decisive precedence over *normative* (that is, the norms of law and ethics) considerations.

Again, as with the cold war, "freedom" is used as a code word by American leaders to mean "on our side." The supposed promotion of freedom and democracy become a large part of the rationale for interventionary wars as in Afghanistan and Iraq. But it also substitutes self-serving geopolitical criteria for normative criteria, that is, assessing the outcomes by reference to the goals of Washington rather than by standards embodied in international human rights. Again, the cold war rhetoric of "the free world" and "free elections" reminds us that authoritarian leaders such as the Shah of Iran and Pinochet were strongly favored by the United States over democratically inclined leaders such as Mossadegh and Allende.[14]

We are faced with difficult issues of assessment. Are the people of Afghanistan and Iraq beneficiaries of war and occupation from the perspective of human rights? It would be premature to offer a definitive answer at this stage, although the future looks more and more definitively dismal for both countries with each passing month. It can be observed that a major incidental cost of the Iraq War, in particular, was to weaken the role of United Nations' authority and of international law.[15] These issues are further entangled with a discussion of the inability to explain the Iraq War convincingly as a response to global terrorism, or as an engagement with the emancipation of oppressed peoples. This war can be best understood as an aspect of the wider American drive for regional and global domination. It is the case that the difficulties of the occupation have increasingly led the United States government to strike a posture of deference to Iraqi sovereignty and of soliciting the widest possible United Nations and international participation. Whether this altered American posture might eventually allow for self-determination on the part of the Iraqi people remains doubtful, as does the political outcome in Iraq as measured by the yardsticks of human rights and democracy. It is possible, of course, that despite imperial objectives that primarily motivated the war, the impact of these wars and subsequent occupations will produce a net gain if appraisal is narrowly based on human rights and democracy.

I am arguing, however, that this narrow appraisal is not adequate, and due account must be given to the negative effects of loosening the bonds of legal, moral, and political constraints on recourse to war. This loosening cannot

---

[14] For the most comprehensive critique along these lines, see Chomsky & Herman 1979.
[15] I have argued along these lines in "What Future for the UN Charter System of War Prevention? Reflections on the Iraq War" (2003b: 195–214).

be disregarded even if the following insistence by President Bush on behalf of the war is accepted, namely, that the people of Iraq, the region, and the world are better off having Saddam Hussein in jail instead of in power. To endorse such a post hoc justification of war would be an exceedingly dangerous precedent, given the unwillingness of available international procedures under U.N. auspices to indicate a *prior* green light for humanitarian intervention, given the regional and popular opposition to the war, given the absence of a palpable humanitarian emergency in Iraq, and given the lack of an established internal opposition to the regime of Saddam Hussein. Such factors should be contrasted with the situation that existed in relation to the NATO Kosovo War of 1999, which itself posed a series of difficult issues because recourse to a non-defensive war was undertaken without a proper legal mandate by the U.N. Security Council.[16]

Some Specific Adverse Effects

The specific adverse effects on human rights are associated with developments that are not derivative from more general policies adopted, especially the priority accorded to security and geopolitical goals, but rather are reflections of deficiencies in the human rights culture of the United States and to a lesser extent in other countries. This is a large subject by itself, and can be encompassed by the rapid and uncritical omnibus legislation known as "The USA PATRIOT Act," which empowered the government to do in the name of anti-terrorism a series of previously prohibited activities intruding on the privacy and liberties of citizens, and even more so, non-citizens. As earlier suggested, there were grounds for tightening security at the expense of rights in light of the severe threats to fundamental security posed after September 11, but such initiatives could have been mainly taken on the basis of pre-existing legislation and carefully crafted supplemental laws.

Beyond the rush to provide the state with omnibus powers over the citizenry, with new proposals being presented for adding still further to the authority of the state, has been the disturbing pattern of practices disclosed, especially in relation to Arab-American and Muslim males. Abusive detention on the basis of unsubstantiated and vague allegations and suspicions has

---

[16] *The Kosovo Report* (Independent International Commission on Kosovo 2002) draws a distinction between "legality" and "legitimacy," and draws the precarious conclusion that the Kosovo War was illegal, yet legitimate. This conditional endorsement was further limited by a framework of principles restricting the claim of legitimacy within principled boundaries. It should be mentioned that I was a member of the commission, and participated in the drafting of the report.

been frequent, accompanied by the vindictive denial of rights to contact with lawyers or family. Such behavior has revealed attitudes of anger, revenge, and racism, and has been inconsistent with claims of prudent law enforcement.

This picture of a gratuitous and vindictive approach to security was strongly reinforced by the style of detention and interrogation adopted by the Pentagon toward individuals detained in combat zones in Afghanistan and Iraq. From the very outset, the establishment of Camp X-Ray in the Cuban enclave of Guantánamo disclosed an American refusal to deal with its prisoners in a manner prescribed by international humanitarian law. The legalistic justification of Washington that these persons were "enemy combatants" and not "prisoners of war," thereby falling outside the protection of the Geneva Convention, was problematic. But even accepting this unilateral and illegal reclassification of such individuals, the manner of their treatment aroused worldwide concerns about the inhumane practices of the prison authorities. This disturbing and discrediting approach was coupled with the establishment of military commissions operating in secret, without appellate procedures for review, with loose rules of evidence, and given the authority to impose capital punishment. The whole structure of such an ad hoc criminal process expressed, above all, a disregard of the rights of the person, and especially a completely coercive approach to individuals who were completely vulnerable in view of their conditions of detention that included harsh methods of interrogation.

What was first disclosed in Guantánamo, and justified by the urgency of obtaining information relating to Al Qaeda, has been confirmed many times over by the pictorial evidence of abuse at Abu Ghraib prison, and other prisons in Afghanistan and Iraq. What is most disturbing about these disclosures, which came to light indirectly in the form of leaks to the media, is the degree to which they represented dysfunctional exercises in sadism and humiliation, which were indirectly, at least, encouraged at the highest levels of government. The great majority of the inmates of Abu Ghraib were not even connected with the Iraqi resistance, much less Al Qaeda or kindred organizations. The depth and breadth of abuse reveals an alarming indifference to human rights. True, these practices have been repudiated, and many of the individuals directly involved will be punished in some ways, but there is no disposition to impose standards of accountability on the higher responsible officials. Donald Rumsfield seems secure in his job, while General Sanchez, the commander in Iraq, is in danger of not receiving his fourth star, hardly sending potent messages of repudiation.

These disclosures contradict in fundamental ways the American claim that it is liberating Iraq and Iraqis, as well as it is the custodian of values diametrically opposed to those of the previous regime of Saddam Hussein. There is even a certain moral erosion of the effort to hold Saddam Hussein responsible for his massive perpetuation of Crimes Against Humanity while exempting George W. Bush and his entourage from scrutiny for their violations of international humanitarian law and, more generally, the laws of war. If Abu Ghraib represents what freedom and democracy mean for the new Iraq, the whole credibility of American leadership in the world is drawn into most serious question. The discourse of democracy, so prominently exhibited in the foreign policy pronouncement of the Bush Administration with respect to the Middle East, has always seemed puzzling, especially when strongly espoused by neocon analysts who are known to be intense supporters of Sharon's Israel (see Frum & Perle 2003). It is not questioned in such pro-Iraq War polemics that "the Arab street" is wildly anti-Israeli and anti-American, and that democracy for the Middle East in the central respect of responsiveness of government to popular will, would directly challenge the most prized features of the grand design of American policy for the region and the world. This advocacy only makes political sense for Washington if "democracy" for the Middle East resembles what the Soviet Union had in mind for its satellites in Eastern Europe when it spoke of "peoples democracy" and "socialism."

Three Alternative Response Patterns

The Turkish Exception: It is interesting to reflect that there is nothing deterministic about encroaching upon human rights in the aftermath of September 11. Turkey is an interesting case. The country was faced with a temporarily dormant insurgency involving the future of the Kurdish minority. As well, several terrorist incidents associated with international jihadism have occurred in Turkey since September 11. Turkey is a country with a strong so-called "deep state" controlled by a minimally accountable military, and Turkey is a member of NATO, a neighbor of Iraq, and a site for important American air bases and a regional strategic ally of the United States. Such a combination of circumstances give rise to expectations that Turkey would seize the occasion of September 11 to justify a tightening of the grip exercised by the state on society, and ignore societal pressures to improve the protection of human rights.

And yet, this expectation has proved to be wrong. Turkey has moved in the period to grant language and cultural rights to the Kurdish minority, it has encouraged the expansion of the right to freedom of expression along with other civil and political rights, it has worked with Europe to improve prison conditions, it has abolished capital punishment, it has enacted a series of laws that strengthen the position of the individual in relation to the state, and most impressive of all, it has made significant reforms intended to weaken the role of the deep state, especially by measures mandating the civilianization of the Turkish National Security Council. This latter important, symbolic, and substantive step was taken with the approval of the military leadership. It may be explained, in part, by the range of Turkish support for moves to satisfy the European Union that Turkey is indeed qualified to become a member.

Given the long unequal strategic relationship, it is also relevant to note that Turkey has not followed the American lead in declaring "war" on terrorism, and despite massive pressures from Washington, refused to allow its territory to be used to invade Iraq in 2003. In this respect, the Turkish government deferred both to its public opinion, which was overwhelmingly opposed to the Iraq War, and to the Parliament that diverged from the recommendation of the Turkish Prime Minister. This exercise of constitutional democracy, although called "disappointing" by a high official in the Pentagon, was not only an impressive exhibition of political independence on the part of Turkey, but also a revelation that democracy-in-practice is not welcomed in Washington when it collides with the pursuit of U.S. strategic objectives.

It is with reason that a leading Turkish official associated with these policies insists that "Turkey is the only country in the world that can claim to have improved its human rights record in the period since September 11."[17]

Of course, there are reasons for this Turkish exception, especially the push/pull influence of the European Union, which the present Ak Party government in Ankara are eager to satisfy so as to begin what promises, at best, to be a long and tortuous accession process. Further, the deep state associated with the Turkish military appears to support the effort to join the EU, as does the United States. Beyond this, the leadership for the sake of its own legitimacy needs to show the compatibility between its soft Islamic identity and its commitment to pluralistic democracy and the rights of individuals to pursue their own beliefs.

What is important under these circumstances is the conclusion that Turkey, despite its encounters with terrorist attacks in its leading city of Istanbul, appears no less secure because of this recent commitment to strengthen human rights. It is also the case that the Turkish state has been vigilant in seeking to use law enforcement methods to prevent and apprehend those engaged in terrorism, and to improve its capacity to prevent terrorism and to apprehend perpetrators. There has been in this period a dramatic tightening of security arrangements in hotels and public buildings, involving monitoring

---

[17] A statement made on a number of public occasions in 2004 by Professor Ahmet Devutoglu, chief advisor to the Prime Minister and Foreign Minister of Turkey.

of entry and nearby parking, but without inducing collective fear by recourse to such tactics as using color code alerts employed in the United States by the office of Homeland Security to convey from time to time a sense of heightened vulnerability. Would the United States have been less secure if it had taken an approach resembling that of Turkey? I think not. That is, there is no evidence to support the claim that the abridgement of human rights and the abuse of detainees and suspects enhances security, and even if some did exist, it would not on this basis alone justify official behavior violative of basic rights. Such supposedly "lesser evil" tactics put any government on a slippery slope that ends with the sort of widespread abuse and torture that has been revealed to have been practiced at Abu Ghraib, Guantánamo, and in prisons throughout Afghanistan and Iraq.

The Spanish Response to March 11: On March 11, 2004, several commuter trains heading for Madrid were exploded by terrorist bombs. The Spanish government, headed by one of the few major European governments to support the Iraq War, initially blamed the explosions on the radical Basque separatist organization ETA, which soon turned out to be a false allegation. Angered by the spin and by Azner's pro-Bush foreign policy, which in relation to the Iraq War ignored the wishes of the overwhelming majority of the Spanish people, the citizenry surprised public opinion polls a few days later by voting the socialists back to power in general elections. The new leadership, headed by Prime Minister Zapatero, immediately indicated that it would withdraw the Spanish contingent of troops from Iraq, and at the same time, would increase police efforts to protect Spanish society by taking steps to apprehend those responsible for the attacks and preventing future attacks. In subsequent weeks, many arrests were made, and the impression created that the new Spanish leadership had fashioned a creative policy that was anti-war *and* anti-terrorist at the same time.

By coincidence I arrived in Barcelona on the day of the attacks to take part in an academic conference. I marched in a large solemn demonstration of one million or so persons on March 12, and was struck by the banners that read "No to war, No to terrorism," "Azner, your war, our lives," and "No to Terrorism by the State." The central mood, also expressed in the talks and a few days later by voters in the national election, was that it was entirely feasible, and quite beneficial, to insist that anti-terrorism did not require a transnational war of undetermined scope.

Again, the question presents itself: Would the United States have less security internally and internationally if it had relied on the Spanish response after September 11? Of course, the facts were different. The attack on the United States was more severe symbolically and substantively, and was accompanied by Al Qaeda declarations of war against the United States and Americans. The nerve center of the perpetrators was immediately identified as Afghanistan, supporting the seemingly plausible contention that a measure of security could be achieved by recourse to a regime-changing war against the Taliban regime in Afghanistan, with the accompanying goal of wiping out the Al Qaeda redoubt. In retrospect, it now seems that the rush to war against Afghanistan was uncritical and possibly counterproductive. It would have been worth exploring the Taliban offer immediately after September 11 to cooperate in a law enforcement mode to apprehend Osama Bin Laden, and end the Al Qaeda presence in the country.

But certainly after Afghanistan, the Spanish model seems far more likely to reconcile security interests with human rights than the American model. As argued above, the transnational scope of the American model can only be understood in relation to goals of foreign policy associated with a grand strategic design, and can only be understood as additional to, and in some respects antithetical to, anti-terrorism. To pursue those wider goals the tactics of fear and oppression are functional, diverting the American citizenry from a politically unacceptable agenda of global domination.

An American Response Based on Enhanced Law Enforcement: Implicit in the prior discussion is a radical questioning of the immediate adoption of a response model based on *war* rather than *law enforcement* by the U.S. government and the mainstream media. It is understandable that this reaction occurred, given the combined sense of urgency and trauma that was associated with the circumstances prevailing on September 12, as well as the war consciousness long associated with the Westphalian approach to world order. I confess to my own early failures of discernment, moving too quickly to accept the rationale for war against Afghanistan, and overlooking the unrealized potential of a law enforcement model (Falk 2003a: 61–72). This potential for inter-governmental cooperation was itself greatly increased by the initial sentiments of solidarity with the United States in the immediate aftermath of the attacks, a solidarity partly based on empathy for the tragedy and its victims, but also reflecting a shared statist opposition to anti-state political violence, especially as was the case with September 11, which was unconnected with any domestic struggle.[18] There existed in that period an unprecedented

[18] Of course, despite this statist opposition to violent penetrations of territorial sovereignty, states had frequently, and none more than the United States, supported anti-state exile movements engaged in transnational violence against established governments. Consider, for instance, support over the years for anti-Castro exiles in Florida and elsewhere culminating in CIA involvement in the Bay of Pigs failed invasion of April 1961, or the extensive help given

opportunity for international cooperation in a genuine effort to protect the basic structure of world order against what might be described as "mega-terrorism." Of course, the law enforcement model as a counter-factual is purely speculative with respect to its effectiveness and effects. What is not speculative are the opportunity costs and harms associated with reliance on the war model, especially as extended to Iraq. Part of these costs involves the sacrifice of human rights, and the difficulty of stopping such a slide once it is underway. It is well accepted that a war mentality tends to displace and over-whelm a human rights mentality both in tightening restraints on freedom in the name of security at home and with regard to the ranking of priorities in foreign policy, and this is precisely what has occurred (Wills 2004: 32–5). Such a displacement was particularly unfortunate as of 2001, as it disrupted an extraordinary pro-human rights momentum that was well underway in the period following the end of the cold war.

It is also not speculative to conclude that the war model as applied to this new form of global conflict has produced many difficulties, some of which have seemed to augment the mega-terrorist danger. And it is not speculative to take note of the non-territorial locus of international jihadism, making war against a sovereign state an indiscriminate and grossly ineffective instrument of response. Even from the perspective of the wider strategic design of regional and world domination it is not at all clear that the militarist strategies favored by the neocon worldview are more effective than the economistic and soft power strategies of the liberal internationalists of the Clinton presidency.[19] What seems evident is that the nature of mega-terrorist threats mounted from concealed and dispersed sites gives a new primacy to information and accurate intelligence even as compared to its vital role in traditional state-to-state conflict, especially with respect to weaponry of mass destruction and missile technology. Such intelligence is exceedingly difficult to achieve, but it seems that American leaders were reluctant to act on intelligence assessments of mega-terrorist threats, both with respect to the pre-September 11 realities and in relation to the Iraq War.[20]

---

to the Contras who were seeking to disrupt by political violence the Sandinista Government of Nicaragua, and more recently the help given to Iraqi exile groups committed to the overthrow of the Saddam Hussein regime in Iraq.

[19] A series of books critical of the Bush foreign policy have argued for the restoration of American leadership in a manner that endorses the economistic and multilateralist approaches of the 1990s by the United States. This restoration involves a resumption of the global empire project, but with more reliance on market forces, a renewed sense of legitimacy, and a reliance on persuasive forms of diplomacy. Useful texts in this regard are Brzezinski 2004; Bacevich 2002; and Etzioni 2004.

[20] Among the most compelling insider books on these failures to follow the trail of intelligence signposts are Clarke 2004; Anonymous 2004; and National Commission 2004. See also the

In criticism of law enforcement it is widely believed by the public and many commentators that it was tried and failed in the 1990s, and that, in any event, it is not responsive to the magnitude and originality of the threat posed by mega-terrorism. It is being claimed that the United States is engaged in World War IV that can only be waged by a full-scale mobilization associated with war that can alone address the challenge to security.[21] I find such a defense of the war model unconvincing and a recipe for a self-defeating approach to security, either reflecting the old thinking of a statist world or the unacceptable new thinking of global empire, and possibly blending the two ideas of order unacceptably. At the same time, the unreflective dismissal of a law enforcement approach is insensitive to the possibilities of enhanced law enforcement based on full-scale global cooperation.[22] The adoption of the law enforcement model would be greatly facilitated if it would be combined with the recognition of the importance of addressing the roots of political and religious extremism, including especially the *legitimate* grievances of the Islamic world against an American-led world order. Such grievances include the failure to promote a just solution for Palestinian self-determination and the embrace of predatory globalization that disadvantages the poorer segments of humanity. Such adjustments would not amount to an acquiescence in the demands of political extremists, but would involve taking steps that should have been undertaken long ago. *Illegitimate* grievances, including relating to the existence and security of Israel and other sovereign states, should be rejected as before.

In favoring enhanced law enforcement, there are also implicit a wide series of opportunities to contribute simultaneously to the establishment of the sort of global architecture required for global governance in a post-Westphalian world in which sovereign states are losing control over many tendencies threatening their well-being, including crime, environment, and migration.[23]

Conclusion

I believe that with some minor exceptions the cause of human rights has been set back by the American response to September 11. This setback was not a

scathing attack on the 9/11 Commission, and its refusal to examine more fully and accurately the context of the attacks, by Griffin 2004.

[21] See Podhoretz 2004, who also is dismissive of reliance on law enforcement without providing any convincing grounds for substituting recourse to global war if indeed the goal is the avoidance of mega-terrorism in the future.

[22] See Clarke 2004 and Anonymous 2004, as well as the National Commission 2004 and surrounding discussion.

[23] An important comprehensive effort to argue the case for an emerging system of global governance that is being fashioned primarily by the state is Slaughter 2004; see also Etzioni 2004.

necessary effect of the attacks. It was a choice shaped as much by geopolitical ambitions as by the challenge of mega-terrorism. As long as these geopolitical ambitions are combined with a war model of response, the prospects for human rights are poor.

If consideration is given to the wider impacts of the attacks and American response, it might have some unanticipated positive effects of a dialectic character. It could move Europe to contrast its political identity with that of the United States by moving even further toward an ethos based on international law and human rights (Kagan 2003; Derrida 2004). It could stimulate the growth of a global anti-war movement that showed signs of robustness by way of the huge demonstration prior to the Iraq War on February 15, 2003, held in more than eighty countries. It could also produce a backlash in the United States that would create a political climate allowing a new leadership to move toward an abandonment of the war model and a concerted effort to address legitimate grievances. It could do all of these things, but these remain as of now remote political possibilities. The more likely political scenario is a continuing downward spiral of political violence, and state repression that drags down human rights at home and eliminates it from foreign policy.

REFERENCES

Anonymous. (2004). *Imperial Hubris: Why the West Is Losing the War on Terror*. Dulles, VA: Brassey's.

Bacevich, A. J. (2002). *American Empire: The Realities & Consequences of U.S. Diplomacy*. Cambridge, MA: Harvard University Press.

Borradori, G. (2003). *Philosophy in a Time of Terror: Dialogues with Jürgen Habermas and Jacques Derrida*. Chicago: University of Chicago Press.

Brinton, C. ([1952] 1957). *The Anatomy of Revolution*. New York: Vintage.

Brzezinski, Z. (2004). *The Choice: Global Domination or Global Leadership*. New York: Basic Books, pp. 24–36.

Chomsky, N. & Herman, E. T. (1979). *The Political Economy of Human Rights: After the Cataclysm: Postwar Indochina and the Reconstruction of Imperial Ideology*, Vol. 2. Boston: South End Press.

Clarke, R. A. (2004). *Against All Enemies: Inside America's War on Terror*. New York: Free Press.

Derrida, J. (2004, August 18). Interview by Jean Birnbaum, 'I am at War with Myself'. *Le Monde*.

Etzioni, A. (2004). *From Empire to Community: A New Approach to International Relations*. New York: Palgrave.

Falk, R. (1998). *Revolutionaries and Functionaries: The Dual Face of Terrorism*. New York: E. F. Dutton, pp. 1–39.

――――. (1999). *Predatory Globalization: A Critique*. Cambridge, UK: Polity Press.

_____. (2003a). *Great Terror War*. Northampton, MA: Olive Branch Press.

_____. (2003b). 'What Future for the UN Charter System of War Prevention? Reflections on the Iraq War'. In I. Abrams & W. Gungwu (Eds.), *The Iraq War and Its Consequences: Thoughts of Nobel Peace Laureates and Eminent Scholars*. Singapore: World Scientific, pp. 195–214.

_____. (2004). *The Declining World Order: America's Neo-Imperial Foreign Policy*. New York: Routledge, pp. 107–36.

Frum, D. & Perle, R. (2003). *An End to Evil: How to Win the War on Terror*. New York: Random House.

George, A. (Ed.). (1991). *Western State Terrorism*. London, UK: Routledge.

Griffin, D. R. (2004). *The 9/11 Commission Report: Omissions and Distortions*. Northampton, MA: Olive Branch Press.

Hardt, M. & Negri, A. (2000). *Empire*. Cambridge, MA: Harvard University Press.

Harvey, D. (2003). *The New Imperialism*. Oxford, UK: Oxford University Press.

Ignatieff, M. (2004). *The Lesser Evil: Political Ethics in an Age of Terror*. Princeton, NJ: Princeton University Press.

Independent International Commission on Kosovo ("Commission"). (2002). *The Kosovo Report: Conflict, International Response, Lessons Learned*. Oxford, UK: Oxford University Press, pp. 185–98.

Joxe, A. (2002). *Empire of Disorder*. Cambridge, MA: MIT Press (Semiotext(e)).

Kagan, R. (2003). *Of Paradise and Power*. New York: Knopf.

Mann, M. (2003). *The Incoherent Empire*. London, UK: Verso.

National Commission on Terrorist Attacks upon the United States. (2004). *The 9/11 Commission Report: Final Report of the National Commission on Terrorist Attacks upon the United States*. New York: Norton.

Podhoretz, N. (2004, September). 'World War IV: How It Started, What It Means, and Why We Have to Win'. *Commentary*.

Selden, M. & So, A. Y. (Eds.). (2004). *War & State Terrorism: The United States, Japan, & Asia-Pacific in the Long Twentieth Century*. Lanham, MD: Rowman & Littlefield.

Slaughter, A.-M. (2004). *A New World Order*. Princeton, NJ: Princeton University Press.

Wills, G. (2004, November 18). 'Iraq: A Just War'. *The NY Review of Books*, pp. 32–5.

12. Eight Fallacies About Liberty and Security

DAVID LUBAN[1]

We often hear it said that in times of danger we confront difficult trade-offs between national security and civil liberties, or between national security and human rights. We nod our heads, and reflect that tough times call for tough measures. An American official, commenting on the harsh and even brutal techniques that U.S. interrogators use on suspected terrorists, put it bluntly. "If you don't violate someone's human rights some of the time, you probably aren't doing your job" (Priest & Gelman 2002).[2] While some people might find such talk appalling, others find it realistic, tough-minded, and oddly reassuring. We face terrible threats posed by ruthless international terrorists who have already proven themselves eager for mass murder – and who may well gain access to weapons of apocalyptic power. Confronted with these threats, excessive concern with human rights and civil liberties seems legalistic and, however well-meaning it is, misguided. Trade-offs are inevitable, and the only important question then becomes where to draw the line. How much liberty should be sacrificed in the name of security? How many human rights can we afford to respect?

The constitutional scholar John Hart Ely once remarked that no answer is what the wrong question begets (Ely 1980: 72). In this chapter, I argue that the questions in the last paragraph are the wrong ones to ask; unfortunately, it is not non-answers they beget, but wrong answers. The whole conversation about "trade-offs" conceals persistent fallacies, and once we take care to

---

[1] Frederick Haas Professor of Law and Philosophy, Georgetown University Law Center. I would like to thank David Cole and Judith Lichtenberg from comments on an earlier draft that saved me from serious errors.
[2] Another official explained, "There was a before 9/11, and there was an after 9/11. After 9/11 the gloves come off" (Priest & Gelman 2002).

eliminate the fallacies, the questions themselves become far less obvious, and in certain ways less urgent.

Fallacy One: The Mel Brooks Fallacy

First, the supposed "trade-off" between security and rights is too easy as long as it's a trade-off of your rights for my security.[3] Mel Brooks once said that tragedy is when I break a fingernail, and comedy is when you fall down a manhole and die. Proponents of the so-called trade-off win specious support by building in an implicit Mel Brooks theory of rights: do unto the rights of others whatever it takes to make me feel more secure. This is no real trade-off. The trade-off question becomes genuine only when we pose it in its legitimate form: how many of *your own* rights are you willing to sacrifice for added security?

Even in this form, the question is deceptively sloppy. As a respectable, middle-aged, native-born, white, tenured professor who leads a dull life, I know the odds are slender that I will ever need to invoke the right against self-incrimination or the right to a speedy, public trial, let alone the right not to be shipped off to the Jordanian police for interrogation. (Knock on wood.) So I am likely to undervalue these rights. In my own mind, I unconsciously classify them as OPR – Other People's Rights. Illicitly, I have returned to the Mel Brooks theory. So long as the government targets only Muslims and foreigners, young men and aging charismatic clerics, paring back on the rights of the accused is no tragedy, in the Mel Brooks sense of tragedy.

Perhaps the question becomes more vivid if we respectable folks imagine that our own children might someday flirt with a radical group that runs afoul of the law.[4] Even then, however, it is easy to dismiss the hypotheticals

---

[3] This is one of the main themes of David Cole's important book *Enemy Aliens: Double Standards and Constitutional Freedoms in the War on Terrorism* (New York: New Press, 2003).

[4] If your college student offspring is careless enough to donate money or even a cellphone to a radical Palestinian group that the government has designated as a foreign terrorist organization, he or she faces many years in prison for providing material support to terrorists. The statutes are startlingly broad. The Secretary of State is authorized to designate as "terrorist organizations" any group of two or more individuals who use or even threaten to use firearms in any country in a way that directly or indirectly endangers life or property (8 U.S.C. § 1182(a)(3)(B)). Anyone who provides material support to a designated organization can receive up to fifteen years in prison (if no one dies at the hands of organization) or life imprisonment (if someone dies) (18 U.S.C. § 2339B). And what is material support? It

because they sound too far-fetched to hit home. Psychologically, it is very difficult to weigh the importance of rights and civil liberties without assuming, consciously or not, the Mel Brooks theory that rights I and my loved ones are unlikely to need are less important than my physical security. But avoiding the Mel Brooks theory is what we must do. Conceptually, we should pose the question using John Rawls' device of an imaginary "veil of ignorance" that at the moment of choice cloaks us from all knowledge of who we are. Suppose that at the moment of choosing your security/rights package, you have no knowledge of whether, when the Veil of Ignorance falls away, you will find yourself a young man of Middle Eastern birth, detained indefinitely without access to counsel or a hearing of any kind, even though you are not a terrorist and are guilty of nothing but minor visa violations. In that case, you are likely to want certain rock-bottom protections to hedge against the possibility of losing your liberty for years because you are the wrong nationality in the wrong place at the wrong time.

Some might reply that it is government's job to protect the interests of its own citizens over those of foreigners. But the human rights of foreigners constitute a moral limit to nationalistic self-preference, and discounting the interests of others can lead to results fairly described as grotesque. When the United States began planning for an American presence in post-genocide Rwanda, Pentagon planners informed the commander of the U.N. force that they needed a body count of the genocide because their superiors considered one American casualty to be the equivalent of 85,000 dead Rwandans (Power 2002: 381). This kind of faux-objective corpse calculus may sound refreshingly hard-nosed to some, a cost-benefit trade-off reminiscent in spirit of Jeremy Bentham, the founder of modern utilitarianism, who regarded human rights as nonsense and inalienable human rights as "nonsense on stilts" (Bentham 1824). But even hard-nosed utilitarians believe that "each counts for one and none for more than one." Fortunately, the Mel-Brooks-like theories of the Rwanda planners are not the official view of the U.S. government, which endorses universal human rights. Indeed, one of President George W. Bush's policy advisors has described the President's view as the "fairly radical belief that a child in an African village whose parents are dying of AIDS has the same importance before God as the president of the United States" (Bumiller

---

includes any amount of money, communications equipment, facilities, or transportation (18 U.S.C. § 2339A(b)). More than that: it includes training, personnel, and expert advice and assistance, startlingly broad categories that can include writing an op-ed in support of the group. See *Humanitarian Law Project v. Reno* (9th Cir. 2000); analysis reaffirmed in *Humanitarian Law Project v. United States DOJ* (9th Cir. 2003).

2003).[5] This is a strong and welcome dose of human rights thinking, and it is a useful corrective to the Mel Brooks fallacy.

Fallacy Two: Thinking That Liberties and Rights Are Different from Security

The Veil of Ignorance thought experiment highlights a feature about civil liberties and human rights that the security-versus-liberty question conceals: rights are themselves forms of security. They are, specifically, security against abuses of the government's police power. The framers of the Constitution were unsentimental men who knew that government officials will inevitably be tempted to abuse the law to get rich, intimidate their opponents, persecute their enemies, or entrench their own power. They also understood that law enforcement is impatient with the niceties of process; enforcement officials will seek the shortest distance between two points. Furthermore, they understood the arrogance of power – the inevitable tendency of those on top to trust their own judgment and assume their own infallibility. For that reason, our Constitution not only protects our rights; it overprotects them. Even if the best source of evidence against a criminal is his own testimony, the framers insisted that he has the right against self-incrimination. Innocent or guilty, he has the right to counsel. Furthermore, as Robert Bork (1990) observes, "Courts often give protection to a constitutional freedom by creating a buffer zone, by prohibiting a government from doing something not in itself forbidden but likely to lead to an invasion of a right specified in the Constitution" – a practice that Bork, hardly a flaming liberal, agrees with.[6] To diminish civil liberties means to diminish our security against abuses and errors of government officials.

Understood in these terms, the trade-off between security and civil liberties might represent a judgment that we fear our own government less than we fear terrorists. Only a paranoid conspiracy-theorist thinks that the government is planning to send in the black helicopters, or is operating with the kind of bad faith and malice that suggests we should fear paring back on Bork's buffer zones.

---

[5] The quotation is from Michael Gerson.

[6] Bork is discussing the case *NAACP v. Alabama*, 357 U.S. 449 (1958), where the Court upheld the right of the NAACP not to turn its membership lists over to the state of Alabama, on the ground that the state's subpoena of the lists would have a chilling effect on membership and thus impinge on the First Amendment right of political association.

But one need not be a paranoid or a conspiracy theorist to believe that government can be error-prone, inefficient, and unwilling to admit mistakes. Indeed, most conservatives who favor paring back on civil liberties in the name of security believe all these things. If the question is, for example, empowering the government to engage in cybersearches to compile profiles of Americans and detect suspicious-looking patterns of behavior, consider the possibility of error and the harm it might do.

Several times in the last few years, I tried to use my credit card and discovered that my bank had frozen it because their theft-detection software found a suspicious pattern of purchases. Twice, it was because I was traveling far from my home. Several times, I had made three or four back-to-back purchases of the kind of goodies thieves buy (gasoline, clothing, electronics). The errors were entirely understandable. That did not make them less inconvenient – and once, stranded abroad, the lack of the credit card put me in a genuine jam.

Is the government's terrorist-detection software likely to be less error-prone than my bank's theft detection software? If anything, the opposite is likely to be true, because the stakes of a false negative are so much higher that analysts will likely err on the side of suspicion. Now imagine that the software error labeled me a potential terrorist, instead of merely blocking my credit card. This might lead to embarrassing interrogations of my employers and friends, an "invitation" to go visit the FBI, or perhaps even an arrest. It might cost me my job. If I happen to have a Muslim name, or to have traveled recently to Pakistan, the odds are worse. If I am an alien who overstayed my visa, I face indefinite secret detention in an immigration gulag.

Even if this isn't a genuine worry (but how, except on the Mel Brooks theory, could it not be?), the government cannot possibly guarantee that information it collects will never be released improperly – for example, sold by a rogue bureaucrat (or a hacker) to my insurance company.[7] The rights-security trade-off – actually, I am arguing, a security-security trade-off – is less hypothetical than may at first appear. "Better safe than sorry!" is not just a pro-security argument, it is a pro-civil-liberties argument as well.

---

[7] See *U.S. v. Czubinski*, 106 F.3d 1069 (1st Cir. 1997), upholding the conviction of an IRS employee who gathered unauthorized confidential tax information about a number of people, including a woman he had dated a few times, a man who had defeated Czubinski in a city council election, and a district attorney who had once prosecuted Czubinski's father. Czubinski apparently did nothing with the information, but that should not make us feel more relieved. None of us has the slightest idea how many other Czubinskis are out there reading our tax forms for their own amusement, and not getting caught.

Fallacy Three: The Fallacy of Tendentious Labeling

We often have a tendency to think that civil libertarians are idealists, while advocates of strong security measures even at the expense of civil liberties are tough-minded realists. In fact, however, the argument is equally strong for saying that it's the other way around: pro-security people have a naive faith in the probity of government (see Fallacy Two), while civil libertarians, who think that government will abuse its power, are the tough-minded realists.

Of course, this too is a one-sided and exaggerated worldview. Better than either is to appreciate that thinking in terms of realists and idealists, the tough-minded and the tender-minded, and other dichotomies of this character, gets us nowhere. It should simply be dropped from the repertoire of respectable argumentation. Labeling those who wish to restrict civil liberties "pragmatists" and denying the label to those who wish to protect them strongly is not helpful.

Fallacy Four: The Fallacy of Small Numbers

The question "how many of your rights are you willing to sacrifice for added security?" is too sloppy because it does not specify how much added security you are likely to gain. The probability of my falling victim to a terrorist attack is, in absolute numerical terms, very slight – how slight is obviously unquantifiable – and so the subjective sense of danger many of us feel bears little relation to any objective measure of likelihood. Psychologists have long known that people overestimate small risks once the risks become psychologically salient, and none of us is immune from this tendency. We are beyond the realm of rational comparison.

It is even more difficult to calculate what increment of added security any given increment in governmental power at the expense of rights can create. But that is the real question. Critics of American intelligence have charged that September 11 should have been detected and stopped before it happened; but defenders of the intelligence community, including the authors of the *9/11 Report*, argue persuasively that what seems plain in hindsight is often impossible to grasp ex ante. When you don't know clearly what you are looking for, isolated scraps of information often appear meaningless.

Let us suppose that the intelligence community's defenders are right about this. The clear implication is that added intelligence-gathering capacity may not provide a big boost in security. Many of us are prone to an understandable mistake: first we picture a terrorist attack that is a sure thing – for example, we picture September 11, which is a sure thing in our own minds because it actually happened. Then we ask ourselves what sacrifice in our liberty we would be willing to undergo in order to prevent it. The answer is obvious: we would be willing to sacrifice a lot of liberty to prevent September 11. But posed that way the question is nonsensical: it is simply a disguised version of a fairy-tale hypothetical – what sacrifice in our rights would we be willing to undergo to undo September 11? September 11 is a low-probability event; the government possesses formidable intelligence and law-enforcement capacity even without new restrictions on civil liberties; and giving the government added powers to investigate and detain people may itself lower that probability only by a little. As a matter of fact, it might actually raise the probability of missing the next terrorist attack, if the new powers inundate the government with useless information, or provoke negative reactions that cause potential informants to withhold information out of fright or anger.

If the trade-off question were posed accurately – that is, without the faulty assumption that loss of liberty makes us significantly safer – it would be this: what sacrifice in our rights would we be willing to undergo to reduce the already-small probability of another September 11 by a factor of, say, one in ten? From, let us say, one percent annually to point-nine percent – an annual saving of less than half a statistical life? And by how much would you be willing to raise the probability of yourself undergoing a false arrest in order to achieve an increment in security that registers only in the third decimal place? That question no longer has an obvious answer. Obviously, my numbers are entirely hypothetical. They are not even guesstimates. But small probabilities, whatever their actual magnitude, are far more realistic than large ones.

Fallacy Five: The Fallacy of the Perpetual Emergency

The U.S. Constitution contains a few provisions for times of emergency, for example by empowering Congress to call forth the national militia to execute the laws, suppress insurrections, and repel invasions (Article I, section 8), or to suspend habeas corpus "when in cases of rebellion or invasion the public safety may require it" (Article I, section 9). Famously, President Lincoln suspended the writ of habeas corpus in the Civil War without Congressional permission. He did so out of fear that unless border-state Confederate sympathizers could be quickly detained they might sabotage essential rail lines: Maryland was too close for comfort to the nation's capital. Suspending habeas corpus was a controversial measure at the time – Lincoln was probably violating the Constitution – but the emergency condition the United States found itself in arguably justified Lincoln's decision.

September 11 likewise marked a true emergency. In the immediate aftermath, when no one knew how wide the conspiracy was, or who was involved, or whether a follow-up attack was already in motion, the FBI detained thousands of Middle Eastern men and interviewed many more. Did the emergency justify a massive short-term dragnet? I think it did. The embarrassment and fright of the interviewees was a small price to pay for an absolutely essential investigation. Even those who were wrongly arrested and detained should have been able to understand that in such a situation investigators had little alternative to sweeping very broadly (although it would have been far better if afterward the government had at least apologized publicly).

But many of them were detained for months, not just hours or days. During the first ten days they were allowed no access to counsel, and subsequently permitted only one outside phone call per week. The Justice Department refused to release their names or even a count of how many there are. To justify its night-and-fog policy, DOJ explained that it did not want to tip off Al Qaeda about which of their operatives were in custody. But this rationale made sense only for the first few days after September 11, when Al Qaeda was presumably scrambling to find out which of its operatives with sensitive information had been arrested. Weeks and months later, the idea that Al Qaeda might still be in the dark about who has gone AWOL is absurd. Nor is this simply harmless error: it turned out that none of those secretly detained were Al Qaeda operatives; and, of the estimated 5,000 detained in the initial dragnet, only five have been charged with terrorism-related crimes, and only one has been convicted (Cole 2003: 25–6).[8]

At this point, the plea of emergency no longer makes sense: calling long-term conditions (like the standing danger of terrorism) an "emergency" is a confusion. Emergencies are temporary departures from normal conditions. September 11 was an emergency. Daily life under long-term risk is not. Any abrogation of rights due to long-term "emergency" conditions should be regarded as permanent, not temporary.

Fallacy Six: The Fallacy of Confusing Substantive Liberties with Their Safeguards

To speak of loss of civil liberties (or rights) actually blends together two distinct issues, because civil liberties encompass both powers and protections.

---

[8] Two others were acquitted, and one was convicted of non-terrorist-related charges. In the first seven weeks after September 11, 12,000 individuals were detained. Nearly 4,000 more have been detained since then.

A power is a substantive liberty: an ability to do something. A protection is a guarantee against official abuses. Freedom of religion is a power: it is the right to practice your religion without government persecution. By contrast, the Sixth Amendment rights "to a speedy and public trial, by an impartial jury of the State and district wherein the crime shall have been committed . . . and to be informed of the nature and cause of the accusation; to be confronted with the witnesses against him [the defendant]; to have compulsory process for obtaining witnesses in his favor, and to have the assistance of counsel . . ." are all protections against the possibility of criminal punishment by mistake or malice.

The distinction between powers and protections is not clear-cut: the right to hire the defense lawyer of my choice is a power as well as a protection (or, more precisely, it is a power contained within a protection). Furthermore, protections can be formally rephrased as powers – thus, the right to a trial by jury can be rephrased as the right to retain my liberty of movement unless convicted by a jury. But less formalistically, the distinction is straightforward common sense. Protections are primarily rights to certain kinds of due process, designed to ward off government error and abuse. They are only derivatively rights to exercise substantive liberties, and the rights they establish are valuable only when the government is after us. Powers, on the other hand, mark out substantive areas of activity that deserve protection so that people can engage in them; they are only derivatively rights to due process if government wants to prevent us from engaging in protected activities. The emphasis is entirely different. Powers, like the rights to free speech, free exercise of religion, freedom of the press, and freedom to associate protect goods that are desirable in and of themselves. Protections, like the rights of criminal defendants, are valuable only if you get in trouble with the law; a trial by jury, unlike a religious service, is not anyone's idea of a morning well spent.

It might be supposed that powers are more important than protections, so that it would be morally worse to constrict powers in the name of security. Actually, the loss of protections is more dangerous. Consider, for example, the most familiar of emergency restrictions on our powers: a curfew, for example during urban riots, or a blackout, or a terrorist attack. Imposing a curfew diminishes people's powers, but it doesn't enormously increase the risk of government abuse. Furthermore, restricting powers is likely to be done cautiously, because it typically affects everyone, which means that there are real political consequences attached to government being too harsh. I don't suggest this is inevitably true: many dictatorships have brutally clamped down on powers for years or even decades. But in the contemporary United States, which is not exactly teetering on the brink of fascism, government is very wary of imposing major inconveniences on Americans across the board. It has become conventional wisdom that if government tried to institute time-consuming, invasive airport security arrangements it would pay a political price. When the government proposed its Total Information Awareness (TIA) and Terrorism Information and Protection System (TIPS), public outrage over privacy invasions and a culture of informants quickly doomed both programs.

Those who argue that perhaps we have too many liberties for the insecure world we live in may have a point when they are referring to powers. Perhaps, for example, none of us can ever again afford the liberty of being able to board airliners without having our shoes x-rayed and our luggage searched. The loss of protections is a different matter. If the right of habeas corpus is suspended, or people are detained incommunicado, or arrested secretly, or assassinated, part of the firewall that protects us from government-inflicted evils has gone. Without the firewall, innocent people may be arrested or killed by mistake (or, what is even worse, *not* by mistake). If they truly are innocent people, then by hypothesis detaining them does nothing to enhance security. It makes them worse off without making anyone better off – the very definition of an unmitigated evil.

The reply is that overinclusive arrests or killings are a necessary evil, because it is simply too difficult or costly to use the procedures that get it right. Better that a hundred innocent people be imprisoned than that one terrorist escape the dragnet, if that terrorist might be carrying a suitcase full of smallpox. Eliminating false positives might let through too many false negatives.

Maybe; but that proposition should never be taken on faith. Its proponents must prove that public safety requires wider latitude for officials to shortcut procedures designed to protect people from being imprisoned or killed by mistake. They must prove that public safety would be threatened unless it is possible to keep the names of detainees secret or hold them incommunicado. The blanket argument that even one false negative might be a terrorist with a suitcase nuke or a crop duster filled with anthrax proves far too much, because the only way to eliminate literally *all* false negatives would be to kill or imprison millions. Or, if the argument is that our ordinary constitutional protections were designed for less perilous times, the response is that all times are perilous. The Civil War, World War II, and the Cold War were all perilous times. In the Civil War-era case *Ex parte Milligan* (1866), the Supreme Court confronted and rejected the argument that ours is a fair-weather Constitution. The Court wrote that the constitutional framers

foresaw that troublous times would arise, when rules and people would become restive under restraint, and seek by sharp and decisive measures to accomplish ends deemed just and proper . . . The history of the world had taught them that what was done in the past might be attempted in the future. The Constitution of the United States is a law for rulers and people, equally in war and in peace, and covers with the shield of its protection all classes of men, at all times, and under all circumstances. No doctrine, involving more pernicious consequences, was ever invented by the wit of man than that any of its provisions can be suspended during any of the great exigencies of government.

Fallacy Seven: Presuming Guilt

We sometimes hear official spokesmen argue that terrorists don't deserve the protection of our rights. Sometimes, the argument adds a rhetorical flourish: "Why should terrorists benefit from the very rights they are trying to destroy?" Such arguments were often used, for example, to justify denying legal process to the Guantanamo detainees. But it assumes that they *are* terrorists, which is the very thing that due process is supposed to settle. Asking "Why should terrorists benefit from the very rights they are trying to destroy?" is like asking, "Why should a guilty criminal get a fair trial?" The answer is obvious: the fair trial is the way we've devised to determine who is and who is not a guilty criminal. Without the trial, all we have is the authorities' say-so that it is indeed a *guilty* criminal we're talking about. The very posing of the rhetorical question already assumes guilt, or, assumes that it is indeed terrorists we are talking about (rather than innocent people wrongly presumed to be terrorists).

Sometimes the fallacy is transparent, for example when we are told for years that the reason Guantanamo internees should not get their Geneva Convention right to a hearing to determine if they really are enemy combatants is that they are Al Qaeda fighters and therefore not entitled to Geneva Convention rights. Of course, the question is whether they are indeed Al Qaeda fighters rather than innocent bystanders swept up by mistake. (During the 1991 Gulf War, two-thirds of those initially detained as possible enemy fighters were released after their hearings.) Our government has admitted that some of the Guantanamo detentions were mistakes, and has repatriated more than eighty detainees – after more than a year of imprisonment, apparently false imprisonment. Many remaining prisoners in Camp X-Ray reportedly have fallen into clinical depression, and suicide attempts have occurred at alarmingly high rates; one suspects that the American public tolerates this out of a lethal mix of the Mel Brooks fallacy and the repeated assertion that Camp X-Ray contains terrorists – the fallacy of presuming guilt, which readily translates into the thought that the inmates deserve the treatment they're getting. In June 2004, the Supreme Court held that the Guantanamo detainees are entitled to hearings on whether they are actually enemy combatants, but as of

November 2004, the government is still fighting against their right to appeal, and has dragged its feet in providing the requisite process (*Rasul v. Bush* 2004).

Another transparent example of the fallacy of presuming guilt is the government's threat to move Zacharias Moussaoui out of the civilian courts and into a military tribunal because it might be too difficult to convict him in civil court (because of that pesky Sixth Amendment right "to have compulsory process for obtaining witnesses in his favor"). Moussaoui is a particularly unappealing case, because he gloats about his Al Qaeda membership and admits that he is America's enemy. But he also claims to have played no role in the September 11 attacks, and that could be true. To offer the need for convicting him as a reason for moving his case to a military tribunal presumes that he is guilty.

These, I have said, are transparent fallacies. But the fallacy of presuming guilt can creep into public discourse in a subtler way. Consider Judge Michael Mukasey's otherwise capable opinion in *Padilla v. Bush* (S.D.N.Y. 2002), which concerns the government's right to hold U.S. citizen Jose Padilla without charges or trial because he is an alleged Al Qaeda fighter who hoped to make a "dirty bomb" to detonate in an American city.[9] The government claims that, as an unlawful enemy combatant, Padilla can be detained until the War on Terror is over – that is, detained indefinitely. Upholding the government's position, Judge Mukasey cited a 1942 case, *Ex parte Quirin*, which concerned a group of German saboteurs (including one U.S. citizen) captured in the United States. The Supreme Court's opinion in *Quirin* upheld the government's right to detain and punish the saboteurs, and Judge Mukasey argued that the government's right to detain Padilla logically follows from the right to detain and punish: the greater power includes the lesser.

This argument sounds entirely plausible – but only until we realize that it *assumes* that if he were tried Padilla would be convicted rather than acquitted, and indeed that after conviction he would be sentenced either to life imprisonment or death, rather than a fixed term of years. If either of these assumptions is false – that is, if he would be acquitted or sentenced to a fixed term of years – then the power to detain Padilla indefinitely without a trial is a greater power, not a lesser one, than the power to detain and punish him

---

[9] The decision was overturned on appeal, but on grounds unrelated to the arguments considered here. In June 2004, the Supreme Court held that Padilla's appeal had been filed in the wrong court and against the wrong defendants (*Rumsfeld v. Padilla*, 124 S. Ct. 2711 (2004)). Thus, his detention status remains unchanged. Given the Court's opinion in *Hamdi*, however, it seems likely that Padilla will eventually be granted a much more expansive hearing than Judge Mukasey's opinion envisages. The case is currently back in the lower courts.

after a trial. The judge's argument assumes guilt in order to deny the right to a trial designed to ascertain guilt. That is a fallacy, and a particularly insidious one.

Fallacy Eight: The Militarization of Civilian Life

In *Padilla*, as in other War on Terror cases, the government appeals to the president's war powers to argue that the judiciary should defer to the executive on military matters such as who to designate an enemy combatant.[10] In June 2004, the Supreme Court partially rebuffed this argument, holding that Yasir Hamdi (an American citizen captured allegedly fighting for the Taliban in Afghanistan, and held as an enemy combatant) must receive a hearing on whether he actually is an enemy combatant (*Hamdi v. Rumsfeld*, 124 S. Ct. 2633 (2004)). Even here, though, the Court did not grant Hamdi the same level of review offered to habeas petitioners in the criminal process: instead of placing the burden of proof on the government, the Court created a rebuttable presumption that the government is right (Ibid. at 2649).[11] So even *Hamdi* accepts the argument that judges should defer to the executive on military matters – an argument to which our judiciary has usually been very receptive. The proposition that judges should not second-guess generals on military matters seems self-evident, and it has been firmly established in our jurisprudence since the *Korematsu* (1944) case upheld the military necessity of interning Japanese-Americans in concentration camps during World War II. The Japanese internment has subsequently come to be regarded as a national disgrace by nearly everyone, although right-wing revisionists have predictably begun to defend it once again.[12] But, national disgrace or not, *Korematsu*'s basic argument for judicial deference has lost none of its luster. Judges need to keep their hubris in check and leave war to the professionals.

But the argument rests on a fallacy, because the President of the United States is a civilian, not a general. We pride ourselves on the principle of civilian

---

[10] Originally, the executive branch claimed that the president's war powers prevent federal judges from scrutinizing such decisions at all, but it was rebuffed by the Fourth Circuit Court of Appeals. Apparently, the executive power grab was too much for the Fourth Circuit, arguably the most conservative in the nation. The argument suggests that worries about executive abuse of the police power to enhance its own power – see Fallacy Two – are not merely hypothetical.

[11] In the fall of 2004, the United States released Hamdi and returned him to Afghanistan, thereby mooting the question of how much due process he would ultimately receive.

[12] See Lowman 2000; Malkin 2004. For a modest defense of *Korematsu*, see Posner 2002: 4–5. Mark Tushnet has "defended" *Korematsu* in what he describes as an "ironic sense" (2003: 274).

control of the military, which (thankfully) differentiates us from the large part of the world governed by military juntas. The president's war power is, fundamentally, a power of civilian control over the uses of the military. It is not grounded in the executive branch's military expertise or prowess, and it is not an argument about who is best suited to make technical military judgments. Thus, it is not hubris for other branches of government to review executive claims that military necessity overrides civil liberties. Both Hamdi and Padilla were classified as enemy combatants by civilians in the executive branch, and the evidence offered to back that classification consisted of affidavits by a civilian employee of the Defense Department. The case had nothing to do with military expertise, and there was really no need for courts to defer to the executive, because the basic task – determining how the law should classify a set of facts – is a pre-eminently judicial function, as Judge Mukasey himself acknowledged.

Why is this important? One of the peculiarities of the war on terror is that it may need to be waged invisibly in American cities, and the "battlefield" could turn out to be the entire country, or indeed anywhere in the world. (Indeed, less than two weeks after September 11, a conservative lawyer in the Justice Department's Office of Legal Counsel produced an opinion justifying presidential use of military force against terrorists within U.S. territory, even if it cost civilian casualties as collateral damage (Golden 2004)). If

(1) the executive is exercising his war powers in short-cutting peacetime civil liberties, and

(2) other branches of government must defer to the executive on war-powers issues, and

(3) the battlefield is coextensive with the U.S., or the world,

a dangerous consequence follows: civil liberties and human rights exist only at the sufferance of the American president, who can unilaterally reduce or suspend them based on factual declarations of military exigency that demand deferential review by the rest of government. All that stands between us and the militarization of civilian life is the president's say-so.

The fallacy lies in confusing the president's formal war powers with military expertise, and deferring to the former because we are thinking of the latter.[13]

---

[13] Even the *Hamdi* opinion conflates the president's status as (civilian) commander in chief with military expertise. The Court states that "our Constitution recognizes that core strategic matters of warmaking belong in the hands of those who are best positioned and most politically accountable for them," apparently not recognizing that "those who are best positioned" – military commanders – and those who are "most politically accountable" for making

This is a particularly dangerous error in fearful times like ours, when our instincts may well make us receptive to arguments of military necessity – even when they come from the lips of civilians who never saw a day of combat in their lives. Military necessity always seems to trump concern for civil liberties, and that should make us especially vigilant against specious claims of military necessity in everyday life.

Conclusion

Let me return to my original question. How much liberty should be sacrificed for security? I began by saying that this is the wrong question, because it rests on mistaken assumptions. Once we take care *not* to suppose that it is somebody else's liberty that will be sacrificed, nor to suppose that only the rights of the guilty and the terrorists are in jeopardy, nor that pro-security is the tough-minded, pragmatic answer, nor that these are military issues best left to the executive, nor that they are merely short-term emergency measures, the question takes a different form. It becomes something like this: *How much of your own protection against bureaucratic errors or malice by the government – errors or malice that could land you in jail – are you willing to sacrifice in return for minute increments in security?* This, it seems to me, is not an easy question to answer, but the most plausible answer is "not much"; and "none" seems like a reasonable place to start.

REFERENCES

Bentham, J. (1824). *Anarchical Fallacies*, Article II.
Bork, R. H. (1990). *The Tempting of America*. New York: Free Press.
Bumiller, E. (2003, October 26). 'Evangelicals Sway White House on Human Rights Issues Abroad'. *New York Times*, p. 1.
Cole, D. (2003). *Enemy Aliens: Double Standards and Constitutional Freedoms in the War on Terrorism*. New York: New Press.
Ely, J. H. (1980). *Democracy and Distrust: A Theory of Judicial Review*. Cambridge, MA: Harvard University Press.
Ex parte Milligan, 71 U.S. 2, 120–1 (1866).

them – elected officials – are not the same people (*Hamdi v. Rumsfeld*, 124 S. Ct. 2633, 2647 (2004)). Furthermore, to support this assertion, the Court cites two earlier decisions – one for the proposition that courts should not "intrude upon the authority of the Executive in military and national security affairs," and the other recognizing "broad powers in military commanders engaged in day-to-day fighting in a theater of war" (Ibid. at 2647–48). Plainly, the executive is not a military commander engaged in day-to-day fighting in a theater of war.

Ex parte Quirin, 317 U.S. 1 (1942).

Golden, T. (2004, October 24). 'After Terror, a Secret Rewriting of Military Law'. *New York Times*, p. A12.

Hamdi v. Rumsfeld, 124 S. Ct. 2633, 159 L. Ed. 2d 578, 72 U.S.L.W. 4607, 2004 LEXIS 4761 (2004).

Humanitarian Law Project v. Reno, 205 F.3d 1130, 1137 (9th Cir. 2000).

Humanitarian Law Project v. United States DOJ, 352 F.3d 382, 404 (9th Cir. 2003).

Korematsu v. United States, 323 U.S. 414 (1944).

Lowman, D. D. (2000). *MAGIC: The Untold Story of U.S. Intelligence and the Evacuation of Japanese Residents from the West Coast During WW II*. Utah: Athena Press.

Malkin, M. (2004). *In Defense of Internment: The Case for "Racial Profiling" in World War II and the War on Terror. NAACP v. Alabama*, 357 U.S. 449 (1958). Regnery.

Padilla v. Bush, 233 F. Supp. 2d 564 (S.D.N.Y. 2002).

Posner, R. A. (2002, Summer). 'The Truth About Our Liberties'. *The Responsive Community*, pp. 4–5.

Power, S. (2002). *"A Problem From Hell": America and the Age of Genocide*. New York: Basic Books.

Priest, D. & Gelman, B. (2002, December 26). 'U.S. Decries Abuse but Defends Interrogations; "Stress and Duress" Tactics Used on Terrorism Suspects Held in Secret Overseas Facilities'. *Washington Post*, p. A1.

Rasul v. Bush, 124 S. Ct. 2686, 159 L. Ed. 2d 548, 72 U.S.L.W. 4596, 2004 LEXIS 4760 (2004).

Rumsfeld v. Padilla, 124 S. Ct. 2711, 159 L. Ed. 2d 513, 72 U.S.L.W. 4584, 2004 LEXIS 4759 (2004).

Tushnet, M. (2003). 'Defending *Korematsu*?: Reflections on Civil Liberties in Wartime'. *Wisconsin Law Review* 2003, pp. 273–307.

U.S. v. Czubinski, 106 F.3d 1069 (1st Cir. 1997).

13. Our Privacy, Ourselves in the Age of Technological Intrusions

PETER GALISON AND MARTHA MINOW

After the terrorist attacks of 9/11, the United States government has elevated terrorism as the most important issue shaping government policies. What has happened and what should happen to legal protections of individual freedom in this context? Privacy is one of the individual freedoms in serious jeopardy due to post-9/11 governmental initiatives, yet it lacks comprehensive and clear definition in law and policy. Philosophically and historically, it may best be understood as a multivalent social and legal concept that refers simultaneously to seclusion, self-determination, and control over other people's access to oneself and to information about oneself. Even though its meanings are multiple and complex, privacy is closely connected with the emergence of a modern sense of self. Its jeopardy signals serious risk to the very conditions people need to enjoy the kind of self that can experiment, relax, form and enjoy intimate connections, and practice the development of ideas and beliefs for valued expression. The fragility of privacy is emblematic of the vulnerability of individual dignity and personal rights in the face of collective responses to terror and other enormous threats, real or perceived. In the face of narratives treating both technological change and security measures as either desired or inexorable, claims that privacy stands as a right outside of history, grounded in nature or divine authority, are not likely to prove persuasive or effective.

A partial, but insufficient, assurance for privacy can come from strengthening legally enforceable rights that safeguard a zone of individual autonomy – including rights that transcend the public/private distinction rather than bolster it. Similarly, some, but insufficient, protection for privacy can be built into designs for physical and electronic architecture affecting visibility and surveillance. And some, but insufficient, protection can come from public pressure

Thanks to Jeffrey Shih for research assistance and to Mario Biagioli, Julie Cohen, Arnold Davidson, and Richard Wilson for helpful comments.

to protect privacy understood as desire, expressed by individuals and groups through consumer markets,[1] politics, and even day-to-day relationships with one another. The same fate could befall the strategy of judicially enforceable individual rights. Unless individuals perceive and object to violations, legal challenges and political objections to invasions of privacy will neither arise nor culminate in judicial enforcement. Moreover, unless judges and legislators understand that large groups within the society expect and value forms of privacy that are under threat, they will not recognize or enforce them.

At the same time, failures to attend to privacy in the design of technology, the articulation and enforcement of laws, and in the mechanisms of markets and politics produce downward spirals, reducing both the scope of experiential privacy and people's expectation of and hope for privacy.[2] A vicious circle ensues: if people repeatedly experience telemarketers passing on their names, phone numbers, addresses, and purchasing records to others; if people are subjected to daily searches of their bodies and belongings as they enter buildings, board airplanes and trains, or drive near national borders; if people watch courts refuse challenges to governmental and corporate collection and sharing of personal information, the actual scope of privacy protections declines, and so does the motivation and willingness to demand privacy in any of these settings. Before we know it, such a downward spiral could affect the very sense of self people have – the sense of room for self-expression and experimentation, the sense of dignity and composure, the sense of ease and relief from public presentation. Although these features of experience have specific historical and cultural roots, and hardly describe all of human

---

[1] Perhaps the most familiar expression of desire these days is through consumer demand, generating market-based responses to private preferences, as suppliers offer privacy protections for a fee. Providers can try to build a taste for privacy by offering products and educating consumers. Whatever the source of the desire, absent individual desires for privacy, the market approach will be unavailing. For only if people demand and show a willingness to pay for privacy protections will consumer purchasing power make a difference. And even if individuals do want to pay, not all forms of privacy are amenable to market-based protection. No fee can be paid (to whom would it go?) to remove substantial information about oneself from the Internet. Political solutions can be prompted similarly by leaders and by grassroots and organized movements, each having the ability to affect the desires of individuals and groups as well as pressuring legislatures and administrators to adopt privacy-protecting rules and practices. Individuals who desire privacy in their everyday life can negotiate for it with their family, friends, and neighbors; in crowded homes, mutual practices of averting one's eyes and agreeing not to look through one another's papers and other belongings can secure some degree of privacy. Yet this approach offers no help where the risk of intrusion comes from strangers. Thus, not all forms of privacy are negotiable person by person.

[2] Recent works exploring the behavioral and normative dimensions of privacy demand and supply on the Internet include Hetcher 2001; Samuelson 2000.

experience, their erosion would amount to a genuine loss of sufficient significance to warrant deliberate concern, attention, and evaluation.

Too often in the past democratic nations have surrendered freedoms in the name of security with enormous cost and too often little benefit. The values of privacy deserve at least some restraints on restrictive measures, even if limited incursions could enhance security over the short term. Similarly, we might marginally increase security by trampling on other rights, such as habeas corpus, but thus far, the country has not made such a sacrifice (see *Rasul v. Bush*, 124 S. Ct. 2686 (2004)). The uncertainty and atmosphere of heightened risk resulting from terrorism should not automatically point toward invading the privacy of individuals. Given the limitations in any single strategy, a mixture of legal, technological, and market solutions offers the best hope for protecting privacy and the goods it stands for in the face of responses to terror, whether those responses are legitimate or illegitimate, and well-considered or ill-advised.

In the past, this and other nations have dramatically curtailed freedoms of speech and association while addressing a sense of internal and external security threats. A recent study of the treatment of freedom of expression during wartime in the United States concludes that in six historic periods, the United States government "went too far in restricting civil liberties" (Stone 2004: 524). Historians, judges, legislators, and other observers have come to condemn as fearful overreactions the Sedition Act of 1789, or President Abraham Lincoln's suspension of the writ of habeas corpus during the Civil War, the internment of Japanese Americans during World War II, the loyalty investigations during the Cold War, and the government treatment of antiwar protests during the Vietnam War (Ibid. at 525). Understandable fears and unscrupulous leaders give rise to repression beyond what circumstances warrant. Excessive restrictions of individual freedoms accompany superstitious beliefs that sacrifice and control of one thing – like personal freedom – would overcome general threats and danger. Privacy, like freedoms of speech and assembly, names a strand of individual liberty that has long faced jeopardy during security crises.

As we explore here, only a complex mix of legal, technological, market, and educational strategies hold realistic promise for confining governmental overreaching and undue restrictions on privacy. Laws can establish procedures that make invasions of privacy more difficult, but they can neither assure complete protection nor devise a perfect algorithm for reconciling privacy and security. Technology can be designed to restrict access to private information in degrees, and can establish filters to guard access to data depending upon the user, but it cannot create the desire for its use; nor does technology function as well retrospectively (after data have been collected) as it does prospectively. Also, in the absence of either legal requirements or market domination, technological privacy protections do not produce coercive or uniform results. Education and market strategies might cultivate a demand for privacy, but both operate diffusely, and leave results to the decisions and behaviors of individuals and institutions. Without deliberate effort, a downward spiral can become a vicious circle, eroding privacy through legal permission, technological access to unprecedented amounts of personal information, and diminishing public expectations of privacy. Deliberate initiatives in law, technology, and market and educational strategies designed to generate desire could, in contrast, promote an upward spiral, moving up while rotating back and forth between positive desires on the one side and legal/technological constraints on the other. At stake is no less than sense of self – contingent in its historical origins and nonetheless highly valued – enabled by assurances of privacy.

I. Prologue: Lessons from the Terrorist Information Awareness Project

In early 2002, the Defense Advanced Research Projects Agency (DARPA), a research and development division within the U.S. Department of Defense, launched an undertaking it initially called the Total Information Awareness project (TIA). For political reasons it was renamed in April 2002 the Terrorist Information Awareness project (TPAC 2004).[3] The project developed advanced informational technology tools to use domestic and foreign databases in both governmental and commercial hands in order to search for "patterns that are related to predicted terrorist activities" (DARPA 2003: 14). TIA used mathematical algorithms and other features of governmental software to "mine" personal data. Its analysts began to develop scenarios for terrorist attacks, based on "historical examples, estimated capabilities and imagination" (Ibid.).[4]

---

[3] Probably the first public indication of the effort appeared in testimony by the Director of DARPA before the Senate Armed Services Committee. Fiscal 2003 Defense Request: Combating Terrorism, Hearing before the Senate Armed Services Committee, April 10, 2002 (statement of Dr. Tony Tether).

[4] This report, developed in response to Congressional and advocacy organization critics, includes consideration of privacy concerns notably in the use of tools such as human face recognition and other tools for identifying individuals (DARPA 2003: 31). The report explains that the Department of Defense would follow existing law to protect privacy and civil liberties, and that the appointment of a Federal Advisory Committee by the Secretary of Defense to address these issues demonstrated the importance the department attaches to privacy (Ibid.).

An early description of the initiative explained how it would "detect, classify, identify, track, understand, and preempt," using biometric data, such as images of faces, fingerprints, iris scans, and transactional data, such as "communications, financial, education, travel, medical, veterinary, country entry, place/event entry, transportation, housing, critical resources, and government" (TPAC 2004: 15).[5] The Lawyers Committee for Human Rights described the data sources to be examined more vividly as encompassing: "religious and political contributions; driving records, high school transcripts; book purchases; medical records; passport applications; car rentals; phone, e-mail and internet search logs" (LCHR 2003).[6] Subject to such searches would be public records held by local, state, and federal government agencies, and databases purchased by the government from commercial vendors, such as credit card companies and retail stores. The project "would make available to government employees vast amounts of personal information about American citizens who are not suspected of any criminal conduct," according to lawyer Floyd Abrams, who served on the Technology and Privacy Advisory Committee ultimately created by Donald Rumsfeld, Secretary of the Department of Defense, to review TIA in response to public outcry (TPAC 2004: 63–4).

Considerable ambiguity about the TIA mission and scope contributed to public confusion and wide opposition to it. Differing descriptions conflicted over whether the project would produce a centralized database in government hands, aggregating data from governmental and the private sector, or the project would instead produce and deploy searching devices across public and private databases while leaving the privately owned data in private control (Markle Foundation 2003: 10).[7] The project generated doubts about the credibility and candor of its managers and about their commitment both to protect civil liberties and to guard against abuses of governmental power.

Whether it resulted from perception or reality, the director chosen to lead the project became a lightening rod for critics. The Director of the Information Awareness Office, established to oversee the initiative, was John Poindexter.

---

[5] Early DARPA ITA Slide, reproduced in TPAC 2004: 15.

[6] Report edited by Fiona Doherty and Deborah Pearlstein, and funded by The Atlantic Philanthropies, the John Merck Fund, the Open Society Institute, Mathew Dontzin, and Equal Justice Works fellowship. The Lawyers Committee changed its name recently to Human Rights First.

[7] Citing for comparison Poindexter 2002 ... ("The relevant information extracted from this data must be made available in large-scale repositories with enhanced semantic content for easy analysis to accomplish this task") with DARPA 2003 ... ("the TIA Program is not attempting to create or access a centralized data base that will store information gathered from public or privately held data bases").

A retired Navy Admiral and National Security Advisor to President Ronald Reagan, he had been convicted of conspiracy, lying to Congress, defrauding the government, and destroying evidence for illegally selling weapons to Iran and using the funds to provide secret and illicit support to a military force in Nicaragua in what became known as "the Iran Contra scandal" (Walsh Report; Weintraub 1986).[8] An appellate court overturned the conviction on the grounds that witnesses who testified against him in the criminal trial may have been affected by Poindexter's own testimony before Congress – and his own testimony was supposed to be protected by a grant of immunity. After the trial and the appeal, Poindexter worked at private sector technology companies, including Synteck Industries, where he helped to develop intelligence data-mining and information-harvesting software on government contracts and for private industry (Sutherland 2002).

In February 2002, Poindexter returned to government service to head the Information Awareness Office of DARPA. In August 2002, at the DARPA-Tech 2002 Conference, he explained TIA's strategy by noting that terrorists would have to engage in transactions, and those transactions would "leave signatures in this information space" (Poindexter 2002). The initiative would pursue more efficient and sophisticated ways to find and mine data for analysis and use. As the Lawyers Committee for Human Rights later pointed out, TIA would proceed with no prior judicial approval. Its searches would not be limited to instances where the government had suspicion about particular individuals or particular terrorist organizations. Instead, it would precipitate unprecedented, constant fishing expeditions into people's lives, and generate millions of searches falling short not only of the standard of probable cause, but actually any cause at all. An American Civil Liberties Union representative warned that data mining by TIA would "amount to a picture of your life so complete it's equivalent to somebody following you around all day with a video camera" (Baer 2003).

This image of the program as total surveillance was actually initially embraced explicitly by the government. DARPA named the project "Total Information Awareness." The initial logo posted on the TIA web-site presented an all-seeing eye on the top of a pyramid transformed from the eighteenth-century eye of providence on the Great Seal to an all-too practically oriented governmental panopticon with the slogan, "Knowledge is Power."[9] Although Director Poindexter noted the importance of protecting privacy

---

[8] The Aide was Oliver North.
[9] It is unclear whether this was meant as a secular version of the Great Seal's Providential eye, a reference to the Masonic sign, or some other cryptic visual reference of omnipresence.

and civil liberties, the DARPA presentation describing the program seemed remarkably indifferent to these issues (Poindexter 2002). Barry Steinhardt, Director of the American Civil Liberties Union Technology and Liberty Program, commented, "It is grimly appropriate that this Orwellian program is being sold to us in such an Orwellian Manner" (Responses 2003).

Sparked by a November 2002 *New York Times* column by William Safire, criticisms of TIA mounted in the press and in Congress. Critics questioned the effectiveness of TIA. They warned that it would generate as many as three million false identifications of individuals as terrorists each year (LCHR 2003: 27).[10] Critics pointed out that the project could create new occasions for governmental misuse of private data (Ibid.). Although the project had defenders, it elicited sharp objections across the political spectrum, from the Eagle Forum lead by Phyllis Schlafly on the right to People for the American Way on the left (Safire 2003). This generated sufficient pressure for the Assistant Secretary of Defense for Intelligence Oversight and the Inspector General of the Department of Defense to initiate review of the program. In December 2002, the Assistant Secretary conducted a review and then brought Intelligence Oversight regulations to the attention of DARPA. In January 2003, the Inspector General initiated an audit of TIA, and called for greater effort to "minimize the possibility for governmental abuse of power" (TPAC 2004: 17).[11]

A separate initiative of DARPA became even more controversial. In July 2003, Democratic Senators Byron Dorgon and Ron Wyden publicly investigated and castigated an experiment in creating a futures market in predicting terrorist events, a joint venture between the DARPA project and the business arm of *The Economist* magazine (CNN.com 2003; Mark 2003). Media coverage linked the terrorist futures venture and TIA as products of DARPA under Poindexter's leadership. In the face of the public outcry Poindexter resigned his post (Rennie 2003). Poindexter later explained that despite public misunderstandings, the TIA initiative had encompassed privacy protections.[12] Yet,

---

[10] Letter from Public Policy Committee, Association for Computing Literacy, to the Senate Committee on the Armed Services, January 20, 2003.

[11] Citing Department of Defense, Office of the Inspector General, Information Technology Management: Terrorism Information Awareness Program (D-2004-033) 4 (2003).

[12] This question by Spencer Reiss and answer by John Poindexter appeared in Reiss 2004:

> [Question:] So how do you persuade people that having the government peer into their lives is a good idea? [Answer:] Most people don't understand what we were trying to do. Too many opinions are formed based on sound bites from those who yell the loudest. One of the things we were working on was a "privacy appliance" that would conceal a person's identity until a case could be made against them. Congress killed that, too.

as columnist Safire pointed out, a person convicted on five felony counts for lying to Congress about the Iran-Contra affair was "hardly the person to ask elected officials to trust with unprecedented, unchecked power" (Safire 2003).

By the time the Inspector General released the results of the audit of TIA in December 2003, and specifically directed the TIA project to build privacy protections into the development process, Congress had already terminated funding for TIA (TPAC 2004: 18). Its Department of Defense Appropriation Act, passed September 25, 2003, permitted TIA work only in relation to counter-terrorism foreign intelligence, and the media optimistically declared that TIA was dead.[13] In fact, as the Technology and Privacy Advisory Committee to the Department of Defense reported, government agencies continued to undertake data-mining projects similar to TIA, but outside of the DARPA framework (Ibid.).

Indeed, in July 2003, the White House announced a multi-agency initiative, the Terrorist Threat Integration Center, to integrate and analyze terrorist-threat-related information, collected domestically and abroad (Ibid. at 28). Some of TIA's activities may have moved there (Ibid.). Placed under the Director of Central Intelligence, this effort is not subject to the oversight of Homeland Security. The initiative also moves police and law enforcement material within the CIA, despite a statutory prohibition against CIA use of police, law enforcement, or internal security powers (Ibid. at 29).[14] So if TIA's activities persist here or in other classified activities, they do so without public review and with real risk of violating existing law.

Other initiatives like TIA proceed as government agencies commission and pay for work in the private sector. Seisint, Inc., a private company, built the Multistate Anti-Terrorism Information Exchange (MATRIX) as a tool for local law enforcement agencies. It enables the data-mining activities launched by TIA based on analysis of drivers' and pilots' licenses, age and gender, ethnicity, and investigation records (*St. Petersburg Times* 31 May 2004; LCHR 2003: 17). Connecting patterns across public and private databases remains a strategy available to other governmental agencies fighting terrorism. It is within the current capability of government agencies to collect and analyze data about individuals within the United States, including citizens, persons with visas, and legal resident aliens (TPAC 2004: xi, 8). Meanwhile, private commercial

---

[13] See, e.g., *Denver Post* 31 May 2004; *Atlanta Journal-Constitution* 10 December 2003. DARPA had identified a range of technologies contributing to TIA, and there is no indication that termination of TIA involved terminating development or use of these other technologies (2003: Appendix B).

[14] Citing The National Security Act, 50 U.S.C. sec. 402-2(d)(1)(2002).

enterprises track the purchasing and Internet surfing behavior of millions of individuals, develop profiles of households containing demographic and lifestyle information[15] – and the government can obtain this information without any legal restriction, simply by purchasing it.

Intense negative response by the media and Congress (and advocacy organizations) to TIA may have led to its official termination, but the underlying activities of government anti-terrorist data mining that generated intense concerns about privacy and error most likely continue and do so with less prospect of public review. Like a ball of mercury, the data-mining activities scatter and grow less visible once subjected to pressure. Public concerns about privacy have generated more secrecy about the government activities that jeopardize personal privacy. The historic national commitment to the pairing of personal privacy and open government now shifts toward governmental secrecy and incursions on individual privacy.

This reversal grows from government actions well beyond TIA.[16] Departing from decades of practice, Attorney General John Ashcroft eliminated rules that had restricted FBI surveillance of religious, civic, and political organizations in the United States. Those rules, adopted after abuses by the FBI during the 1950s and 1960s, confined investigations to crimes that had already been committed. Now, in contrast, the FBI can infiltrate groups, monitor meetings, and collect and analyze data looking for patterns and other possible predictors of future terrorist activities even in the absence of evidence of a crime (Borger 2002; *Times-Picayune* 3 June 2002). After 9/11, without much debate,[17] Congress enacted the USA PATRIOT Act (2001). That law relieves the FBI of the obligation to produce individualized evidence in order to justify searching library and bookstore records, rental car records, school grades, medical records, financial records, and Internet sites. The Act allows the FBI to obtain telephone and Internet service records without any judicial oversight. To search the records of libraries, medical and financial institutions, and schools, the FBI now needs only to submit a request in secret to a special semi-secret tribunal, the Foreign Intelligence Surveillance Court, which hears in closed-door sessions the government's requests ex parte, without

---

[15] See, e.g., Directionsmag.com 3 December 1998; R. L. Polk & Co. 2005. See also McClurg 2003 (discussing Double-click and other consumer profiling and tracking enterprises).

[16] See LCHR 2003: i–xviii, 3–14 (reviewing government policies to restrict release of information to the public about governmental activities, to expand treatment of materials as classified for security reasons, and to limit Congressional oversight).

[17] Michael Moore's documentary film, 'Fahrenheit 9–11', charges that most of the legislators adopted the law without reading it – but one representative captured on film reported that did not differentiate this bill from others.

participation of the target or the target's lawyer (LCHR 2003: 16–17).[18] Congressional efforts to examine how the FBI is actually using these powers have been rebuffed by the Department of Justice (Ibid. at 17). State governments have already produced and used the multistate crime and terrorism database known as the MATRIX to look for patterns in data to identify potential terrorists.[19] Most of these actions have triggered little public reaction. Even when there has been criticism in the media or Congress, the expansive governmental powers persist, without oversight or accountability. For example, public criticisms of airline watch lists developed by the Transportation Security Administration after 9/11 remain exempt from judicial review and existing laws ensuring individuals access to and opportunity to correct government records (LCHR 2003: 26). Government contracts with private companies for the collection of personal information may elude legal rules constraining government and protecting individual privacy (see Hoofnagle 2004).

When exposed to view, airline watch lists and the Total Information Awareness project trigger criticism by advocacy groups, elected representatives, and media. This suggests both widespread low-level discomfort with invasions of privacy and the frailty of privacy rights. (During the first part of 2004, Senator

---

[18] Discussing sections 215 and 505 of the USA PATRIOT Act. Some defend the PATRIOT Act provisions as necessary; others argue that they do not alter the standards protecting individual privacy (see *National Law Journal Roundtable* 2003: 19). For example, Alice Fisher, former deputy assistant attorney general in the Department of Justice, explained that "A grand jury can issue a subpoena for just these records in a library in a regular criminal investigation, and it often has." But Ann Beeson, associated legal director of the American Civil Liberties Union, argues that the Section 215 orders operate like warrants, unlike subpoenas, because they cannot be challenged prior to compliance and instead are immediately executable. David Sobel comments that the USA PATRIOT Act transforms the role of the Justice Department from prosecuting crimes to "anticipating and preventing them," which changes the role of intelligence and investigation pursued by the government. (Ibid. at 21).

[19] The Multi-State Anti-Terrorism Information Exchange (MATRIX) is described on its website this way:

> This technology helps to identify, develop, and analyze terrorist activity and other crimes for investigative leads. Information accessible includes criminal history records, driver's license data, vehicle registration records, and incarceration/corrections records, including digitized photographs, with significant amounts of public data records. This capability will save countless investigative hours and drastically improve the opportunity to successfully resolve investigations. The ultimate goal is to expand this capability to all states. http://www.matrix-at.org/, visited August 24, 2004.

The American Civil Liberties Union filed suit challenging the use of the MATRIX by Michigan because it allegedly violates a 1980 law prohibiting police from sharing confidential information without legislative permission or approval from a citizen oversight group (Baldas 2004) (describing MATRIX, and suit, filed as *Milliken v. Sturdivant*, No. 04-423728CZ, Wayne Co. Mich. Cir. Ct.).

Edward Kennedy found himself on the no-fly list some five times – and eventually cleared up the error by phoning Ashcroft, not an option available to most citizens.) As government initiatives in data gathering and analysis become less available to review by the media, the Congress, and by private individuals, privacy erodes. So does public awareness of these developments. What might this mean for democracy, for self-government, and for checking centralized governmental authority? And what might these developments mean for the conceptions and experiences of the self?

II. Privacy: Conceptual and Legal Frailties

The vulnerability the legal conception of privacy produces is a result of its plural and diffuse nature. Predicated on plural and at times inconsistent social values, constructed by judges without a clear grounding in legal text or tradition, and wedged within a distinction between public and private spheres that limits the scope of legal remedies, legal privacy faces predictable competition and likely defeat. The very structure of privacy as an individual right, subject to countervailing state interests, is too crude to deal effectively with shifting social relationships; it is also adrift from foundational ideas that could withstand the politics of the moment. Jeopardy to privacy is jeopardy to the space for individual self-invention that our society celebrates.

A. Multiple and Contingent Values. Noting the multiple complexity and even contradictory notions encompassed by privacy has become commonplace among scholars. Robert Post commented, "Privacy is a value so complex, so entangled in competing and contradictory dimensions, so engorged with various and distinct meanings, that I sometimes despair whether it can be usefully addressed at all" (2001: 2087). The content of privacy and the very idea that something called privacy is of value remain historically and culturally contingent. It is possible to trace a boundary between public and private life to practices in ancient Greek and Roman societies, with the private referring to home, dominated by the patriarch, and the public referring to the realm of self-governance, reserved for citizens (see Arendt 1958; Solove & Rotenberg 2003: 27). This divide between public and private is less helpful in describing many non-Western societies. It also does not capture well the conception of individual privacy that people invoke against intrusive searches by government agents, surveillance of consumer transactions and health status by commercial entities, and monitoring Internet use of web-sites by an individual user. Privacy as a claim by an individual is a call to control access to one's self or information about oneself in relation to neighbors, strangers, employers, and government actors. Yet it also refers to the ability to make a personal decision about reproduction, contraception, marriage, or adoption without interference from others, and especially without restrictions imposed by the government.

As these descriptions suggest, the term "privacy" evokes a cluster of ideas, rather than a sharply chiseled concept. Some scholars propose conjunctive definitions. They acknowledge that privacy has come to denote related but distinct concepts, such as the ability of individuals to find seclusion and also control over access to their person and to information about themselves (Allen 1988: 46–7; Westin 1967; Solove & Rotenberg 2003: 31–2; DeCew 1997: 75; Kang 1998: 1202). Others try to find a core theory underlying distinct concepts,[20] such as the right to be let alone, or personhood, or intimacy, but none has secured widespread agreement.

Robert Post notes that contrasting and at times conflicting theories animate different conceptions of privacy. Privacy could be an avenue for dignity and a vehicle for expressing shared norms about self-respect and respect for others, but it also could be a route for freedom and experimentation, including resistance to shared norms (Post 2001: 2095). "Privacy as dignity seeks to eliminate differences by bringing all persons within the bounds of a single normalized community; privacy as freedom protects individual autonomy by nullifying the reach of that community" (Ibid.). Although it is not so obvious that dignity requires conformity rather than social enforcement, Post's analysis offers an intriguing lens unto somewhat paradoxical features of a norm that requires for its effectiveness widely shared practices and, once effective, affords individuals latitude for unique and even rebellious action.

Daniel Solove argues for abandoning the search for the essence of privacy and instead proposes viewing privacy as a set of ideas that bear "family resemblances" to one another, in the sense that Ludwig Wittgenstein developed; then he argues we can address issues of privacy pragmatically in light of particular circumstances (2002: 1098, 1128). Somewhat analogously, turning to the translation of conceptions of privacy in the law of privacy, Jerry Kang and Benedikt Buchner propose abandoning arguments over whether to locate privacy rights within a framework of property law or instead within a framework of fundamental human rights (2004). Instead, they suggest that analysis should proceed functionally by asking whether and when societal interests should override individual choices, when should governmental rules fortify individual preferences for privacy (Ibid.). Even that approach leaves

---

[20] Daniel J. Solove drew this useful contrast between the cluster approaches and the core concept approaches to privacy (2002: 1087).

undecided the scope of concerns to be registered by a privacy analysis, and the resolution of conflicts between privacy and public interests such as security and public health.

The emergence of privacy as a right within American law reflects development of a sense of the private self that needs seclusion and finds violation in the capture and distribution of information without consent. In 1965, the United States Supreme Court struck down as unconstitutional a statute criminalizing the distribution of information and medical advice about contraception (*Griswold v. Connecticut*, 382 U.S. 479 (1965)). The plaintiffs' lawyers organized a test case, now known as *Griswold v. Connecticut*, to challenge the arrest of individuals who had counseled married couples about contraception. This circumstance held considerable appeal for the Court because the law intruded upon "the intimate relation of husband and wife," and therefore violated a right of privacy older than the Constitution itself (Ibid. at 482). Thus the Court focused on the locus of greatest protection for privacy – the marital home – although specifically under scrutiny was the communication between the couple and the physician.

The Court's majority had trouble, however, finding language inside the Constitution to root a right to privacy. The opinion by Justice Douglas cast about for a hook and listed several that seemed close (Ibid. at 484).[21] But, finding no clear basis for a right to privacy, Justice Douglas proceeded in his opinion for the majority to scout out "penumbral rights of privacy and repose," lying around the edges of rights explicitly stated in the Constitution (Ibid. at 480). Conducting a tour of the Constitution, his opinion pointed to First Amendment freedoms of association, privacy in one's associations, and freedoms to teach and to learn and to choose how one's children should learn; the Third Amendment's prohibition against the quartering of soldiers in private homes; the Fourth Amendment's ban against unreasonable searches or seizures; the Fifth Amendment protection against self-incrimination; and the Ninth Amendment's reservations of rights retained by the people, even if not enumerated in the text. One commentator suggested that Justice Douglas here "skipped through the Bill of Rights like a cheerleader: 'give me a P . . . give me an R . . . an I . . . ,' and so on, and found P-R-I-V-A-C-Y as a derivative or

---

[21] Citing the First Amendment right of association, the Third Amendment prohibition against the quartering of soldiers in any house, the Fifth Amendment protection against self-incrimination, and the Ninth Amendment retention of rights not enumerated in the Constitution. See also Ibid. at 482 (discussing prior decisions recognizing the right of parents to select the child's schools and the right to study a particular foreign language). The Court here reread these cases to form a right to privacy even though the cases themselves arose centrally as conflicts over the treatment of religious and ethnic identities in schooling. See Minow 1987.

penumbral right" (Dixon 1976: 84). Another argued as a matter both of logic and legal drafting, the explicit textual reference to some but not other features of privacy – including the right against self-incrimination, but not a right to reproductive choice – would indicate that the framers of the Constitution did not intend to protect the unmentioned features (Henkin 1974: 1422).

The unsatisfying nature of the majority opinion prompted even the individual justices who agreed with the result to write concurring opinions. Each groped for a place in the Constitution's text on which to ground the right used to reject the ban on contraceptive advice (*Griswold*, 381 U.S. at 486, 499). Two of the nine justices found the entire enterprise preposterous and objected in their dissenting opinion that the Court's majority arrogated power, without the authority of Constitutional language, to impose federal judicial policy preferences (Ibid. at 507, 527). Justice Black, joined by Justice Stewart, explicitly criticized the Court's majority for seeking to turn into constitutional principle the effort by Warren and Brandeis to recast common law tort remedies as "right to privacy" (Ibid.).

What has emerged through case-by-case constitutional adjudication is not one right to privacy but instead several distinct lines of cases. One, emanating from *Griswold v. Connecticut*, protects decision making by individuals over the intimate matters of marriage and procreation from "undue burden" or other intrusions by state regulation.[22] A related strand protects individuals in their intimate relationships including, but not limited to, marriage (*Lawrence v. Texas*, 539 U.S. 558 (2003)). Neither of these ideas produces absolute protection and instead they call for "balancing" the private interest and competing public purposes.

A distinct legal notion of privacy – mentioned by Justice Douglas in *Griswold* – stems from the Fourth Amendment protection against unreasonable searches or seizures.[23] Once limited to physical intrusions into an area protected by the Constitution, this notion of privacy was recast by the Supreme Court to "protect people and not simply physical 'areas'" (*Katz v. United States*, 389 U.S. 347 (1967)). In seeming to broaden protection of privacy from the physical locales of home or office to persons, the Court actually

---

[22] See *Eisenstadt v. Baird* (1972); *Roe v. Wade* (1973); *Webster v. Reproductive Health Services* (1989); *Planned Parenthood of Southeastern Pennsylvania v. Casey* (1992).

[23] "The right of the people to be secure in their persons, houses, papers, and effects, against unreasonable searches and seizures, shall not be violated, and no Warrants shall issue, but upon probable cause, supported by Oath or affirmation and particularly describing the place to be searched, and the persons or things to be seized." U.S. Constitution, Amendment IV. The Supreme Court developed a doctrine excluding from the evidentiary base in criminal trials evidence obtained in violation of this guarantee, but debates over the scope and viability of that doctrine have grown broad and intense. See, e.g., *United States v. Leon*, 468 U.S. 897 (1984).

also introduced considerations that can erode privacy protections. Justice
Harlan articulated the scope of the Fourth Amendment protection in terms
of two requirements: an actual subjective expectation of privacy, held by the
individual, and an assessment that society should treat that expectation as
"reasonable" (Ibid. at 360). These requirements are patently flexible. They lend
themselves to downward reductions of the amount of privacy either by the
simple assertion of a judge – whose rejection of a privacy claim immediately
shrinks what is reasonable to expect – or by shifting social and commercial
practices. The Supreme Court has acknowledged that individuals may expect
the contents of their garbage to be private but nonetheless denied constitutional protection to trash left for collection in an area accessible to the public
(*California v. Greenwood*, 486 U.S. 35 (1988)). In that one act, the Court
told people not to expect privacy in the refuse they leave out for garbage
collection. Similarly, helicopter surveillance of the interior of a partially
covered greenhouse in the backyard of a residential home does not violate
constitutionally protected privacy because five members of the Supreme
Court concluded it would not be reasonable to expect privacy there (*Florida v.
Riley*, 488 U.S. 445 (1989)).

The Courts can further diminish the scope of legal privacy protections by
narrowly interpreting what counts as a "search" that should trigger Fourth
Amendment protections, and by linking the definition of a search, like the
content of reasonable expectations, to shifting social practices and growing
uses of new technologies. The Court did treat a thermal-imaging device outside a home as a search because it would identify the presence of heat lamps,
often used in marijuana production that would otherwise not be visible from
outside the building (*Kyllo v. United States*, 533 U.S. 27 (2001)). The Court's
definition of a search in that context emphasized that the thermal-imaging
device "is not in general public use." Hence, changing uses could alter what
counts as a search (Ibid. at 41).

Mindful of plural qualities of privacy as a normative ideal, judges have
created legal doctrines that are attentive to competing considerations and
evolving circumstances. Yet in so doing, the judges may have produced legal
concepts that are circular or even self-defeating. The very requirements articulated by judges to implement a legal conception of privacy may lead to
its demise. Jeffrey Rosen recently argued that the "reasonable expectation of
privacy" is a circular notion, offering no independent purchase on knotty
problems and therefore no real protection for privacy (2000: 60).[24] Robert
Post, in reply, has agreed that there is a kind of circularity in the notion,

---

[24] Scholars and judges have criticized the standard as circular. See LaFave 1966: 393–4; Posner
1979: 188; *Minnesota v. Carter*, 525 U.S. 93, 97 (1998).

but nonetheless argues that the reasonable expectation test is not determined entirely by law but also by social norms derived outside of law (2001: 2094).

Here, Post argues that legal privacy grows from two distinct and even conflicting social norms (without specifying their cultural roots or historical origins). On the one hand, there is a social norm of dignity behind privacy: "Privacy as dignity locates privacy in precisely the aspects of social life that are shared and mutual. Invading privacy causes injury because we are socialized to experience common norms as essential prerequisites of our own identity and self-respect" (Ibid. at 2094). On the other hand, privacy refers to a valued space for freedom, a location for trying out and exposing parts of our identity that we conceal before other people (Ibid. at 2095). "Privacy as dignity safeguards the socialized aspects of the self; privacy as freedom safeguards the spontaneous, independent, and uniquely individual aspects of the self" (Ibid. at 2096). If Post is right, the legal conception of privacy is inherently unstable as it contains internally conflicting social norms.

Whether they are as Post describes or take some other shape, the social norms behind the legal conception of privacy are historically contingent. When buffeted by other social forces, such as wartime public and media frenzy or collective fears about terrorism (often abetted by political figures), the social values behind privacy provide even less sturdy legs for holding up an enforceable legal conception. Legal conceptions of privacy that depend on social expectations lack both the coherence and content to resist pressures to cut back on individual privacy. Especially when those pressures come from security demands, or from the seeming inexorability of new technologies, they are likely to diminish or even elide both the social wellsprings and the legal protections for personal privacy.

B. The Public-Private Distinction and the State Action Doctrine. Echoing ancient Greek and Roman ideas, American law assumes and enforces a distinction between the public sphere and the private sphere, and this very distinction is a source of vulnerability for legal enforcement of personal privacy for several reasons. First, as critics for at least 100 years have emphasized, the use of law to define and regulate the boundaries between public and private puts law – and public officials like judges and police officers – in control of the very scope of privacy, rendering what is private subject to public control.[25] Jamie Boyle argues that, "the central fear of the liberal political vision

---

[25] Theorists known as legal realists launched many critiques of the public/private distinction in their work that flourished between 1890 and 1945. See generally Horwitz 1982; Fisher, Horwitz & Reed 1993.

is that unrestrained state power will invade the private sphere. And yet the only force available to police the state is the state" (1992: 1434; see also Peller 1985). This warning is most powerful when, as is increasingly the case now, the state combines secrecy with invasions of privacy.

Second, persistent ambiguity over the meaning of the public/private distinction makes it an unreliable tool for protecting privacy. Does "public" refer to government? Or to anything that is not private? Does private refer to the family and home, or to anything that is not government? The ambiguity revolves around the status of the marketplace and civil society. Should employment settings be viewed as public or private? How about commercial exchanges? Or clubs? If viewed as public, each of these settings is properly subject to public values, such as nondiscrimination. If viewed as private, then each should be granted latitude and even seclusion from public surveillance and norms. Third, courts created the "state action doctrine" to monitor the scope of constitutional rights such as equal protection, liberty, and freedom from intrusive searches. Those rights, therefore, attach only when state actors threaten private persons – and they do not apply even when profoundly jeopardized by corporations, religious entities, or other private actors.

Thus, the United States Constitution makes state action a prior requirement for most constitutional provisions affecting liberty, and it is within the concept of liberty that courts tend to identify privacy.[26] State action is required to trigger the protections of freedoms of speech, religion, and assembly, the right to be secure against unreasonable searches or seizures, the right to due process before deprivations of life, liberty, or property, the right to equal protection of the law, and the right to vote. The protection of privacy, as recognized by judges under the Fourteenth Amendment's due process clause, is tethered to the state action requirement and thus applies only to threats by government actors.

In efforts to aid the civil rights movement, many courts during the 1960s construed the scope of state action broadly to apply to an ostensibly private entity if in practice it performed a government function or worked entwined with governmental aid or involvement. Over the past few decades, the Supreme Court has cut back on the scope of state action and therefore reduce the reach of rights predicated on it. This enlarges the ability of governments to bypass constitutional requirements simply by shifting previous government tasks to the private sector. A private school, educating children and financed almost exclusively by government funding, can manage

---

[26] This discussion draws upon Minow, *Privacy and Privatization* (draft Aug. 2004).

its employment disputes like a private employer and avoid the due process rules governing government bodies because private as well as public entities historically have provided education (*Rendell-Baker v. Kohn*, 457 U.S. 830 (1982)). A commercial company can pursue its own enforcement for breach of contract without following due process rules, even if such rules would apply if a sheriff or court played a role in such enforcement (*Flagg Brothers, Inc. v. Brooks*, 436 U.S. 149 (1978)).[27] The Court thus has come to define the government function test for state action restrictively by asking if the function is exclusively assigned to government rather than by looking, as scholars have suggested, to the kind and scope of power exercised (see Friendly 1969: 222; Choper 1979).

The definition of state action affects whether the collection and distribution of personal information must be subject to the strictures of the Constitution, such as the warrant requirement of the Fourth Amendment or the protection against self-incrimination in the Fifth Amendment. Because data collected by supermarkets and drug stores in exchange for discount cards are then available for sale to government as well as other purchasers, the government can easily acquire information in two steps without complying with the rules that attach if it pursued the information directly.

Privacy rights can be installed beyond the Constitution's commands. They can be enforced without state action through statutes when legislators have the power and will to act. Congress has adopted statutes regulating private conduct in the absence of state action.[28] Yet commercial lobbying groups may secure limitations in the statutes or in the regulations or enforcement patterns that vitiate the goal of protecting individual privacy. When legislation leaves privacy protections up to individual consent, companies condition purchases and services on waivers of individual privacy claims; that is cheaper for the companies and also affords access to the consumers' information to enhance marketing and sales. Recently, the U.S. Congress adopted the Graham-Leach-Bliley Act to authorize financial institutions to share personal information, especially to facilitate business between affiliated financial institutions. The

---

[27] For a probing analysis of the issues raised by the case, see Brest 1982.

[28] See, e.g., Section 605, Federal Communications Act of 1934. Later, Congress articulated the norm in the Omnibus Crime Control and Safe Streets Act of 1968, 18 U.S.C. sections 2510–20, but it exempts wiretaps for national security purposes. The Electronic Communications Privacy Act of 1986 establishes the current framework that includes an avenue for suppressing contents of intercepted electronic communication. The law does permit electronic surveillance if one of the parties to the communication consents. Congress also adopted the Right to Financial Privacy Act, 39 U.S.C. sections 3401–22, to prevent banks and other financial institutions from disclosing a person's financial information to the government, absent a subpoena or search warrant.

law empowers federal agencies to establish standards to strengthen the security and confidentiality of personal information held by financial institutions and to protect against unauthorized access. Yet, the dominant approach taken by the agencies thus far is to presume that the financial institutions can share consumer information, as long as consumers have a chance to opt out of the sharing systems. Practically speaking, by placing the default position to favor sharing, most of the information will indeed be available for distribution. People too often do not understand the stakes or take the effort to opt out through densely written release forms.

The limitations of constitutional analysis, the vagaries of statutory coverage, and the frailty of individual vigilance, taken together, expose personal privacy to massive challenge by corporate and market activities. Governmental purchases of commercial information accomplish an end-run around the checks otherwise applicable when government seeks personal information. Government uses of subcontracting, vouchers, and other techniques of privatization similarly water down or bypass privacy restrictions that attach to public action.

C. The Weakness of an Individual Rights Framework. Constituting legal protection of privacy through an individual right tethers privacy protections to an uncertain anchor. This uncertainty is pronounced in this age when rights are subjected to constant balance, against societal interests, and when the theoretical foundations for rights are disputed or absent. The contemporary style of judicial interpretation of constitutional rights in the United States has led Alexander Aleinikoff to call this an "age of balancing" (1987). He argues that the metaphor aligns constitutional adjudication with a calculus of utilities and with an ad hoc approach to issues that impairs the development of stable and predictable legal rules (Ibid.). Framed as an entitlement of the individual, to be weighed against the interests of the state, an individual's privacy must do battle with potentially powerful needs of majorities (Greer 2003). It also presumes a degree of individual autonomy and bargaining power that departs from many people's lived experiences, and leaves the enforcement of privacy to the assertion of claims by people with sufficient motivation, time, and money. Also, the rights framework affords little latitude for conceptualizing, much less for resolving, conflicts among multiple rights-bearing individuals.

The individual rights framework is especially weak in the absence of explicit textual support for the right and in a moment of history when allusions to natural rights or God-given rights do not resonate widely. Michael Ignatieff, who has asked whether an era of human rights is ending because of the global fight against terrorism,[29] offered a searing challenge to the "idolatry" of international human rights, and his challenge reverberates for all systems of individual rights (2002b). A secular state cannot rely on religious ideas to bolster rights, but turning legal rights into a new secular religion would mistakenly treat law as the source for defining all that is good and desirable. Instead, Ignatieff argues, rights should be predicated on the minimal respect for a space of individual decision making.

Even this minimal conception of rights partakes of the pretense that rights are "out there" rather than names for commitments people want to hold onto even in the face of countervailing arguments. What is missing is the language to acknowledge their contingency even while using rights as tools or techniques to resolve knotty problems. Conventionally, privacy protections invoke images of walls or swords and shields. Perhaps such images are necessary to reinforce the essentially rights claims that can irritate the minority. Yet the balancing methodology, and the perpetual availability of countervailing arguments render privacy weak from start to finish. Perhaps acknowledging the frailty of rights would avoid disillusionment with legal action that does find a compromise or directly caters to anti-privacy interests. Despite ambiguity and complexity, privacy has grown up alongside a notion of the self that can be fashioned – and jeopardy to privacy spells danger for that sense of self as well.[30]

D. Privacy and the Self. In different ways and in different contexts, we find ourselves with a conception of privacy that keeps running aground. First, we looked at the seemingly unavoidable clash between an understanding of privacy that depends on subordinating individuals within a community to shared norms, and on the other side the devotion precisely to freedom for the individual to depart from the norms of that same community. Then we found ourselves caught in a second, seemingly paradoxical situation, in which the individual seeking privacy from the state is forced to look to the state to define the boundary between private and public and then to keep the state squarely on the far side of that border. The paradox plays itself out even in the internal workings of legal doctrine, where only state actors are constitutionally liable for privacy violations even as government actors – judges – decide who is and

---

[29] Ignatieff 2002a.
[30] For a useful effort to explore more flexible elements in a concept of privacy, see Nissbenbaum 2004.

who is not a state actor for these purposes. Finally, as we look to privacy as a right or collection of rights, we find ourselves unsuccessfully looking for permanent, free-standing principles beyond history or politics, and yet no potential principles seem robust enough to reach across present contexts and changing political realities – let alone across time.

We suggest starting with, rather than fleeing from, the recognition of the historical contingency of privacy notions. The roots of privacy in specifically liberal political ideas serves to elevate the significance of the individual, enforce the distinction between a public and private realm, and constrain the state to protect individuals through laws and rights. Privacy centrally advances and protects a concept of a distinctive self, unmoored from station, time and destiny, that emerges from a prior century of liberal thought into social practices in parts of the United States and Europe by the late nineteenth century. The centrality of a particular notion of self to the resulting legal and political norms cannot be overstated. Self-expression, self-assertion, self-determination – all these and others make that dependence explicit, but the dependence is there even when the word "self" is not. Indeed, the origins of a "self" as a concept are far older than the specific form of modern selfhood that we intuitively want to protect with concepts of privacy. The pre-Socratics most certainly were concerned with a self that needed cultivation through isolation and testing. And medieval writers certainly took much to turn on the nature of the individual soul as key to selfhood. A reflective self figures as a theme in the Renaissance (Bloom 1999). But only in a Pickwickian sense could we say that people of ancient or medieval times thought about the plastic invented self, implied in our current usage of privacy.

The history of the self has different aspects, but its history in the United States and Europe has been played out, largely (though in important ways not exclusively) through the body. When the ancients sought to cultivate the self by meditation or isolation, by deprivation; when the German Bildungsroman of the nineteenth century moved the hero toward a completion of the self through a voyage; when the French formed their secondary schools in the early nineteenth century to teach its young men how to assert "le moi" – these were all techniques to create a self in a particular image (Goldstein 1994). Indeed, there are many techniques for reinforcing certain forms of selfhood. Architecture can be built to annihilate the sense of individual importance or can be constructed to glorify the individual, even to repeat the human face and body in the structures in which we live. A legal system can elevate or subordinate the individual; elevation has been the direction of law in the United States with increasing force after the Civil War and subsequent constitutional amendments.

One of the architectural markers of apartments in the late nineteenth century was a radical distinction between public and private places. Certainly in the wealthier houses (bit by bit imitated in more modest homes) public sectors of the living space were dedicated to display. A foyer (sometimes dining room) offered a kind of routing station after the reception area, beyond which only the family would pass. After these open and quasi-open spaces, were the sacred precincts of the bedrooms. These were hidden from public view, beds and sexuality needing cover from sight (Guerrand 1990).

Within the bourgeois apartment, the restriction of smells came more slowly. Britain mandated flush toilets, hygienists pressed for sanitary kitchen facilities – air, clean water, removal of odors became an obsession principally during the last half of the century (Ibid. at 370–4). It is against this sociospatial background that Samuel Warren and Louis Brandeis' 1890 "Right to Privacy" needs to be viewed. These authors began by invoking the ancient protection of life and property: assault on body, cattle, or land could be defended. It was their ambition, however, to *extend* "property" to the intangible domain. "Much later," they wrote, "came a qualified protection of the individual against offensive noises and odors, against dust and smoke, and excessive vibration." Here Brandeis and Warren were indeed taking up a very current campaign that was in the process of re-making the boundary of the self, hygienic and architectural transformations that extended the protective cocoon of selfhood from the body and possessions as such and widened them considerably. Judges, invoking common law, could sanctify this new sphere of the self: "thoughts, emotions, and sensations demanded legal recognition" (Warren & Brandeis 1890).

If privacy was augmented, then intrusions – trespasses – too would appear in a correspondingly broader scope. The particular kind of trespass using [the] penny press to circulate portraits and gossip were felt especially by members of the upper classes who found themselves the target of scurrilous rumors, but the very phenomenon of this kind of "mechanical devices" was itself of relatively recent construction, and even more recent registration as an emotional intrusion. "To satisfy a prurient taste the details of sexual relations are spread broadcast in the columns of the daily papers," and some retreat, some refuge from this "advancing civilization" would demand a sanctum sanctorum, a zone into which prying eyes could not peer (Ibid. at 196).

Caring for this zone of privacy took many forms. Collecting became a hugely important activity of the late nineteenth century – family archives, stamps, rocks, seashells, antiques, art. These were all at once a gesture (alongside, for example, diary keeping) against death, a retreat into domesticity, a small-scale imitation of aristocratic splendor, and a rejection of the exterior social world. Collecting was a way of making the self – a technology as it were – completely irrelevant as a form of self-construction in the time of the Stoics. As Michelle Perrot has put it, "the ubiquity of collecting is one of the most telling facts of nineteenth-century upper-class history" (Perrot 1990: 545). This may make it plainer why Warren and Brandeis took up the issue in the historic essay:

> Suppose a man has a collection of gems or curiosities which he keeps private: it would hardly be contended that any person could publish a catalogue of them, and yet the articles enumerated are certainly not intellectual property in the legal sense, any more than a collection of stoves or of chairs (1890: 203).

Precisely because the self was in flux in the late nineteenth century, the work necessary to preserve and develop it was visible. In times of stability such efforts might fade into the unseen. Warren and Brandeis toyed with the idea that conscious creation of artistic or literary works might be worthy of protection but everyday conduct not. Such a distinction, it might be said, would encourage creative work.

> This contention, however plausible, has, in fact, little to recommend it. If the amount of labor involved be adopted as the test, we might well find that the effort to conduct one's self properly in business and in domestic relations had been far greater than that involved in painting a picture or writing a book.... (Ibid. at 204).

Making a (private) life was, so to speak, its own aesthetic creation, and the protection of that life-as-art was in and of itself worthy, perhaps *most* worthy, of protection. It would be insufficient, in their view, to find protection only in the scope of property law to guard against the publication of private expression – for example, in a written letter; a right to privacy would be needed for the sake of peace of mind and the sense of "inviolate personality," not merely for any economic value (Ibid. at 210, 205).

This creation had its locus in part in property – the prying eye of the press camera, for example, might be seen as an extended trespass. But some aspects (lists of items in one's collection) were not in any literal sense a material trespass. In short, Warren and Brandeis' defense of privacy are in a transition moment of the self; privacy as defense of that expanded self was – and is – in historical flux. This is crucial not just theoretically, but practically. Once we see how the boundaries of the self change, we also should come to understand how the associated boundaries dividing public from private and state from individual cannot be legislated or judged once and for all time. But the slow variability of the self over the course of the nineteenth century, for example, should not be conflated with moment-to-moment arbitrariness. The sense of self is not ephemeral in that way. Even when we want to change the boundaries of the private, it may not be something willed otherwise in a moment – as our sense of shame and modesty makes abundantly clear.

Bringing to visibility the techniques of the self – as Michel Foucault and Pierre Hadot have argued[31] – shows how the self is historical, not transcendental. Because it has changed over time and place, privacy – designed to create a penumbral region around the self – is also variable. That the sense of privacy should vary as much as it does from culture to culture today, even among Anglo-American and continental European countries, is less of a surprise if we recognize that there are also differing senses of self. For example, long-standing differences in conceptions of the relation of each person to duty and state characterize even a cursory contrast between the United States and Germany. So when we, with Robert Post, reflect on the tensions between privacy associated with conformism and privacy associated with freedom, we need to return to the specific underlying concept of the self that is so indissociably attached to privacy.

To look at the self as constituted through technologies is to open up a series of questions. What are our methods (ethics) now, individually or collectively, for *intentionally* cultivating the self? How do our educational institutions, churches, courts, armed forces, and psychiatric hospitals function (discipline) in this regard? How do developments affect the shaping of the self even without intentional aim to do so? The full range of these techniques leave open other possibilities, including self-shaping technologies that are chosen for many different reasons – but are not at all necessarily in *order* to shape the self. These days one thinks of new technologies, from films and surveillance devices to Internet searches, on-line games, on-line affinity groups, and chat rooms. In a variety of ways, these produce subtle shifts but also potentially profound changes in how a self is created, presented, and subject to surveillance, display, or manipulation.

For example, older concepts of the self were bound up with kinship relations determined more by affect than by biology. Indeed, for quite some time, courts insisted upon the father-child relationship even in cases where the biology (determined by blood type) proved that the father had not, so to speak, "fathered" the child. According to anthropologist Marilyn Strathern, kinship relations have recently undergone a major transformation as genetic information increasingly defines connections where before they had not. Genetic

---

[31] On the notion of the 'technique of self' from Foucault and Hadot, see Focault 1986: 43–5; Foucault, L'Herme/neutique du subject (2001); Hadot 1995. See also Davidson 1994; Martin, Gutman & Hutton 1988. For application to scientific techniques of the self, see Galison 2004.

information has led to new duties – including some codified legally – to pass along information about genetic (medical) predictions of dangerous conditions to genetic relatives. The family, as she puts it, becomes "informational" (Strathern 2003: 180–4). As we might by now anticipate, when features of the self as deep-going as kinship are affected, privacy issues cannot be far behind, entering as soon, for example, as people start demanding the protection of DNA sequences that might predict future medical difficulties. At the practical level will employers be allowed to discriminate based on genetic defects? Would carrying a BRCA mutation that might predispose one to breast or ovarian cancer open up the possibility of social exclusion? Does privacy in the physician-patient relation break down when genetic disease might affect a relative – is there an obligation here to break confidentiality? Alteration in privacy codes affecting DNA data could, in these and other ways, re-shape our sense of who we and others are; conversely, if we come to identify ourselves increasingly in terms of our DNA, that may generate new pressures to enforce genetic privacy (Weaver 1997; Green & Thomas 1998; Sudell 2001).

New technologies may render unavailing the late nineteenth-century notions of privacy as a guardian against unwanted journalistic or neighborly prying eyes. That older conception was in essence *territorial*; many recent extensions of property try to generalize a simple "no trespass" rule: from don't cross my field, don't touch my cattle, to don't survey my hard drive, don't check my library records. Some specific metaphors, such as firewalls, can be helpful in articulating notions of privacy in worlds created by new technologies (Pohlmann & Crothers 2002). But it would be a mistake to treat such metaphors as fully mapping onto the new realms and risks permitted by new technologies. Data mining, analogized to invasion of territorial space, would be nothing more than an extension of someone looking through a crack in your fence, each individual bit of information obtained simply adding to a heap of wrongly obtained bits. Yet, such territorial conception seems seriously incomplete in the contexts of virtual reality, information technology, and markets for personal information. The territorial conception of privacy critically understates what is lost if such data mining proceeds without any limitations. To understand what is at risk requires attending to how the computer has made possible the combination of different forms of information that would have been, a century ago, unimaginable. Getting a list in a few seconds of anyone in the United States who subscribes to a Middle Eastern newspaper, watches Al-Jazeera, is between ages 20 and 35, and who traveled to Washington on the day of a major political demonstration is but a few clicks away. When that bureaucrat at TIA or one of its successors performs such a search and you are named by the state, it is not just "information" that has been gathered. This e-interpellation goes farther than the information separately considered – by the very act of naming you as a suspect (or "person of interest") you have changed status in the eyes of others who know about this, and if you come to know or fear, in your eyes as well. Correlating state databases (including taxes, criminal records, social security, voting registration) with private databases (purchases, travel, on-line clicks) does more than merely assemble a tad more information here or there. It undermines the very concept of a private life.

Can privacy, linked to a conception of private spaces, be sufficient to guard the jeopardy to selves that ensues from such surveillance of personal data mining? There is something far too crude in the image of the physical invasion of specific locales as the threat to privacy. Simple extensions of the legal conception of privacy neglect the degree to which retrospective assertion of a right comes too late, once databases are linked and mined, or secret governmental hearings are in process. Such an "invasive" picture fits many kinds of privacy violation, but it ignores the slow, but nonetheless powerful changes in the self that have occurred since the late nineteenth century and continue today. Is a fallen hair still your property and is its sequencing rightly described as an act of trespassing? Or, more dramatically, if your brother's DNA is sampled – perhaps because he was arrested, perhaps because he was caught up in a DNA dragnetting sweep, perhaps because he was in the military – then *your* DNA is also largely known. But your DNA was known *without* any territorial intrusion on your body or property: the sequencing could even have taken place without your knowledge and based on no strand of your hair or scraping of your skin. By sampling your brother, your DNA code could well have been cracked while you were, in fact, on the other side of the world. Similarly, if publicly available data sets are mined in concert, where – in what *place* would one locate the "intrusion"? No, territorial concepts of self and privacy simply are not expansive enough to capture the totality of issues surrounding our current condition (Grand 2002; Kaye 2001).

Still, if we believe that privacy talk enters with historically fluid concepts of the self, then we may be able to understand the weakness of privacy-as-right. As popular as it may be to see many features of social life as contingent on particular historical and cultural practices, acknowledging this feature of privacy and the sense of self it presupposes and supports seems particularly problematic because we expect stability in privacy and the self. Granted the conception of self has changed over time; this explains why the privacy right always seems too particular to capture the putative universality of rights talk that Michael Ignatieff calls rights as secular religion. But the self does not change moment to moment; we must not infer from this that the contingency of the concept necessarily implies the uselessness of a defensible, mid-scale notion of privacy. A venerable oak may have a history, it surely was not always there, but it can just as surely occupy a central position in our town square's landscape. Pursuing a concept of privacy (and its associated sense of self) that is neither eternal nor ephemeral offers an avenue toward protections that are robust, without positing an imagined, and quickly deflected, universal ought.

III. A Complex Strategy for the Pursuit of Privacy Protections

The double danger that threatens the concept of privacy is this: on one side, if privacy is taken to be a universal, eternal notion then we are tempted to posit rigid principles that define it. But this very rigidity makes privacy frail – to take privacy as territorial, for example, is to be thoroughly unprepared for a new world of data mining, infra-red searches, DNA dragnetting, or computer hacking.[32] On the other side, if privacy is taken to be a matter for every local subculture, every passing fad and every individual whim, then we are left at the beck and call of every new technique of surveillance, market intrusion, or nosy neighbor. Our view is twofold: first, that privacy is not well defined in isolation – it takes its significance from its association with a widely (but not universally) shared notion of self. And second, the self is itself historically embedded, changing slowly relative to the headlines of the daily paper, but significantly over historical time – the self of the Renaissance or Greek Antiquity is not the self of the late nineteenth century. Privacy and the self are neither eternal nor ephemeral. On this picture privacy is the label we give to the protective penumbra that surrounds this historicized self – privacy marks the penumbral edge of selfhood.

Certainly it is all too easy to expect categories to fall into the eternal or the ephemeral: something is true for all time or a mere and local construction. But privacy, like race, may be neither. For years we have known that race as an immutable hereditary essence is nineteenth century in origin – we can even prize apart the conditions of its appearance and growth in European and American culture. But to track the genealogy of race is not to dismiss its power: race grips us today as it did a century ago. Our experiences with the built environment, hygiene, sexuality, or warfare have similar middle-term histories: here are worlds neither eternal in their structure nor changeable at the drop of a hat. What categories like these (privacy, self, race, sexuality) have in common is that they are often taken to be trans-historical – unlike,

---

[32] For discussions of these technologies and the legal issues they raise, see Dodson 2000; Ditzion, Geddes & Rhodes 2003; Regnier 2004.

say, clothing fashion or architectural idiom. Privacy and the self need to be understood precisely as of this mid-range type: powerful, robust, relatively long-lived – and yet changing markedly over the course of the centuries.

Both the notion of privacy and the sense of self it protects are contingent on historical, technological, and political shifts; privacy is linked to the historical development of a sense of self during late nineteenth century in the United States and Western Europe.[33] Perhaps implicit in its contingency lies the greatest promise of privacy. Entwined with the emerging notions of a sense of individual self capable of free choice, experimentation, and self-invention, the specific conception of privacy emerging in American law enables the creativity and the spirit of liberty that exemplify the nation's contributions to human civilization. No doubt the self is continuing to change. There is no reason to expect that the bourgeois architecture of the late nineteenth century and the patterns of collecting, cleaning, diary-writing, alongside sound- and smell-proofing, were the final word on defining selfhood. Our current world is making use of new technologies that may well re-define the self. Who is to say what the long-term effect will be as an ever-increasing number of people spend more and more hours trying on new personalities and even identities on-line, around the non-virtual globe?[34] The conception of the self nurtured in private, experimenting with choice and self-invention could well be extending and shifting in the new environment, even as it depends on the sphere of the private invented only over the past century or so.

With this historicized conception of privacy in mind, we come at the end of this chapter to three conclusions. First, the idea that by sacrificing personal privacy we will achieve security at best reflects faulty analysis or magical thinking and at worst seeks to excuse failures to attend to immediate and difficult security dangers that require no sacrifice of privacy. Sacrificing personal privacy does nothing to defend those ferociously toxic chemical plants that stand upwind from major cities or to secure the major repositories of plutonium, highly enriched uranium, nuclear weapons, or radioactive waste.

---

[33] We do not mean to make claims of either similarity or difference with conceptions of the self in other parts of the world – but do mean to note the historical and regional contingency of such conceptions. In addition to historical contingency, privacy as an idea is likened to contingent privileges of class and contingent features of gender identity. Thus, privacy may embody privileges associated with wealth. The ability to seclude oneself, to control who has access to viewing oneself, or to imagine freedom to shape one's identity free from intrusions by others imply control over sufficient resources even to develop these as aspirations. Privacy may also carry important gendered dimensions; certainly, control over one's reproductive choice has been largely conceived as a special concern for women, given the disparate burdens pregnancy carries for women compared with men.

[34] See Haraway 1991; Mitchell 2003; Turkel 1997.

These fundamental dangers to our security have yet to receive priority. At the same time, successful law enforcement efforts, such as arrests of major al Qaeda leaders, did not result from trolling through millions of private e-mails, correlating their contents with the book borrowing or video rentals; it has come from targeted cell phones and pavement-pounding police work. To date, it is at most a tiny minority of terrorists who have been convicted as a result of data mining consumer and government records. It is not clear that even such techniques – rather than targeted searches based on reasonable suspicions of individuals – have generated any arrests or detentions (see Schneier 2003; CSTCT 2002). It strikes us as worse than foolish to imagine that the sacrifice of something we value – privacy – is in and of itself the means to increase security. Sacrifice for the sake of sacrifice is magical thinking, a kind of haywire homeland potlatch. Instead of blindly opening up our reading, our communication, our purchases, and our travel to commercial and governmental mining, we can and should demand that priority be given to the real security failings that represent real and enormous threats. In the absence of such steps, it is tempting to interpret the invasions of privacy through massive governmental surveillance and data mining as part of the efforts by leaders to claim they have advanced security, when they have not, to heighten fears in order to maintain political control, or to appeal to an irrational notion that sacrifice and pain will exchange for safety and deliverance.

Second, given the complexity of the self, trying to reduce the privacy concept to a purely utilitarian framework is like steamrolling a statue to capture its essence in the simpler space of the two-dimensional plane. Such flattening may make security and privacy look like a simple balancing act – twelve ounces of each on the two sides of the scale – but it does nothing to acknowledge the space people need to deliberate, to try out new ways of acting or different ways of speaking. To imagine we could weigh against security what we call privacy pretends that we can transform these ends into quasi-quantifiable means, and to conduct a charade that anything could ever win against security. Because in such a flatland view, utility always will make security measures trump, even if the security gains are at best marginal or speculative, or a political performance designed to reassure us that we are doing something in the face of panic and unease. It is all too easy for each of us to exaggerate fear and minimize values like privacy, or the associated sense of freedom for self-development and the experience of dignity. To ask "what is the utility of dignity" is to offer it up for sacrifice.

Finally, we believe that no single kind of intervention – not law by itself, not technology by itself, and not the individual exercise of our desires and choices by themselves will be adequate to protect privacy. If we take seriously the protection of privacy – protection of the dignity of the self – we must pursue complex and multiple means. Our best chance at this will necessarily involve a kind of complementarity among the law, technology, and desire. Law provides institutional checks on power, transparency of decision making and results, and recompense for violations and mistakes. Technology steers action and can provide complete deterrence of invasive action through the hardware and software designed to collect and analyze data or monitor conduct and presence. Technology also creates possibilities for open expression. Desire – whether expressed in markets, political action, or private conduct – is generative, imaginative, pressurizing. Our desired choices can shape the self. The role of each is not, of course, completely independent – experience with certain technologies can certainly shape the self, the law can sometimes deter, and our desires themselves can drive us towards transparency.

But each has its limits. Law can all too often be beholden to politics. It is, by its very means, slow, reactive, and responsive to pressures of politics and power. Legal protections, even if successfully adopted, require the desires and courage of victims to complain and judges for enforcement. Technology can be too rigid – no sooner is there a measure to protect e-privacy then a hacker arrives with a countermeasure. If technology is too rigid, desire can be so flexible that we can find ourselves giving up privacy in the enthusiasm of a demagogic moment. We can draw on the strengths of law, technology, and desire to complement and substitute for each other's limitations.

The idea of such complementarity may be more familiar from more mundane concerns. After all, defending such an abstract aspect of what we care about is at least as hard as protecting our bodies in automobiles. On the road we rely on hardware (soft dashboards, shatterproof glass, airbags, and seatbelts). We count on laws that restrict speeding, limit alcohol, and channel traffic. And we demand proactive good sense, the right management of desires on the part of drivers as they handle intrinsically dangerous machines: prosaic as it is, courtesy does matter at 65 miles per hour.

In coming to terms with privacy we will need a mix of this kind, even if it will need to be significantly more complicated. We need legal rules that anticipate rather than merely react – that affect the structure of technology, for example.[35]

---

[35] "In thinking about guidelines, the government should start with the basic architecture – what is the appropriate level of protection for different types of information, and what kinds of standards and procedures might provide that protection. The current legal framework governing access to and use of privately held data is a patchwork quilt of different standards for information with similar sensitivity (such as wire, cable, and Internet

We need new technologies that will no doubt include anonymizing software, cryptography, and hardware that make much more difficult what currently are easy intrusions into the monitoring of our on-line lives, purchases, and travel. Privacy in the coming generation will require architecture, both of the electronic and bricks-and-mortar type designed to provide refuge from inquiry more sophisticated by far than any of the prying eyes of the press presented to Warren and Brandeis seventy-five years ago. And we will have to make use of our own decisions, our own desires, as we express our choices in the marketplace, to be sure, but not only there. We need to educate ourselves about our tendencies to overemphasize dangers and the short term and inadequately to imagine the circle of concern.[36] And we will need to demand publicity about decisions affecting our privacy. Without the investigative work of a newspaper columnist, the details of the Terrorist Information Awareness project may well never have surfaced publicly, though when they did, people demanded change. That democratic process of oversight becomes all but impossible as new developments moved behind the wall of classified secrets. Opportunities for knowing what is going on are central to the development and expressions of desires – and here maintaining scrutiny of governmental secrecy and vigilance over personal privacy remain vital legal strategies. Some sense of a right to privacy will be needed, even while we recognize that rights talk will have to be flexible enough to change with changing technological and political times. No single measure will protect us on the interstate; no magic

communications) and inappropriate or nonexistence standards for other kinds of information. See www.markletaskforce.org for matrices about this. The complexity of these rules, and the confusion they engender, may cause government officials to be reluctant to take lawful and necessary action to gather important counterterrorism information for fear of crossing a vague line. At the same time, these rights offer little assurance to the public that their rights are adequately protected. . . . New guidelines should, at a minimum, address the following: (1.) government acquisition and use of private sector data; (2.) government retention of the data; (3.) sharing of the data by the acquiring agency with other agencies for purposes other than counterterrorism; and (4.) accountability and oversight" (Markle Foundation 2003: 32–6). It is tempting to explore the common law as an avenue for relief/checking by private individuals against commercial entities (see McClurg 2003). Yet contractual terms can easily evade common law duties.

36 "By sensationalizing 'newsworthy,' but low-risk, dangers, [the media] generate a sense of panic that quickly cascades through society. People routinely overreact to vivid depictions of frightening, but low-probability, dangers. Lurid reports of sniper shootings, for example, send ripples of fear through a community, triggering excessively cautious responses. This can have a devastating effect on society when the precipitating event is a terrorist attack or espionage in wartime. In such circumstances, the 'excessively cautious' response may not be merely to avoid the sniper's haunts but to insist that government detain and depart aliens, anarchists, or Muslims because of an exaggerated sense of the danger they pose to the nation" (Stone 2004: 533). See also Nussbaum 2003.

bullet, technological, juridical, or decisional, can sufficiently guard our sense of self.

How much we want to protect privacy implicates what space and latitude we preserve for selfhood. How we *want* to exercise the self, so to speak, is more than a personal question. Our decisions about the Terrorist Information Awareness project and the USA PATRIOT Act redefine the reach and ambition of government surveillance; they re-align the boundary between public and private, and the very scope for self-creation for everyone in the nation. James Scott's powerful book, *Seeing Like A State* (1998), depicts the statistical vision of the rising nation-state from the early eighteenth century forward (see Anderson 1991). We are now in a position to determine how we want the state to see today and therefore how the state and individual should relate to one another both in pragmatic roles – who can read what – and symbolically – what would we prefer that the state *not* see such that an individual can explore the world with a measure of openness?

Reading privacy together with the conception of the self brings forward other values, like human dignity, which we do not want to throw away simply to signal commitment against an amorphous network of criminal terror-ists. Our sense of dignity, our sense of self are tied up with our most valued freedoms to grow, to raise our children with self-respect, to nurture the delib-erative democracy we have been proud of for 225 years. Posing the question of privacy in terms of self and dignity not only helps us understand the historicity of these notions, but it also underscores the stakes we have in their protection.

Devastating as it was, the bombing of the World Trade Center was also a warning. It was not only a warning from the terrorists, but also a warning from inside our own political culture that we must reckon, urgently, with the aspects of our civil life that we value most deeply. Privacy is not a dangerous luxury to be thrown away like cigarettes on the deck of a wartime freighter plying the dark North Atlantic night. Privacy is the name we give the edge of the dignified self, a boundary we need to protect even if, especially if, we find ourselves once again under siege.

REFERENCES

Aleinikoff, T. A. (1987). 'Constitutional Law in the Age of Balancing'. 96 *Yale Law Journal* 943.

Allen, A. L. (1988). *Uneasy Access: Privacy for Women in a Free Society*. Totowa, NJ: Rowland & Littlefield.

Anderson, B. (1991). *Imagined Communities: Reflections on the Origin and Spread of Nationalism* (revised edition). New York: Verso.

Arendt, H. (1958). *The Human Condition*. New York: Doubleday.

Atlanta Journal-Constitution. 'Balance Information With Privacy'. 10 December 2003, p. 22A.

Baer, S. (2003, January 5). 'Broader U.S. Spy Initiative Debated; Poindexter Leads Project to Assess Electronic Data, Detect Possible Terrorists; Civil Liberties Concerns Raised'. *Baltimore Sun*, p. 1A (quoting Jay Stanley of the American Civil Liberties Union).

Baldas, T. (2004, August 9). 'ACLU Takes on "Matrix" Crime, Terrorism Database'. *National Law Journal*, p. 4.

Bloom, H. (1998). *Shakespeare: The Invention of the Human.* New York: Riverhead Books.

Borger, J. (2002, May 21). 'Shamed FBI's Snooping Powers Increased'. *The Guardian* (London), p. 18.

Boyle, J. (1992). 'A Theory of Law and Information: Copyright, Spleens, Blackmail, and Insider Trading'. 80 *California Law Review* 1413.

Brest, P. (1982). 'State Action and Liberal Theory: A Casenote on Flagg Brothers v. Brooks'. 130 *University of Pennsylvania Law Review* 1296.

California v. Greenwood, 486 U.S. 35 (1988).

Choper, J. (1979). 'Thoughts on State Action: The "Government Function," and "Power Theory" Approaches'. *Washington University Law Quarterly* 757.

CNN.com. (2003, July 30). 'Amid furor, Pentagon kills terrorism futures market'. Inside Politics. Available at: http://www.cnn.com/2003/ALLPOLITICS/07/29/terror.market/index.html.

Committee on Science and Technology for Countering Terrorism (CSTCT). (2002). *Making the Nation Safer: The Role of Science and Technology in Countering Terrorism.* National Research Council of the National Academies. Washington, D.C.: National Academies Press.

DARPA (2003, May 20). *Report to Congress Regarding the Terrorism Information Awareness Program.* Available at: http://www.globalsecurity.org/security/library/report/2003/tia- di_report_20may2003.pdf.

Davidson, A. (1994). 'Ethics as Ascetics: Foucault, The History of Ethics and Ancient Thought'. In J. E. Goldstein (Ed.), *Foucault and the Writing of History.* Cambridge: Blackwell.

DeCew, J. W. (1997). *In Pursuit of Privacy: Law, Ethics, and the Rise of Technology.* Ithaca, NY: Cornell University Press.

Denver Post. 'Virtual Borders vs. Civil Liberties'. 31 May 2004, p. C-07.

Directionsmag.com. (1998). 'Acxiom's InfoBase Profiler Via the Acxiom Data Network is First Consumer Data Product to Provide Census and Household-Level Demographic Data and Scores in Sub-Second Time'. 3 December 1998, Press Release, Acxiom Corp. Available at http://www.directionsmag.com/press.releases/index.php?duty=Show&id=80.

Ditzion, R., Geddes, E., & Rhodes, M. (2003, Spring). 'Computer Crimes'. *American Criminal Law Review*, vol. 40, issue 2, p. 285(52).

Dixon, R. (1976). 'The "New" Substantive Due Process and the Democratic Ethic: A Prolegomenon'. *Brigham Young University Law Review* 43.

Dodson, A. J. (2000, Winter). 'DNA "Line-Ups" Based on a Reasonable Suspicion Standard'. *University of Colorado Law Review*, vol. 71, issue 1, pp. 221–54.

Eisenstadt v. Baird, 405 U.S. 438 (1972).

Executive Summary of the Independent Counsel Investigation (the Walsh Report). Available at: http://www.fas.org/irp/offdocs/walsh/execsum.htm.

Fisher III, W. W., Horwitz, M. J., & Reed, T. (Eds.). (1993). *American Legal Realism*. New York: Oxford University Press.

Flagg Brothers, Inc. v. Brooks, 436 U.S. 149 (1978).

Florida v. Riley, 488 U.S. 445 (1989).

Foucault, M. (1986). *History of Sexuality, vol. 3: The Care of the Self* (R. Hurley, Trans.). New York: Vintage.

Friendly, H. (1969). *'The Dartmouth College Case and the Public-Private Penumbra'*. Austin: University of Texas.

Galison, P. (2004). 'Image of Self'. In L. Daston (Ed.), *Things that Talk*. Cambridge: Zone Books.

Goldstein, J. (1994). 'Foucault and the Post-Revolutionary Self: The Uses of Cousinian Pedagogy in Nineteenth-Century France'. In J. Goldstein (Ed.), *Foucault and the Writing of History*, pp. 99–115. Oxford: Blackwell.

Grand, J. S. (2002, August). 'The Blooding of America: Privacy and the DNA Dragnet'. *Cardozo Law Review*, vol. 23, issue 6, pp. 2277–323.

Green, R. M. & Thomas, A. M. (1998). 'DNA: Five Distinguishing Features for Policy Analysis'. 11 *Harvard Journal of Law and Technology* 571.

Greer, S. (2003, September). 'Constitutionalizing Adjudication Under the European Convention on Human Rights'. *Oxford Journal of Legal Studies*, vol. 23, issue 3, pp. 405–433(29).

Griswold v. Connecticut, 381 U.S. 479 (1965).

Guerrand, R.-H. (1990). 'Private Spaces'. In M. Perrot (Ed.), A. Goldhammer, (Transl.), *A History of Private Life, vol. 4: From the Fires of Revolution to the Great War*, pp. 359–74. P. Ariès and G. Duby (general Eds.). Cambridge, MA: Belknap Press, Harvard University Press.

Hadot, P. (1995). *Philosophy as a Way of Life*. New York: Blackwell.

Haraway, D. J. (1991). *Simians, Cyborgs, and Women*. Routledge.

Henkin, L. (1974). 'Privacy and Autonomy'. 74 *Columbia Law Review* 1410.

Hetcher, S. (2001). 'Changing the Social Meaning of Privacy in Cyberspace'. 15 *Harvard Journal of Law and Technology* 149.

Hoofnagle, C. J. (2004, Summer). 'Big Brother's Little Helpers: How ChoicePoint and Other Commercial Data Brokers Collect, Process, and Package Your Data for Law Enforcement'. *University of North Carolina Journal of International Law and Commercial Regulation*, vol. 29, no. 4, pp. 595–637.

Horwitz, M. (1982). 'The History of the Public/Private Distinction'. 130 *University of Pennsylvania Law Review* 1423.

Ignatieff, M. (2002a, February 5). 'Is the Human Rights Era Ending?' *New York Times*, p. A29.

———. (2002b). *Human Rights as Politics and Idolatry*. Princeton, NJ: Princeton University Press.

Kang, J. (1998). 'Information Privacy in Cyberspace Transactions'. 50 *Stanford Law Review* 1193.

Kang, J. & Buchner, B. (2004, Fall). 'Privacy in Atlantis: A Dialogue of Form and Substance'. *Harvard Journal of Law and Technology*, vol. 18, no. 1. Available at http://papers.ssrn.com/sol3/papers.cfm?abstract_id=626942.

Katz v. United States, 389 U.S. 347 (1967).

Kaye, D. H. (2001, Summer). 'The Constitutionality of DNA Sampling on Arrest'. *Cornell Journal of Law and Public Policy*, vol. 10, issue 3, p. 455(55).

Kyllo v. United States, 533 U.S. 27 (2001).

LaFave, W. (1966). *1 Search and Seizure* (3rd ed.), section 2.1(d), pp. 393–4.

Lawrence v. Texas, 539 U.S. 558 (2003).

Lawyers Committee for Human Rights (herein "LCHR"). (2003). *Assessing the New Normal: Liberty and Security for the Post-September 11 United States*. New York. Available at: http://www.humanrightsfirst.org/pubs/descriptions/Assessing/AssessingtheNewNormal.pdf.

Mark, R. (2003, July 29). 'Pentagon Folds Hand in Online Terrorism Futures Scheme'. Available at: http://dc.internet.com/news/article.php/2241421.

Markle Foundation (2003). *Creating a Trusted Information Network for Homeland Security: Second Report of the Markle Foundation Task Force*. Available at: http://www.markletaskforce.org/Report2_Full_Report.pdf.

Martin, L. H., Gutman, H., & Hutton, P. H. (Eds.). (1988). *'Technologies of the Self: A Seminar with Michel Foucault'*. Amherst, MA: University of Massachusetts Press.

McClurg, A. J. (2003). 'A Thousand Words Are Worth a Picture: A Privacy Tort Response to Consumer Data Profiling'. 98 *Northwestern University Law Review* 63.

Minnesota v. Carter, 525 U.S. 93, 97 (1998).

Minow, M. (1987). 'We, The Family: Constitutional Rights and American Families'. *Journal of American History*, vol. 74, no. 3, p. 959.

Mitchell, W. J. (2003). Me^{++}: *The Cyborg Self and the Networked City*. Cambridge, MA: MIT Press.

Multi-State Anti-Terrorism Information Exchange (MATRIX). Available at: http://www.matrix-at.org/. Accessed on 24 August 2004.

National Law Journal Roundtable (2003, April 26). 'Patriot Act Attacked'. 26 April 2003, p. 19.

Nissbenbaum, H. (2004). 'Privacy as Contextual Integrity'. 79 *Washington Law Review* 119.

Nussbaum, M. (2003). 'Compassion and Terror'. In J. P. Sterba (Ed.), *Terrorism and International Justice*, pp. 229–52. Oxford: Oxford University Press.

Peller, G. (1985). 'The Metaphysics of American Law'. 73 *California Law Review* 1151.

Perrot, M. (1990). 'The Secret of the Individual'. In M. Perrot (Ed.), A. Goldhammer, (Transl.), *A History of Private Life, vol. 4: From the Fires of Revolution to the Great War*, pp. 457–548. P. Ariès and G. Duby (general Eds.). Cambridge, MA: Belknap Press, Harvard University Press.

Planned Parenthood of Southeastern Pennsylvania v. Casey, 505 U.S. 833 (1992).

Pohlmann, N. & Crothers, T. (2002). *Firewall Architecture for the Enterprise*. John Wiley & Sons, Inc.

Poindexter, J. (2002, August 2). 'Overview of the Information Awareness Office'. Prepared remarks for delivery at DARPATech 2002, Anaheim, CA, Aug. 2, 2002. Available at: http://www.fas.org/irp/agency/dod/poindexter.html.

Posner, R. (1979). 'The Uncertain Protection of Privacy by the Supreme Court'. *Supreme Court Review* 173, 188.

Post, R. C. (2001). 'Three Concepts of Privacy'. 89 *Georgetown Law Journal* 2087.

Rasul v. Bush, 124 S. Ct. 2686, 159 L. Ed. 2d 548, 72 U.S.L.W. 4596, 2004 U.S. LEXIS 4760 (2004).

Regnier, T. (2004, Spring). 'The "Loyal Foot Soldier": Can the Fourth Amendment Survive the Supreme Court's War on Drugs?' *UKMC Law Review*, vol. 72, issue 3, pp. 631–68.

Reiss, S. (2004, May). 'Poindexter Confidential'. *Wired Magazine*, Issue 12.05. Available at: http://www.wired.com/wired/archive/12.05/poindexter.html.

Rendell-Baker v. Kohn, 457 U.S. 830 (1982).

Rennie, D. (2003, August 1). 'Admiral Behind Terrorist Futures Market "To Quit"'. *Daily Telegraph* (London), p. 20.

'Responses by Center for Democracy and Technology and Other Civil Liberties Organizations to TIA Report' (herein "Responses") (2003, August 20). Available at: http://www.cdt.org/security/usapatriot/030520cdt.shtml.

R. L. Polk & Co. (2005). 'Automotive Profiling System'. Available at: http://www.polk.com/products/aps.asp.

Roe v. Wade, 410 U.S. 113 (1973).

Rosen, J. (2000). *The Unwanted Gaze: The Destruction of Privacy in America*. New York: Vintage.

Safire, W. (2003, February 13). 'Privacy Invasion Curtailed'. *New York Times*, p. 41.

Samuelson, P. (2000). 'Privacy as Intellectual Property?' 52 *Stanford Law Review* 1125.

Schneier, B. (2003). *Beyond Fear: Thinking Sensibly About Security in an Uncertain World*. New York: Springer-Verlag.

Scott, J. C. (1998). *Seeing Like a State: How Certain Conditions to Improve the Human Condition Have Failed*. New Haven: Yale University Press.

Solove, D. J. (2002). 'Conceptualizing Privacy'. 90 *California Law Review* 1087.

Solove, D. J. & Rotenberg, M. (2003). *Information Privacy Law*, p. 27. New York: Aspen Publishers.

St. Petersburg Times (Florida). 'Total Information Awareness II?' 31 May 2004, p. 12A.

Stone, G. R. (2004). *Perilous Times: Free Speech in Wartime from the Sedition Act of 1789 to the War on Terrorism*. New York: W. W. Norton & Co.

Strathern, M. (2003). 'Emergent Relations'. In M. Biagioli & P. Galison (Eds.). *Scientific Authorship*, pp. 169–94, chapter 7. New York: Routledge.

Sudell, A. (2001). 'Comment: To Tell or Not to Tell: The Scope of Physician-Patient Confidentiality When Relatives Are at Risk of Genetic Disease'. 18 *Journal of Contemporary Health Law and Policy* 273.

Sutherland, J. (2002, February 18). 'No more Mr Scrupulous Guy'. *The Guardian* (United Kingdom). Available at: http://www.guardian.co.uk/g2/story/0,3604,651950,00.html.

Technology and Privacy Advisory Committee (herein "TPAC") (2004, March 1). *Safeguarding Privacy in the Fight Against Terrorism: Report of the Technology and Privacy Advisory Committee to the Department of Defense*. Available at: http://www.mipt.org/pdf/Safeguarding-Privacy-Fight-Against-Terrorism.pdf.

Times-Picayune (New Orleans, LA). 'Plots at Public Meetings?' 3 June 2002, p. 4.

Turkel, S. (1997). *Life on the Screen: Identity in the Age of the Internet*. New York: Touchstone.

United States v. Leon, 468 U.S. 897 (1984).

Uniting and Strengthening America by Providing Appropriate Tools Required to Intercept and Obstruct Terrorism Act of 2001 (herein "USA PATRIOT Act"), Pub. L. No. 107–56, 302(a) (1), 115 Stat. 272 (2001).

Warren, S. D. & Brandeis, L. D. (1890). 'The Right to Privacy'. 4 *Harvard Law Review* 193.

Weaver, K. D. (1997). 'Genetic Screening and the Right Not to Know'. *Issues in Law & Medicine*, vol. 13. no. 3, p. 243.

Webster v. Reproductive Health Services, 492 U.S. 490 (1989).

Weintraub, B. (1986, November 26). 'Iran Payment Found Diverted to Contras; Reagan Security Advisor and Aide Are Out'. *New York Times*, p. A1.

Westin, A. F. (1967). *Privacy and Freedom*. London: Bodley Head.

14. Are Human Rights Universal in an Age of Terrorism?

WIKTOR OSIATYNSKI

To answer the question posed in the title it is useful to distinguish between human rights as the set of rules and human rights as principles. It also distinguishes between human rights and the philosophy of human rights. In 1948, there existed a cross-cultural consensus on rights as principles and on basic tenets of the philosophy of human rights. Recently, the consensus over principles and over the philosophy of human rights has broken down. The events of September 11 did not start this process; it merely accelerated it, and the war on terrorism brought it to a point that could be beyond repair. Therefore, our task today should not be to restore the consensus over the philosophy of human rights, but to detach the rules from – once universal, albeit no more – principles so that we could rescue human rights norms and find the most adequate means to enforce them.

To understand better this thesis, a brief overview of the development of human rights is in order.

The Original Consensus on Human Rights

The Universal Declaration of Human Rights (UDHR) adopted by the United Nations in December 1948 reflected a broad consensus between various ideas, values, and cultures. Even though the idea of individual rights was of Western origin, it was the non-Western countries that pushed for the adoption of the Declaration, against some reluctance of the Western governments (Lauren 1998: 165–71). Leaders and philosophers from Latin America, Asia, and the Middle East joined Western intellectuals and activists in support of human rights (Glendon 2001).

The final version of the Declaration proclaimed the values of individual liberty, democracy, and participation, as well as social and economic rights. Latin American governments also placed great emphasis on labor rights and

295

adequate conditions for work, and these initiatives were supported by the European Left. The Declaration implied an active state, and on a number of occasions mentioned the fulfillment of the individual's potential as an obligation of the state. It offered protection for the family and hailed self-determination. But the main goal of the Declaration was to safeguard peace.

Thus, the Declaration was a compromise in a number of ways: It was a compromise between American and European (Continental) traditions of rights and freedom. It was a compromise between liberal and dignity-based conceptions of rights (Glendon 2001: 227).[1] It was a compromise between various ideologies; present in the Declaration were liberal, conservative, Christian, and socialist ideas. Self-determination, social rights, and the concept of the active state also made the UDHR a compromise between the Western concept of freedom and the needs of non-Western people who wanted freedom from colonialism and development.

The Declaration was adopted with no opposition and a small number of abstentions. Among the abstainers were the Soviet Union, Belarus, Ukraine, and the Soviet satellites in East Central Europe, for which the broad range of civil liberties and political rights was unacceptable. The Republic of South Africa had legalized apartheid just before the adoption of the UDHR, rejecting its principle of racial equality. Finally, Saudi Arabia pointed out that articles permitting the free choice of religion and defining the family as a voluntary contract between equal partners were incompatible with Islam. Other Arab states and countries with large Muslim populations did not share these objections and their representatives acted, sometimes fiercely as in the case of Indonesia and Egypt, for the adoption of the UDHR. While there were many political differences, there was no large cross-cultural conflict at the time of the passage of the Declaration.

In 1948, however, there existed no procedural consensus about the enforcement of human rights. In fact, the lack of enforceability was the price of the compromises regarding the content. It was pretty obvious that some of the rights included, such as social rights, labor rights, and family rights, could not be enforced with the same rigor as civil liberties or political rights. Therefore, the Declaration was formulated as a set of standards for humankind, with no enforcement mechanisms whatsoever. Soon afterwards, Western European states reached a procedural consensus by re-defining human rights, that is, by narrowing them down to civil liberties and political rights, and attaching

---

[1] Glendon uses the word "dignitarian" to describe rights tradition prevailing in continental Europe and more appealing to the rest of the world than liberal tradition of rights.

procedural guarantees in the European Convention of Human Rights (1950). In the Economic and Social Charter (1960), social rights were treated primarily as the goals for the public social policies of states, rather than as individual rights enforceable in courts.

This approach was copied in the separation of international human rights into two U.N. covenants adopted in 1966 and ratified ten years later; the International Covenant on Civil and Political Rights, and the Covenant on Economic, Social, and Cultural Rights. Civil and political rights (the so-called first generation rights) were treated as binding the signatory governments *hic at nunc*, while social, economic, and cultural rights were perceived as aspirations to be realized progressively by states according to their economic capabilities. The second covenant, on Economic, Social and Cultural Rights, did not impose enforceable obligations on the wealthier countries to share resources with nations for whom the realization of these aspirations was impossible. Therefore, even though the pacts were international, the rights included were treated as being primarily domestic.

In contrast, the mechanisms for the enforcement of human rights in the framework of the United Nations' covenants were primarily international. While in domestic law a claim against the government is brought in by the particular victim of abuse, the international human rights mechanism originally removed victims into a foreground. For a very long time, individual petitions to the Human Rights Committee were inadmissible. Claims were brought by one state against another, on the grounds that this state had violated the rights of its own citizens. This solution was supposed to provide external support for the victims. In fact, however, it turned human rights into one of the instruments of international politics. The ability to choose when to put forward an accusation was a tempting tool of foreign policy. It is no wonder that international human rights have been compromised by selective enforcement.

Before this cynical application became widespread, however, human rights receded altogether under the pressures of the Cold War. The Cold War was fought by military deployments in Europe and all over the world, by the arms race and by the threat of nuclear war. It was only in the 1970s that human rights re-emerged on the international scene.

The Re-Definition of Human Rights in the 1970s

By the 1970s, Western countries had finally removed the human rights liabilities that had made governments somewhat skeptical to the idea of human rights immediately after World War II. Great Britain and other Western states finally agreed to the independence of their colonies. The United States illegalized racial separation and granted equal citizens' rights to its black minority. But the Soviet Union, by contrast, was still imprisoning millions of people and forcibly subordinating those who fell under Soviet control in Yalta in 1945. Human rights suddenly became a useful instrument of foreign policy for the West in their plight against the Communist bloc. President Gerald Ford made human rights an official goal of the United States foreign policy and appointed an Undersecretary of State for Human Rights. At the same time, human rights were acknowledged internationally within the Helsinki Agreement (1975). In that agreement, the West recognized the post-World War II boundaries in Europe and opened the door for the Soviet bloc to have access to Western funds and technology in return for the recognition of human rights by all countries that signed the Helsinki Agreement.

The Helsinki Agreement included an article stating that "everyone has the right to know one's rights." This provision has provided a legal basis for the formation of monitoring groups in the Soviet bloc. In 1975, a group of Soviet dissidents founded the Moscow Helsinki Committee, thus establishing the first official human rights organization in the Communist world. The Committee soon found support not only among Western governments, but also amid the broader human rights movement organized by citizens' groups and non-governmental organizations worldwide. This movement had begun to gain momentum after the September 1973 military coup in Chile, when mass crimes were being committed by General Pinochet's security forces. For the first time in human history, modern media made it possible for the entire world to actually witness the crimes as they were being committed by state officials. The human rights movement then spread to Asia after Indira Gandhi introduced martial law in India. In 1977, the Nobel Peace Prize was awarded to Amnesty International, providing recognition for human rights activists worldwide and boosting their confidence. Human rights had truly entered the international scene.

But this re-discovered concept of human rights was different from the one that had been formulated in the UDHR some thirty years earlier. The Soviets and the Pinochets of the world were violating civil liberties and political rights, not the social and economic ones. So it was on these rights that Western governments focused their attention. Similarly, the emerging international human rights movement also focused its monitoring and protest activities on civil liberties and political rights. Social and economic rights and other rights provided for in the UDHR (the so-called second and third generation rights) were no longer in the picture.

Early Challenges to the Universality of Human Rights

It was this re-definition of the human rights concept that provided arguments for the critics of human rights in the 1970s. The first challenge was the so-called "socialist concept of human rights," which belittled the significance of civil and political rights and emphasized social rights (Wieruszewski 1988). It also rejected the procedural guarantees of rights, replacing the judicial mechanisms of enforcement with so-called "material guarantees" of human rights. It gave priority to social and economic rights. Civil liberties and political rights, by contrast, could be curtailed whenever their realization would hamper the greater, national aims of economic growth and well-being of the population. Communist propaganda of the time claimed that civil liberties and political rights were demanded only by a small group of oppositionists and class enemies: the discontented intelligentsia wants freedom, these critics said, while the people want bread and meat. The regime would provide the meat and gag the opposition.[2]

In the mid-seventies, the opposition in Poland managed to persuade the majority of people that without civil and political rights there could be no social or economic progress, particularly in a centrally planned economy. By 1980, many ordinary people were convinced that the lack of rights was a significant cause of the deepening economic crisis in Poland: "There is no bread without freedom," the slogan went, and it became the rallying cry during the Solidarity strikes on the Baltic coast in 1980 (Kurczewski 1993: 190–218). The majority of the demands made by the workers concerned civil and political rights in addition to the more typical social and economic issues and demands for better working conditions. By the end of 1980s, the socialist concept of human rights had been abandoned. Soon afterwards, the Communist bloc collapsed and all post-Soviet countries adopted new constitutions in which all categories of rights were given recognition.

The second challenge to human rights, based on cultural relativism, has been more durable. Around the same time when the socialist concept was emerging, a number of leaders of Asian and African countries began to claim that human rights were a mask for neocolonialism. Some leftist intellectuals from the West rushed to support them. For example, in the late seventies, Adamantia Pollis and Peter Schwab (1979) from the New School for Social Research in New York City claimed that in the Third World, human

---

[2] On socialist concept of rights see Wieruszewski, 1988: 28–31. See also Socialist Concept of Rights, 1966.

rights were less important than economic development and the formation of nation-states. Because individualism is a construct of Western culture, they argued, the rights of individuals are perceived as a foreign concept in the post-colonial world. Here, the individual is viewed as an integral part of a social group, not separated from others, and the individual's identity is inseparable from the local and tribal community. What followed decolonization in Africa and Asia was the supremacy of a society over an individual. Economic growth and development require the continuation of this supremacy, claimed the authors. The dominant role of tribes and local communities, however, should be replaced by the state, usually the only body capable of introducing socioeconomic reforms and guaranteeing progress and prosperity for the people of the Third World. Any human rights violations that might occur are to be seen as the inevitable price that must be paid for progress. Because no tradition of rights exists, the price is not so high. According to the authors, their arguments prove that the right to development should have priority over human rights.

A little over a decade later, these scholarly arguments reappeared in a more applied political form. Prime Minister Lee Kwan Yew of Singapore, the Malaysian Prime Minister Mahatir Mohammed, and the Indonesian dictator General Suharto openly labeled human rights a neocolonial ideology and opposed it with "Asian values." Subordination of the individual to his or her family, local community, and employers was meant to guarantee the people of Southeast Asia happiness and prosperity in accordance with traditional values. The same function was to be played by traditional mechanisms for maintaining discipline and social harmony, and by state capitalism and authoritarian forms of government.

The global economic crisis of 1997 shook those Asian values, and proved the vulnerability of an economy based on the alliance of the state with large corporations. Even before the crisis, the leaders of many independent African states used the idea of the traditional supremacy of society over the individual to violently shift group loyalty to the State. Such leaders also used force to destroy local communities and to rob the populations of their own countries, turning parts of the continent into battlefields of never-ending and brutal wars. Human rights abuses neither strengthened nation-states nor accelerated economic development (Pollis 1996). By ignoring human rights, such leaders condemned the majority of Africans to hunger and dependence on international humanitarian aid. In the absence of democracy, freedom of the press, and political rights, such aid does not reach the starving and the needy. On the contrary, it inevitably falls into the hands of warring tribal leaders and faction commanders.

It is worth noting that the supporters of cultural relativism tended to represent the viewpoint of those in power who violate the rights of their citizens rather than the perspective of the victims. The views of dictators tended to emphasize the different traditions in Africa and Asia, whereas their opponents and independent civil organizations in Africa and Asia have stressed the universal nature of human rights.

After the collapse of Communism, the idea of human rights ceased to be a weapon in the Cold War between the East and West, but it has remained a contentious topic on the North-South conflict. The countries of the South that controlled the majority of votes in the U.N. General Assembly insisted that the U.N. human rights programs concentrate primarily on social and economic rights that are included in the right to development. The final declaration of the World Conference on Human Rights in Vienna in 1993 announced that "all human rights are universal, indivisible and interdependent, and interrelated. The international community must treat human rights globally in a fair and equal manner, on the same footing and with the same emphasis."

The 1990s had a mixed record in human rights. Better known and more widely accepted than before, human rights were acknowledged in the constitutions and statutes of many new democracies. There were at least two military interventions to defend human rights, in Kosovo and East Timor. In 1998, General Augusto Pinochet's case was brought to international attention. First, the Spanish Supreme Court, the *Audiencia Nacional*, declared that crimes committed by heads of state could be prosecuted in foreign countries for violations of the international law of human rights (Wilson 1999). Then, the British House of Lords declared that ordering and even accepting torture, and officially sanctioning killings and treacherous political assassinations do not fall under the duties of a head of state and therefore such acts by a head of state are not protected by immunity. As a result, the principle of responsibility has begun to outweigh the principle of sovereignty that had prevailed until now. The same principle formed the basis for the International Criminal Court that was established after the ratification of the Treaty of Rome in 1998.

On the other hand, there were also negative developments in the 1990s. The Human Rights Committee of the United Nations had become almost completely ineffective. First, it did not re-elect a representative of the United States and then it chose for its chairman the delegate of Libya, a country with a rather grim human rights record. International politics was marked by double standards and selective enforcement of human rights. Moreover, even in those cases where agreement was eventually reached, the appropriate actions were taken only after the violations reached genocidal proportions. Human rights were also inflated by their over-application to all kinds of claims, including

animal rights. This human rights inflation was also institutional: all over
the world, numerous new human rights non-governmental organizations
(NGOs) were emerging and some of them focused solely on getting grants
from international donors with little benefit to vulnerable populations.

There was also a growing gap within the international human rights movement. While large international human rights organizations still focused on
the traditional agenda derived from the first generation of rights, many local
human rights groups, particularly in Latin America, Asia, and Africa, were
concerned primarily with social and economic rights. For many groups in
Africa, the central issue has been ensuring real participation in decision making, for which the traditional framing of political rights seemed insufficient.

It was with this mixed record that the human rights community entered
the twenty-first century and began to seek balance between the conflicting
claims, varying needs, and limited resources. But hopes for such a balance
were placed in jeopardy by the most recent outburst of terrorism, and the
U.S. reaction to it, namely the war on terror.

Terrorism and Human Rights

The most immediate reaction to terrorism was the limitation of rights in the
countries affected or threatened by terrorism. The USA PATRIOT Act passed
in 2001 drastically curtailed the rights of U.S. citizens and paved the way
for further limitations by the executive. It also limited the rights of resident
aliens in the United States. The rights of the suspects accused of terrorism were
drastically limited, as best demonstrated by the debate about the conditions
on the U.S. base in Guantanamo. Some of the limitations of civil liberties
seemed, in fact, justified by the state's obligation to provide their citizens
with security against potential terrorist threats. This was the reason why these
measures actually garnered the support of U.S. legislators and public opinion
more widely. The extent to which the authorities adhered to the principle
of minimal and necessary limitation of rights is the subject of a majority of
chapters in this book. Therefore, I will focus on the other aspects of terrorism
and the response to it that have influenced the possibility of a cross-cultural
consensus on human rights.

One clearly visible aspect of the war on terror is the new anti-terrorist
international alliance. With the military action against Afghanistan, a number of autocratic regimes have become allies to the United States. Pakistan,
Uzbekistan, and other Central Asian countries have indisputably negative
human rights records. But now that their governments have been offering
military bases to the U.S. troops, the character of these regimes is overlooked

and there remain increasingly fewer prospects for the United States to challenge their human rights practices. Moreover, the leaders of a number of the new U.S. allies have recently intensified their ruthless actions against their domestic opposition, calling all opponents terrorists. Thus, the practice of selective enforcement, which had already been a major obstacle in implementing international human rights, has in fact become more widespread in the past several years.

The war in Afghanistan, and even more so the war in Iraq, have also compromised the very concept of human rights. One cannot overemphasize the destruction caused by the U.S. government's change of the justification of the war against Iraq. Initially, the justification for the military action was the threat that Saddam Hussein was developing weapons of mass destruction. It was only after the invasion, when no proof of such activity was discovered, that the U.S. leaders shifted the emphasis to the struggle against tyranny and the protection of the rights of the Iraqi people. It is obvious that human rights were treated instrumentally, as a second-best justification when the first one was discredited.[3] Finally, the incidents of torture in the Abu Ghraib prison have further compromised the human rights aspect of the war on terror in Iraq.

When the Bush Administration shifted the war on terror to Iraq, Samuel Huntington's thesis on the clash of civilizations became a self-fulfilling prophecy (1993). Initially, terrorism was primarily related to the internal conflict within Muslim countries and it was used by the opponents of modernization. But the war on Iraq is being perceived by a growing number of Muslims worldwide as a jihad against the West, particularly against the United States and its allies. It has accelerated the growth of anti-Americanism worldwide.

There are many causes for the most recent wave of anti-Americanism. I will not get into all of the details here. The fact is that a political leader can count on a great number of votes solely on the basis of an anti-American agenda, and not only in Pakistan or Turkey, but even in Germany. With the exception of the European countries, anti-Americanism influences negatively the entire global attitude toward human rights. Because those rights have almost always been identified with the United States, even if erroneously, anti-Americanism calls for the rejection of human rights. The record of the United States in Iraq and Guantanamo provides a number of arguments to support such a blanket rejection.

---

[3] There would have been no sufficient reason for the intervention on human rights grounds as international law does not permit intervention some years after genocide takes place.

Is a Consensus Still Possible?

These developments influence the prospects for the cross-cultural consensus on human rights. The outburst of terrorism and the war on terror have exacerbated the tendencies toward fundamentalism in the modern world. By fundamentalism I mean primarily a peculiar attitude that limits rational discussion in the public life by demanding adherence to an ultimate and literal truth, as in the case of religious or ideological fundamentalism. A similar attitude, however, can also be fostered by the excessive use of symbols of any kind, or emotions that hamper debate and tend to impose one point of view over the other. Fundamentalist attitudes threaten human rights because they tend to demand the imposition of a single interpretation of policies and morality and to neglect the opponents' rights to disagree and act on their beliefs. Moreover, fundamentalism limits the very spirit of open rational debate. Regardless of the spiritual sources and aspects, human rights is a rational political framework incompatible with fundamentalism of any sort.

In recent decades, fundamentalism has been identified almost exclusively with religious movements, and in the past several years, primarily with radical Islam. However, while thinking about the future of the idea of human rights we should not disregard strong tendencies that move the public away from rational discussion toward symbolic politics, even in established democracies. Electronic media has conditioned people to ever shorter attention spans, in turn pushing politicians to adopt the use of symbols. Economic globalization has pushed many decisions out of the reach of national governments, thus further encouraging politicians to deal with moral issues using emotive symbolism. It is significant that for a long time the internal politics of the sole remaining superpower were dominated by a discussion of the personal sexual activities of the president. The growth of populism in a number of European democracies shifts public debate away from rational arguments and instead it pushes it toward symbols, threats, and fears. Finally, the war mentality itself neither nourishes rational debate nor does it promote human rights.

While Western quasi-fundamentalism is related to the inadequacy of the traditional theories and institutions of democracy in the electronic age, fundamentalism in the South is primarily a reaction to the failure of the promise of modernization. This failure helps to explain why so many Third World governments that had actively pressed for the adoption of the Universal Declaration of Human Rights in the 1940s are opposing human rights today and saying that the philosophy of rights had been imposed on them by the West. It seems that the answer lies in the changed character of the dominant ideologies in the developing world. At the end of the colonial period, the dominant ideologies of the Third World elites were developmental. With the absence of a strong local business class, usually this ideology was a statism of some sort. With Abdul Gamal Nasser in Egypt, socialism entered the post-colonial states. Nevertheless, both statism and socialism could be reconciled with the broad compromise that was the UDHR.

By the mid-1970s, this picture had changed. The hopes for fast modernization, development, and independence never materialized. In many countries, the multi-party system collapsed and military governments took over. Their practices were increasingly incompatible with human rights standards, and they invoked cultural relativism as justification for the violations. Iran's Ayatollah Khomeini was the first to conclude that there exist no adequate resources for modernization, and that the West would not provide them. He turned to the more traditional resources, which could assure some degree of dignity for the people, like religion. The fundamentalism fostered by Khomeini and followed by the imams was not developmental. And it was irreconcilable with the philosophy of human rights. The objections raised by Saudi Arabia in 1948, which at that time had been rejected by Iran and other Islamic countries, now became the core of the new fundamentalism.

There were some indications that religious fundamentalism in Iran and in other Islamic countries was on the defensive before 2001, although it was impossible to predict whether it would be replaced with a political dispensation that would be more compatible with the idea of human rights. It seems, however, that the inept pursuit of the war on terror has only enhanced fundamentalism throughout Muslim world. To counter this tendency would require immense efforts to make modernization actually work. For ordinary people in the South, this task seems more difficult today than ever.

What If There Is No Consensus?

It may be that it is impossible to restore the consensus. This need not mean that human rights are doomed. We may have to distinguish between the philosophy of human rights and human rights themselves. The 1948 consensus included both. Today, there are even more reasons to believe that the philosophy of human rights is not universal. Different cultures protect dignity in different ways and some of these methods do not require placing the individual in the center and cherishing his or her human rights.

But this does not mean that the values protected by human rights have to be abandoned. Whatever the philosophical justification, human rights protect individuals from the abuse of a coercive power of state. They put limits on such coercion by defining the spheres of individual autonomy and choice. It is conceivable that the same result can be achieved in a different way: Let us assume that all governments sign a new covenant that does not mention human rights but simply lists those things that state authorities cannot do to their citizens. This new agreement could be named "On the Limitations of Public Authorities." It would be something resembling a penal code. Such a penal code does not have to state its philosophy; it has to say what it is that individuals are prohibited from doing under the threat of punishment. There could be another such code for the individual states and their officials, which would list the prohibited behaviors. One can speculate that such a bill would include a lot of what we today called human rights. Those who believe in human rights would have an additional reason to obey such a code. The dictators who violate the code would not be able to justify their behavior by saying that they do not adhere to the Western philosophy of human rights.

Such a penal code for state authorities could build on the momentum that had led to the ratification of the ICC treaty. It seems, however, that this would not be adequate by itself. It would leave intact the issue of social and economic exclusion, which, after all, also breeds terrorism, or at least provides justification for it. Therefore, it could be augmented by a second covenant, "On the Responsibilities of Public Authorities," defining what it is that governments are obliged to do for their citizens. Included would be the provision of access to justice, the mechanism for participation in decision making, and some other services that today fall under positive rights. The international agreement could also provide for the global redistribution of resources that could help to meet the minimal obligations everywhere in the world. This mechanism of redistribution could also serve as the enforcement of the first covenant: the countries that violate the prohibitions would be dropped from the resource redistribution mechanism.

But one thing would still remain unsolved: Not all violations of human rights are perpetrated by the states. There also exists oppression by cultures, which too poses a distinct threat to human rights. While the legitimacy of the tyrants is very weak and fades away the instant they are removed from power, cultural customs and religious norms are often accepted by society. And in this realm people's hostility is directed not toward the abusers but against the defenders of human rights who would do away with what is viewed as tradition, either by enlightened legislation, or by force.

Experience suggests caution in such cases. The much-needed discussion must try to define the type of situation in which norms can be invoked against cultural traditions. It seems that such norms should be imposed only as a last resort – whenever a tradition is truly cruel, when it threatens individual lives, and when it is questioned by at least some of those concerned. In other cases, action should be directed at education, the development of conditions that encourage the acceptance of universal standards, and aid for those victims of the abuse who are willing to accept aid. Decree, force, and sanctions cannot change conservative traditions. Such means are effective only in those cases where violations of rights are the result of the abuse of the state's power, for such abuses usually lack wide social support.

The use of force, however, might be necessary to stop the violation of rights by non-state groups of terrorists, even when they invoke cultural or religious arguments to justify their actions. This is one additional lesson for the defenders of rights in the age of terror. The problem is deciding what kind of force will be justified and effective, as well as when and against whom it should be legitimately used (Holzgrefe & Keohane 2003).

REFERENCES

Glendon, M. A. (2001). *A World Made New: Eleanor Roosevelt and the Universal Declaration of Human Rights*. New York: Random House.

Holzgrefe, J. L. & Keohane, R. O. (Eds.). (2003). *Humanitarian Intervention: Ethical, Legal and Political Dilemmas*. Cambridge: Cambridge University Press.

Huntington, S. (1993). 'The Clash of Civilizations?' *Foreign Affairs* 72.3, pp. 22–49.

Kurczewski, J. (1993). *The Resurrection of Rights in Poland*. Oxford: Clarendon Press.

Lauren, P. G. (1998). *The Evolution of International Human Rights: Visions Seen*. Philadelphia: University of Pennsylvania Press.

Pollis, A. (1996). 'Cultural Relativism Revisited: Through a State Prism'. *Human Rights Quarterly*, 18.2, pp. 316–44.

Pollis, A. & Schwab, P. (Eds.). (1979). *Human Rights: Cultural and Ideological Perspectives*. New York: Praeger Publishers.

Socialist Concept of Rights. (1966). (Collective work). Budapest: Akademiai Kiado.

Wieruszewski, R. (1988). 'The Evolution of the Socialist Concept of Human Rights'. *Netherlands Quarterly of Human Rights* 6(1) (*SIM Newsletter* 1/1988), pp. 27–37.

Wilson, R. J. (1999). 'Prosecuting Pinochet: International Crimes in Spanish Domestic Law'. *Human Rights Quarterly*, 21.4, pp. 927–79.

15. Connecting Human Rights, Human Development, and Human Security

MARY ROBINSON

The subject matter of this edited volume on "Human Rights in the 'War on Terror'" could not be more significant for the human rights community. Sufficient time has passed since the terrible attacks of September 11, 2001, for us to answer in more depth Michael Ignatieff's question as to "whether the era of human rights has come and gone?"

I first answered that question in June 2002, as U.N. High Commissioner for Human Rights, when I delivered the Fifth Commonwealth Lecture in London, as follows:

> Not gone, is my response, but we are challenged in new ways to respond to profound concerns over human security in our world today. My own sense is that there is an enormous responsibility to uphold rigorously international human rights standards, recognizing that they, too, are the object of terrorist attacks. At the same time, I believe there must be more commitment to the implementation of those standards in practice through strong support for human rights capacity building at national level.

As Arthur Chaskalson, Chief Justice of the Constitutional Court of South Africa, puts it, "We have to be vigilant from the very beginning; if you concede the first step, every next step will lead to the further erosion of the rule of law and disregard of human dignity."

The failure of the U.S. Congress and the media, among others, to be vigilant in the aftermath of 9/11 led to a rapid erosion of civil liberties and the misuse of immigration laws, as was well documented in the report *Assessing the New Normal* (2003) by Lawyers Committee for Human Rights (now Human Rights First). It also led to the disregard of human dignity evident in the mistreatment of prisoners in the Abu Ghraib prison in Iraq.

Our answer now must be a firm, well-thoughtout, and coherent response to current security concerns. A good start was made by the International

Commission of Jurists, when, during its biennial conference at the end of August 2004, 160 international lawyers from around the world adopted a Declaration on Upholding Human Rights and the Rule of Law in Combating Terrorism. That Declaration acknowledges that terrorism poses a serious threat to human rights, and affirms that all states have an obligation to take effective measures against acts of terrorism, but it sets out the boundaries as follows:

> In adopting measures aimed at suppressing acts of terrorism, states must adhere strictly to the rule of law, including the core principles of criminal and international law and the specific standards and obligations of international human rights law, refugee law and, where applicable, humanitarian law. These principles, standards and obligations define the boundaries of permissible and legitimate state action against terrorism. The odious nature of terrorist acts cannot serve as a basis or pretext for states to disregard their international obligations, in particular in the protection of fundamental human rights (ICJ 2004: 1).

A pervasive security-oriented discourse promotes the sacrifice of fundamental rights and freedoms in the name of eradicating terrorism. There is no conflict between the duty of states to protect the rights of persons threatened by terrorism and their responsibility to ensure that protecting security does not undermine other rights. On the contrary, safeguarding persons from terrorist acts and respecting human rights both form part of a seamless web of protection incumbent upon the state. Both contemporary human rights and humanitarian law allow states a reasonably wide margin of flexibility to combat terrorism without contravening human rights and humanitarian legal obligations (Ibid.).

The Declaration then affirms eleven principles that states must give full effect to in the suppression of terrorism and calls on all jurists to act to uphold the rule of law and human rights while countering terrorism (ICJ 2004). This Berlin Declaration (available at www.icj.org) restores the balance that was lost in the aftermath of 9/11. It is a declaration that should hang in law offices and judges' chambers throughout the world. It is the rule of law charter to counter the imbalances of the "new normal." But it is not sufficient.

To combat terrorism it is necessary to probe more deeply and tackle the root causes of the humiliation, anger, and frustration that can be manipulated to draw recruits for terrorist action.

In a constantly changing foreign policy environment, it may be too soon to find clear, unequivocal assessments of the human rights benefits and costs of what has been called the war on terrorism. I have been arguing consistently that it may have been a strategic error to characterize the attacks of September 11 as requiring a "war on terrorism" rather than as "crimes against humanity" that required intense international military, police, and intelligence cooperation to bring the perpetrators to justice.

Language is crucial in shaping our reactions to critical events. The words that we use to characterize an event may determine the nature of the response to it. The terrible attacks of 9/11 fell, in my view, within the definition under international human rights jurisprudence of "crimes against humanity," which would have been a more effective rubric under which to organize and sustain an effective response. International cooperation and resolve are required under international human rights law to combat such crimes.

That the language of being "at war with terrorism" was used from the beginning has had direct, and nefarious, implications. It has brought a subtle – or not so subtle – change of emphasis in many parts of the world: order and security have become priorities that trump all other concerns. As was often the case in the past during times of war, the emphasis on national order and security frequently involves curtailment of democracy and human rights. An honest debate about the costs and benefits has not yet really taken place. Abrogations in the United States, where there are many checks and balances in the wider society, have been copied with very negative effects for human rights in many countries of the world. Questions arise as to when, if ever, this war on terrorism will be won. Are we, as the novelist and commentator Gore Vidal (2002) has characterized it, embarked on a *perpetual war for perpetual peace*?

To prevent this, we must dig deeper and explore the issue of security. Our post-9/11 world is preoccupied with different experiences of insecurity. The atrocities in Darfur, Sudan, the misery of the millions living with, and orphaned by, HIV and AIDS in sub-Saharan Africa, Asia, and elsewhere, the long hardships suffered by indigenous peoples in the Americas, the humiliating poverty in slums and rural areas in the developing world – they all tell us a deplorable truth: that governments in different regions of the world are failing to provide even the rudiments of human security.

In the United States and Europe, the focus is on state security and combatting acts of terrorism. But the stark reality is that the terrible attacks of 9/11 had no discernable impact on the millions of people already at daily risk from violence, disease, and abject poverty. Their insecurity continues to stem from worry about where the next meal will come from, how to acquire medicines for a dying child, how to avoid the criminal with a gun, how to manage the household as a ten-year-old AIDS orphan – the comprehensive insecurity of the powerless.

The statistics from this year's *Human Development Report* confirm that our world is, in very basic terms and despite our aggregate wealth, more insecure than secure:

> More than 800 million people suffer from undernourishment. Some 100 million children who should be in school are not, 60 million of them girls. More than a billion people survive on less than one dollar a day. Some 1.8 billion people live in countries where political regimes do not fully accommodate democratic, political, and civil freedoms. And about 900 million people belong to ethnic, religious, racial or linguistic groups that face discrimination (UNDP 2004: 129) . . . The picture that emerges is increasingly one of two very different groups of countries: those that have benefited from development, and those that have been left behind (Ibid. at 132) . . . An unprecedented number of countries saw development slide backwards in the 1990s. In 46 countries people are poorer today than in 1990. In 25 countries more people go hungry today than a decade ago (Ibid.).

Approximately 25,000 people in the last six years have died due to terrorist attacks throughout the world. Compare this with the number of people who have died over the same period due to hunger, malaria, and other preventable diseases. That number is closer to 25,000 per day. On which of these problems is the political energy of the multilateral system focused at the moment?

For women, gender is itself a risk factor threatening human security: the secret violence of household abuse, the private oppressions of lack of property or inheritance rights, the lifelong deprivations that go with lack of schooling, and the structural problem of political exclusion.

Women are particularly vulnerable in zones of conflict and in post-conflict situations where many are terrorized on a daily basis. We need to go much further in addressing this widespread form of terrorism. In September 2004 in New York, there was a major conference on gender justice in post-conflict situations under the title "Peace Needs Women, and Women Need Justice." The objective was to take stock of the extent of the problem, and to develop a broad action program for gender justice. An independent assessment prepared for the conference, titled *Women, War, Peace: The Independent Experts' Assessments on the Impact of Armed Conflict on Women and Women's Role in Peace-Building (Vol. 1)*, notes:

> Our visits to conflict situations confirmed the stark reality that women are being denied justice. With few exceptions, those who commit heinous crimes against women in war are not punished, nor are women granted redress. Worse yet, with alarming consistency, little is being done to prevent new abuses (Rehn & Sirleaf 2002: 88) . . . Throughout history soldiers have abducted, raped, tortured and

enslaved women in wartime. But attacks against women and girls in contemporary conflicts seem to occur on a greater scale and have reached an even higher level of depravity. They spread terror, destroy families and shatter community cohesiveness. Violence does not happen randomly – it is determined and deliberate (Ibid.)... Increased levels of violence against women continue into the post-conflict period. Criminal activity often thrives in such situations, where law enforcement is generally weak and there is rarely an effective judicial system. Women are exposed to physical and sexual violence in camps, on the street or in their homes. Perpetrators may be returning combatants, neighbours or family members. Women have nowhere to turn: law enforcement agents, military officials, peacekeeping forces or civilian police may be complicit or themselves guilty of these acts. The failure to prevent and punish such crimes is a betrayal of women on a massive scale (Ibid. at 89).

The problem of accountability – or rather, lack of accountability – is addressed:

Accountability on the part of states and societies for crimes against women means more than punishing perpetrators. It means establishing the rule of law and a just social and political order. Without this, there can be no lasting peace. Impunity weakens the foundation of societies emerging from conflict by legitimizing violence and inequality (Rehn & Sirleaf 2002: 89) ... Rarely have women been consulted about the form, scope and modalities for seeking accountability. Women's stake in these processes has been minimized or denied and, in most cases, crimes against them go unrecorded (Ibid.).

Redress is also important.

Ensuring accountability to women within the justice system will require a range of strategies. These can be carried out at national, regional or international levels, and through a variety of judicial methods: the ICC, ad hoc tribunals, special courts and tribunals and national justice systems. Non-judicial methods, such as truth and reconciliation commissions and traditional mechanisms, can also play an important role in establishing accountability for crimes against women in war. A combination of methods may be appropriate in order to ensure that all victims secure redress (Rehn & Sirleaf 2002: 91) ... Reparations are also important for achieving justice and accountability for women. They may take the form of restitution, compensation, rehabilitation or guarantees that similar crimes will not be committed (Ibid. at 90).

Essentially, this agenda for gender justice requires that we prioritize, take seriously, and implement the measures necessary to involve women as actors for change in conflict and post-conflict situations, to protect women in conflict and post-conflict situations with zero tolerance for and accountability of perpetrators of violence, and that effective measures of reparation are built in.

To bring about a truly secure world, we must adopt a new paradigm that shifts priority to the security of individuals and of communities – that is, to achieving human security. This will require a renewed commitment both to human rights and human development – and a shared sense of responsibility for all people, in all parts of the world.

What we need now is a major course correction – a new approach – which begins with a broader understanding of what defines human and global security. We must craft a policy that manages and balances our increasing interdependence with our increased vulnerability. Governments from both the North and the South must expand their thinking and policies to encompass a broader understanding of security beyond the security of states.

What I began to appreciate as president of Ireland – on visits, for example, to Somalia and Rwanda – and became convinced of during my five years in the United Nations, is that the underlying causes of practically all human insecurity are an absence of capacity to influence change at personal or community level, exclusion from voting or participating in any way in national decision making, and economic or social marginalization. The key to change lies in empowering people to secure their own lives. For this they need the means to try to hold their governments accountable, at local and national levels.

This broader understanding of human security was examined by an independent Commission on Human Security, co-chaired by Amartya Sen and Sadako Ogata. Their report, *Human Security Now* (2003), explains that human security involves a new paradigm that shifts from the security of the state to the security of the people – to human security. The emphasis is on the extent to which human security brings together the human elements of security, of rights, and of development (CHS 2003).

The report identifies two underlying concepts, protection and empowerment, which lie at the heart of human security (Ibid. at 10–12). The first of these, protection, is primarily a state responsibility, and sometimes an international responsibility, as examined and clarified by the International Commission on Intervention and State Sovereignty in their report, *The Responsibility to Protect* (2001), which reminds us of the

> ... growing and widespread recognition that armed conflicts cannot be understood without reference to such root causes as poverty, political repression, and uneven distribution of resources. "Every step taken towards reducing poverty and achieving broad-based economic growth," the Secretary-General has stated in his recent report, "is a step toward conflict prevention." Preventive strategies must therefore work "to promote human rights, to protect minority rights and to institute political arrangements in which all groups are represented." Ignoring

these underlying factors amounts to addressing the symptoms rather than the causes of deadly conflict (pp. 22–3).

The Commission on Human Security describes the second concept, empowerment, as

> People's ability to act on their own behalf – and on behalf of others... People empowered can demand respect for their dignity when it is violated. They can create new opportunities for work and address many problems locally. And they can mobilize for the security of others (2003: 11).

This is a concept around which the human rights community and academic legal scholars can join together and promote innovative examples. Essentially, we need to make more visible, and build on, the grassroots movements that are challenging unfair global governance, and using the human rights framework to hold their governments more accountable for implementing rights to food, to safe water, to health and education, and for doing so without discrimination.

I witnessed this grassroots work in every country I visited as High Commissioner. Human rights groups, women's groups, those working on child rights, with minorities, or tackling poverty were using tools of budget analysis and policy research to expose failures to implement progressively these rights, or to challenge expenditures on unnecessary military equipment or projects benefitting only a small elite. Invariably, the work was underresourced, undervalued, and often resented by those in power. Now these groups have additional tools available in the commitments both developed and developing countries have made to achieve the Millennium Development Goals by 2015, which will be reviewed during next year and debated at the General Assembly in September 2005. An opportunity presents itself, for human rights activists and lawyers, among others, to reinforce the empowerment of grassroots organizations in every region, by helping them to link their country's undertaking to achieve the Millennium Development Goals, and the country's legal commitments to progressively implement economic and social rights under the relevant international treaties, together with developed countries' commitment to substantial new resources for financing this development.

There is a further link that needs to be made here in the United States. I have noted that when President Bush emphasizes the importance of fighting terrorism and promoting freedom, he explains that it is not America's freedom he is referring to, but "Almighty God's freedom." I confess that I am troubled by this notion, and I prefer the approach that was advocated by President Mkapa of Tanzania in a speech he gave to the Helsinki Group on Globalization and Democracy during our meeting in Dar es Salaam at the end of August 2004:

> To be the anchor of global peace and security, globalization must be promulgated by accepted universal values. But this imperative should not be translated as one set of countries imposing one set of values – whether political, economic, or cultural – on the rest of the world. Global values must be embedded in global dialogue, from best practices adapted to local conditions. We must all be contributory and determinative of the process towards the universal common good.

Human rights advocates should make it clear that freedom in this sense cannot be imposed and should encompass the broader idea of human security. In the words of Amartya Sen, in his much acclaimed work, *Development as Freedom* (1999):

> Sometimes the lack of substantive freedoms relates directly to economic poverty, which robs people of the freedom to satisfy hunger, or to achieve sufficient nutrition, or to obtain remedies for treatable illnesses, or the opportunity to be adequately clothed and sheltered, or to enjoy clean water or sanitary facilities. In other cases, the unfreedom links closely to the lack of public facilities and social care, such as the absence of epidemiological programs, or of organized arrangements for health care or educational facilities, or of effective institutions for the maintenance of local peace and order. In still other cases, the violation of freedom results directly from a denial of political and civil liberties by authoritarian regimes and from imposed restrictions on the freedom to participate in the social, political and economic life of the community (p. 4).

Linking freedom and human security in this way could also have a positive impact on the allocation of resources. Additional money to support the Millennium Goals was pledged by the United States at the International Conference on Financing for Development held from March 18–22, 2002, in Monterrey, NL, Mexico, through the Millennium Challenge Account. The European Union has also increased its commitment. However, there is still a wide disparity between the global spending on official development assistance, which amounts to around $60 billion a year, the annual amount developed countries spend on agricultural subsidies of $300 billion, and global military expenditure of $900 billion. It was estimated at Monterrey, by an eminent panel of economists chaired by Ernest Zedillo, that an additional $50–60 billion annually on development assistance would be needed to ensure full implementation of the Millennium Development Goals by 2015. If this extra expenditure would in fact make the world more secure, does it not seem like a good investment?

Let me conclude by highlighting the emphasis placed by Shirin Ebadi of Iran, the 2003 Nobel Peace Prize winner, on the universality of human rights. In her contribution to the *Human Development Report 2004*, she begins by identifying the differences in people that are part of cultural diversity. She then emphasizes that human rights embody the fundamental values of human civilizations and concludes:

> So cultural relativity should never be used as a pretext to violate human rights, since these rights embody the most fundamental values of human civilizations. The Universal Declaration of Human Rights is needed universally, applicable to both East and West. It is compatible with every faith and religion. Failing to respect our human rights only undermines our humanity ... Let us not destroy this fundamental truth; if we do, the weak will have nowhere to turn (UNDP 2004: 23).

REFERENCES

Commission on Human Security (CHS). (2003). *Human Security Now.* New York. Available at: http://www.humansecurity-chs.org/finalreport/index.html.

International Commission of Jurists (ICJ). (2004, August 28). *The Berlin Declaration: The ICJ Declaration on Upholding Human Rights and the Rule of Law in Combating Terrorism.* Available at: http://icj.org/IMG/pdf/Berlin_Declaration.pdf.

International Commission on Intervention and State Sovereignty (ICISS). (2001, December). *The Responsibility to Protect.* Ottawa, ON, Canada: International Development Research Centre. Available at: http://www.dfait-maeci.gc.ca/iciss-ciise/pdf/Commission-Report.pdf.

Lawyers Committee for Human Rights (LCHR). (2003). *Assessing the New Normal: Liberty and Security for the Post-September 11 United States.* New York. Available at: http://www.humanrightsfirst.org/pubs/descriptions/Assessing/AssessingtheNewNormal.pdf.

Rehn, E., & Sirleaf, E. J. (2002). *Women, War, Peace: The Independent Experts' Assessments on the Impact of Armed Conflict on Women and Women's Role in Peace-Building (Vol. 1).* New York: United Nations Development Fund for Women (UNIFEM). Available at: http://www.unifem.org/index.php?f_page_pid=149.

Sen, A. K. (1999). *Development as Freedom.* New York: Knopf.

United Nations Development Programme (UNDP). (2004). *Human Development Report 2004: Cultural Liberty in Today's Diverse World.* New York: Hoechstetter Printing Co. Available at: http://hdr.undp.org/reports/global/2004/pdf/hdr04_complete.pdf.

Vidal, Gore. (2002). *Perpetual War for Perpetual Peace: How We Got to Be So Hated.* New York: Thunder's Mouth Press.

16. Human Rights and Civil Society in a New Age of American Exceptionalism

JULIE A. MERTUS

What does it mean to be a human rights advocate in an age of extreme American exceptionalism? More broadly, what role can civil society play in supporting human rights goals and combating exceptionalist policies? American exceptionalism has a long history,[1] and human rights advocates have continually struggled against it, but three factors have made human rights practice extraordinarily difficult in our post-Cold War, post-September 11 era: (i) American military and economic supremacy and a willingness and ability to use it unilaterally to advance U.S. interests; (ii) American disregard for international institutions and international norms, with unparalleled intensity and consistency, and (iii) the co-option of human rights talk by the government to serve narrow state interests contrary to human rights principles. Advocates for human rights in civil society must address all three of these factors, but this brief essay will focus on efforts to address the third factor, namely, the co-option of human rights discourse by the government and the challenge this poses for human rights advocates.

This discussion is divided into three parts. First, it begins by describing the state of the United States in the immediate aftermath of the election of George W. Bush to a second term as president. This part serves as an introduction to some of the key challenges confronting human rights advocates in light of government intrusions on civil liberties post-September 11th. The second section analyzes the manipulation of human rights discourse by the government and its application of a "bait and switch" in its actual practice. Drawing from the international relations theory of norm diffusion, this section offers

---

[1] As Michael Hirsh observes, "America's success in building a continental empire [has] only fed into the certainty that it could act with total freedom of action. Its pride in its values and ideals [has] made Americans certain that they were always right."

explanations for civil society's seeming impotence in this area and suggests ways in which it could move toward a more effective response. The final section of this essay then reviews some steps that advocates have already taken in this direction and concludes with a note of optimism: In the face of a bleak human rights outlook at present, the U.S.-based human rights movement has been challenged to build a firmer foundation for human rights, at home and abroad, in the future.

I. The Dire Present: Challenges to Human Rights Advocates

A general crackdown on human rights in the United States post-September 11th has effectively fed *on* and *into* the climate of fear permeating the country. Color-coded terrorist alerts have been accompanied by the introduction of regressive legislation, curtailing civil liberties and enlarging government powers. One of the most significant legislative measures that has furthered a sense of imminent threat to the United States among the general public and paved the way for serious cutbacks on civil liberties includes the passage of the USA PATRIOT Act by Congress in 2001. In particular, the Act expands the ability of the Federal Bureau of Investigation (FBI) to secretly access a wide range of personal information without showing that the target has any established link to terrorist or related criminal activity that would jeopardize national security (LCHR 2003: 15–30). Thus, the Act allows secret monitoring of telephone conversations as well as internet, library, medical, education, and financial records (Ibid.). The result is a substantial expansion of surveillance activities going well beyond many of the privacy rights that the U.S. population was entitled to before the passage of the Act (Ibid. at iii).

In addition to becoming more intrusive, the U.S. government has become more secretive. At the heart of the trend towards expanding the secrecy of government conduct has been a series of executive branch initiatives impinging on public access to information. These efforts combine to restrict access to information through a simultaneous increase in the classification of documents and a decrease in the declassification of documents (Ibid. at ii). As a result, information that human rights organizations rely on for their watchdog roles is more difficult to obtain and, once obtained, is incomplete or distorted.

At the same time, the White House has made challenges to such measures more difficult by sidestepping Congress and the judicial system whenever possible. Among the more notorious examples of the administration's exertion of executive power in the name of safeguarding national security is its resort to extra-legal mechanisms, including military commissions, for certain terrorism suspects.[2] Such procedures sidestep the regular judicial process by subjecting detainees to decision making by military personnel reporting directly to the president, with no possibility of appeal to the federal judiciary (LCHR 2003: ii; see also Levy 2002). These actions not only undercut the judicial system, but they also undermine the entire constitutional system of checks and balances – the foundation of American democracy.

Paramount to the increased governmental control over U.S. citizens, the administration has tightened its policies against immigrants and refugees. In the atmosphere of fear choking the United States, immigrants and refugees provide a handy scapegoat for those wishing to find and punish enemy "others." For all foreigners who travel into the United States, fingerprints and photographs are now standard procedures upon entry into the country. "[T]hrough a series of nationality-specific information and detention sweeps – from special registration requirement, to 'voluntary' interviews, to the detention of all those seeking asylum from a list of predominantly Muslim countries – the administration has acted on an assumption that all such individuals are of concern" (LCHR 2003: iv). Further, foreigners already inside U.S. borders are now subject to deportation without an administratively accountable process. Judicial reviews are no longer necessary for such cases, and suspected illegal immigrants may be held in detention, without notification of their families, for unspecified amounts of time, while their cases are pending.[3]

The work of human rights advocates to address these regressive measures would be difficult enough without the Bush administration trying to strong-arm advocates to stay in line. Several accounts from human rights organizations contend that the government has pressured the organizations and their funders to downplay their reporting of America's own human rights abusers.[4] Coupled with this, new procedures exist that make it mandatory for all of the non-governmental organizations (NGOs) who receive federal funds through the Combined Federal Campaign (CFC)[5] to verify that their employees are not on a government-created blacklist. Should any employees

---

[2] On November 13, 2001, President Bush issued an executive order announcing the establishment of military commissions for trying non-citizens alleged to have violated "the laws of war and other applicable laws" in cases where the President finds "reason to believe that such individual . . . has engaged in, aided or abetted, or conspired to commit, acts of international terrorism, or acts in preparation therefore" (Presidential Military Order of November 13, 2001).

[3] Author interview with Jeffrey Walker, former U.S. Air Force Lieutinent Colonel, presently defense attorney for captives in Guantanamo, October 10, 2004.

[4] Author interviews with advocates, November and December 2004.

[5] Note that the CFC is a program that collects and distributes charitable contributions from federal employees.

be on this list, employers are then caught in the trap of the governmental stip-ulations, which mandate that they ask the employees questions that "violate the privacy rights of employees and ask inappropriate questions that trample employees' associational rights" (Romero 2004a). Such blacklists have been found to be "riddled with inaccuracies" according to lawsuits filed against the government by the ACLU. Further, people on the list are systemically unable to correct false information.[6] The pressuring of human rights organizations to comply with these strident CFC regulations threatens their own ability to uphold civil rights at the risk of losing important federal funding.

To some extent, the workings of the imperial presidency are nothing new. In fact, these measures are hallmarks of all U.S. presidencies run on a climate of fear. Matthew Bowles, a field director for the American Civil Liberties Union, explains:

> On many levels, what is going on post-9/11 is merely a reformulation of previous policies of state repression with new racial scapegoats and a repackaged discourse of who the 'evil enemy' is. Instead of interning Japanese Americans we are interning Arabs and Muslims, instead of the evil ideology of 'communism' we are denouncing the evil ideology of 'Islamic Extremism,' instead of the Alien and Sedition Act we have the USA PATRIOT Act . . .[7]

There is a sense of *déjà vu* in the latest internal U.S. crackdown on human rights. Just as the campaign against communism gave many countries appar-ent liberty to abridge the rights of all people labeled "terrorists" or even "terrorist suspects," the campaign against terrorism is giving license to other states to infringe upon international human rights in the name of national security (Roth 2004; Donnelly 2004). The environment in which the abuses are taking place, however, is substantially different than in the McCarthy era or in any other period in U.S. foreign policy dominated by fearmongering and repression of perceived enemies. Today, unlike in earlier periods, the regres-sive measures are taking place during a time wherein human rights adherents wielded unprecedented influence over the policy agenda and played a role in decision making. By all accounts, however, it appears as if the human rights approach is failing to address the climate of fear choking civil liberties and the policies of the imperial presidency that make this possible.

II. The Underachieving Human Rights Movement

What's going wrong with human rights? There is nothing wrong with human rights per se. There are good reasons for human rights as the tool of choice

---

[6] Author interview with Matthew Bowles, December 1, 2004.
[7] Author interview with Matthew Bowles, December 1, 2004.

for framing arguments and making policy choices. The notion of individual dignity and moral equality that lie at the heart of human rights ideology is something worthy of promoting. The disempowered turn to human rights discourse because it so "successfully manages to articulate (evolving) political claims" (Dembour 1996). Rights are not wrong. What is wrong is that human rights remain only an option and has not achieved the status of an imperative. In interplay with other options, human rights are vulnerable to being tossed out by powerful states that use fearmongering to bully their citizens into submission.

What Is Wrong. The ability of human rights advocates to impact the human rights policies of their governments should be advanced by the professionalization of the field and the increased mobility of individuals from the government sector to civil society. In the United States today, individuals working on human rights issues are likely to be former members of the Clinton administration and other previous administrations, former State Department employees who quit in protest over U.S. policies, and former ambassadors and military officers, as well as individuals who cut their teeth working on humanitarian projects in Afghanistan, election monitoring in Bosnia, or the founding of the Truth Commission in South Africa. Tapping this expertise, human rights organizations should now have the potential to reach deeper into the foreign policy establishments and their periphery. In contrast to the traditional human rights technique of public shaming, these new insider efforts often involve private meetings and cooperative information sharing, the provision of concrete policy proposals, and the offer of technical assistance. While some advocates have sought to push political leaders to interpret the existing policy agenda through a human rights lens (e.g., to weigh human rights factors into intervention decision making), others seek to add new issues to the agenda (e.g., human trafficking). Because this new generation of human rights advocates has been able to target their advocacy more precisely and work at times *within* (instead of *against*) government structures, they have succeeded in framing issues in human rights terms. For example, it has become routine for the U.S. government to invoke human rights as a rationale for its foreign policy decisions and military ventures (see Lang 2003). When measured by the sheer volume of human rights speak, advocates' efforts appear wildly successful.

Yet the danger to these insider approaches to human rights advocacy are great. Transparency is particularly low, and the danger of morphing from *cooperation* to *co-option* is great. Also at risk is the tendency of social movements to lose their more radical edge once their demands are reshaped in the centrally liberal and seemingly less challenging framework of human rights.

Perhaps even more troubling is the lack of evidence that these insider efforts to frame policy issues in human rights terms have had a great impact on human rights behavior. U.S. policymakers still consistently apply a double standard for human rights norms: one the rest of the world must observe, but that the United States can safely ignore. Human rights advocates have shaped the discourse, without the desired influence on policy options.

The scandal over the U.S. government memoranda attempting to justify the torture of accused terrorists is just one case in point. In August 2002, the Department of Justice Office of Legal Counsel produced a fifty-page memorandum stating the President could authorize torture even though our laws and treaties prohibit it (Mertus 2004). The Justice Department (2002) concluded that "the treaty's text [the Convention Against Torture] prohibits only the most extreme acts by reserving criminal penalties solely for torture and declining to require such penalties for cruel, inhuman, or degrading treatment or punishment" and that "under the current circumstances, necessity or self-defense may justify interrogation methods that might violate [these prohibitions]." International law, through the Convention Against Torture (CAT), the Universal Declaration of Human Rights, and the International Covenant on Civil and Political Rights, prohibits torture and forms of cruel, inhumane, or degrading punishment and the right to personal integrity. The CAT (to which the United States is a party) specifically requires that state's parties incorporate the crime of torture in their domestic legal codes and punish accordingly any acts of torture committed by their own citizens. The CAT makes no allowances for any exceptional circumstances, such as a state of war or political unrest, or other times of public emergency. Violations of the right to be free from torture are violations of both domestic legal provisions and international human rights law.

Through a tortured interpretation of international law, the memorandum supported the view that the president of the United States is somehow above international law (Clark & Mertus 2004). This is not so. Under the Constitution, the president and members of the executive branch are bound to faithfully execute the law, which includes treaty law and customary international law. International law is not somehow optional. The law here is clear: The United States is prohibited from invoking national security arguments to justify torture.[8]

One cannot claim to believe in the idea of human rights, and also believe that these rights apply to only *some* individuals, or that only *some* states have

---

[8] For further analysis, see generally Weiss 2004.

a responsibility to respect human rights (Paarekh 1999). Talk of "human rights" has become the political equivalent of a "bait and switch." Like the car salesman promoting an amazing but bogus deal in order to get people into the showroom, politicians promise human rights in order to induce desired behaviors in others. Then, as soon as the desired behavior happens, a substitute is provided – one human rights standard for the United States and another for the rest of the world. Instead of promoting just solutions to contemporary foreign policy dilemmas, rights talk is becoming just another way to dupe otherwise unwilling citizens to support U.S. foreign policy.

To extend the car dealer analogy: The car is a desired commodity promised by the dealer in an attractive package. Once inside the showroom, the customer finds that the option actually offered is not the same as the advertised special. The car dealer misleads people through his power of influence, created by both the fact that he has something someone else wants and that his wealth gives him a magnified voice. Like the car dealer, the United States can use its wealth and influence to mislead the populace about its commitment to the human rights framework, appearing to support universal human rights standards when actually it is applying double standards.

Recognizing the ethical problems with "bait and switch" car dealers, consumer protection laws seek to set advertising requirements that diminish the possibility for such behavior. Perhaps even more influential is the limited tolerance of the American consumer for such nonsense and trickery. What is needed with respect to human rights is some kind of similar safety guarantee to eliminate or at least highly restrict the possibility that they will be trumped by lesser competing norms. But the problem is that while Americans have very high expectations with respect to their car dealers, they have low expectations with regard to human rights. Especially in a climate of fear, Americans are willing to tolerate surprisingly deep intrusions into their own civil liberties, and even greater intrusions into the rights of others (e.g., foreign nationals), all in the name of fighting terrorism.[9]

Toward a More Effective Strategy. This problem of low expectations for human rights policy options strikes at the heart of international relations theory about how norms spread and gain influence. For a long time, the most popular theory of norm diffusion has been the socialization and persuasion approach championed by such international relations thinkers as Thomas Risse and Kathryn Sikkink. According to this perspective, dialogue,

---

[9] For analysis of government manipulation of the climate of fear, see generally Sterba 2003; Daalder & Lindsay 2003.

communication, and argumentation are essential mechanisms for the socialization of norms (Risse & Sikkink 1999). Promoting human rights not only shames states into action in individual instances, but also, as human rights norms are internalized, prompts a transformative shift in identity, interest, and expectations. Rights win out when they promote awareness and genuine openness to the oppression of others. Thus, so the theory goes, successful advocates are those who advance the most convincing or skillful argument to policymakers favoring one norm over another (Risse 2000; Risse & Sikkink 1999).

This socialization theory of norm diffusion used to explain the influence of human rights norms does have serious shortcomings. At the outset, there are empirical problems. In the cases in which human rights advocates are deemed successful, have they really persuaded anyone in a broad or transformative sense or have they only managed to convince someone to apply their approach to specific, isolated cases? Given the instrumental and selective manner in which the Bush administration employs human rights, can we really point to a shift in the identity, interests, and expectations of anyone in the White House? Can we ever really tell if someone's sentiments have shifted? More important, does a sentiment shift matter if behavior does not change? Why is it that U.S. foreign policy, regardless of administration, continues to address in a selective and self-serving manner the violation of human rights by other countries while refusing to apply the same international standards to its own behavior?

One interesting response to these shortcomings of the socialization theory of norm diffusion does not require an explicit showing of a philosophical shift, rather, just enough "rhetorical coercion" to compel the endorsement of a normative stance. Under the model of norm diffusion proposed by international relations upstarts Patrick Jackson and Ronald Krebs, claimants deploy arguments less in the hope of naïve persuasion than in the realistic expectation that they can, thorough skillful framing, back their opponents into a "rhetorical corner" (Jackson & Krebs 2003). The goal then is not to persuade but to coerce by limiting policy options.

According to this theory of norm diffusion, human rights advocates who focus on persuasion and primarily target decision makers have it all wrong. Instead of trying to change minds in government, advocates should focus on changing minds in the general public. Only a cultural shift in favor of human rights would create the conditions that compel rights-based policy choices. In a participatory democracy, one good way to limit policy options is through a demanding electorate and active civil society (Belloni 2000; see also Diamond 2001). This approach seeks to leverage public pressure in order to limit policy options to those consistent with human rights principles.

How could this be done? The answer, provided in both new applications of international relations normative theory and suggested as well in emerging U.S.-based human rights practice, lies in creating a human rights culture. To the extent that human rights advocates concentrate on changing perspectives, those that are most relevant belong not to policy-making elites, but to the general public. If we analogize rights-based concerns to consumer protection conditions, the expectations of consumers are elevated and the options for impinging upon consumer protections are sharply reduced by an expectant and demanding public. For human rights advocates, the creation of a human rights culture could serve a similar function by providing an environment in which human rights double standards are not tolerated.

A *human rights culture* is the vehicle through which a particular set of shared beliefs and understandings – human rights norms – take root in and influence a population (Witte 2001).[10] The adoption of human rights language is an essential step in building a human rights culture, but this alone is insufficient. Human rights concepts enter culture slowly as a population develops its own shared (although often contested) understanding of the prominence and importance of the norms. Incrementally, they become part of the identity, interests, and expectations of individuals and groups. In Jack Donnelly's words, "[h]uman rights is the language of the victims and the dispossessed" (1998: 20). As the disempowered shape human rights ideology and use it for their own goals, they exercise their moral agency. Over time, the individuals and groups that adopt human rights language and thinking *become* a human rights people. The human rights framework becomes a taken-for-granted lens through which to view and understand the world and their role in it (Preis 1996: 315).

Human rights cultures exist when human rights are one of "the forms through which people make sense of their lives" (Rosaldo 1993: 26). In other words, a human rights culture is a way of seeing the world through the lens of human rights and consequently with the principles of human dignity and equality. It is through human rights culture that human rights norms take root in and influence a population (Witte 2001: 707–12; see also Pollis 1996). Tom Malinowski, the Advocacy Director for Human Rights Watch, has recognized that "NGOs 'win' not only when they get international institutions to do something, but when they get people to think in a certain way."[11] Just as one major aspect of the environmental movement is to encourage people to "think green," the human rights movement seeks to encourage people to think human rights.

---

[10] Witte states that human rights norms "need a human rights culture to be effective."
[11] Author interview with Tom Malinowski, June 2003.

III. Toward Creating a Culture of Human Rights

The prospects for building a more robust foundation for human rights at home in the United States may seem hopelessly naïve at best. Far from encouraging the development of a culture of human rights, the U.S. government has consistently found it advantageous to suppress human rights awareness at home, while invoking human rights abuses abroad as a rationale for imposing sanctions and even invasions. While America may have human rights talk, it does not have a human rights culture. The level of awareness of human rights in the United States is extremely low. According to Amnesty International, 94 percent of American adults and 96 percent of American youth have no awareness of the Universal Declaration of Human Rights.[12] Without a human rights culture, American citizenry cannot be expected to evaluate and criticize U.S. foreign policy decisions on human rights terms.

Until recently, human rights culture-building activities have been undertaken by smaller organizations and by constituency-driven organizations, not by Human Rights Watch. Many of these smaller organizations emphasize human rights education as a tool for building human rights culture; such organizations include Human Rights Advocates and the People's Decade for Human Rights Education, as well as organizations associated with social movements for social justice, such as the National Center for Human Rights Education (NCHRE).[13] Activists trained by NCHRE work on a multitude of issues – combating racism, homophobia, poverty and discrimination against people with disabilities, promoting women's rights, protecting the environment, defending reproductive rights. As the result of these training efforts, many activists who previously identified themselves more narrowly as civil rights activists now identify themselves as part of the global human rights movement.

In the post-September 11th climate, the crackdown on civil liberties has encouraged many mainstream human rights organizations to direct their energies closer to home, going against their traditional practice of focusing on human rights abuses well beyond U.S borders. These efforts are likely to gain even greater momentum following the re-election of President George W. Bush. "Policies that once seemed like temporary measures, now have the real possibility of becoming permanent," explained Fanny Benedetti-Howell, of Global Rights.[14] "The reorientation of major human rights organizations

---

[12] See http://www.hrusa.org/features.shtm. The survey was commissioned in 1997 by Human Rights USA Partners – Amnesty International USA, National Center for Human Rights Education, Street Law, Inc., and the University of Minnesota Human Rights Center.

[13] National Center for Human Rights Education (NCHRE). See http://www.nchre.org/.

[14] Author interview with Fanny Benedetti-Howell, Global Rights, December 1, 2004.

to focus on U.S. activities could be on the horizon," predicted one high-ranking member of a U.S.-based human rights NGO who preferred to remain anonymous. While the shift is not a complete reorientation, it is notable nonetheless. Significantly, several states, as well as more than 360 towns, counties, and cities have adopted resolutions reaffirming their commitment to individual civil liberties in the face of the USA PATRIOT Act and related measures (see ACLU 2004).

On the treaty-monitoring front, groups like Global Rights are now seeking to promote the active engagement of U.S. civil rights and social justice groups in the implementation of treaties ratified by the United States (IHRLG). At the top of its agenda is the Convention on the Elimination of all Forms of Racial Discrimination (CEDAW), the central international treaty prohibiting race discrimination, which the United States ratified in 1994. Among other activities, Global Rights has been instrumental in educating civil rights groups in CERD and in facilitating these groups' involvement in the monitoring of U.S. compliance. According to Global Rights, as a result of these and other efforts to bring human rights home, "today, the anti-racism movement in the United States is linked more closely than ever to the global movement against racial discrimination, and new advocacy strategies offer new opportunities to press the U.S. government for reforms."[15]

On the legislative front, to circumvent the continuing erosion of human rights at a federal level, advocates are increasingly seeking to integrate international human rights norms into the law and policy of state and local communities. For example, under pressure of the advocacy group WILD (Women's Institute for Leadership Development), San Francisco incorporated the principles of the UN Convention on the Elimination of all forms of Discrimination Against Women (CEDAW) into city law.[16] The new city law requires city departments to use a gender and human rights analysis to review city policy in employment, funding allocations, and delivery of direct and indirect services.

Other local human rights laws have been directed at taking local action against U.S. corporations committing abuses abroad. For example, the Massachusetts General Assembly passed legislation in 1996 prohibiting its state and any of its agencies from contracting with any person doing business with Myanmar. Twenty-six cities, including Santa Monica, San Francisco, Berkeley, Oakland, Boulder, and Ann Arbor, have passed similar ordinances limiting business with Myanmar (Milliken 1999: 188). Other local ordinances

---

[15] Global Rights, "Global Rights in the United States," Available at: http://www.globalrights.org/site/PageServer?pagename=www_ame_index_57.

[16] WILD for Human Rights, http://www.wildforhumanrights.org/human_rights_advocacy.html.

have targeted Nigeria, China, Indonesia, and Cuba for their record of human rights abuses. While still extremely rare, these kinds of local efforts have served to enhance local awareness of human rights norms (Flowers 2002).

Among the broadest of these home-based human rights initiatives is the Ford Foundation's recent support of U.S.-based human rights activism, and the establishment of a U.S. Network on Human Rights in 2003. These developments demonstrate the developing interest by civil liberties groups (such as the ACLU) in the discourse and practice of human rights, and the growing involvement of human rights groups (such as Amnesty International) in matters previously within the province of civil rights groups.

Amnesty International (AI) has long used human rights arguments to oppose the death penalty in many U.S. states and, on an occasional basis, AI has at times applied its human rights approach within the United States. In 1999, for example, in cities across the country, it held hearings on the international human rights dimensions of police brutality.[17] It was the terrorist attacks on September 11th and the subsequent crackdown on civil liberties within the United States, however, that led AI to expand its human rights education program within the United States and to focus its attention more concertedly on building a human rights culture at home.[18]

In contrast, the ACLU, an organization traditionally devoted to applying civil rights law domestically, has turned more to international human rights law. These efforts expanded rapidly post-September 11th and today the ACLU's efforts to pressure the U.S. government to respect human rights, both at home and abroad, include:[19]

- Filing a complaint with the United Nations Working Group on Arbitrary Detention on behalf of thirteen men who were arbitrarily arrested and detained after the September 11th attacks;
- Requesting information about the use of torture and other illegal interrogation techniques in U.S. detention facilities abroad, in violation of the Convention Against Torture and other laws;
- Documenting and challenging the U.S. government's misuse of the material witness statute to detain Muslim men without charges (in a joint project with Human Rights Watch);
- Monitoring military commissions in Guantánamo Bay, Cuba, and posting daily dispatches about the proceedings;

---

[17] Author interview with Cosette Thompson, Amnesty International, September 6, 2003.
[18] Author interview with Nancy Flowers, Amnesty International consultant, November 4, 2004.
[19] This is drawn directly from: "ACLU Intensifies International Human Rights Advocacy," http://www.aclu.org/International/InternationalMain.cfm (released Dec. 6, 2004).

- Promoting groundbreaking New York City legislation that would implement the principles of the Convention on the Elimination of all forms of Discrimination Against Women (CEDAW) and the Convention on the Elimination of all forms of Racial Discrimination (CERD); and
- Fighting federal legislation that would make it an impeachable offense for federal judges to rely on international law in their decisions.

While such developments are fostering linkages between civil rights and human rights practices and organizations, the Bush administration is decidedly opposed to the building of a strong culture of rights and its actions suggest that it is actively pursuing a strategy of undermining the work of human rights organizations. Through establishing policies that impose matching employees' names to a blacklist of terrorist suspects for any organization that receives Combined Federal Campaign (CFC) funding, human and civil rights are being forced to compromise their own principles of upholding strong standards of rights.

The "climate of fear and intimidation" in the country is leading some other major grant-givers, who are traditionally allies of civil and human rights, to force their grant recipients to accept grants based on conditions that would potentially violate rights to privacy and free speech (Romero 2004b). As far as the ACLU is concerned, rather than capitulate to the blacklisting and antiterrorism rules, in 2004 the organization turned down $1.15 million in future funding from the Ford Foundation (Memorandum 2004; see also Romero 2004b). The new language required in grant stipulation letters was held by the ACLU to introduce onerous, potentially rights-violating stipulations tied to their funds that were connected with the war on terrorism.[20]

While some human rights organizations like the ACLU have made the decision to turn down large funding opportunities rather than be strong-armed by the government to compromise their principles, others have complied with government demands. "It's a matter of survival," is the most common response of those who go along with the new demands.[21] The result could be the widening of a divide in the U.S.-based human rights movement, between those who cooperate and those who resist, accompanied by increased tensions and multiple points of friction. In addition to the cooperation/co-option question, another strong point of friction in the human rights movement

---

[20] The language reads as follows: "By countersigning this grant letter, you agree that your organization will not promote or engage in violence, terrorism, bigotry or the destruction of any state, nor will it make sub-grants to any entity that engages in these activities" (Memorandum 2004).

[21] Observation drawn from author interviews, November and December 2004.

today is the question of the scope of rights that should be addressed, the kinds of strategies that should be pursued, and the types of actors who should be involved.

Another potential divide in the U.S.-based human rights movement today concerns the scope of issues addressed. Included on the agenda of many human rights advocates is a broader array of human rights issues, including economic, social, and cultural rights. The traditional model of investigation and public exposure of misconduct that is effective in cases involving state responsibility for violation of civil and political rights is unlikely to be as effective in cases involving economic and social rights, where there may be relative uncertainty in the identification of violation, violator, and remedy. Violations of economic, social, and cultural rights have been viewed as difficult to address, both because of the often diffuse, structural nature of such violations, and because of the communal impact on affected populations (Korey 1998; Alston 1994). The new human rights advocacy often reaches beyond the state as duty bearer and violator of human rights, targeting also international financial institutions (IFI), transnational corporations, trade regimes, and other institutions. Among other methods, these "new rights advocates" tackle issues of social justice and call into question the international practices that weaken states' capacity to meet social and economic rights (Nelson & Dorsey 2004).

In addition to broadening the scope of *what* they do, human rights organizations are expanding *where* activities occur and *how* they take place. Human rights organizations are increasingly involved in hands-on technical assistance projects in country and field offices. This reflects a shift in international human rights practice from the monitoring of violations to the building of institutions and capacities to facilitate compliance. Especially in the post-September 11th climate, there is more urgency than ever to include victims in human rights program design and implementation. In traditional accounts of human rights, victims are passive recipients of the wisdom and good work of human rights NGOs and benevolent diplomats. The new focus on field-oriented, in-country human rights programs, however, must rely on human rights victims becoming active, empowered participants in human rights practice. Human rights projects that ignore local expertise and rely instead on "experts" who are parachuted in for a quick fix are not merely normatively flawed, their programs are designed for failure.[22] Primary responsibility for the implementation of human rights at the national level is directly linked

---

[22] See, e.g., the Kosovo and Bosnia examples presented in Clark 2000 and in Chandler 1999.

to national ownership of human rights promotion and protection systems (Carothers 1999: 15; Desai & Howes 2002: 261). National systems cannot simply be imported from outside. A more participatory approach will necessarily be a more effective means of promoting and protecting human rights.

Conclusion: What Does It Mean to be a Human Rights Advocate in These Days of Extreme American Exceptionalism?

There is no one single way to be an effective advocate today; the strength of the movement lies in the collective. Practicing human rights in a time of exceptionalism is exceptionally difficult, but human rights advocates must find a way to reclaim human rights and stop the bait and switch. The impact of the Bush administration on human rights at home has been devastating, but it has served as a wake-up call to many U.S.-based human rights advocates who had previously paid little attention to the abuses at their doorstep. From the largest and most mainstream organizations to the smallest and most radical, human rights organizations are finally moving at least some of their activities closer to home. The U.S. human rights and civil rights movements may have emerged on separate paths (Anderson 2003), but now they are forging new linkages with one another, and with broader international movements (see Boulding 1988). Their ability to cooperate and to learn from one another will have great bearing on whether they can find a way to bring their common message to the street, to mobilize citizens from all walks of life to fight for freedom – their own and others.

REFERENCES

Alston, P. (1994). 'Economic and Social Rights'. In Henkin and Hargrove (Eds.), *Human Rights: An Agenda for the Next Century*. The American Society of International Law, Studies in Transnational Legal Policy, No. 26.

American Civil Liberties Union (ACLU). 'Safe and Free: List of Communities that have Passed Resolutions'. Available at: http://www.aclu.org/SafeandFree/SafeandFree. cfm?ID=11294&c=207. (Accessed December 12, 2004).

Anderson, C. (2003). *Eyes off the Prize: The United Nations and the African American Struggle for Human Rights, 1944–1955*. Cambridge: Cambridge University Press.

Belloni, R. (2000, January 12). 'Building Civil Society in Bosnia-Herzegovina'. *Human Rights Working Papers*, No. 2. Available at: http://www.du.edu/humanrights/ workingpapers/papers/02-belloni-01-00.pdf.

Boulding, E. (1988). *Building a Global Civic Culture*. Syracuse: Syracuse University Press.

Carothers, T. (1999). *Aiding Democracy Abroad: The Learning Curve*. Carnegie Endowment for International Peace, Washington D.C., p. 15.

Chandler, D. (1999). *Bosnia: Faking Democracy after Dayton*. London: Pluto Press.

Clark, H. (2000). *Civil Resistance in Kosovo*. London: Pluto Press.

Clark, K. & Mertus, J. (2004, June 20). 'Torturing the Law: The Justice Department's Legal Contortions on Interrogation'. *Washington Post*, B03. Available at: http://www.washingtonpost.com/ac2/wp-dyn/A54025-2004Jun19?language=printer.

Daalder, I. & Lindsay, J. M. (2003). *America Unbound: The Bush Revolution in Foreign Policy*. Washington, D.C.: Brookings Institution Press.

Dembour, M.-B. (1996). 'Human Rights Talk and Anthropological Ambivalence: The Particular Contexts of Universal Claims'. In O. Harris (Ed.), *Inside and Outside the Law: Anthropological Studies of Authority and Ambiguity*, p. 35. London, New York: Routledge.

Desai, V. & Howes, M. (2002). 'Accountability and Participation: A Case from Bombay'. In M. Edwards and D. Hulme (Eds.), *Nongovernmental Organizations – Performance and Accountability*, p. 84. London: Earthscan Publications.

Diamond, L. (2001). 'What Civil Society Can Do to Reform, Deepen, and Improve Democracy'. Paper presented to the "Workshop on Civil Society, Social Capital, and Civic Engagement in Japan and the United States." Sponsored by the Japan Foundation Center for Global Partnership, The Asia Foundation, and the Program for U.S. Japan Relations at Harvard University, June 12–13, 2001, Tokyo.

Donnelly, J. (2004). 'International Human Rights: Unintended Consequences of the War on Terrorism'. In T. G. Weiss et al. (Eds.), *Wars on Terrorism and Iraq: Human Rights Unilateralism and U.S. Foreign Policy*, p. 98. New York: Routledge.

————. (1998). *International Human Rights*, 2nd ed., p. 20. Boulder: Westview Press.

Flowers, N. (2002, March). 'Human Rights Education In the USA'. *Issues of Democracy*, vol. 7, no. 1 (electronic publication of the U.S. State Department). Available at: http://usinfo.state.gov/journals/itdhr/0302/ijde/flowers.htm.

Global Rights. 'Global Rights in the United States'. Available at: http://www.globalrights.org/site/PageServer?pagename=www_ame_index_57.

International Human Rights Law Group (IHRLG). 'Combating Racial Discrimination in the U.S.'. Available at: http://www.hrlawgroup.org/country_programs/united_states/default.asp.

Jackson, P. T. & Krebs, R. R. (2003). 'Twisting Tongues and Twisting Arms: The Power of Political Rhetoric'. Paper prepared for delivery at the 2003 Annual Meeting of the American Political Science Association, August 28–31, 2003.

Korey, W. (1998). *NGOs and the Universal Declaration of Human Rights: A Curious Grapevine*, pp. 34–50. New York: St. Martin's Press.

Lang, A. F., Jr. (Ed.). (2003). *Just Intervention*. Washington, DC: Georgetown University Press.

Lawyers Committee for Human Rights (LCHR) (2003). *Assessing the New Normal: Liberty and Security for the Post-September 11 United States*. New York. Available at: http://www.humanrightsfirst.org/pubs/descriptions/Assessing/AssessingtheNew-Normal.pdf.

Levy, R. A. (2002, November 25). 'Indefensible – The Case Against Military Tribunals'. *Wall Street Journal*.

Memorandum from Ford Foundation to Grantees (herein "Memorandum") (2004, January 8). Available at: http://www.fordfound.org/about/docs/ff_grantee_memo.pdf.

Mertus, J. A. (2004). *Bait and Switch: Human Rights and U.S. Foreign Policy*. New York: Routledge.

Milliken, E. E. (1999). 'National Foreign Trade Council v. Natsios: Massachusetts as a Participant or a Regulator in the International Market'. *Journal of Law and Commerce*, Fall, vol. 19, pp. 187–99.

Nelson, P. & Dorsey, E. (2004). 'The New Rights Advocacy'. Paper presented at the 2004 Annual Meeting of the International Studies Association, Montreal, Canada.

Paarekh, B. (1999). 'Non-ethnocentric Universalism'. In T. Dunne and N. J. Wheeler (Eds.), *Human Rights in Global Politics*, p. 149. Cambridge: Cambridge University Press.

Pollis, A. (1996). 'Cultural Relativism Revisited: Through a State Prism'. *Human Rights Quarterly* 18, no. 2, pp. 316–44.

Preis, A. S. (1996). 'Human Rights as Cultural Practice'. *Human Rights Quarterly* 18, p. 315.

Presidential Military Order of November 13, 2001: Detention, Treatment, and Trial of Certain Non-Citizens in the War Against Terrorism. *Federal Register*, vol. 66, No. 222, p. 57,833. Available at: http://www.fas.org/sgp/news/2001/11/bush111301. html.

Risse, T. (2000, Winter). 'Let's Argue! Communicative Action and International Relations'. *International Organization* 54, pp. 1–39.

Risse, T. & Sikkink, K. (1999). *The Power of Principles: The Socialization of Human Rights Norms in Domestic Practice*. New York: Cambridge University Press.

Romero, A. (2004a, July 31). 'John Ashcroft Cannot Force the ACLU to Check Employees Against a "Black List" – ACLU Will Reject CFC Funds and Challenge Government Policy in Court'. Statement by Anthony Romero, Regarding Patriot Act Restrictions on Combined Federal Campaign Donations. Available at: http:// www.aclu.org/SafeandFree/SafeandFree.cfm?ID=16185&c=206.

————. (2004b, October 17). 'ACLU Declines Ford and Rockefeller Grants Due to Restrictive Funding Agreement; Painful but Principled Decision to Put Civil Liberties First'. Available at: http://www.aclu.org/news/NewsPrint.cfm?ID= 16838&c=206.

Rosaldo, R. (1993). *Culture and Truth: The Remaking of Social Analysis*. Boston: Beacon Press.

Roth, K. (2004). 'The Fight Against Terrorism'. In T. G. Weiss et al. (Eds.), *Wars on Terrorism and Iraq: Human Rights Unilateralsim and U.S. Foreign Policy*, p. 113. New York: Routledge.

Sterba, J. P. (2003). *Terrorism and International Justice*. New York: Oxford University Press.

U.S. Department of Justice, Office of Legal Counsel (2002, August 1). 'Memorandum for Alberto R. Gonzales, Counsel to the President. Re: Standards of Conduct for Interrogation under 18 U.S.C. §§ 2340–2340A'. Available at: http://www. washingtonpost.com/wp-srv/nation/documents/dojinterrogationmemo20020801. pdf.

Weiss, T. G. et al. (Eds.). (2004). *Wars on Terrorism and Iraq: Human Rights Unilateralsim and U.S. Foreign Policy*. New York: Routledge.

Witte, J. (2001). 'A Dickensian Era of Religious Rights: An Update on Religious Human Rights in Global Perspective'. *William and Mary Law Review* 42, pp. 707, 712.

Index